CHALLENGES AND CHANGING BUSINESS PRACTICES IN RECENT TIMES

EDITORS

Namrata Acharya | Ritu Chakraborty | Priyanka Oza

INDIA • SINGAPORE • MALAYSIA

ISBN 979-8-89133-432-8

Conference Proceedings
of
13th International Conference
on
Challenges and Changing Business Practices in Recent Times
Papers Published
February 28, 2023

ISBN - 979-8-89133-432-8

Patron: Dr. Vijay Bhangale
Editors: Dr, Namrata Acharya, Prof. Ritu Chakraborty and Prof. Priyanka Oza

IES's Management College & Research Centre
791, SK Marg, HIG Colony, Nityanand Nagar, ONGC Colony,
Bandra West, Mumbai, Maharashtra 400050
Contact: 022 50001729 Email: info@ies.edu

Conference Proceedings
of
13th International Conference
on
Challenges and Changing Business Practices in Recent Times
Papers Published
February 28, 2023

ISBN - 979-8-89133-432-8

REVIEWERS:

Dr. Sushma Verma	Associate Professor Vivekanand Education Society's Institute of Management, Mumbai, Maharashtra
Dr. Padma Singhal	Associate Professor Chetana's Institute of Management and Research, Mumbai, Maharashtra
Dr. Vinima Gambhir	Associate Professor Atlas SkillTech University, Mumbai, Maharashtra
Dr. Vinay Gudi	Chief Financial Officer Symbiosis Skills and Professional University
Dr. Baisakhi Mitra Mustaphi	Associate Professor N L Dalmia Institute of Management Studies and Research, Mumbai, Maharashtra
Dr. Indira Singh	Assistant Professor Chetana's Institute of Management and Research, Mumbai, Maharashtra

IES's Management College & Research Centre
791, SK Marg, HIG Colony, Nityanand Nagar, ONGC Colony, Bandra West, Mumbai, Maharashtra 400050 Contact: 022 50001729 Email: info@ies.edu

ABOUT THE INSTITUTE

IES is one of India's oldest Public Charitable Trusts committed to education and successfully running 64 Institutions. IES's Management College and Research Centre (IESMCRC) is recognized as a premier business school, committed to academic excellence and value based education. In our endeavor to shape and develop business leaders, we offer several full time courses which include Post graduate Diploma in Management (PGDM) and Post Graduate Diploma in Management (Pharmaceutical Management) approved by AICTE.

Armed with proficient and experienced faculty members and state-of-the-art academic infrastructure, IES MCRC provides an excellent environment for research and development activities. We offer the latest in management education through a unique pedagogy to enable the students to become successful and socially responsible professionals.

IES MCRC's commitment to "Value Addition through Education" is manifested through a whole spectrum of programs and Industry-oriented activities. In addition, our students take up various projects with NGOs and organize CSR activities under various platforms. The Institution has produced many distinguished alumni, who have contributed significantly to the industry and the society and earned accolades and respect in their chosen careers.

MESSAGE FROM THE DIRECTOR

We are glad to introduce IES's Management College and Research Centre (IES MCRC), a premier management institute in Mumbai. Our value proposition at IES MCRC is to offer the latest in management in order to enable the students to become successful and socially responsible professionals. We promote quality education in a wide array of specializations in the field of management like Finance, Marketing, HR, Operations, Business Analytics, Entrepreneurship and Pharma Management. We aim to provide top class management education and training which will ensure that students/ course participants are equipped to meet the present and future challenging requirements of the trade and industries, not only in India but also globally.

This year we organized the 13th International Conference on "Challenges and changing business practices in recent times" on Feb 28, 2023. The global economy is getting back on track after the pandemic which has been a major crisis for many businesses. This crisis enabled organizations to look for changes in business practices and relooking it in these challenging times. Recognizing and overcoming the common drawbacks linked to growth is essential if a business is expected to thrive and grow. Studies suggest that the common global business environment changes are related to technology, customers, competitors and regulations.

The conference was organized with an objective to understand and define the above challenges and changing business practices. Through this conference, we attempted to provide a common platform for industry and academia to come together and contemplate on various ideas around the theme. We received over 70 research papers from research scholars, faculty members, industry practitioners as well as students. The papers were screened and reviewed by the external panel members and finally shortlisted for publication.

It gives me immense pleasure to present to you the rich compilation of the selected papers that were presented in the 13th International Conference on "Challenges and changing business practices in recent times".

Happy Learning!!
Dr. Vijay Bhangale

MESSAGE FROM THE CHIEF GUEST

Change is unavoidable in business when there are challenges. As entrepreneurs, instances are everywhere; process owners are overwhelmingly concerned with the ever-changing dynamics associated with important aspects. Let us attempt to compile a list of criteria's that many would consider essential. Changes brought about by innovations, which are frequently neglected or excessively underestimated, will be at the top of my list. Stakeholders normally expect some nice surprises in everything, whether it's a product or a service. A novelty component is always valuable. Today, India ranks third in the number of unicorns, second in the total number of start-ups, and first in the number of new start-ups launched per day. The majority of these businesses rely on innovation. However, advancements are expensive. Fortunately, access to the world of funds has become simpler, and India is seeing a massive influx- a Positive change is desperately required. FDI, for example, has been at an all-time high for the past eight years. This money came from 162 countries and was distributed to about 30 states. As a result, my second point is about positive changes in the investment climate. The majority of firms rely substantially on technology. In other words, 'connectivity,' which is the third most essential change component in my opinion. India used to be ranked low, around 120, because we were a bad data consumer. We became the world's largest data consumer in less than a decade. Furthermore, we capture approximately 42% of total global digital transactions. The other factor is the shift in mobility. Along with digital speed, we have one of the world's fastest developing physical connectivity networks. We are getting more tightly connected, with a national highway network of approximately 1.5 lakh kilometers and a record rail network of 4500 kilometers this year. Finally, some argue that size does important. We took around 67 years to reach a trillion-dollar economy, eight years to reach a two-trillion-dollar economy, and only five years to reach a three-trillion-dollar economy. It is projected that by the end of the year, we will have surpassed Germany to become the world's fourth largest economy. Rolling stones, as they say, gather no moss! Change is in the air, and the only constant is 'change'!

Dr. Arindam Saha, Managing Director, Vista Intelligence Private Limited,

MESSAGE FROM THE CONVENER

The world has witnessed an unprecedented series of challenges in recent times, with the global pandemic being a significant catalyst for change. The research conference organized by IES MCRC was aimed to understand the multifaceted challenges faced by businesses and the subsequent adaptations and transformations in their practices. The past few years have brought forth a multitude of disruptive factors, from global pandemics and economic fluctuations to technological advancements and shifting consumer behaviors. These circumstances challenged the organizations to reevaluate their strategies, adapt to new paradigms, and find innovative solutions to survive and thrive. Thus this book has brought together a diverse group of researchers, industry professionals, and thought leaders to shed light on the ever-evolving business landscape.

The discussion by authors move around one of the central topics on the impact of digitalization and emerging technologies on business models. The rapid advancements in technology have necessitated a paradigm shift in the way organizations operate. Discussions revolved around harnessing the power of data, leveraging automation and artificial intelligence, and embracing digital platforms to enhance productivity, improve customer experiences, and drive innovation.

The book also further delves into the growing importance of sustainability and corporate social responsibility (CSR) in shaping business practices. Authors have explored strategies for integrating sustainability into core business operations, addressing environmental and social challenges, and aligning CSR initiatives with corporate values. The authors have highlighted the significance of creating shared value, engaging stakeholders, and embracing a long-term perspective for sustainable success.

The changing dynamics of the workforce emerged as another critical aspect of the research theme. The authors have examined the impact of remote work, flexible arrangements, and the gig economy on organizational structures and culture. The topics explored are strategies for fostering employee well-being, managing virtual teams, promoting diversity and inclusion, and cultivating an agile and adaptive work environment.

Effective leadership in times of uncertainty is a recurring theme throughout the book. The discussion is centered around the qualities and skills required of leaders to navigate crises, drive organizational change, and inspire teams in turbulent times. Authors have explored adaptive leadership styles, the importance of communication and transparency, and the role of resilience and emotional intelligence in leading through uncertainty.

The insights generated during the conference have significant implications for businesses operating in the current landscape. Organizations must embrace agility, innovation, and a forward-thinking mindset to adapt to rapidly changing circumstances. They must invest in digital capabilities, integrate sustainability into their strategies, foster a supportive and inclusive workplace culture, and cultivate effective leadership at all levels.

This book sheds the light on the pressing issues faced by businesses today and emphasized the importance of agility, innovation, sustainability, and effective leadership. As we move forward, it is crucial for organizations to leverage these insights and embrace the transformative opportunities presented by the evolving business landscape.

Dr. Namrata Acharya

SHORT DESCRIPTION OF THE BOOK

The theme of the IES MCRC's 13th International Conference focused on "Challenges and Changing Business Practices in Recent Times" as we all had witnessed a radical change in the way businesses responded to the crisis. It was observed that the crisis accelerated the use of technology to a great extent, brought a shift in customer behavior and changed how employees can get work done remotely.

The pandemic also has been a testing time for businesses as they had to make tough decisions with regards to rethinking supply chains, preserve their bottom line and decide on office spaces and work culture. The business world is taking transformative decisions and hence the focus of this conference was majorly on the changing business practices.

In the above context, researchers are also contributing about how the organizations can manage challenges in a better way through changing business practices. To enable these researchers a platform to showcase their work, IES's Management College and Research Centre, Mumbai, organized its 13th International Conference on Feb 28, 2023. The conference was attended by academicians, research scholars, consultants, management practitioners and students. They also got a chance to submit their original, unpublished research work on the theme of the conference.

The conference was well received by the research community as well as the participants and it received an overwhelming response. The conference was conducted in hybrid mode and hence we could receive participation from all over India.

Out of all the papers presented in the conference, we have considered a selected few papers for publication in this book. The book focusses on how the challenges of the recent times can be handles through various innovative solutions and how organizations can take up changing business practices to overcome these challenges.

Contents

Work Life Balance And Its Impact On Working Professional

CHAPTER 01

Author – Prof. Roma Khanna, Assistant Professor, TMIMT, Uttar Pradesh, Dr. Raghuvir Singh, Vice Chancellor, TMU, Uttar Pradesh & Dr. Himanshu Jain, Associate Professor, Panipat Institute of Engineering and Technology, Haryana

ABSTRACT

Work life balance has become a need of hour in every sector. Especially academicians who provide good citizens to the country are required to have good WLB but now a days they are also facing problems in balancing work and personal life that the main reasons for workplace balance are exploitations faced mentally and physically mainly suffered by females. Therefore study focuses on 50 female academicians to find the factors affecting WLB and also highlights the relation of age with WLB. For the study convenient sampling has been used and the data collected is analyzed with the help of percentage analysis and chi-square test.

Key words- Work life balance, factors, age

INTRODUCTION

WLB) is defined as a state of balance, where the demands of a person's occupation and personal life are equal (**Sharkey J. 2019). Greenhouse and colleagues (2003**) define work-family balance as the "extent to which an individual is equally engaged in -and equally satisfied with- his or her work role and family role".

In simple words Work life balance can be explained as a normal feeling occurred in the individual when able to balance certain demands of work and family. The causes of these demands and events can be many such as work, relationships, financial pressure etc.

The studies on work life balance examined that the main reasons for workplace balance are exploitations faced mentally and physically mainly suffered by females. Other common symptoms in women include headaches, difficulty in sleeping, tiredness, back pain, stomach pain, improper eating habits, problems `related to skin, lack of energy, upset stomach, loss of temperament, low positive thinking, lack of concentration.

A Working Professional woman's has to perform responsibility of both her family and her work, At times performing and balancing between them can be problem. This is the very well known fact which cannot be avoided that females are more sensitive than males. The brain of females are highly active, which makes it makes difficult for a female to avoid all incidents and due to this active brain females are not able to avoid any situation moreover the suffers from pressure in performing multiple role and this leads to stress in them.

OBJECTIVES OF THE STUDY

1. To Know the factors leading to Work life balance.
2. To Know the different perspective of Work life balance with respect to age group.

Need Of The Study -Females play a vital role in the society and for them maintaining a balance in life is necessary but females suffers from stress due to multiple role performed by females. As stress is a factor which creates imbalance but it is required to understand identify the causes of work life balance also the methods which can reduce stress.

REVIEW OF LITERATURE

Mayya S.M *et. al.* (2021) tried to indicate relation of better WLB with the upper age group, gender, and faculties of science discipline and after multiple regression analysis it was found that WLB was associated with gender and age.

Singh. H., and Sharma. R., (2020) Study further depicts that in Punjab there were more number of male faculties. Work life Balance of faculties is impacted by presence of children and being married and ultimately affect their performance in job.

Meharunisa S. (2019) worked on the factors affecting stress and its impact on balancing work life and personal life in female faculties. The study was conducted on Northern India with a sample size 208 female faculty. It was concluded that stress is responsible for low performance of employee and affect their work life. For the study samples were selecting through random purposive technique and the tools used were correlation, regression, ANOVA analysis. The study found several factors affecting stress and work life like hectic work schedule, discrimination and lack of training which also impact employee productivity

Dikshit S. and Acharya S. A. (2017) tried to examined the effect of workplace stress on WLB. Study also examined the relationship between demographic factors and stress in maintaining balance in life. Role ambiguity was a factor which was found to be different for male and females. It was concluded that factors of stress differ in both private and public colleges teachers.

Joseph A., Kumar P. ((2017) reviews descriptive study and analysed that most of faculty feel stress in managing work and personal life as they do not have time for family and also maximum faculty have problem with working hours. The study provided suggestions to implement programs which help faculties to balance stress and stress.

Zaheer A., Islam J., Darakhshan N. (2016). Aimed to find level of work life balance in working women working in academics. Purposive sampling was chosen for the study. Maximum respondent were married, fall into the age group of 36-45 and have experience of 5 to 10 years. Study reveals that average relationship exist between stress and WLB in faculty. Efficiency and effectiveness of organization will improve if it works on WLB of faculties.

Sundaresan, S.(2014) In this study, working women's work-life balance is examined, as well as the effects of having an unsatisfactory balance. Poor work-life balance has a number of negative effects, including high levels of stress and anxiety, domestic strife, job burnout, and the inability to reach one's full potential.

Uddin R. M.(2013). To determine the true situation of work-life balance institutions, a survey is carried out in 62 educational institutions in Bangladesh using a sample of 320 professors. According to the study, there is a modest work-life balance issue that can be resolved by providing female instructors with flexible work schedules, transportation options, housing options, child care facilities, flexible work arrangements, lowered workloads, and child-care facilities.

Senthilkumar K.G., Chandrakumaramangalam, S. and Manivannan L. (2012). The study aims to find various demographic variable and their relationship with the stress level in maintain balance among personal and professional life. It was concluded that females suffers from stress more and maximum respondents are not satisfied with WLB. So to be successful in the environment an organization should implement programmes which enable faculties to have WLB as it is a combined effort of both employers and employees.

RESEARCH METHODOLOGY

The study is descriptive in nature and the data is collected through primary source i.e. with the help of questionnaire. The sample of 50 working professionals has been taken for the research selected through random sampling and the data collected analyzed with the help of percentage analysis and chi-square test.

HYPOTHESIS

Hyothesis 1:-There is no relation between factors that lead to Work life balance and age group of a respondent.
Hypothesis 2:-There is no relation between age group and mental effect of Work life balance.

DATA ANALYSIS

Table-1 Age group

Age	Up to 25 yrs	26years-35years	36 years-40 years	Above 40 years
Respondents	10	25	10	05
Percentage	20	50	20	10

The above table illustrates that maximum respondents belong to age group 26-35 years.

Table2:-Ratio of Working Professional Women's

S.no	Number of women
Working	50
Non-Working	0

The table shows that all the respondents of the study are working female Professionals.

Table3: Factors mostly lead to cause Work life balance

s.no	Factors	Number	Percentage
1	Organizational Related Factors	16	32
2	Interpersonal Factors	11	22
3	Work Related Factors	6	12
4	Finance Related Factors	08	16
5	Family Related Factors	07	14
6	Others	2	04

It can be analyzed from the data that organizational factors are mainly responsible for causing Work life balance among working professional. Another factor that lead to WLB are Interpersonal factors and finance related factors.

Table4: Mental Effect of Work Life Imbalance

S.No	Factors	Number	Percentage
1	Easily Loose Temper	20	40
2	Negative Attitude	5	10
3	Impatient at the Time of Idleness	12	24
4	Lack of Concentration	13	26

Respondents mainly loose temper due to Work life Imbalance. Other effects found among respondents were Lack of concentration and Impatient at the time of idleness.

Table5: Effect of Work Life Balance on Health

s.no	Factors	Number	Percentage
1	Allergy	5	10
2	Asthma	0	00
3	Headache	30	60
4	Spinal Pain	0	00
5	Diabetes	4	08
6	Others	6	12
7	No Effect	5	10

Maximum respondents suffer from headache due to imbalance in work and life while respondents do not have problem of Asthma and spinal pain.

Table6: Impact of Work life balance on Other Areas

s.no	Factors	Number	Percentage
1	Performance	10	20
2	Higher Absenteeism	5	10
3	Poor Performance	5	10
4	Shift Job Frequently	0	00
5	Job Dissatisfaction	30	60

Job dissatisfaction and effect on performance is found maximum among respondents as an impact of stress while respondents do not shift job frequently due to stress.

ANALYSIS OF HYPOTHESIS

Hypothesis1:- There is no relation between factors that lead to stress and age group of a respondent.

Age group of the respondent * Factors the cause Stress in you								
Count								
Organizational Related Factors		Factors the cause Stress in you						Total
		Interpersonal Factors	Work Related Factors	Finance Related Factors	Family Related Factors	Others		
Age group of the respondent	Up to 25 yrs	4	1	1	1	0	3	10
	26years-35years	11	2	0	3	7	2	25
	36 years-40 years	0	8	2	0	0	0	10
	Above 40 years	3	2	0	0	0	0	5
Total		18	13	3	4	7	5	50

Chi-Square Tests			
	Value	df	Asymptotic Significance (2-sided)
Pearson Chi-Square	40.265[a]	15	.000
Likelihood Ratio	45.523	15	.000
Linear-by-Linear Association	3.906	1	.048
N of Valid Cases	50		
a. 22 cells (91.7%) have expected count less than 5. The minimum expected count is.30.			

Result:-As per analysis the table value found to be.048 which is less than the significant value of.05 therefore hypothesis has been rejected which means that there is age group and causes of stress are related to each other.

Hypothesis 2:- There is no relation between age group and mental effect of stress

Age group of the respondent * Mental affect of the Stress Cross tabulation						
Easily Loose Temper		**Mental affect of the Stress**				Total
		Negative Attitude	Impatient at the Time of Idleness	Lack of Concentration		
Age group of the respondent	**Up to 25 yrs**	5	0	2	3	10
	26years-35years	8	1	8	8	25
	36 years-40 years	4	3	3	0	10
	Above 40 years	1	0	1	3	5
Total		18	4	14	14	50

Chi-Square Tests			
	Value	df	Asymptotic Significance (2-sided)
Pearson Chi-Square	14.091[a]	9	.119
Likelihood Ratio	15.267	9	.084
N of Valid Cases	50		
a. 13 cells (81.3%) have expected count less than 5. The minimum expected count is.40.			

Result:-As per analysis the table value found to be.084 which is more than the significant value of.05 therefore hypothesis has been accepted which

means that age group and mental effect of balancing work and life are not related with each other.

FINDINGS

- According to research maximum working women belonging to age 26-35.
- The research indicated that most of the working individuals loose temper and suffer from headache which reflect not able to balance work and family
- Data collected reflects that organizational factors are mainly responsible for balancing work and family.

DISCUSSION AND CONCLUSION

Work life imbalance is found for every working person but it is found more prevalent in women.**(Sumathi V. and Velmurugan R. 2018)** So it is important to identify factors affecting work life balance and the problems arising because of imbalance and promote healthy environment at workplace. The study conclude that age has significant correlation with the WLB.**(Uddin R. M.2014)** Organizational factors which are important at workplace are responsible for WLB. So for successful employers effective leadership is required which deals with the challenges of balancing work and life. An imbalance in life can lead to several physical and mental problems like headache and loss of temperament in working persons which effect on performance in working place.

LIMITATIONS OF THE STUDY

Limited sample size and sample area is one of the major constraint of research. Further only age as a variable is studied so there is a scope of that other demographic variable can be taken and its relation with Work life balance.

REFERENCES

Dikshit S. and Acharya S. K., (2017). Impact of Occupational Stress on the Work Life Balance of Teaching Professionals in Higher Education with Special Reference to Bhubaneswar City, Odisha. Advances in Economics and Business Management (AEBM).p-ISSN: 2394-1545; e-ISSN: 2394-1553; Volume 4, Issue 6; April-June, 2017, pp. 357-361.

Dhanabhakyam M.. And Anitha V.(2011). A study on stress management of working women in Coimbatore district. International journal of multidisciplinary research,1 (7),1-8.

Dhaliwal. M.and Kaur M (Joseph A., Kumar P. ((2017). Work Life Balance of Women Employees with Reference to Teaching Faculties. *International Journal of Innovative Research in Science, Engineering and Technology.* Vol. 6, Issue 7, *pp 13272-13276.*

Maya S.M e.tal(2021). Work-Life Balance and Gender Differences: A Study of College and University Teachers From Karnataka. SAGE Open October-December 2021, pp 1-11

Meharunisa S. (2019). Work-Life Balance and Job Stress Among Female Faculties in India's Higher Education Institutions. International Journal of Recent Technology and Engineering (IJRTE) ISSN: 2277-3878,Volume-8, Issue-2S11, pp 846-852.

Rani.U.R., and Bhuvaneshwari. K.(2014). An Analysis on the Main Factors of Occupational Stress among Indian Women – A Soft Computing Approach. International Journal of Computational Intelligence and Informatics, 4(2),155-162.

Singh. H., & Sharma. R., (2020) Work life balance of University teachers of Punjab state – with special reference to demographic factors. *Dogo Rangsang Research Journal.* ISSN: 2347-7180 Vol-10 Issue-07 No.8 July 2020. *Pp 20-34.*

Senthilkumar K.G., S. Chandrakumaramangalam and Manivannan L. (2012). An Empirical Study on Teaching Professionals' Work-Life Balance in Higher Learning Institutions with Special Reference to Namakkal District, Tamilnadu. Bonfring International Journal of Industrial Engineering and Management Science, Vol. 2, No. 3, pp 39-41.

Sharma.B. and,Manju N.(2015) A qualitative study on causes and effects of stress among working women in management colleges in Jaipur. International Journal of current advanced research. ol 4, Issue 6, pp 152-157.

Sundaresan S.(2014). Work-Life Balance – Implications For Working Women. *Oida International Journal of Sustainable Development,*7(7), pp 93-101.

Sumathi V. and Velmurugan R.(2018). Work Life Balance of Female Faculty in Arts and Science Colleges in Coimbatore District. *International Journal of Pure and Applied Mathematics,* 119(15), pp1395-1406.

Uddin R. M.(2013). Work-Life Balance: A Study on Female Teachers of Private Education Institutions of Bangladesh. International Journal of African and Asian Studies - An Open Access International Journal, 1, pp 101-107.

Zaheer A., Islam J., Darakhshan N. (2016). Occupational Stress and Work-Life Balance: A Study of Female Faculties of Central Universities in Delhi, India. *Journal of Human Resource Management.* ISSN: 2331-0707 (Print); ISSN: 2331-0715, Volume 4(1), pp 1-5.

WEBLIOGRAPHY

Adam Felman.(Feb 2023). Why stress happens and how to manage it from https://www.medicalnewstoday.com/articles/145855

Jan 2023. Women and stress from https://my.clevelandclinic.org/health/articles/5545-women-and-stress

Times of India.(May 24, 2019)Do you know why women are more stressed than men? We tell you from http://timesofindia.indiatimes.com/articleshow/69463836.cms?utm_source=contentofinterest&utm_medium=text&utm_campaign=cppst

A Study on the Covid-19 Pandemic's Impact on the International Trade of the Usa and India

Author – Vishwa Yashodhar Bhatt, Research Scholar, S D School of Commerce, Ahmedabad & Dr. Dharmendra S. Mistry, Professor and Principal, M C Shah Commerce College, Ahmedabad

ABSTRACT

For the year 2020, foreign trade was down, but by 2021, it had rebounded greatly. While global commerce is already above pre-pandemic levels, the consequences of trade on various commodities, industries, and trading partners are vastly different and exert pressure on certain industries. Usually, a four- to five-year shift in the organization of commerce would occur as a result of the Coronavirus epidemic. However, not all of the losses from the prior sharp drops had been recovered when trade imbalances remained in 2021. Consumers, corporations, and the government all have a greater motivation to deploy new or reinforce existing risk mitigation techniques because of the vast range of trade consequences and trade flows between products and origins and destinations.

In the literature review of trade in the USA and India, Economic and trade Challenges were discussed using different research papers. The research methodology of the paper is a secondary qualitative method. The result shows in all cases, the pandemic's negative demand repercussions outweigh its negative supply implications. Extra fixed effects are important since their absolute values diminish.

KEYWORDS

International Trade, USA, India, Covid-19, Economy, Export-Import

INTRODUCTION

In 2020, international trade declined, but it rebounded significantly in 2021. Even though total trade flows are already comfortably above pre-pandemic levels, trade effects on specific items, industries and trade partners are immensely diverse and exert pressures on specific industries and supply chains (Hayakwa & Mukunoki, 2021). The Coronavirus epidemic caused a significant shift in the commerce structure that would normally occur over four to five years in a single year. Trade imbalances remained at the end of 2021, but not all of the losses from the earlier steep declines had been recovered. There is a high degree of unpredictability and adjustment costs associated with the wide range of trade impacts and trade flows across products, origins, and destinations, which means those consumers, businesses, and the government all have an increased incentive to implement new or strengthen existing risk mitigation strategies.

To put it another way, 2020 was the year when trade and production volumes fell to their lowest levels since World War 2 (Pei et al., 2021). During the first half of 2020, both global industrial output and goods trade fell to levels not seen since the Financial Crisis bottom in 2008. However, the recovery will take a V-shape in 2020 as a result of their quick emergence and subsequent breakdown. It was in 2021 that trade grew fast, recouping some but not all of the losses that had been inflicted by the sharp declines that had occurred earlier. However, there was no drop in global merchandise commerce in 2020 of the magnitude predicted during the epidemic era. Towards the middle of 2020, global trade volume will begin to return to pre-pandemic levels.

Coronavirus has had a significant impact on the global economy. Economic harm in several other countries was larger than in the United States in 2020, despite one of the harshest contractions in its history. We have seen a robust rebound in the United States thanks in large part to an early and rapid vaccination rollout, as well as substantial economic assistance. Strong demand, skewed toward commodities rather than services, combined with supply chain difficulties creates inflationary pressures in the United States and practically all of our major trading partners.

The U.S. trade deficit has grown as a result of the country's quick recovery compared to the rest of the globe. Imports have risen as a result of the resurgence of business and consumer demand in the United States, thanks in part to the strength of the country's economic recovery. The recovery of many of the countries that buy American goods has lagged behind that of exports, despite exports reaching historic highs. International travel has been hit hard by the latest outbreaks of infection, which has hampered the return of several key exports for the United States, such as travel and tourism. Long-standing economic challenges, notably those originating from the integration of the global economy, have been highlighted by the pandemic. Since many American workers and communities have had to bear the costs of transferring production abroad while not fully benefiting from it, widening inequality has resulted from a lack of supportive public policy in the past.

By establishing laws that expand the benefits of trade and level the economic competitive landscape across national borders, we can correct these mistakes. It's important to reduce uncertainty and engage with economic and commercial partners to ensure that all Americans benefit from global commerce. By applying these policy measures, this can be achieved.

LITERATURE REVIEW

A pandemic of Coronavirus has entrapped the planet. As a Chinese and Southeast Asian problem, it was initially misunderstood. In the wake of earlier epidemics, such as SARS, decision- makers around the world felt that the disease could be confined and controlled inside the affected area (Socrates, 2020). Because of natural, political, and regulatory causes, the illness quickly expanded over the world and was eventually recognised as a pandemic by WHO. The expansion was undoubtedly made easier by the already-existing ties between countries.

Since the outbreak began, the pandemic has been considered a public health issue. As of April 3 2020, there have been more than a million confirmed cases worldwide, with nearly 60,000 deaths documented (Hayakwa & Mukunoki, 2021). Shortly, these numbers are likely to climb significantly. While some nations look to be gaining control of the problem, are either still fighting to prevent the spread of the disease or are in the early phases, which are often characterised by explosive increases in cases (eg the USA and India). There are, however, several possibly far more significant repercussions that will only become apparent as time goes on. Economic and political crises that are mutually reinforcing may lead to major significantly interfere as the costs of the pandemic will not only be large but also unfairly distributed, both within countries and among different social groups in states.

As far as the economy is concerned, most experts foresee a global recession in 2020 that could be severe in some nations or areas. Between –10 and –25 per cent, JP Morgan Research expects a two- quarter GDP drop in the United States, and between –15 and –22 per cent, for the Eurozone (Pei et al., 2021). The amount and pace of healing are still unanswered questions. The political crisis can spread beyond the country's borders and affect governments at the regional or international level. As a result, several analysts are concerned about the survival of the European integration effort, citing the European institutions' inability to respond. Coronavirus is viewed as a danger to liberal democracy by some. Autocratic tendencies are already showing symptoms of strengthening in the future, as some early indicators suggest.

The present pandemic has the potential to harm global commerce as well. Because it is too early to know the full impact of the numerous processes now taking place, this text's goal is limited (Berthou, & Stumpner, 2022). A probable course of action that appears to be evolving in the field will be highlighted rather than multiple possibilities being identified and analysed for their probabilities.

THE US TRADE

The world's biggest producer of petroleum products as well as an important exporter and importer. Each year, more than 10% of the total trade balance from the U. S. is made by American companies. In the first ten months of 2021, crude oil and natural gas prices rose considerably, with WTI crude oil completing the year more than 55percentage points above its end-2020 level and global natural gas prices increasing approximately several folds between November and November 2021(Berthou, & Stumpner, 2022). The dollar value of U.S. petroleum exports was approximately 50% higher than its 2020 level, while the dollar value of imports was up more than 75% as a result of rising prices and increasing volumes of imports and exports.

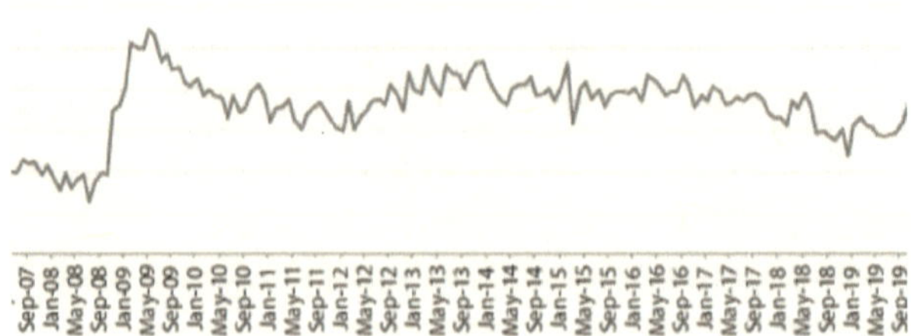

In 2021, both domestic and international causes were responsible for the rise in energy prices. Government efforts to reign in the use of coal were stifling overall supply in the US, but the energy consumption of manufacturing facilities soared as production increased.US's increased demand for natural gas has resulted in an increase in natural gas prices throughout Europe and Asia. Due to the decline in demand caused by the pandemic, OPEC+ (Organization of the Petroleum Exporting Countries Plus) cut oil output in 2020 by 10 million barrels per day (approximately 10% of global production), which pushed up global energy prices Investments in new energy sources in the United States were sluggish in 2020, which had an impact on energy supply in 2021, when the economy was recovering (D'Aguanno, et al.,2021). Another factor affecting U.S. oil production was the abnormally cold winter in Texas and the hurricanes Ida and Nicolas in the Gulf of Mexico.

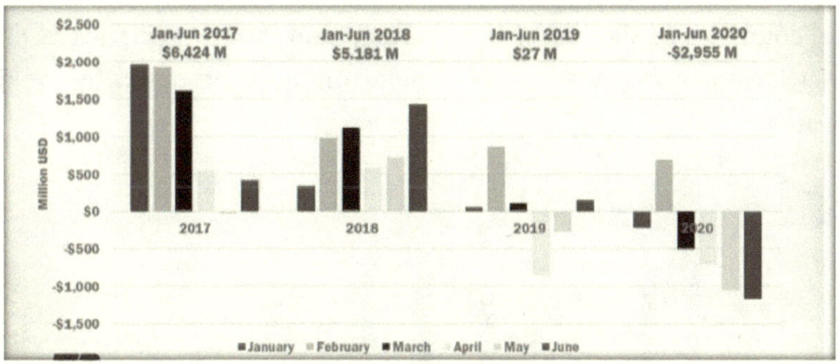

Figure 1 US decline in trade

The return of travel as well as some commutes as a result of vaccines becoming widely available in the spring of 2021 increased demand for gasoline on the supply side (Hardy, and Logan. 2020). Car travel and commuting soared in the wake of the H1N1 pandemic, which shifted people away from mass transit and plane travel in favour of driving.

US ECONOMIC AND TRADE CHALLENGE

It's easy to see how America's strong financial support aided our economy's swift return to health after the Coronavirus outbreak when viewed from across the globe. The demand-driven recovery, however, has a darker side. Unfortunate deaths occurred as a result, and prices rose as a result. The prior year's global economic trend is best understood in the context of the current coronavirus outbreak. This is by far the most obvious indication of the number of individuals killed by Coronavirus is an important indicator of the pandemic's impact on the world population. By the end of 2021, the virus had claimed the lives of more than 5 million individuals. In the United States alone, there are more than 827,000 persons (D'Aguanno, et al., 2021). The true global death toll is likely to be much higher as a result of the data collection.

If the United States is not the only country dealing with these issues, many other countries may be in a similar situation. Under-reporting has been a major problem. Consider the figure of $1 billion, as an example. About 4 million people died in India alone as a result of the disaster. The pandemic and the US economy are intertwined. In addition to Subramanian, in the year 2021. As a percentage of the entire population, death rates are more accurate. The global financial crisis has disproportionately impacted low- and middle-income countries. Asia, the Middle East, and South America. Different countries have varying death rates, which might be obscured by looking at total deaths.

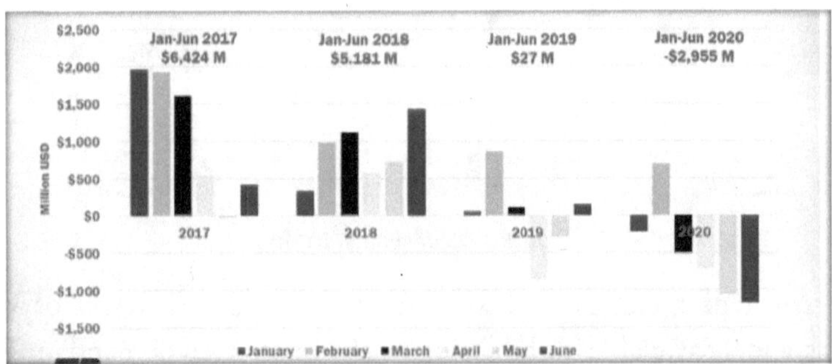

Figure 2 US export and import

Many storms have hit each with a different level of intensity. A country's fortunes have fluctuated dramatically at any given time. The verified facts the US, the UK, and the EU have each at one point had the greatest number of cases per thousand people recorded. In the early phases of the epidemic, the United States had the largest number of cases per capita. There were more deaths in the United Kingdom than in any other country. In the second half of 2021, things began to turn around. True. In addition, the Eurozone recorded the highest number of illnesses per capita in the spring. Most major economies will have some variation in this by 2021.

At some point, the epidemic had a significant impact on you. Even the pace of vaccination has changed throughout time (Hardy, and Logan. 2020). To or from a different country U.S.A. and the United Kingdom were successful in expediting vaccine rollouts and have made them the most populous countries. There was an increase in deployments in Canada and the European Union. Both locations' immunisation rates will soar by summer 2021. Exports from the United States have grown dramatically in recent years when compared to other major trading partners.

The second half of 2021 should see an increase in the vaccination rate in many middle-income countries. In countries like Mexico, the rate of inflation has overtaken that of the United States. In low- income developing countries, it stays much lower (not depicted). According to the OED, the year is 2021.

COVID 19 AND INDIAN TRADE

The textile, clothing, and transportation industries account for about 18% of India's total exports, making them the most exposed sectors in India to COVID-19. More than 40% of India's exports are made up of the top three categories of fuels, chemicals, and stone and glass, all of which have a moderate level of exposure (Anderson & Wincoop, 2021). Vegetables, rubber products, animals, food goods, etc., face the lowest danger of exposure to foreign markets. India's minimal reliance on US's intermediary imports makes it less vulnerable to US's economic power. An additional cushion will be provided by the low price of crude oil, India's largest import (Campbell et al., 2021). Demand shocks, not supply shocks, have the greatest influence on the economy in the countries hardest hit by COVID- 19.

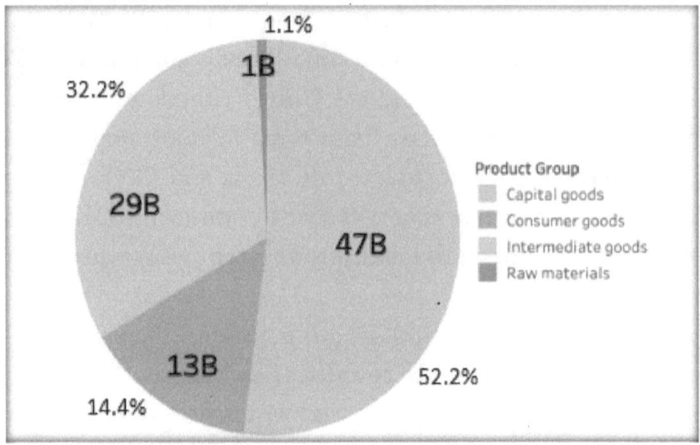

Figure 3Indian trade 2021

India's share of trade in GDP is 43 per cent, which indicates a moderately open economy compared to other nations.US, on the other hand, has a huge food trade deficit with India (Hanson, 2021). The percentage of Coronavirus cases in India is also low. India, on the other hand, is more likely than the other countries in the group to suffer a high number of human casualties as a result of the pandemic due to its high population density and inadequate access to healthcare facilities, as demonstrated by the low population of doctors. To meet the global post-pandemic demand, US industries are preparing to reopen as soon as possible and in time.

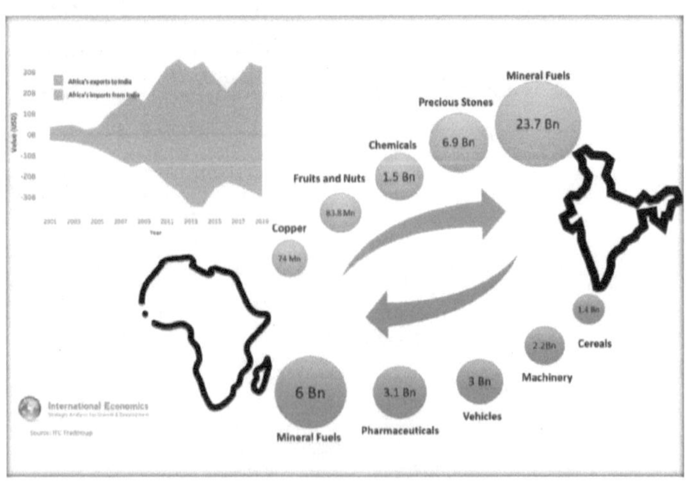

IEC; Data from ITC Trade Map

The resumption of activity would give the US a first-mover advantage, which could hurt Indian MSMEs (Socrates, 2020). In the event of a financial constraint caused by the pandemic, many small businesses will be unable to make up for a lost market share. Uncertainty in the Indian financial market has been exacerbated by mounting doubts about the future and the consequences of COVID-19, which has resulted in massive crashes and the depreciation of capital. The stock fell by 4,000 points in a single day on March 24, 2020, when the increasing uncertainty of business activity caused the most significant market crash in India's history. A low point of 77.60 Indian Rupees against the US Dollar was also set in April 2020.

RESEARCH GAP

- What kind of economic impact and challenges on the United States and India during Covid?
- The impact of Coronavirus on Indian and US exports and imports.

THE OBJECTIVE OF THE STUDY

To research "India and the United States of America: Implications of the Coronavirus Pandemic on Global Trade"

RESEARCH METHODOLOGY

GRAVITY APPROACH

Using national COVID incidence, national lockdown limitations, and the same parameters for the nation's major trading partners, we do a gravity-like calculation. Imports from the US for all locations to which the US exports in 2019 and 2020, at the item (HS 6-digit) level, are our dependent variable. There is a definite negative correlation between COVID incidence (the number of fatalities per capita) and COVID-inducing government measures (an index of the strictness of lockdowns). Our baseline specification suggests that a country with the largest per capita number of Coronavirus deaths attained in our sample will see a 13 per cent drop in imports from the US in 2019. 17.6 per cent of imports would be reduced by switching from 0% lockdowns to maximum lockdown stringency.

Studies that focus on the US are few and far between and their data only go up to the middle of 2020, meaning that they halt before the end of the first wave of the pandemic. In other cases, researchers use data from other nations, such as India or data from several different economies. International trade has been adversely affected by the outbreak.

The research uses both Coronavirus death instances and lockdown procedures when most other studies only use one or the other (Campbell et al., 2021). Lockdowns are enforced in response to the pandemic, usually when the number of deaths is high or predicted to climb, even if Coronavirus deaths are an obvious proxy for its impact. In other words, the occurrence of COVID drives the implementation of lockdown measures. A lack of lockdown measures in the study of Coronavirus deaths, for example, can lead to falsely inflated negative effects related to Coronavirus deaths and vice versa. Because we include both variables as regressors, our analysis is resistant to this form of endogeneity.

In addition, we specifically consider the impact of the epidemic on international trade flows in the paper. (Anderson & Wincoop, 2021) discussed multilateral resistance, and yet most existing works have not explored the influence of other countries on gravity estimation. 6 Quantitatively, they're critical, as we've discovered.

DATA AND EMPIRICAL STRATEGY

As developed by the "Oxford" Coronavirus Government Response Tracker (OxCGRT) compiles publicly available information on several COVID incidents and policy indicators. For example, nine indicators monitor containment strategies, such as the closures of schools, workplaces, and international borders. 10 One way to gauge the degree to which "lockdown style" laws restrict people's freedom of movement is by creating an index using these indicators (Hobijn, and Şahin 2021). The original strictness index is between 0 and 100. To aid in the comprehension of regression coefficients, then divide the original index by 100. An increasing number of restrictions are placed on individuals and businesses when the shutdown methodological rigour index is high.

DISCUSSION

When comparing death rates between nations and across time, the Coronavirus mortality data obtained by "OxCGRT" appears to be the most accurate. Testing capacity and reporting process have a significant impact on other outcomes, such as the total number of tests and positive instances. The capacity of governments to do so has changed dramatically in 2020. Our proxy for Coronavirus prevalence is based on the number of deaths per thousand persons (Covid) (Hanson, 2021). "OxCGRT's" original Coronavirus data is updated every day. When data are unavailable for a day, the number of new deaths is averaged across the last seven days. To arrive at a monthly average, we gather all of the data.

$$Stringency\_Row_{ipt} = \frac{\sum_{j=1}^{N} M_{ijp,2018} Stringency_{jt}}{\sum_{j=1}^{N} M_{ijp,2018}},$$

RESULT

It examines the impact of our key factors on monthly log differences in Chinese imports, defined at the 6-digit level. Just two variables in columns 1 and 2: Stringency and Covid. We simply include month dummies in the first column to get a sense of how they relate to the dependent variable. Our second column then includes fixed impacts for both countries and products (absorbed). As a result, the regression is better able to capture the data. The pandemic's adverse demand consequences outweigh its adverse supply implications in both scenarios, showing that the negative demand effect is stronger. For this reason, it is critical to take into account extra fixed effects, as their absolute values drop significantly.

LIMITATIONS

Primary data can now be acquired, thanks to Covid; hence, research can be based on secondary resources. so its credibility and validity are not sure. Internet-based communication tools (e.g., email, an online survey platform) are used to collect data from participants who reply to the research link (e.g. E-mail, online survey platform). Because of the COVID-19 pandemic, academics have been increasingly interested in adopting internet-based data collecting methods to gather information. This is demonstrated by the rise in the number of studies that have used online surveys to gather information since the epidemic began.

FURTHER SCOPE OF THIS STUDY

Expansion of the scope of the research This study will be used in a variety of projects in the future to help reduce the negative effects that Covid has on trade. In addition, students use this study to improve their understanding of the subject of COVID-19. The merchants from both the United States and India used this research to get a better grasp of export and import during the worldwide pandemic, given that this study discusses the commerce that occurs between the two countries

CONCLUSION

Trade is a vital part of the economy, and governments must weigh the benefits of limiting the spread of a pandemic against the costs incurred by abandoning commercial activity in the fight against the virus. A pandemic like Coronavirus made it clear that anticipating the health and economic implications of disease and governments' responses to it is a challenging endeavour, in part because there are few parallels. As a result of the global epidemic, we've come up with the initial estimations of how it will affect international trade in 2020. Estimates like this are essential to establish the most effective policies to handle future pandemics. For example, many systemic models have been created since the beginning of the Coronavirus dilemma. As part of this endeavour, our findings can serve as valid benchmarks for direct pandemic effects and efforts to avoid their spread on trade flows. These estimations could be used to calibrate the models using the elasticity derived from these estimates.

As a result of our findings, we believe that any conceptual framework should consider the influence of the pandemic in other nations on bilateral trade flows. Indeed, the third-country effects show that the best approaches to cope with a pandemic need to be synchronized across nations. These interdependencies can be intuitive, but accurate estimations are needed by policymakers. We use data on the US's exports to every country and area of the world to estimate trade flows at the country-product level. This enables us to detach the pandemic's impact on countries that import it.

REFERENCES

Anderson, J., & Wincoop, E. (2021). Gravity with gravitas: A solution to the border puzzle. *American Economic Review*, **93**(1), 170 192.

Berthou, A., & Stumpner, S. (2022). Trade under lockdown. Banque de France Working Paper No. 867

Campbell, E., A. McDarris and W. Pizer. (2021). "Border Carbon Adjustments 101." Resources for the Future. https://www.rff.org/publications/explainers/ border-carbon- adjustments-101/

CRS (Congressional Research Service). (2020). "'Made in US 2025' Industrial Policies: Issues for Congress." https://sgp.fas.org/crs/row/IF10964.pdf.

D'Aguanno, L., O. Davies, A. Dogan, R. Freeman, S. Lloyd, D. Reinhardt, R. Sajedi, and R. Zymek. (2021). "Global Value Chains, Volatility and Safe Openness: Is Trade a Double- Edged Sword?" Financial Stability Paper 46, Bank of England, London.

Eaton, J., Kortum, S., Neiman, B., & Romalis, J. (2018). Trade and the global recession. *American Economic Review*, **106**(11), 3401– 3438. https://doi.org/10.1257/aer.20101557

Hanson, G.(2021). "Can Trade Work for Workers?" Foreign Affairs, May–June. https:// www.foreignaffairs.com/articles/united-states/2021-04-20/ can-trade-work-workers.

Hardy, B., and T. Logan. (2020). "Racial Economic Inequality Amid the CORONAVIRUSCrisis." Hamilton Project, Washington. https://www.brookings.edu/research/ racial-economic-inequality-amid-the-covid-19-crisis/.

Hayakwa, K., & Mukunoki, H. (2021). Impacts of CORONAVIRUSon global value chains. *The Developing Economies*, **59**(2), 154– 177.

Heise, S., J. Pierce, G. Schaur, and P. Schott. (2021). "Tariff Rate Uncertainty and the Structure of Supply Chains." Working paper, Yale School of Management, New Haven, CT.

Hobijn, B., and A. Şahin. (2021). Maximum Employment and the Participation Cycle. NBER Working Paper 29222. Cambridge MA: National Bureau of Economic Research. https://www.nber.org/system/files/working_papers/w29222/w29222. Pdf

Le Moigne, M., & Ossa, R. (2021). Crumbling Economy, Booming Trade: The Surprising Resilience of World Trade in 2020. Working Paper 01-21 Kühne Center Impact Series.

Pei, J., de Vries, G., & Zhang, M. (2021). International trade and Covid-19: City-level evidence from US's lockdown policy. *Journal of Regional Economics*, Forthcoming, 1– 26.

Sforza, A. & Steininger, M. (2020). Globalization in the Time of Covid-19. CESifo working paper 8184.

Socrates, M. K. (2020). The effect of lockdown policies on international trade flows from developing countries: Event study evidence from India. Working Paper. University of Delhi

Analyzing Indian Rupee / UD Dollar (INR/USD) Exchange Rate Movements Under Managed Float: A Cointegration Approach

Author – Dr. Shalini Devi, Associate Professor, Keshav Mahavidyalaya, University of Delhi

ABSTRACT

The paper tests the validity of monetary model of exchange rate in the long run and behavior of INR/USD exchange rate in the short run during managed float regime in India. Augmented Dicky Fuller (ADF) test is applied to test stationarity of variables used. Johansen cointegration test is applied to examine long run association between exchange rate and relevant monetary fundamentals. Short run dynamics of exchange rate is studied with help of error correction model (ECM). The study validates long run relationship between INR/USD exchange rate and monetary variables. It is observed that exchange rate converges towards long run equilibrium value with 36.05% speed of adjustment. The study concludes that in the long run, besides relative interest rate, the relative money supply is also an important macro-economic variable that should be regularly and carefully managed by the authorities to control the adverse exchange rate movements and to maintain the exchange rate within control limits as we are following the managed float. Also, these variables can be used for the purpose of exchange rate forecasting.

KEYWORDS

Exchange Rate, Relative Money Supply, Real Income Differential, Flexible Exchange Rate Regime, Cointegration, Error Correction Model

JEL Classification: E 41, F 31

INTRODUCTION

The price of foreign currency in terms of domestic currency is termed as exchange rate. Exchange rate links an economy with the rest of the world through trade and investments. Exchange rate determines the level of trade of an economy in the world. A strong exchange rate is an indicator of good health of an economy whereas weak exchange rate is an indicator of weak economy. Therefore, the exchange rate is among the most carefully monitored, analysed and controlled macro-economic variable. Exchange rate is important not only at the macro level but it also affects the real return on an investor's portfolio, the profitability of specific sectors, firms etc. Thus, the exchange rate management policies are framed with the objective of having a stable exchange rate. Exchange rate now a days is one of the most challenging fields for empirical studies, particularly after adopting flexible exchange rate regime by majority of the economies across the world. Under flexible exchange rate regime, the demand and supply forces determine the exchange rate just like any other asset price. Any change in the factors affecting demand and supply level of foreign exchange will cause a change in the exchange rate. This relationship between exchange rate and changes in money supply level is explained under monetary approach to exchange rate determination. The monetary approach establishes a relationship between exchange rate and monetary fundamentals of an economy. The Indian rupee (INR) was at par with the US dollar at the time of independence. Since then the Indian rupee has depreciated number of times and now the continuous decline of rupee has become a matter of concern for India. When the domestic currency depreciates, it makes imports costlier. It becomes a worry for emerging economies like India which is an import intensive country. India meets most of its oil demand through imports and depreciating rupee creates pressure on overall domestic inflation and the current account balance. Exchange rate fluctuations also affect the foreign investments. Therefore, it becomes important to study the factors that affect exchange rate in the short run as well as in the long run so that appropriate measures may be taken to avoid excessive exchange rate volatility. The present study is an attempt into this direction.

THE MONETARY MODEL

Exchange rate for an economy may be defined as the price at which the foreign currency is sold in terms of the domestic currency. Therefore, just like any other asset price, the exchange rate should also be determined by the market forces of demand and supply for that particular currency. Further since it is the relative price between the two moneys, it should be related to the demand and supply forces of these two moneys.

In order to sustain equilibrium in the domestic money market, the existing level of money supply must be willingly held (demanded). According to neo-classical theory, the demand function for money in logarithmic form for domestic economy is stated as:

$$m = p + a + \alpha y - \beta r$$

$$m = p + \alpha y - \beta r \qquad (1)$$

having 'm' as the domestic money supply, 'y' as the domestic real gross domestic product and 'r' as the domestic interest rate. Except 'r', all other small alphabets represent natural logarithm of the corresponding variables.

Similarly, for the foreign economy, the money market equilibrium condition is stated as:

$$m^* = p^* + \alpha y^* - \beta r^* \qquad (2)$$

where the asterisks (*) denotes the foreign variables.

For simplicity, we assume that the elasticity with respect to income that is, α and semi-elasticity with respect to interest rate that is, β are equal across the two countries.

The money market equilibrium conditions as given in equation (1) and (2) do not show explicitly that how the equilibrium level of the exchange rate is established i.e. how do the exchange rate changes contribute to equilibrate the money demand and supply levels. It is explained by the absolute purchasing power parity (PPP) relationship, which postulates equality between the domestic prices P and the foreign prices converted into domestic currency, that is, P*. In symbolic terms,

$$S = \frac{P}{P^*}$$

where 'S' = spot exchange rate, 'P' = domestic price level and 'P*'= price level of the foreign economy.

Or $$\log S = \log P - \log P^*$$

$$s = p - p^* \qquad (3)$$

where small case alphabets are the logarithmic values of the corresponding variables.

The flexi-price version of monetary approach was given by Frankel (1976) and Mussa (1976), and Bilson (1978) which assumes that the goods prices are perfectly flexible and therefore the purchasing power parity as shown by equation (3) holds instantaneously.

Now, equation (3) establishes a relationship amongst the exchange rate and relative price levels of the two economies. It implies that the higher the domestic price level relative to foreign prices, the higher will be the exchange rate so that the purchasing power parity between the domestic and the foreign money holds.

The purchasing power parity relationship as shown by equation (3) implies that the exchange rate can affect the money market equilibrium level through its association with the relative price level of the domestic and foreign economies.

From equation (1), we have:

$$p = m - \alpha y + \beta r \qquad (4)$$

From equation (2), we have:

$$p^* = m^* - \alpha y^* + \beta r^* \qquad (5)$$

Putting equations (4) and (5) in equation (3), we get:

$$s = p - p^* = m - \alpha y + \beta r - m^* + \alpha y^* - \beta r^*$$

$$s = (m - m^*) - \alpha\,(y - y^*) + \beta\,(r - r^*) \qquad (6)$$

The above equation is generally called the 'flexi price reduced form' equation of monetary model of exchange rate determination. Equation (6) asserts that the exchange rate of an economy depends on the differential of the rate of growth of money supply, rate of growth of national income and the interest rate differential of the two economies.

For the purpose of estimation, the model as given by equation (6) is specified as:

$$s = \alpha 0 + (m - m^*) - \alpha 1(y - y^*) + \alpha 2\,(r - r^*) + \epsilon t \qquad (7)$$

with the assumption of common elasticities for both the countries under consideration. The model also assumes that the elasticity of exchange rate with respect to money supply of the two countries is unity. These conditions are restrictive and have been empirically tested in various studies.

OBJECTIVES OF THE STUDY

An attempt is made to empirically test and analyse the flexi price monetary model of exchange rate determination. Numerous studies have been done in this area but only very few studies have been conducted for India for the post liberalization period. Therefore, this study aims:

(1) to empirically test the long run relationship between monetary fundamentals and exchange rate, as given by the flexi price monetary model, for explaining the Indian Rupee-U.S. Dollar (INR/USD) exchange rate movements in flexible exchange rate regime

(2) to analyse the dynamics of INR/USD exchange rate in the short run and how the exchange rate moves towards its long run equilibrium level in case of disequilibrium

REVIEW OF LITERATURE

Most of the studies in the area of exchange rate determination prior to 1970s were based on fixed price assumption. But with the adoption of flexible exchange rate regime in 1970s by the major economies of the world, the monetary approach to exchange rate determination was developed. The monetary approach assumes the prices to be flexible. Frankel's (1976) study consists of the doctrinal aspects as well as the empirical evidence of the monetary approach to the exchange rate and probably it is the best expository study in this area. It deals with the determinants of exchange rate.

Bilson (1978) examined the empirical validity of a simple asset market model between duetsche/pound rate during 1970-1977. His findings suggest that the actual behaviour of the duetsche/pound rate is broadly consistent with the predictions of the monetary model. Bilson also argued that the monetary model may be useful in the analysis of short-run behaviour and may be considered as a guide to the intervention policy.

Woo (1985) studied monetary approach to exchange rate determination with a partial adjustment mechanism and found empirical support for the monetary model. Paul M. Boothe and Stephen S. Poloz (1988) conducted a study to investigate the validity of monetary model of exchange rate determination by allowing the unrestricted dynamics and taking care of the shift in demand for money due to the financial innovations and developments. He tested for the Canada-U.S. exchange rate using simulation technique and found strong evidence for the model. Ronald MacDonald and Mark P. Taylor (1993) re-examined the monetary approach to exchange rate determination, using monthly data on the duetsche-mark- U.S. dollar exchange rate and found that the monetary model is valid as a long run equilibrium condition.

Mathias Moersch and Dieter Nautz (2001) developed an alternative to the widely used reduced form monetary model of exchange rate determination. They showed that various parameter restrictions assumed under the monetary approach can be easily avoided by estimating the long run money demand function separately. Groen (2002) tested monetary models for Canada, Japan and US on quarterly data for the period 1975-2000 using panel vector error correction (VEC) technique and they found that the forecasting performance of monetary models outperform the random walk model forecasts. Zhang and Lowinger (2005) empirically examined monetary model for developed countries including Japan, United Kingdom, Germany and United States using cointegration methodology and found linear relationship between fundamental macro-economic variables namely, money supply, real GDP, interest rates and exchange rate in short run and in the long run relationship was established between expected inflation rate and exchange rate. Islam and Hasan (2006) tested monetary model for Japanese Yen/US dollar exchange rate using quarterly data for the period 1974 to 2003 using cointegration and vector error correction (VEC) technique and found support for long run validity of monetary model. They also concluded that in terms of forecasting performance, the monetary model outperformed the random walk model. Abas and Yusof (2009), Liew et al. (2009) and Chin et al. (2007) proved the long-run validity of the monetary models in Malaysia, Thailand and the Philippines, respectively. Dua and Ranjan (2011) proved that different versions of the monetary model forecasts outperform the forecasts generated by the random walk model in case of India. Evans (2013) examined empirically the monetary model of exchange rate determination for Nigeria using Autoregressive Distributed Lag (ARDL) technique for the period 1998Q1 to 2011Q2 and found support for long run relationship between macroeconomic variables and exchange rate. They recommended that the macroeconomic variable namely, money supplies, real incomes, and interest rates can be used to forecast the exchange rate movements.

Sharma and Setia (2015) and Padake, Karamcheti and Geeta (2018) empirically tested and confirmed that monetary approach to exchange rate determination is a long run phenomenon and it does not hold in the short run. Huy and Hoang Ba (2020) tested monetary approach for five Pacific Basin countries using quarterly data for the post Asian financial crisis period. They found that the monetary model did not work for Thailand and Indonesia, found long run validity of the model for Korea and Malaysia and for Vietnam, the monetary model was found to be well fitted both in terms of coefficients as well as the expected signs of the variables. Thus, the empirical evidence of monetary models based on individual time series data are mixed depending upon different approaches such as use of panel data or time series data, increase in the time span and testing of non-linear models etc.

RESEARCH METHODOLOGY AND DATA SOURCES

Since the data we have used is time series variables, first the stationarity of all the variables used in the study is tested using the Augmented Dicky Fuller (ADF) test. The ADF statistic used in this test is a negative number. The more negative the value of this statistic, the stronger the rejection of the null hypothesis that there is a unit root. If we do not have unit root problem in the variable, the variable is said to be stationary and it is I(0). If the variable has unit root problem, we apply the ADF test on first difference of the variable. If the variable becomes stationary at first difference, it is I(1). Johansen cointegration technique is used to test for the existence of long run relationship amongst the variables and the short run dynamics of exchange rate is studied with the help of error correction model (ECM). If the coefficient of lagged error term (ECMt-1) has negative value, the dependent variable i.e. the exchange rate is said to converge towards its equilibrium value in the long run. If the value is positive, then this becomes the case of divergence i.e. the exchange rate will move away from the equilibrium value. Initially, we have tested the naïve version of the reduced form monetary model as given below:

$$s e t = \alpha + \beta (m - m^*) + \gamma (y - y^*) + \eta (r - r^*) + \epsilon t \qquad (8)$$

where se t is the equilibrium level of logarithmic value of spot exchange rate.

with the restriction and expected signs as:

$\beta = 1, \gamma < 0$, and $\eta > 0$.

The error correction model (ECM) estimated in the study is given as:

$$\Delta st = \beta 1 + \beta 2\ \Delta(m - m^*) + \beta 3\ \Delta(y - y^*) + \beta 4\ \Delta(r - r^*) + \beta 5\ ECMt\text{-}1 + \epsilon t$$

where 'Δ' represents the first difference of the corresponding variables.

VARIABLES USED AND DATA SOURCES

The study tests the validity of flexi price reduced form monetary model of exchange rate determination that includes the money supply differential (m - m*), real income differential (y - y*) and interest rate differential (r - r*) as the independent variables. The study uses quarterly data for the period 2004Q1 to 2021Q2. United States of America (USA) is taken as the foreign economy. All the data except the interest rates, are considered in logarithmic form. For money supply, M1 (narrow money) definition of money has been used. The Consumer Price Index (CPI) is used to convert the nominal GDP into real GDP. For interest rates of the both the economies, discount rate is used. Exchange rate is the quarterly average exchange rate.

The required data is obtained from secondary sources including International Financial Statistics – publication of IMF, Handbook of Statistics on Indian Economy, and Statistical release of Federal Reserve Bank. E-views software has been used for the purpose of estimation.

EMPIRICAL ESTIMATION AND ANALYSIS

CORRELATION MATRIX

Before start testing the time series property of stationarity of the variables, first we have computed the correlation amongst the variables as given below in the correlation matrix in Table 7.1.

Table 7.1: Correlation Matrix

Variables	st	(m – m*)	(y – y*)	(r – r*)
st	1.0000	0.3513	0.6879	0.6847
(m – m*)	0.3513	1.0000	0.8687	0.5494
(y – y*)	0.6879	0.8687	1.0000	0.7592
(r – r*)	0.6847	0.5494	0.7592	1.0000

Source: *The Author*

UNIT ROOT TEST

Since the data used in this study is the time series data, the test for presence of unit root becomes the first essential step. The Augmented Dicky Fuller (ADF) test was applied on each variable to test whether the variable is stationary or not. In case of variables having unit root at levels, the ADF test was applied on the first difference of the variables to check for stationarity and the order of integration. If variables are stationary at levels, they are I(0) and if the variables are stationary at first difference, they are I(1). Table 7.2 shows ADF test results for the order of integration of the variables used in the analysis.

Table 7.2: Unit Root Test (ADF Test) Results

Variables	ADF Values for Levels	ADF Values for First Difference	Critical Values	Order of Integration
st	-2.9258 (with constant & trend)	-6.5028	-3.4773 (5% level) -4.0987 (1% level)	I(1)
(m - m*)	-1.7019 (with constant)	-6.5422	-2.9055 (5% level) -3.5316 (1% level)	I(1)
(y - y*)	-2.4428 (with constant & trend)	-10.7058	-2.9055 (5% level) -3.5316 (1% level)	I(1)
(r - r*)	-1.0214 (with constant & trend)	-7.6275	-3.4794 (5% level) –4.1032 (1% level)	I(1)

Source: *The Author*

The above table shows that the order of integration of all the variables is I(1). Since all variables are I(1), the Johansen cointegration test is used to test the long run validity of the model and error correction model (ECM) is used to test the short run dynamics of exchange rate movements.

JOHANSEN COINTEGRATION TEST

Since all the variables are I(1), the Johansen cointegration test is used to check for the presence of long run relationship amongst the variables. Both the Trace statistic and Max Eigen Value statistic are used under the Johansen test for cointegration analysis. The cointegration test results are reported in table 7.3(a) and 7.3(b). The Akaike Information Criteria (AIC) is used to determine the optimal lag length. The trace test and max eigen value test statistics show the existence of one cointegrating equation at 5% level implying that there is long run relationship among exchange rate, money supply differential, real income differential and interest rate differential.

Table 7.3(a): Johansen Cointegration Test (Trace Test)

(H0: There is no cointegration)

Hypothesized No. of CE(s)	Eigen Value	Trace Statistic	0.05 Critical Value	Prob.**
None *	0.464177	63.90122	55.24578	0.0072
At most 1	0.363588	31.45573	35.01090	0.1144
At most 2	0.123650	7.956441	18.39771	0.6874
At most 3	0.020799	1.092961	3.841466	0.2958

Trace test indicates 1 cointegrating equation at the 0.05 level.

* denotes rejection of the hypothesis at the 0.05 level

**MacKinnon-Haug-Michelis (1999) p-values

Source: The Author

Table 7.3(b): Johansen Cointegration Test (Max Eigen Value Test)

(H0: There is no cointegration)

Hypothesized No. of CE(s)	Eigen Value	Max-Eigen Statistic	0.05 Critical Value	Prob.**
None *	0.464177	32.44549	30.81507	0.0313
At most 1	0.363588	23.49929	24.25202	0.0626
At most 2	0.123650	6.863480	17.14769	0.7278
At most 3	0.020799	1.092961	3.841466	0.2958

Max-eigenvalue indicates 1 cointegrating equation at the 0.05 level.
* denotes rejection of the hypothesis at the 0.05 level
**MacKinnon-Haug-Michelis (1999) p-values
Source: TheAuthor

ESTIMATION OF COINTEGRATING RELATIONSHIP

The long run cointegrating relationship between exchange rate and other dependent variables of the monetary model is as given below. This long run estimation result shows the long run effects of the explanatory variables on the exchange rate. It is found that all the variables namely money supply differential, real income differential and interest rate differential have expected signs in the long run as explained under the monetary approach to exchange rate determination. Positive sign of the relative money supply indicates that an increase in the domestic money supply relative to foreign economy money supply results in depreciation of the domestic currency in terms of that foreign currency. The relative money supply and relative interest rate variables are significant in the long run at 5% level of significance. However, the relative real income variable is found to be insignificant, and it could be because of high correlation (0.87) between real income differential and relative money supply (Table 7.1).

$$st = 0.386776\,(m - m^*) - 0.030023(y - y^*) + 0.013633(r - r^*)$$

(3.1628) (0.1684) (3.1628)

Log Likelihood Ratio = 310.1940

ESTIMATION OF ERROR CORRECTION MODEL (ECM)

After cointegrating relationship, the error correction model (ECM) was estimated. The ECM explains the short run behavior of exchange rate with respect to money supply differential, real income differential and interest rate differential. The cointegration relationship will be supported if the one period lag of the error term i.e. ECMt-1 carries a negative sign and is statistically significant. The coefficient of lagged error term ECMt-1 shows the proportion of disequilibrium in the exchange rate in one period that gets corrected in the next period implying the speed of adjustment i.e. how much proportion of the disequilibrium of exchange rate gets corrected in one time period. The estimated error correction model is given below:

$\Delta st = \beta 1 + \beta 2\ \Delta(m - m^*) + \beta 3\ \Delta(y - y^*) + \beta 4\ \Delta(r - r^*) + \beta 5\ ECMt\text{-}1 + \epsilon t$

$\Delta st = 0.0112 - 0.1580\ \Delta(m - m^*) - 0.2264\ \Delta(y - y^*) + 0.0153\ \Delta(r - r^*)^{**}$

(2.3794) (-1.6075) (-1.0951) (2.7236)

• - 0.3605 ECMt-1 **

(-3.1701)

(values in the parentheses represent t - statistic value

** indicates that the coefficient is significant at 5% level.)

$R^2 = 0.3679$ $Rbar^2 = 0.3152$ DW-Statistic = 2.1388

In the above estimated ECM, we found that the coefficient of lagged error term ECMt-1 has a negative sign and is statistically significant at 5% level of significance. The value of the coefficient of lagged error term in the above ECM shows that the speed of adjustment is 36.05% meaning that 36.05% of the disequilibrium in INR/USD exchange rate from its long run equilibrium value gets corrected in one quarter. From the estimated ECM, we see that the coefficient of interest rate differential variable is statistically significant. It implies that the interest rate differential variable is more responsive to correct the long run disequilibrium in exchange rate values. The coefficients of money supply differential and real income differential are statistically insignificant implying that these variables are not so responsive to correct the disequilibrium as the interest rate differential variable is.

FINDINGS AND CONCLUSION

The study tested the validity of flexible price monetary approach to exchange rate determination under flexible exchange rate regime in India. Johansen cointegration technique is used to check for exchange rate movements in the long run and error correction model is used to study the short run dynamics. The empirical results of the study show that there is cointegration or long run relationship between exchange rate and other monetary variables namely money supply differential, real income differential and interest rate differential. This finding of the study is similar to the findings of Uddin et.al.'s (2013). In the estimated cointegrating equation, all the variables have expected signs. An increase in the domestic money supply relative to money supply of the foreign economy results in increase in the exchange rate which implies depreciation of the of the domestic currency. We can observe this relationship on the events that happened in the Indian economy. On August 28, 2013, there was biggest single day percentage fall of 3.7% in the value of Indian rupee against US dollar. Indian rupee was recorded as the most affected Asian currency. This drastic depreciation of the Indian rupee against US dollar in 2013 can be attributed to the removal of quantitative easing by the US Federal Reserve. Following the 2008 financial crisis, in order to provide more money to fuel the US economy, Federal Reserve started buying bonds from the commercial banks and private financial institutions. It resulted in increase in the US monetary base. A major portion of this new money created in US reached India in the form of investments by FIIs. In 2012-13, when US started removing the quantitative easing by increasing the interest rates in US, a large portion of the capital was withdrawn by the FIIs from the Indian financial market. It generated huge demand for US dollars and resulted in historic depreciation of the Indian Rupee against US dollar. Similar relation can be traced for other variables as well. The error correction model show that only interest rate differential variable has significant impact on exchange rate in the short run. It has positive sign implying that when domestic interest rate is higher than the Us interest rate, people will invest more in the Indian financial market which will increase the monetary base of India and will result in increase in the exchange rate i.e. depreciation of the Indian rupee. The ECM show that the relative money supply and relative real income variables do not have significant impact on exchange rate in the short run. The ECM also show that the speed of adjustment is 36.05% meaning that 36.05% of the deviations from equilibrium value of exchange rate gets corrected in one quarter.

Thus, the study found that in the short run, interest rate is more significant macroeconomic variable affecting the exchange rate and therefore, it must be very carefully and continuously monitored and controlled by the regulatory authority to keep the exchange rate movements within desirable limits. However, in the long run, besides relative interest rate, the relative money supply is also identified as an important macro-economic variable that should be regularly and carefully managed by the authorities to control the adverse exchange rate movements and to maintain the exchange rate within control limits as we are following the managed float. Also, these variables can be used for the purpose of exchange rate forecasting.

REFERENCES

Abas, K. H., & Z. Yusof, (2009). Exchange Rate and Monetary Fundamental: Evidence from Malaysia and Japan. Conference Proceedings, International Conference on Business and Information, 2009.

Bilson, John F.O. (1978). Recent Developments in Monetary Models of Exchange Rate Determination. IMF Staff Paper, Vol.24, pp. 201-221.

Boothe, Paul M., & Stephen S. Poloz (1988). Unstable Money Demand and the Monetary Model of the Exchange Rate. Canadian Journal of Economics, November, pp. 785-798.

Charemza Wojciech W. and Derek F. Deadman (1992). New Directions in Econometric Practice – General to Specific Modeling, Cointegration and Vector Autoregression. Edward Elgar, Cheltenham, U.K., Lyme, U.S.

Chin, L. M.Azali, B. Zulkornain, & M. B. Yusoff, (2007). The monetary model of exchange rate: evidence from the Philippines. Applied Economics Letters, Vol. 14, pp 993–997.

Dua, P. & R. Ranjan, (2011). Modelling and Forecasting the Indian Re/US Dollar Exchange Rate. Working Paper 197, Centre for Development Economics, Delhi School of Economics, India.

Evans Olaniyi (2013). The Monetary Model of Exchange Rate in Nigeria: An Autoregressive Distributed Lag (ARDL) Approach. Munich Personal RePec Archive (MPRA), Paper No. 52457. URL: http://mpra.ub.uni-muenchen.de/52457.

Frankel, Jeffery (1980). Tests of Rational Expectations in the Forward Exchange Market. Southern Economic Journal, Vol.46, April, pp- 1083-1101.

Frenkel, Jacob A. (1976). A Monetary Approach to the Exchange Rate: Doctorinal Aspects and Empirical Evidence. Scandanavian Journal of Economics, pp- 201- 224.

Frenkel, Jacob A. & H.G. Johnson, eds. (1978). The Economics of Exchange Rates. Reading, Mass: Addison-Wesley.

Frenkel, J. (1979). On the Mark: A Theory of Floating Exchange Rates Based on Real Interest Differential. American Economic Review, Vol.69, pp. 610-622.

Groen, J. J. J. (2002). Cointegration and the Monetary Exchange Rate Model Revisited. Oxford Bulletin of Economics and Statistics, Vol.64, pp. 361–380.

Huy, C. L. & Hoang Ba, H.L. (2020). The monetary approach to exchange rate determination: empirical observations from the Pacific Basin Economies. Decision Science Letters, Vol. 9, pp 453-464.

Islam, M.F. & M.S. Hasan, (2006). The Monetary Model of the Dollar- Yen Exchange Rate Determination: A Cointegration approach. International Journal of Business and Economics, Vol. 5, No. 2, pp 129–145.

MacDonald, Ronald, & Mark P. Taylor (1993). The Monetary Approach to Exchange Rate: Rational Expectations, Long Run Equilibrium and Forecasting. IMF Staff Papers, Vol.40, No.1, March, pp 89-107.

Moersch Mathias & Dieter Nautz (2001). A Note on Testing the Monetary Model of the Exchange Rate. Applied Financial Economics, Vol.11, pp 261-268.

Mundell, R. A. (1968). International Economics. Macmillan, New York.

Padake, V., Karamcheti, B. & Geetha, T. (2018). The INR/USD Exchange Rate Determination: An Empirical Investigation of the flexible Price Monetary Model in a Vector Auto Regression Framework. Theoretical Economic Letters, vol. 8, pp 1070-1082.

Sharma, C. & Setia, R. (2015). Macroeconomic Fundamentals and Dynamics of the Indian Rupee-Dollar Exchange Rate. Journal of Financial Economic Policy, Vol. 7, pp 301-326. https://doi.org/10.1108/JFEP-11-2014-0069.

Uddin, M., Quaosar, G. & Nandi, D. (2013). Factors Affecting the Fluctuation in Exchange Rate of Bangladesh: A Cointegration Approach. International Journal of Social Sciences, 18(1), 1-12.

Woo, Wing T. (1985). The Monetary Approach to Exchange Rate Determination Under Rational Expectations: The Dollar-Deutschmark Rate. Journal of International Economics. Vol.18, February, pp- 1-16.

Zhang, S.D., & Lowinger, T.C. (2005). Cointegration in a Monetary Model of Exchange Rate Determination. ASBBS E-Journal, 1, pp 1-18.

Influence Of Developments Of Artificial Intelligence On The Recruitment Process: A Review

Author – Dr. Vinima Gambhir, Associate Professor, Atlas Skilltech University, Mumbai & Shailaja Tiwary, Research Scholar, Amity University, Mumbai

ABSTRACT

'Technology has always held an influence within the recruitment scene, reducing costs and delivering increased effectiveness in recruiting candidates (Okolie, 2017)'. The organisations throughout the world are increasingly getting technologically dependent due to globalisation. Hence if they need to survive, they have to keep up with the competition, thereby making the HR department responsible to bring in employees with newer skillsets and knowledge. This change has made human resource management especially recruitments to take the centre stage. The impact of technology on the field of HRM and particularly the recruitment process, therefore needs to be carefully considered and assessed.

This research paper will try to understand the effects of technological breakthroughs, particularly Artificial Intelligence (AI), on influencing employers and candidates, specifically in the initial stages of recruitment process. It intends to look into how AI can be included into the current hiring process to potentially improve efficiency and what are the ramifications of doing so would be.

Key words: Artificial Intelligence, Recruitments, Improvement, Ramifications

INTRODUCTION

In the business world, hiring is essential for acquiring ability. The recruitment team is in charge of speaking with prospective hires, interviewing candidates, and selecting the best candidates. These workers can add to the company's or organization's overall business success, which will be advantageous when done successfully.

Efficiency and hiring quality are the two main measures that recruiters typically use. They need to hire people as quickly as they can to fill open positions or finish new roles. However, they need to make sure they hire the individuals who are best suited for the positions or roles.

However, there are some difficulties in recruiting that HR department frequently face. They must first spend a lot of time contacting possibilities, screening a large number of applicants, and closing deals with potential employees. Additionally, they frequently hire the incorrect candidates in the job market. The use of artificial intelligence has created new innovational trends for many companies across a variety of industries, thanks to technological advancements. However, using AI to find potential still requires caution on the part of recruiters.

OBJECTIVES OF THE STUDY

- To study the influence of artificial intelligence on recruitment process.

REVIEW OF LITERATURE

'Artificial Intelligence in Recruitment: Opportunities and Challenges of Implementing Artificial Intelligence in today's Recruitment Processes', a thesis submitted by Helena Lundvall in September 2022 comes to the conclusion that the lack of qualified applicants that is currently constraining the labour market is driving the creation of a more effective and secure hiring procedure where AI plays an increasingly significant role. To enable the implementation of AI, organizations need to actively encourage the acquisition of knowledge about the technology among their HRM professionals, because, without their understanding of the technology and how it benefits them, its prominent advantages cannot be achieved by the organization.

Sunil Kumar Srivastava, 26 July 2018, 'Artificial Intelligence: way forward for India', suggests that AI is probably going to change the manner in which we live and work. Because of its high potential, its reception is being treated as the fourth modern upset. Similarly as with any significant headway in innovation, it carries with it a range of chances just as difficulties.

Dhamija, Pavitra,' E-Recruitment A Roadmap towards E- Human Resource Management', 2012, proposes that the main indispensable incentive for an endeavor is the experience, aptitudes, inventiveness and bits of knowledge of its kin. HR is the key segments in each association. It speaks to add up to information, ability, and demeanor, innovative capacity, inclination and conviction of an individual associated with the issues of an association. In the ongoing years, the field of human asset the board has experienced various innovative progressions. Web has had an effect on the general working of human asset division. HR procedures and techniques have been upheld by everything from muddled record organizer frameworks to computerization, going from utilization different frameworks and databases to a solitary form of the entire framework.

Dave Bartram, 28 June 2008, Internet Recruitment and Selection: Kissing Frogs to find Princes states that The Internet has affected the manner by which recruitment and selection are completed in North America and the effect is progressively being felt as far as changes practically speaking in Europe and Asia-Pacific

V Yakubovich, D Lup - Organization science, 2006, Stages of the recruitment process and the referrer's performance effect states that in spite of the fact that the current hypothesis predicts that a referral's odds of being employed increment with the activity execution of the referrer, no experimental proof is accessible to help this case. To address this error, they disintegrate the enrollment procedure into target choice, emotional determination, and self-choice and hypothesize that the probability of passing a specific enlistment stage increments with the presentation of the referrer under target choice and self-choice, yet stays dubious at a phase of abstract choice.

O Kaya, J Schildbach, DB AG, S Schneider on Artificial intelligence, 2019, stated that Artificial Intelligence (AI) is a critical advance forward in the digitalization and change of present day organizations. To put it plainly, it alludes to PCs' ability to procure and apply information without developers' mediation. Until this point in time however, AI usage in banking has been humble. Computer based intelligence is being tried for constant distinguishing proof and counteraction of extortion in internet banking just as in know-your-client (KYC) forms. Robot-guides are moreover developing after some time to turn out to be genuine AI arrangements.

J. McCarthy,P.J.Hayes, 1981, Some Philosophical Problems from the Standpoint of Artificial Intelligence states that A PC program fit for acting wisely on the planet must have a general portrayal of the world regarding which its information sources are deciphered. Planning such a program requires responsibilities about what information is and how it is gotten. In this way, a portion of the major conventional issues of reasoning emerge in man-made reasoning. lish a specific objective.

Cappelli, Peter in the article "Your Approach to Hiring is all wrong" says that Organizations have never done as much employing as they do today and have never made a more terrible showing of it, says Peter Cappelli of Wharton. A great part of the procedure is redistributed to organizations.

J McCarthy, 1981 - Elsevier, Readings in artificial intelligence states Man-made reasoning or artificial intelligence (AI) issue has been isolated into two sections—an epistemological part and a heuristic part. This section further clarifies this division, clarifies a portion of the epistemological issues, and presents some new outcomes and approaches.

H Lu, Y Li, M Chen, et al, 2018, Springer Brain Intelligence: Go beyond Artificial Intelligence states that as of late, AI has stood out as a key for development in created nations, for example, Europe and the United States and creating nations, for example, China and India. The consideration has been centered basically around growing new computerized reasoning data correspondence innovation (ICT) and robot innovation (RT).

V Jeet, D Sayeeduzzafar, 2014, a study of HRM practices and its impact on employees' job satisfaction in private sector banks states that In current period of profoundly unstable business condition associations are confronting developing difficulties in type of securing and advancement of human asset. Being important and scant capacities, HR are considered as a wellspring of manageable upper hand.

DISCUSSION

Artificial Intelligence and Recruitment

As it's been said, 'need is the mother of creation', human resources are currently discovering comfort in new-age advancements, for example, computerized reasoning (AI), block chain. The expression "man-made reasoning" or famously known as "artificial intelligence" was first utilized in the mid-1950s. Albeit numerous definitions are available.

Accenture defines AI as, "Computer systems that can sense, comprehend, act and learn. In other words, a system that can perceive the world around it, analyze and understand the information it receives, take actions based on that understanding, and improve its performance by learning from what happened. And by enabling machines to interact more naturally – with their environment, with people and with data – the technology can extend the capabilities of both humans and machines far beyond what each can do on their own."

Artificial intelligence (AI) has a lot of potential and significant interest in the future of the hiring process. Even though AI is still in its infancy, by automating many of the tasks presently performed by human recruiters, it has the potential to completely transform the hiring process. AI-powered recruitment bots may be used in the future to screen applicants, determine who is the best fit for a position, and even perform preliminary interviews. As a result, human recruiters would have more time to devote to strategic duties like cultivating rapport with candidates and learning more about the corporate culture.

AI could also be used to give applicants input in real-time during the application process, which would enhance the procedure for everyone. Overall, the use of AI in hiring appears to have a bright future. AI has the potential to improve the recruitment process by automating many of the tasks presently carried out by human recruiters.

IMPACT OF AI ON RECRUITMENT

Artificial intelligence (AI) will certainly have a significant impact on the hiring process in the future. AI is currently used to identify prospective job candidates and to automate some steps in the application process. But as AI technology advances, it's possible that in the future it will contribute even more to the hiring procedure. A candidate's skills and qualifications could possibly be evaluated by AI much more precisely than by a human. A applicant who might be a good match for a position but who would not have been found using conventional methods like resumes or job applications could also be found using AI. AI could also be used to streamline processes.

Artificial intelligence in the hiring process appears to have a bright future. AI can assist in ensuring that hiring choices are impartial and fair. This is a huge plus because it can be challenging to discover qualified candidates without any bias. AI can also contribute to process acceleration by automating repetitive duties like sorting through resumes. This allows recruiters to concentrate on the more crucial job of speaking with candidates. Overall, it appears that AI will have a significant positive effect on the employment market. It will aid in ensuring that the finest candidates are hired, as well as accelerating the procedure so that recruiters can for focus on important tasks.

CONCLUSION

Artificial intelligence involves creating machines that mimic human intellect. As a result, machines are now capable of acting or thinking like people. They can carry out the duties assigned to the employees or take on some of their responsibilities. Having said that, AI employment merely incorporates artificial intelligence into the process of hiring talent. Recruiters can find potential prospects, narrow down the applicant pool, and even automate manual tasks using AI technology. The end result is to streamline the complete hiring procedure.

Artificial intelligence will undoubtedly have a significant impact on hiring practices in the future. AI can expedite the process and deliver more precise results, which will undoubtedly improve the effectiveness and efficiency of the hiring process. The human component of recruitment should not be completely replaced by AI; rather, AI should be used as a tool to enhance it. The human touch is essentially what makes recruitment successful.

BIBLIOGRAPHY

Dhamija, Pavitra,' E-Recruitment A Roadmap towards E- Human Resource Management', 2012

Fraij, Jihad & Várallyai, László. (2021). literature Review: Artificial Intelligence Impact on the Recruitment Process. International Journal of Engineering and Management Sciences. 6. 108-119. 10.21791/IJEMS.2021.1.10.

Heric (2018) Digital technologies have become essential for HR to engage top talent and add value to the business, October 10th, 2018

Jarrahi, M. H. (2018). Artificial Intelligence and the Future of Work: Human-AI Symbiosis in Organizational Decision Making. Business Horizons, 61(4), 1-10. doi:10.1016/j.bushor.2018.03.007

Merlin.P, R., & Jayam.R. (2018). Artificial Intelligence in Human Resource Management. International Journal of Pure and Applied Mathematics, 119(14), 1891-1895. Retrieved from http://www.acadpubl.eu/hub/

O Kaya, J Schildbach, DB AG, S Schneider on Artificial intelligence, 2019

Peter (2018) The impact of AI on Hr function, Published in institute of employement studies, November 2018.

Prachant Srivastava (2018) Impact of AI on strategic Hr Decision Making, April 6th, 2018

Prasanna Tambe,Peter Cappeli and Valery Yakubovish (2018) AI in HRM challenges and a path forward AI, January 2018.

Rajeev Bharadwaj (2019) How AI is revolutionising the human resource functions, January 5th,2019

Sarah Fister Gale (2019) AI is coming-and Hr is not prepared, January 4th, 2019

Barriers To Entry At Workplace For Individuals With Disabilities In India

Author – Dr. Devpriya Dey, Assistant Professor, Alliance University, Bangalore

ABSTRACT

In India, there are around 3 crore people with disabilities, of which about 1.3 crore are employable, but sadly, 34 lakhs have found employment in a variety of fields, including organized, unorganized, and self-employment. In the private sector, there are just 0.28 percent of workers who are disabled. As per the "Rights of Persons with Disabilities Act, 2016", there are certain provisions of incentives for the private employers. In Government sector, reservation for persons with disabilities exists. Institutions such as NASSCOM and CII are also working towards the creating employment opportunities for the disabled workforce. In addition to this, there are few more private sector employers running training and development centers exclusively for disabled people. In spite of such efforts taken, the current employment situation of the persons with disabilities looks quite dim.

This exploratory research paper attempts to understand the reasons for roadblock to entry at workplace for the persons with disabilities in India. Qualitative approach of data collection has been adopted for this research. Reports from reputed bodies such as ILO, World Bank, Government websites as well as research papers, articles from online media have been carefully considered for data analysis. Overall, this research will form a foundation for conducting in-depth research exploring the factors causing hindrance in the employment pathways of persons with disabilities in India.

Key Words: Persons with disabilities, Employment, Diversity, Inclusion

INTRODUCTION

One fifth of the world's population comprises of individuals with disabilities. Across the globe, these individuals are occupied in various professions but majority of them are not involved in mainstream employment on an equal basis (Shenoy, 2011). The employment rates of the persons with disabilities are lower in all countries than for the non-PwD population (O'Keefe et.al, 2009). There is a large difference in the India's employment rate for people with and without disabilities too. Therefore promoting the employment of disabled people is important (DEOC, 2009). Employment is necessary for everyone since it provides an income and social security, especially for the persons with disabilities (PwD) since it also gives them a meaning of livelihood and develops their self-esteem. It also helps them to overcome the feeling of self-isolation in the society. Inclusion of PwD at workplace gives them an equal status and respect. From an employer perspective, there are multiple benefits of hiring PwD. Employers feel that the PwD are committed and dedicated workers. Overall performance of the employees with disabilities is quite favorable. They demonstrate a greater ability to improve their performance over a period. Moreover, they work together with their co-workers and share a positive relationship with their supervisors too. Workers with disability are in fact rated higher than the non-disabled ones based on a number of factors such as they arrive on time from their breaks, accept authority, punctual to work, reliable and dependable. More over the inclusion of PwD at workplace enhances the ability of the organization to compete with the competitors (Kregel, 1999). The retention rate of the employees with disabilities is quite higher. In fact, it develops the community image of the employer too (Unger, 2002).

LITERATURE REVIEW

According to the last Census 2011, 26.8 million persons with disabilities exist in India. The Government of India has increased the categories of disabilities to twenty-one in 2016. People with thalassemia, Parkinson's disease, dwarfism or even acid attack victims also have been added under the persons with disability category (GoI, 2016). Out of the total disabled population, only 9.7 million are employed. 69 percent of the disabled population resides in the rural areas and the remaining 31 percent in the urban territory of the country. Approximately 21 percent of the employed individuals with disabilities belong with seeing, hearing and movement category. 50 percent of the total persons with disabilities fall under the age group of 20 years to 59 years which the potential age to pursue an employment (GoI, 2011).

Several employment avenues are available for the persons with disabilities in India. One of such mediums is the employment exchange. As on 2014, there are 978 employment exchanges are available which assists to people to gain employment opportunities (DEOC, 2009). These employment exchanges help people in getting job market related information, give suggestions about vocational training centers for skill development and even counsel regarding available career options. These facilities are open for persons with disabilities too. The placement percentage of the employment exchanges is approximately 6 percent. Among the individuals with disabilities who are placed, 80 percent belong to orthopedically impaired category. Even among the disabled people who registered in the live register in employment exchange, 70 percent are from orthopedics category. Remaining 16 percent are hearing impaired and last 13 percent are from visually impaired category. The other categories are neither not registered nor placed (O'Keefe et.al, 2009).

Apart from the employment exchanges, there are special exchanges and special cells that aim to help the persons with disabilities to secure employment. 42 special exchanges and 38 special cells have been established until 2014 in India (DEOC, 2009). The placement condition of these special exchanges has been equally dim as the employment exchanges. National Career Service report, 2016 mentions that only 200 individuals with disabilities got an employment opportunity out of 5700 registered disabled applicants that makes the placement percentage to 3.51 percent. Even like the employment exchange, all 200 placed PwD belonged to orthopedically impaired category. The other categories have either not registered or not placed. Concerning the employment of the PwD through the special cells, the percentage is 0.6 since 583 individuals with disabilities have been placed out of 92736 in the live register. The World Bank report, 2009 mentions that only 27 percent of the individuals with disabilities have registered in the special exchanges and special cells.

As per the "Rights of Persons with Disabilities Act, 2016" there is a provision of 4 percent reservations in the government jobs spread across visual, hearing, speech impaired, locomotor disability and intellectual disability categories. As per the World Bank report, 2009, only 0.44 percentages of the vacant positions, which were meant for the individual with disabilities, got filled. National Institute for the Hearing Handicapped has been set as an autonomous institute that functions under the Ministry of Social Justice and Empowerment. This body is engaged in managing reservation issues with persons with disabilities and helps in filling up the pending vacancies reserved for the disabled people. This institution i.e. "jobfordeaf.nic.in" has developed a website where in the hearing impaired people can register their profile for employment opportunities. This website is currently not functional for unknown reasons. Recruitment of gazetted and non-gazetted employees is conducted by "Union Public Service Commission (UPSC)" and "Staff Selection Commission (SSC)" bureau. Persons with disabilities are granted concessions in these examinations. These bureaus also organize special recruitment drives only for PwD. Even there is a provision of age relaxation for PwD in these examinations depending upon the level of job that they apply for (DOEC, 2009). Regarding the special recruitment drives for PwD, only one drive was conducted where 296 disabled people were selected since 2015

Even according to the Apprentices Act, 1961, a reservation of 3 percent has been allocated for physically handicapped people only. As per this legislation, training is provided to enhance the employability in the private sector. In spite of this facility, there is no information available on the participation of persons with disabilities in the apprentice training from 2004-05 onwards (O'Keefe et.al, 2009).

In order to enhance the employability skills of the individual with disabilities, 21 vocational rehabilitation centers (VRC) have been established in India. These VRCs' assist the PwD in rendering skill based industry specific training. The duration of such training, programs are generally short term that may be extended to 12 months also. Those individuals with disabilities who do not possess required academic qualification can also enroll at the VRCs' to receive trainings in informal mode that will enable themselves into formal training based organizations such as Industrial Training Institutes (ITIs) or Polytechnics. Among these 21 VRCs', there are some who provides placement opportunities too. In addition to the VRCs' 7 training workshops have been also been established for skill enhancement. There has been a plan to set up a VRC in each state that is yet to a reality. 11 rural rehabilitation extension centers (RREC) has also been established to cater the needs of the individual with disabilities in the rural since the VRCs' were located in the urban territories of the country. These RRECs' have collaboration with several NGOs and organize Community Based Rehabilitation (CBR). Here assessment camps are conducted with the help of mobile rehabilitation counselors in a periodic manner. In order to support the VRCs and RRECs, composite regional centers (CRC) have been set up in 7 locations of the country. The role of the CRC is to establish the infrastructure required for the VRC, development of manpower, conduct research and rehabilitate the individuals with disabilities. In this process, the skill level of the PwD get enhanced that leads to enhancement of employment opportunities. In spite of setting up these skill enhancement centers across the country, only 12363 individuals with disabilities out of 17 million unemployed as on 2014 got rehabilitated through the VRCs. This statistics raises a question mark on the capacity of these skill building avenues. The impact of the trainings offered by VRC or RREC is nowhere mentioned i.e. the growth of employability of PwD post the training received is not available as per the World Bank report, 2009.

METHODOLOGY

This research is exploratory in nature where the aim is to comprehend the various factors that acts as a barrier for the persons with disabilities towards securing an employment opportunity. A qualitative approach of data analysis have been adopted to understand the objectives of the study in an in-depth manner. Research papers and articles from online media, as well as reports from reputable organisations like the ILO, World Bank, and government websites, have all been carefully evaluated for data analysis. Overall, the findings of this study will serve as a basis for further study into the variables obstructing the persons with disabilities from pursuing work.

FINDINGS

The roadblocks that are faced by the persons with disabilities have been categorized into internal and external factors.

Internal Factors

Majority of the individuals with disabilities are located in the rural areas, most of them are unaware about the training and job opportunities available in the urban areas. Most of the government schemes and employment related information is confined to the urban areas only. PwD from rural areas fail to fetch such vital information. Due to this limited access to the labour markets many of them do not register for the special exchange or special cells' facility available. They are not exposed to the outer world.

Those who are aware the opportunities are either reluctant to leave their home and stay separately in cities or their parents become over protective with their wards since they have never left them alone. The parents are skeptical about their overall behaviour outside since they have been dependent of any of the family members even for minor tasks (ILO, 2011). This mindset makes it more difficult for the PwD to seek any employment opportunity independently.

When it comes to seek employment from private sector employers, many persons with disabilities are reluctant about the thought. Since there are reservations available with the government sector jobs for the PwD, their preference towards the government jobs are more. They tend to apply for the government jobs year after year, get rejected but still do not opt for private sector jobs (ILO, 2011).

There has been instances where the own mindset of the individuals with disabilities have created an obstacle for securing an employment opportunity. The availability of the social security schemes encourages the PwD in not seeking for any employment opportunities. People are eligible for some economic benefits or subsidies by few government initiatives. Some of them are unemployment allowance, disability pension schemes etc. One of the popular social security scheme implemented widely in India is Mahatma Gandhi National Rural Employment Guarantee (MGNREGA) Act, 2005. Under this act, 100 days of assured pay to every adult unskilled worker in rural area is guaranteed. This also acts as a source of income for many people including individuals with disabilities. In fact, as per the "Rights of persons with Disabilities Act, 2016", if an individual with disabilities is unemployed for more 2 years in spite of being registered with the special employment exchange, the concern citizen is eligible for unemployment allowance. For e.g. a person with disability is entitled to get Rs. 2000 to Rs. 4000 per month as disability pension in Goa. In fact, the system of free housing, free medical facilities, mid-day meals, free education for kids is applicable in many states of India with an additional benefit under MGNREGA, unemployment allowance, disability pension etc. In such case, a huge probability stands still that such individual with disabilities would not like to leave their home and come to urban area to work for a call center or a retail store and earn Rs. 5000 to Rs. 10000 per month (ILO, 2011). This reflects a lack of self-motivation to become employed.

Many individuals with disabilities are rejected in the interview even before they appear for a job interview due to lack of self-esteem. This is because from an early stage of their life, they have been staying at social isolation condition. Parents were reluctant to take them to any social gatherings; they had limited social networks, friends and family members. At times, few of have would have got bullied or ridiculed too. Due to this development of their behavior, low self-esteem has cropped up within them. (ILO, 2011)As a result, their inner ability to be employed even before trying to get an employment opportunity has become extinct.

The minimum education level that any employer would look into a candidate for a standard job is a graduate level. This is due to the lack of accessible education. The reality for the persons with disabilities is that hardly 5 percent of the total PwD population has passed their graduation. This is primarily because from an early stage, children with disabilities were not encouraged to join regular school pattern. Moreover, the limited awareness among parents, lack of special school for the disabled, availability of good instructors, lack of infrastructure in higher education levels in schools made the overall literacy level at low level for the persons with disabilities (ILO, 2011). In fact lack of financial resources to avail specific schools that are meant for individuals with disabilities is one the reasons for low literacy levels among the persons with disabilities

Although majority of the vacancies are applicable for the orthopedic handicapped people, they are not prepared to pass the written exam or the interview stage. This reflects the lack of competence among them in comparison to non-PwD candidates.

Those individuals with disabilities who are below graduate level end up looking for elementary jobs with various companies. Their competition starts with the non-disabled ones. Recruiters find many PwD lacking in their life skills such as managing their personal hygiene, grooming etc. Moreover, necessary skills for working such as time management, participating in teams, money management etc. are not present among the low-level educated or unskilled persons with disabilities (ILO, 2011). This leads to a further obstacle in the way of seeking an employment for the PwD.

The employers look for trained people with basic job related skills such time management; money management etc. so that they can be further trained according to the job requirements. Majority of the PwD reside at the rural territory where the avenues for training are not available for disabled ones. Even those PwD who manage to gain a reasonable educational qualification, they lack in spoken and written English skills or computer related knowledge (ILO, 2011). This becomes a challenge for the prospective employer to make them industry ready for elementary level jobs such as data entry operator where minimum knowledge of English and usage of computer is required.

External Factors 80 percent of the individuals belong to severe disabilities category such as mental retardation, mental illness and multiple disabilities (GoI, 2011). Persons with such severe disabilities become a rare choice among the employers.

One of the reasons for low registration in the employment exchanges are due to the competency levels of the employment exchanges staffs who are not trained or lack in experience in handling queries from individuals with disabilities that might result in offending the disabled ones and discourage them in approaching subsequently to the employment exchanges.

The issue with these country-wise recruitment initiatives by UPSC and SSC bureau is that, only physically challenged people get a priority on others. The recruitment advertisements or the forms have "PH" i.e. physically handicapped mentioned instead of "PwD" (UPSC, 2018). In some cases, hearing handicapped, visually impaired and cerebral palsy is being mentioned as an additional category. In such situations, other categories of individuals with disabilities such as autism, mental illness, speech impaired, dwarfism etc. remains left out in securing an employment opportunity (SSC, 2018). Even the training facility as per the Apprentices Act, 1961 is reserved only for the "PH" category only. Moreover, designations such as police, security, the PwD are non-applicable. Not only this, there is no uniformity across all the states about the eligibility for the PwD for the same designations.

Earlier there were many clerical jobs such as typists, steno, telephone operator etc. available in public sector, but these types of roles have almost become extinct. There are still few jobs in the government domain, which demands typewriting skills. Now it is a dilemma among the individuals with disabilities regarding the necessity of knowing typewriting over computer. Even if the PwD would like to learn typewriting, it is a challenge since most of the typewriting institutes have closed down due to lack of demand. Secondly, those who would like to learn computer they face these obstacles. First, since most the PwD reside in rural areas, locating a computer institute is a challenge.

Secondly, those institutes who have computer in the rural areas fight with the power shortage issues most of the time. Third, irrespective of the territory of the computer institute, they are unaware of the software to be installed so that the individuals with disabilities can cope up in learning about computer. Fourth, many disabled individuals hail from a poor economic background who cannot afford the fees of these institutes. Most of the government jobs demand online application mode from the applicants, which again becomes a roadblock to entry at workplace for the persons with disabilities.

Majority of the disabled ones who is rehabilitated falls under the orthopedically impaired category. The other categories participation is either minimum or negligible. Due to the non-inclusion of other categories of PwD in the vocational training programs, the chances of employability reduce among the persons with disabilities, which become a roadblock to enter at workplace. In fact, there is a provision of 3 percent reservation for the PwD to get enrolled in the VRCs' yet the number of PwD rehabilitated is quite low. One of the prime reason behind the low participation is the urban based location of the VRCs' since around 70 percent of the PwD reside in the rural areas whereas the VRCs' are situated in the urban areas. Secondly, the VRCs' are not well equipped to accommodate all categories of the disabilities due to inadequate infrastructure and incompetent trainers. Third, since the VRCs' are located in urban areas, the parents are hesitant to leave their wards at an unknown place. Fourth, even of an individual with disability completes their training from a VRC; there is no assurance that the trainee will secure an employment. This message of non-assurance further demotivates others to approach any VRC. The skill enhancement programs by RREC may not be motivational enough to attract more individuals with disability. Moreover, there are only 11 RREC to cater to 28 states in the country. In addition to this, the training offered by RREC periodic in nature in collaboration with the NGOs'.

Finally, those persons with disabilities who reside in the urban areas also at times are reluctant or even forced to sit at home rather than seeking employment opportunities outside. It is primarily due to the environment accessibility concerns. The physical environment facilities in indoor and outside of workplaces does not suit the requirement of an individual with disability such as conditions of the roads, improper footpaths, existing transport systems, unavailability of accessible toilets, required warning symbols at various surface levels, Braille markings at the suitable places, lack of accessible ramps and easy parking spaces.

CONCLUSION

Roadblock or a barrier is relative term and can be perceived from perspectives of various stakeholders responsible in this process of inclusion of persons with disabilities at workplace. For e.g. the PwD opine that the employment opportunities are limited for them whereas the employers state that the differently abled people lack in the required level of education for a particular role. Secondly, Government has established many vocational rehabilitation centers for the skill development of the people with disabilities whereas the PwD mention that the rehabilitation centers lack in required assistive technology of trained faculties.

Some of the employers take the initiative of hiring the PwD through practicing several inclusionary efforts. These efforts get affected sometimes due to the size and scale of the businesses. Small and medium scale organisations lack in awareness towards the actual expense that is required to modify infrastructure, provide reasonable accommodation and assistive technologies. Many employers are trapped between the intentions of inclusion of PwD i.e. some employers hire PwD as a part of their corporate social responsibility and few of them hire to improve their bottom line of the business. These were some of thought points from the demand side of the business.

From the supply side of the business, many PwD are equally not inclined to work in private organisations. There can several reasons behind this attitude. It can due to the inclination towards availing jobs in Government sector or due to the incentives that avail from various social schemes. It can be also due to the lack of life-skills and lack of self-esteem among the PwD. This attitude has developed due to the over protective behaviour from their parents. These underlying barriers play an eminent role in the inclusion process of the PwD at workplace and affect the inclusionary efforts taken by the employers. Hence, the internal factors and the external factors that acts a roadblock to entry at workplace for individuals with disabilities in India are imperative to comprehend since the bottom line of employment gets affected.

REFERENCES

DEOC. (2009). *Employment of Disabled People in India.* Retrieved from http://www.dnis.org/Employment.pdf

GoI. (2007). *Scheme for providing Employment to Persons with Disabilities in the Private Sector - Incentives to the Employers.* Ministry of Social Justice & Empowerment. Retrieved from http://disabilityaffairs.gov.in/upload/uploadfiles/files/incentive_rev.pdf

GoI. (2008). *Employment of Persons with Disabilities in Public Sectors in India.* Society for Disability and Rehabilitation Studies. Retrieved from http://planningcommission.nic.in/reports/sereport/ser/ser_pdp1206.pdf

GoI. (2008). *Scheme of Providing Incentives to Employers in the Private Sector for Providing Employment to Persons with Disabilities.* Ministry of Social Justice & Empowerment and Ministry of Labour & Employment. Retrieved from http://ayjnihh.nic.in/scheme.pdf

GoI. (2011). *2011 Census Data.* Ministry of Home Affairs,Government of India. Retrieved from http://censusindia.gov.in/2011-Common/CensusData2011.html

GoI. (2016). *The Rights of Persons with Disabilities Act, 2016.* Retrieved from http://www.disabilityaffairs.gov.in: http://www.disabilityaffairs.gov.in/content/page/policy.php

GoI. (2016). *Disabled Persons in India: A Statistical profile 2016.* Ministry of Statistics and Programme Implementation. Retrieved from http://mospi.nic.in/sites/default/files/publication_reports/Disabled_persons_in_India_2016.pdf

GoI. (2016). *Reports & Documents.* Retrieved from www.ncs.gov.in: https://www.ncs.gov.in/Pages/NCSPolicyDocuments.aspx

GoI. (2018). *Constitutional Provisions.* Ministry of Social Justice and Empowerment. Retrieved from http://socialjustice.nic.in: http://socialjustice.nic.in/ViewData/Details?mid=76656&catID=69

GoI. (2018). *Department of Adult Independent Living.* Retrieved from niepmd.tn.nic.in: https://niepmd.tn.nic.in/department.php?pageid=3

GoI. (2018). *Faq related to the Apprentices Act, 1961.* Retrieved from http://www.talimrojgar.gujarat.gov.in: http://www.talimrojgar.gujarat.gov.in/pages/faq_ats.pdf

ILO. (2003). *India Country Profile.* Retrieved from https://digitalcommons.ilr.cornell.edu/cgi/viewcontent.cgi?referer=https://www.google.co.in/&httpsredir=1&article=1198&context=gladnetcollect

ILO. (2004). *Training and Employment of People with Disabilities: India 2002.* ILO. Retrieved from https://digitalcommons.ilr.cornell.edu/gladnetcollect/197

ILO. (2011). *Persons with disability and The indian labour market: Challenges and opportunities.* ILO. Retrieved from https://www.ilo.org/wcmsp5/groups/public/---asia/---ro-bangkok/---sro-new_delhi/documents/publication/wcms_229259.pdf

Jagaran Josh. (2016, September 26). *10 Facts about PwD Reservation Quota in Government Jobs.* Retrieved from www.jagranjosh.com: https://www.jagranjosh.com/articles/10-facts-about-pwd-reservation-quota-in-government-jobs-1474893425-1

Kregel, J. (1999). Why It Pays to Hire Workers with Developmental Disabilities. *Focus on autism and other developmental disabilities, 14*(3), 130-132. Retrieved from http://citeseerx.ist.psu.edu/viewdoc/download?doi=10.1.1.612.3830&rep=rep1&type=pdf

Nagarajan, R. (2013, December 2). *Disabled people clear UPSC, but wait for service allocation.* Retrieved from timesofindia.indiatimes.com: https://timesofindia.indiatimes.com/india/Disabled-people-clear-UPSC-but-wait-for-service-allocation/articleshow/26713017.cms

Naraharisetti, R., & Castro, M. C. (2016). Factors associated with persons with disability employment in India: a cross-sectional study. *BMC Public Health, 16*(1).

O'Keefe, Philip; O'Keefe, Philip;. (2009). *People with Disabilities in India From Commitments to Outcomes (English).*Washington, DC: World Bank. Retrieved from http://documents.worldbank.org/curated/en/577801468259486686/People-with-disabilities-in-India-from-commitments-to-outcomes

PTI. (2016, July 4). *3% Reservation to Disabled Persons Must in Government Job: SC.* Retrieved from www.news18.com: https://www.news18.com/news/india/3-reservation-to-disabled-persons-must-in-government-job-sc-1265687.html

Sharma, N. (2018, January 25). *Government jobs for those with learning disabilities too.* Retrieved from https://economictimes.indiatimes.com:

https://economictimes.indiatimes.com/jobs/government-jobs-for-those-with-learning-disabilities-too/articleshow/62643622.cms

Shenoy, M. (2011). *Persons with disability and The indian labour market_ Challenges and opportunities.* ILO. Retrieved from https://www.ilo.org/newdelhi/whatwedo/publications/WCMS_229259/lang--en/index.htm

SSC. (2018). *SSC Recruitment 2018.* Retrieved from http://www.sarkarinaukridaily.in: http://www.sarkarinaukridaily.in/ssc-recruitment

UNCRPD. (2016). *Convention on the Rights of Persons with Disabilities.* Retrieved from www.un.org: https://www.un.org/development/desa/disabilities/convention-on-the-rights-of-persons-with-disabilities.html

Unger, D. D. (2002). Employers' Attitudes Toward Persons with Disabilities in the Workforce: Myths or Realities? *Journal of Vocational Rehabilitation, 17*(1), 2-10. Retrieved from https://journals.sagepub.com/doi/10.1177/108835760201700101

UPSC. (2018). *Recruitment Advertisements.* Retrieved from http://www.upsc.gov.in: http://www.upsc.gov.in/recruitment/recruitment-advertisement

WHO. (2011). *World Report on Disability.* World Health Organization. Retrieved from http://www.who.int/disabilities/world_report/2011/report.pdf

Measuring The Accuracy Of Machine Learning Models For Heart Attack Prediction

CHAPTER 06

Author – Prof. Akshay Rele (Business Analytics), Visiting Faculty, IES's Management College and Research Centre, Mumbai

ABSTRACT

Heart Attack has been a serious cause of death in humans in the world's population. Medical Professionals working in the field of heart diseases, apart from using various medical instruments and devices, they require a support system for accurate predictions. In order to reduce the mortality due to heart attacks, Machine Learning (ML) and data sciences have open new doors for precise prediction of heart attack considering several risk factors and body parameters. Various ML algorithms viz; Logistic Regression, Naïve Bayes, Random Forest Classifier, K-Nearest Neighbor, Decision Tree and Support Vector Machines were deployed on the dataset. The accuracies of the mentioned ML algorithms for the prediction of heart attacks were compared using programming tools. Based on the results obtained from the comparison, the best suitable ML algorithm was trained to perform optimized predictions of heart attacks. Hence, data sciences and ML can provide effective and efficient healthcare research and predictions.

KEYWORDS

Heart Attack, Machine Learning, Machine Learning Algorithms, Data Sciences, Prediction, Healthcare

1 INTRODUCTION

A Heart attack happens when something blocks the flow of blood to the heart which damages the muscles of the heart. Heart Attack is considered as the most serious disease in the segment of cardiovascular disorders. It accounts to more deaths than any other disease. For doctors, to diagnose the several heart diseases has always been a challenge and indeed a crucial task. A numerous medical diagnostic tests with the help of advanced instruments and scientific technologies are adopted by the doctors, but sometimes even with the help of these technological advancements, doctors fail to take accurate decisions for the prediction of heart attacks. Different factors which cause a risk of heart diseases includes high blood pressure, cholesterol, blood sugar, obesity, poor diet, etc. The healthcare sector generates a huge amount of data every day from the several medical equipments regarding patient details, diseases, diagnosis, symptoms. This data if properly analyzed with Data Sciences and Machine Learning (ML) algorithms, can help doctors to accurately predict the heart attacks. The key to the ML algorithms is to find a pattern behind the observed data and build several ML algorithms on that data. Logistic Regression, Naïve Bayes, Random Forest Classifier, K-Nearest Neighbor, Decision Tree and Support Vector Machines are the ML algorithms used in this paper and the accuracies of each of these algorithms are measured.

LITERATURE REVIEW

Golande [6] used Machine Learning Techniques, in which the author has used a few data mining policies to help doctors to identify heart attacks. Decision trees, k-nearest neighbor, and Naive Bayes were common techniques that were used. Decision trees had more accuracy.

Ravindhar [7], used four ML algorithms and one Neural Network model, compared performance quantities to cardiac disease detection. The Deep NN algorithm correctly identified heart disease 98% of the time.

Krishnan [3] The author has used classification methods to predict heart attacks in patients. Heart attack was predicted using Naive Bayes and Decision Tree. Decision Trees, such as ID3 Algorithms, and Naive Bayes Techniques, are the most repeatedly used techniques for prediction. According to the author, Naïve Bayes classifier achieves more accuracy.

Kumar [12] used ML classification techniques to forecast chronic illness. The Hoeffding classifier correctly predicted heart disease with an accuracy of 88.56% in their study. According to their findings, when collective with the specified characteristics, the hybrid model achieved an accuracy of 87.41%.

Santhana [8], used a datasets which was classified in terms of medical parameters. Their system evaluated those parameters using data mining classification technique. The datasets were processed in python programming using two main Machine Learning Algorithm namely Decision Tree Algorithm and Naive Bayes Algorithm which shows the best algorithm among these two in terms of accuracy level of heart disease.

RESEARCH METHODOLOGY

The System design methodology is as depicted in the Figure 1. The first step is the data acquisition which is downloaded from [1]. We have total 14 attributes including the target variable (Output). The description of every attribute is shown in Table 1.

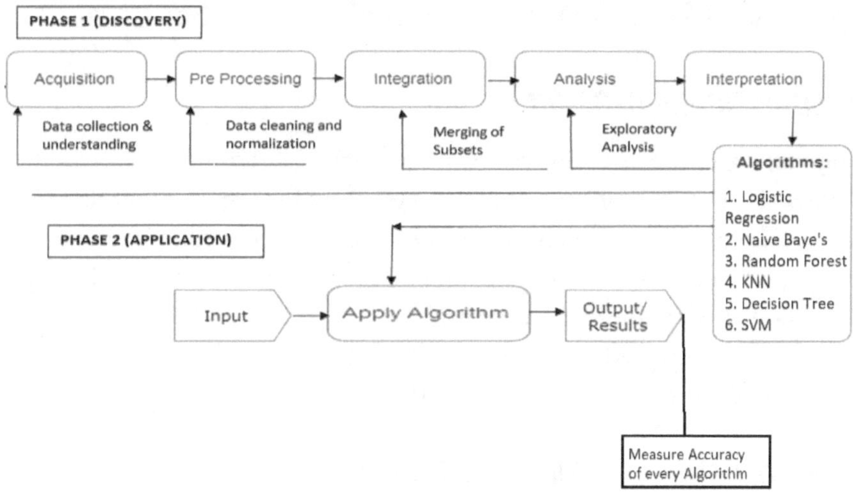

Fig 1: *System Design Methodology*

The second step is 'pre-processing where we perform data cleaning, add missing values and removal of redundancies and outliers. The data has been cleaned using various pre-processing techniques, missing values replaced with mean values and duplicates were removed.

The third step is integration where libraries, packages and different modules were imported in python and merging them to perform necessary actions.

The fourth step is Exploratory Data Analysis(EDA) was performed to understand the relationships among different attributes of data (Table 1). Pattern identification and decision making, understanding correlation between variables were analyzed.

The fifth step is interpretation with the help of 'matplotlib' python library inorder to understand the impact of various parameters in the data set on the output variable.

The sixth step is application of various ML algorithms viz; Logistic Regression, Naïve Baye's, Random Forest, KNN, Decision Tree and SVM.

The seventh step includes these ML algorithms which were applied one by one for prediction of Heart Attack and the accuracy is measured with the accuracy_score function. Accuracy score is used to measure the model performance in terms of measuring the ratio of sum of true positive and true negatives out of all the predictions made.

MACHINE LEARNING MODELS USED FOR ANALYZING DATASET

1. LOGISTIC REGRESSION

Logistic regression is a supervised classification algorithm where the target variable (or output) can take only discrete values for a given set of features (or inputs). Logistic regression is a regression model which predicts the probability that a given data entry belongs to the category numbered as 1 or 0. Logistic regression models the data using the sigmoid function. The target variable which we want to predict is that prediction of heart attack; whether the person will suffer from heart attack based on the input parameters in the data set.

2. NAÏVE BAYES CLASSIFIER ALGORITHM

Naïve Bayes algorithm, a supervised learning algorithm based on **Bayes theorem** is used for solving classification problems. It is mainly used in *classification* that includes a high-dimensional training dataset.

It is a probabilistic approach based on conditional probability expressed with the help of the formula as shown in equation (1)

$$P(A|B) = \frac{P(B|A) * P(A)}{P(B)} \quad \textbf{(1)}$$

3. RANDOM FOREST ALGORITHM

Random Forest is a supervised learning technique which uses a combination of both Classification and Regression. **Random Forest is a classifier that**

contains a number of decision trees on various subsets of the given dataset and takes the average to improve the predictive accuracy of that dataset. Instead of depending on only one decision tree, the random forest takes the prediction from each tree and based on the majority votes of predictions, and it predicts the final output.

A random forest is a meta estimator that fits a number of decision tree classifiers on various sub-samples of the dataset and uses averaging to improve the predictive accuracy and control over-fitting. The sub-sample size is controlled with the max_samples parameter if bootstrap=True (default), otherwise the whole dataset is used to build each tree. [9]

4. K-NEAREST NEIGHBOUR ALGORITHM

K-Nearest Neighbour is a Supervised Learning technique. K-NN algorithm assumes the similarity between the new case/data and available cases and put the new case into the category that is most similar to the available categories. It uses proximity to make classifications or predictions about the grouping of an individual data point. While it can be used for either regression or classification problems, it is typically used as a classification [10]. KNN algorithm at the training phase just stores the dataset and when it gets new data, then it classifies that data into a category that is much similar to the new data.

5. Decision Tree Algorithm

Decision Tree is a Supervised learning technique that can be used for both classification and Regression problems, but mostly it is preferred for solving Classification problems. It is a tree-structured classifier, where internal nodes represent the features of a dataset, branches represent the decision rules and each leaf node represents the outcome.

In a Decision tree, there are two nodes, which are the Decision Node and Leaf Node. Decision nodes are used to make any decision and have multiple branches, whereas Leaf nodes are the output of those decisions and do not contain any further branches.

While there are multiple ways to select the best attribute at each node, two methods, information gain and Gini impurity, act as popular splitting criterion for decision tree models. They help to evaluate the quality of each test condition and how well it will be able to classify samples into a class. [9]

6. Support Vector Machine Algorithm

Support Vector Machine or SVM is one of the most popular Supervised Learning algorithms, which is used for Classification as well as Regression problems.

The goal of the SVM algorithm is to create the best line or decision boundary that can segregate n-dimensional space into classes so that we can easily put the new data point in the correct category in the future. This best decision boundary is called a hyperplane.

SVM chooses the extreme points/vectors that help in creating the hyperplane. These extreme cases are called as support vectors, and hence algorithm is termed as Support Vector Machine.

DATASET

The dataset is attained from the UCI Machine Learning Repository which is a collection of databases, domain theories, and data generators that are used by the machine learning community for the empirical analysis of machine learning algorithms. This dataset can be accessed online from the link https://archive.ics.uci.edu/ml/datasets/Heart+Disease

The data set (sample rows) is as shown in the Figure 2 with 14 attributes, the description of which is summarized in Table 1.

	A	B	C	D	E	F	G	H	I	J	K	L	M	N
1	age	sex	cp	trtbps	chol	fbs	restecg	thalachh	exng	oldpeak	slp	caa	thall	output
2	63	1	3	145	233	1	0	150	0	2.3	0	0	1	1
3	37	1	2	130	250	0	1	187	0	3.5	0	0	2	1
4	41	0	1	130	204	0	0	172	0	1.4	2	0	2	1
5	56	1	1	120	236	0	1	178	0	0.8	2	0	2	1
6	57	0	0	120	354	0	1	163	1	0.6	2	0	2	1
7	57	1	0	140	192	0	1	148	0	0.4	1	0	1	1

Figure 2: *Dataset attributes*

No.	Features	Description	Value
1.	Age	Age is an important aspect of health care.	Its value is an integer.
2	Sex	Gender	Female = 0, Male = 1
3.	Chest pain(cp)	The patient is suffering from chest pain.	Asymptomatic = 4, typicalangina = 1, atypicalangina = 2, non-anginal pain = 3
4.	RestingBloodPressure (trestbps)	High blood pressure ensues with some other factors which increase the risk.	It has either an integer or float value.

No.	Features	Description	Value
5.	Cholesterol(Chol)	Serum cholesterol	It has either an integer or float value
6.	FastingBloodSugar(Fbs)	Fasting blood sugar is more than 120 mg/dL	0 = false; 1 = true
7.	RestingECG (restech)	ElectroCardioGraphic Resting	ST-T wave abnormality Normal Left ventricular hypertrophy=1,
8.	Max Heart Rate Achieved (thalach)	This is the highest heart rate you have ever had.	It has either an integer or float value.
9.	Exercise-Induced Angina (exang)	Angina instigated by exercise	no = 0, yes = 1
10.	Oldpeak	Exercise-tempted ST depression compared to rest	It shows the value as either an integer or a float.
11.	Slope	slope of peak exercise ST segment	flat = 1, downsloping = 2, Upsloping=0
12.	Coronary Artery (ca)	Fluoroscopy has colored a large number of major vessels	It has either an integer or float value.
13.	Thalassemia (thal)	Normal, reversible defect, fixed defect,	Measuring scales: 3 = normal; 7 = reversable defect; 6 = fixed defect
14.	Output	Heart Attack Prediction	0 indicates No Heart Attack, 1 indicates Heart Attack

Table 1: Description and values of all the Data set attributes

FINDINGS

Algorithm	Accuracy
Logistic	85.25%
Naïve Baye's	85.23%
Random Forest	95.34%
KNN	72.14%
Decision Tree	83.45%
SVM	87.44%

Table 2: Accuracy of ML Models

The accuracy of the ML Models is measured as the number of correct predictions divided by the total number of predictions as in Equation (1)

$$\text{accuracy} = \frac{\text{total number of correct predictions}}{\text{total number of predictions}} \quad \textbf{(1)}$$

DISCUSSION

The performance of various ML models used in the research is calculated and the accuracy is as predicted in table 2. It was observed that Random Forest had the highest accuracy of 95.34% followed by SVM. Logistic Regression and Naïve Baye's algorithm along with Decision Tree showed the same accuracy of 85% and 83% respectively. KNN was found be less accurate among all the ML models.

FUTURE SCOPE

Heart attack prediction using machine learning is an active area of research with significant potential for advancements. Some potential areas for future research and improvements in this field include multi-modal data fusion where investigating the integration of multiple data sources, such as medical imaging, electrocardiograms (ECG), wearable sensor data, and electronic health records, could provide a more comprehensive and accurate representation of an individual's cardiac health status. In addition to this, moving beyond binary prediction (heart attack/no heart attack), future research can focus on patient-centric risk stratification, which provides more granular risk assessments tailored to individual patients' specific risk profiles.

Moreover, we can develop real-time prediction models that can quickly process streaming data, such as wearable device data or continuous monitoring data which could enable early detection and timely intervention for heart attack prevention. Integrating genetic and molecular data into machine learning models may unlock new insights into genetic predisposition and biomarkers associated with heart attacks, leading to more personalized risk assessments.

SUMMARY AND CONCLUSIONS

In this paper, various ML models were used to predict the heart attacks. The dataset was attained from [1]. The data was preprocessed, after which ML models were applied using Python. We used Jupyter Notebook as our open-source application to perform the various operations on the dataset, apply ML models and find the accuracy. Random Forest was found to be the most accurate among all the ML models used. Heart Attack prediction can be accurately predicted using our work.

In future, deep learning and neural networks will be used to accurately and effectively evaluate the presence of heart attacks, as well as to enhance the accuracy of the existing models used in the paper.

REFERENCES

1. Available online: https://archive.ics.uci.edu/ml/datasets/Heart+Disease (accessed on 20th February 2023).
2. Ghulab Nabi, Ahmad Shafiullah, Mixed Machine Learning Approach for Efficient Prediction of Human Heart Disease by Identifying the Numerical and Categorical Features, Appl. Sci. 2022, 12, 7449, MDPI.
3. P.Santhi a, R.Ajayb,D.Harshini, A Survey on Heart Attack Prediction Using Machine Learning, Turkish Journal of Computer and Mathematics Education Vol.12 No.2 (2021), 2303 – 2308.
4. Akram Mustafa and Mostafa Rahimi Azghadi, Automated Machine Learning for Healthcare and Clinical Notes Analysis, Computers 2021, 10, 24, MDPI.
5. Dr. Krishan Kumar Goyal, Aejaz Hassan Paray, A Survey of Different Approaches of Machine Learning in Healthcare Management System,Int. J. Advanced Networking and Applications Volume: 11 Issue: 03 Pages: 4270-4276 (2019).
6. Avinash Golande, Pavan Kumar T. Heart Disease Prediction Using Effective Machine Learning Techniques, International Journal of Recent Technology and Engineering (IJRTE) ISSN: 2277-3878,Volume-8, Issue-1S4, June 2019.
7. Ravindhar, N.V.; Anand, H.S.; Ragavendran, G.W. Intelligent diagnosis of cardiac disease prediction using machine learning. Int.J. Innov. Technol. Explor. Eng. **2019**, 8, 1417–1421, ISSN 2278-3075.
8. Mr.Santhana Krishnan.J, Dr.Geetha.S. Prediction of Heart Disease Using Machine Learning Algorithms, 2019 1st International Conference on Innovations in Information and Communication Technology(ICIICT),ICIICT1.2019.8741465.

9. Available online: https://scikitlearn.org/stable/modules/generated/sklearn.ensemble.RandomForestClassifier.html (accessed on 26th Feb 2023).
10. Available Online. https://www.ibm.com/in-en/topics/knn (accessed on 24th Feb 2023).
11. Available online https://www.javatpoint.com/machine-learning-support-vector-machine-algorithm (accessed on 21st Feb 2023).
12. Kumar, N.; Sikamani, K. Prediction of chronic and infectious diseases using machine learning classiers-A systematic approach Int. J. Intell. Eng. Syst. 2020.

Study on Organizational Capabilities – A Literature Review

CHAPTER 07

Author – Prof. M. Rangathan, Research Scholar, NMIMS, Mumbai

ABSTRACT

A good strategy is defined as a theory about how to gain advantages over other players in the chosen industry. By conducting a sequential set of analysis and choices, known as Strategic Management Process, organizations increase the likely hood of selecting good strategy (Barney & Hesterly, Strategic Management and Competitive Advantage, 2010). Therefore, the basic purpose of Strategic Management in an organization is to stay ahead of the other players in the chosen industry. Organizations, often, acquire and develop one or a combination of attributes, which becomes the differentiating factor(s) of that organization. Frequently, organizations acquire and develop attributes such as access to natural resources, or inexpensive power or access to highly trained and skilled personnel and human resources, or inexpensive capital, or access to technology etc. as their sources of differentiating factor(s). The other source of differentiating factor(s) for the organizations is the Organizational Capabilities. (Collis, 1994) defines organizational capabilities as processes which are socially complex and which determine the efficiency with which firms physically transform inputs into outputs. (Grant, The Resource- Based Theory of Competitive Advantage: Implications for Strategy Formulation, 1991) defines Organizational Capability as the capacity to perform some task or activity by utilizing or deploying a resource or team of resources. Many studies have established Organizational Capability as an important source of differentiating factor for any firm. This is a Literature Review of development of Organizational Capabilities in Industry.

KEY WORDS

ORGANIZATIONAL CAPABILITY, RESOURCE BASED VIEW, ORGANIZATIONAL RESOURCES, TANGIBLE ASSETS, INTANGIBLE ASSETS

INTRODUCTION

Barney, refers to organizational capabilities as those characteristics in the organization that 'enable an organization to conceive, choose and implement strategies', while Henderson and Cockburn refer to them as 'the abilities of the organization to deploy the firm's resources as well as to develop new ones' (Collis, 1994). Apart from utilizing and deploying the resources, Organizational capability also involves adapting to changing customer and strategic needs. This is done by establishing internal structures and processes that enable its members to create organization-specific competencies. Employees are a critical resource for sustainable competitiveness (Lake, 1991). The capacity of a firm to perform some internal activity competently is termed as capability (Arthur A. Thompson M. A.). Firms develop and enable Organizational capabilities through the deployment of a company's resources.

Capabilities vary in form, quality, and competitive importance; some capabilities are more competitively valuable than others, within the same organization. Apple's product innovation, Nordstrom's superior incentive management capabilities and PepsiCo's marketing and brand management capabilities are widely recognized as being far superior to those of its competitors (Thompson). (Barney & Hesterly, Strategic Management and Competitive Advantage, 2010) **defines Capabilities** as the tangible and intangible assets that enable a firm to take full advantage of the other resources it controls. While Capabilities on their own, do not enable a firm to conceive and implement its strategies, they enable a firm to use other resources of the firm to conceive and implement such strategies. Deriving from above, internal sources of an organization, specifically, capabilities and knowledge, play a vital role in developing Competencies for any firm which are superior to its competition.

The components of Internal Analysis Leading to superior performance of a firm is explained through the following figure (This figure is a modification made from the figure originally prescribed by Hitt et al. – Figure 3.1 in their book Strategic Management – A South-Asian Perspective (Hitt, 2018)

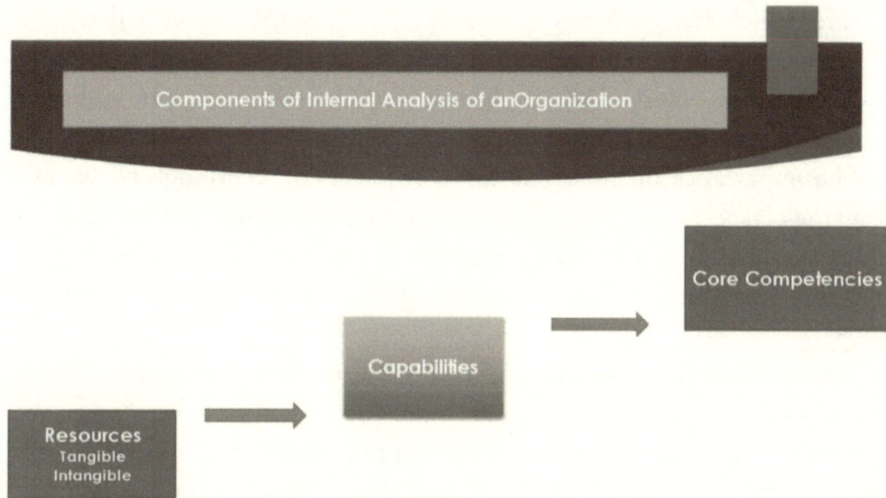

Organizations develop several Capabilities in the process of conducting its business (in order to develop competencies for the firm). From literature, several capabilities have been identified, which well managed companies tend to have: such as, Competitive Intelligence, Dynamic and IT enabled CRM, Internationalization, Talent / Talent Management, Speed / Agility, Shared Mindset / Coherent Brand Identity, Accountability, Collaboration, Learning, Leadership, Ability to connect with customers, Innovation, Efficiency, Strategic Unity, HR Capability, Knowledge Management Capability and Technological Capability.

LITERATURE REVIEW

(DAVID J. TEECE, 1997) stipulates that Resources should be inimitable which implies that they have to be firm- specific assets. Some examples are Trade secrets and certain specialized production facilities and engineering experience. Such assets are difficult to transfer among firms because these assets may contain tacit knowledge.

(Hall, 1992) classifies Intangible Resources may be classified as 'assets' or 'skills'. Assets are obvious things which can be owned, such as IP Rights of patents, copyright, trademarks, and registered designs and may also include trade secrets, contracts, and data bases. Reputation may also be classified as an Intangible asset, however, it cannot be bought or sold except that it may reside in a brand name. Intangible resources are by and large Skills of a firm such as the know-how of employees, suppliers, distributors; and the organizational culture (which enables it to cope with change, put the customer first, etc.). When a company is sold the acquirer gets the acquiree's intangible resources such as patents, brand name etc., but the acquirer cannot be certain that the intangible resources of know-how, culture, or networks are retained.

The importance of intangible assets is increasing continuously not only from the perspective of financial point of view but also from the point of view of tax and accounting. As the firms compete for limited and scarce resources, they will focus on improving their intangible asset management (Madhani, 2009).

Taking this further, we need to distinguish between competence, ability, and capability. In technical areas, an individual is said to possess functional competence whereas an organization is said to possess core competencies. On social issues, we refer to an individual's leadership ability or to an organization's capabilities (Smallwood & Ulrich, 2004). Organizational capabilities play the most important role in developing a solution (in the form of product) by delivering on the combined competencies and abilities of its individuals. This is summarized in following figure (reproduced from Capitalizing on Capabilities by Norm Smallwood and Dave Ulrich – June 2004 issue of HBR:

	INDIVIDUAL	**ORGANIZATIONAL**
TECHNICAL	**1. An individual's functional competence**	**3. An organization's core competencies**
SOCIAL	**2. An Individual's Leadership ability**	**4. An Organization's capabilities**

DEVELOPMENT OF THE TOPIC, IDENTITIFCATION OF IMPORTANT ISSUES AND OBJECTIVES

David J Teece in his 1997 paper describes three existing paradigms of strategy and describes the fourth paradigm called dynamic capabilities. The existing three paradigms are: 1. Competitive Forces Approach, Michael Porter 1980; 2. Strategic Conflict Approach (Shapiro 1989; and 3. building CA thru firm-level efficiency advantages, (Resource-based perspective). The fourth paradigm, which is explained in this paper is firm-specific capabilities that can be sources of CA. This approach emphasizes on development of management capabilities and difficult to imitate combinations of organizational, functional, and technological skills. The fourth paradigm, the dynamic capabilities approach demands there is a need to understand how CA is achieved. Firms that have been winners in the global market place demonstrate timely responsiveness and rapid and flexible product innovation; these firms exhibit management capability to effectively co-ordinate and redeploy internal and external competences. The ability to achieve these new forms of CA is referred as **DYNAMIC CAPABILITIES** in this paper. The term DYNAMIC refers to the capacity to renew competences in order to achieve congruence to the changing business environment. The term CAPABILITIES refer to the key role of strategic management in appropriately adapting, integrating and reconfiguring internal and external organizational skills, resources, and functional competences to match the requirements of a changing business environment (DAVID J. TEECE, 1997).

Capabilities are built, developed, and nurtured by organizations over a long period of time through conscious actions such as investments in staffing, training, compensation, communication, and other human resources areas (Smallwood & Ulrich, 2004). Capabilities often tell us the ways in which people and resources are brought together to accomplish work, by an organization. It defines what a company is good at doing. When organizations nurture their capabilities over a period, it becomes difficult for competitors to copy them. Thus, Intangible assets explain why investors are willing to attach higher value to a company (in comparison with its competitors), as they represent the future earning potential of the company.

Important issues that are identified in this paper are that what are the capabilities that well managed firms adopt and practice and among several capabilities possessed by well managed companies, which are the core capabilities of the organizations that differentiate them.

Objectives of this study are (i) identifying capabilities which are adopted and practiced by well managed companies – this paper outlines fifteen such capabilities which may not be an exhaustive list and (ii) among these fifteen capabilities which are the core capabilities practiced by well managed companies to differentiate themselves – this study outlines six such core capabilities.

Well managed companies tend to exhibit / practice several capabilities such as Competitive Intelligence, Dynamic and IT enabled CRM, Internationalization, Talent / Talent Management, Speed

/ Agility, Shared Mindset / Coherent Brand Identity, Accountability, Collaboration, Learning, Leadership, Ability to connect with customers, Strategic Unity, Innovation, Efficiency, HR Capability and Knowledge Management Capability to name a few. Referring to the previous studies made by several authors, we explain these capabilities below.

COMPETITIVE INTELLIGENCE AS AN ORGANIZATIONAL CAPABILITY

(Adidam & Shukla, 2012) studied, how the competitive intelligence (CI) practices impact the firm's performance in the emerging market context of India. Environmental scanning is the first step in CI which is a method of gathering information. CI uses the information thus collected and converts it into knowledge about the firm's competitor(s). This knowledge is used by various functional as well as corporate departments within an organization to make strategic decisions. (Wright, 2008) highlights CI as a continuous and evolving process which enables the companies to assess the behavior and capabilities of its current and potential competitors in order to develop as a competency.

Dynamic and IT enabled Customer Relationship Management (CRM) as an Organizational Capability

(Darshan Desai, 2007) explores why a static CRM (as a strategic initiative) cannot drive the firm towards competencies which enables a firm to have advantage over its competition. In dynamic markets, the domain of CRM is characterized by lots of changes. Drawing from the dynamic capability approach, this study identifies sources of competitive performance for the process of CRM in dynamic situations. Dynamic capability is defined as an organization's ability to continuously improve, innovate, and reconfigure resources to match the evolving environmental needs. Information technology (IT) competence is an important moderator of the relationship between dynamic capability and competitive performance. Some of the important findings of the study are: (i) In the emerging markets of Asia, dynamic capability played a crucial role in gaining competitive CRM performance among three industries namely, telecom, banking, and retail. (ii) In the highly dynamic and competitive Indian telecom industry, the dynamic capability played the most important role. (iii) Important drivers of dynamic capability also include social networking capability along with capabilities related to integration and market orientation. (iv) CRM technology had positive effects on competitive CRM performance.

INTERNATIONALIZATION CAPABILITIES OF COMPANIES AS AN ORGANIZATIONAL CAPABILITY

(Singh, 2001) studied the Foreign Direct Investments (FDI) by Developing Countries with specific reference to India and investigates the factors which encourage Indian Companies to invest in other countries. The author studies the Pull Factors (benefits offered by the host country to encourage FDI in their country) as well as Push Factors (the factors arising from restrictions on monopolistic practices, restrictions on diversification, environmental regulation, market saturation or slack in the home countries of investors). The study finds that production experience, managerial skills, conglomerate ownership, and size are the main sources of competencies for Indian firms investing overseas.

TALENT / TALENT MANAGEMENT AS AN ORGANIZATIONAL CAPABILITY

(Smallwood & Ulrich, 2004) defines talent as the ability to attract, motivate, and retain competent and committed people. Competencies are developed as organizations buy (acquire new talent), build (develop existing talent), borrow (access thought leaders through alliances or partnerships), bounce (remove poor performers), and bind (keep the best talent). This organizational capability (talent) is measured through productivity measures, retention statistics, employee surveys, and direct observation.

SPEED AS AN ORGANIZATIONAL CAPABILITY

(Smallwood & Ulrich, 2004) defines speed as the ability of an organization to make *important changes rapidly*. Speed refers to the organization's ability to recognize opportunities and act quickly. Organizations exhibit speed when exploiting new markets, creating new products, establishing new employee contracts, or implementing new business processes. Speed is measured in the following ways: (i) how long it takes to go from concept to commercialization, (ii) time taken from collection of customer data to changes in customer relations, (iii) increases in inventory turns (which show that physical assets are well used), (iv) time savings which demonstrate improvements in labor productivity, etc.

SHARED MINDSET AND COHERENT BRAND IDENTITY AS AN ORGANIZATIONAL CAPABILITY

Shared mind-set is gauged by asking each member of your team to answer the question, what are the top three things we want to be known for in the future by our best customers? Many companies score 50% to 60% on shared mind-set, while leading companies score in the 80% to 90% range. The next step is to invite key customers to provide feedback on brand identity. The greater the degree of alignment between internal and external mind-sets, the greater the value of this capability.

ACCOUNTABILITY AS AN ORGANIZATIONAL CAPABILITY

(Smallwood & Ulrich, 2004) Performance accountability becomes an organizational capability When employees realize that failure to meet their goals would be unacceptable to the company, then that performance accountability becomes an organizational capability.

COLLABORATION AS AN ORGANIZATIONAL CAPABILITY

Collaboration is the ability of an organization to gain efficiencies of operation through the pooling of services or technologies, through economies of scale, or through the sharing of ideas and talent across boundaries. Sharing services has been found to produce a savings of 15% to 25% in administrative costs (Smallwood & Ulrich, 2004).

LEARNING AS AN ORGANIZATIONAL CAPABILITY

Learning in an organizational context refers not only to generating and generalizing ideas with impact. For individuals, learning means letting go of old practices and adopting new ones (Smallwood & Ulrich, 2004)

LEADERSHIP AS AN ORGANIZATIONAL CAPABILITY

Companies that consistently nurture produce effective leaders generally have a clear leadership brand (leadership in many organizations are defined by the common understanding of what leaders should know, be, and do). It is not only about developing and nurturing the current leadership, but also about nurturing and developing a pool of future leaders or leaders in the pipeline. The future leadership potential measured by number of backups we have for top 100 employees in any organization (called as substitute – to – star ratio.; higher the ratio, better it is) - (Smallwood & Ulrich, 2004).

ABILITY TO CONNECT WITH CUSTOMER AS AN ORGANIZATIONAL CAPABILITY

Building enduring relationships of trust with targeted customers is an important aspect for an organization's success. The ability to connect with targeted customers is a strength, since most frequently, 20% of customers account for 80% of profits. Dedicated customer account teams, databases of customers (that track their preferences), or the involvement of customers in HR practices and many other initiatives enhance your customer connectivity.

STRATEGIC UNITY AS AN ORGANIZATIONAL CAPABILITY

The three levels of strategic unity are intellectual, behavioral, and procedural. At intellectual level, organizations must make sure employees from top to bottom know what the strategy is and why it is important. To gauge strategic unity at the behavioral level, measure how much of employees' time is spent in support of the strategy and observe whether employees' suggestions for improvement are heard and acted on. For strategic unity at procedural level, continually invest in procedures that are essential to your strategy (Smallwood & Ulrich, 2004)

INNOVATION AS AN ORGANIZATIONAL CAPABILITY

Innovation is about doing something new in both content and process. Innovation focuses on the future rather than on past successes. It excites employees, delights customers, and builds confidence among investors. Innovation capability of organizations is tracked through a vitality index (for instance, one that records revenues or profits from products or services created in the last three years) (Smallwood & Ulrich, 2004).

EFFICIENCY AS AN ORGANIZATIONAL CAPABILITY

Efficiency in a broader sense is about managing costs. Organizations which fail to manage costs will not likely could grow the top line. Efficiency as a capability is the easiest to track. Inventories, direct and indirect labor, capital employed, and costs of goods sold can all be viewed on balance sheets and income statements (Smallwood & Ulrich, 2004).

HUMAN RESOURCE CAPABILITY AS AN ORGANIZATIONAL CAPABILITY

Human Resources Capabilities are positively correlated to Organizational Performance. Human Resource Capability is a significant predictor of Sustainable advantage for a firm vis a vis its competition (Sharma A. K., 2005).

KNOWLEDGE MANAGEMENT CAPABILITY AS AN ORGANIZATIONAL CAPABILITY

There is a significant relationship between Knowledge Management Process Capability and Organizational Performance.

CORE CAPABILITIES

Core Capabilities are those capabilities on possession of which, companies are able to differentiate them strategically (LEONARD-BARTON, 1992). According to Teece, Pisano and Shuen, Core Capabilities provide the basis for a firm's competitiveness and sustainable advantage through differentiated skills, complementary assets, and routines. Dorothy Leonard Barton, emphasizes on the knowledge element of the Core Capability. Core capability is simply the knowledge set that leads to competencies that translates into advantage over the competition. Dorothy Leonard Barton further defines the four dimensions of this knowledge set. These four dimensions are, (1) knowledge and skills embodied in people (2) knowledge embedded in technical systems (accumulated experience, tacit knowledge in people etc.), (3) knowledge created, controlled, and guided by the Managerial Systems and (4) the values and norms of the firm associated with this knowledge. (LEONARD-BARTON, 1992)

From the above literature, the emphasis is on knowledge residing within the people, technical systems, and Managerial Systems in order to define a capability as a core capability. Therefore, based on the extent to which knowledge element is embedded in it, we may classify the core capabilities among the fifteen organizational capabilities identified earlier. The core capabilities thus identified are: Competitive Intelligence, Learning, Leadership, Ability to connect with customers, HR Capability and Knowledge Management Capability. The remaining capabilities, which we may call as add-on capabilities are listed here: Dynamic and IT enabled CRM, Internationalization, Speed / Agility, Accountability, Collaboration, Strategic Unity, Innovation, Efficiency, Talent

/ Talent Management and Shared Mindset / Coherent Brand Identity.

The other important element is that when a capability is identified and carefully nurtured over a long period of time, it becomes a core capability. Therefore, many Organizations, big and small embark upon a long journey to develop a capability into a core capability.

CONCLUSION

Firms desirous of developing Sustainable Competitive Advantage may look deep inside (within their own organization) and identify the core capabilities of the organization. Organizations consciously develop and nurture few core capabilities not only to develop sustainable Competitive Advantage but also to stay relevant in the business context. Thus, organizations which can respond to the changing business context and customer preferences by suitably adapting to their capabilities will remain relevant and competitive in the market place. When Managers respond to Opportunities and Threats posed by external environment through the analysis and utilization of internal resources (and capabilities), they create value for the customers and in turn for the company (Barney, Looking inside for competitive advantage, 1995)

REFERENCES

Masurali A., S. P. (2018). *Perception and Awarness level of Potential Customers towards Electric Cars.* INTERNATIONAL JOURNAL FOR RESEARCH IN APPLIED SCIENCE AND ENGINEERING TECHNOLOGY.

Pritam K. Gujarathi, V. A. (2018). *Electric Vehicles in India: Market Analysis with Consumer Perspective,.* Surat: River Publishers.

Putri, B. &. (2021). *Factors Affecting E-Scooter Sharing Purchase Intention: An Analysis Using Unified Theory of Acceptance and Use of Technology 2.* International Journal of Creative Business and Management.

roche, M. M. (2010). *Public attitude towards demand for hydrogen fuel cell vehicles: a review of the evidence and methodological implications.*

Singh, S. (n.d.). *Investigating the Characteristics and Choice of Electric Scooter Users.* Tiruchirappalli .

Eating Your Stress or Being Eaten By Your Stress: The Work-Life Balance Dilemma

Authors: Iqra Fatima, Research Fellow, Jamia Millia Islamia, Delhi, Chayan Poddar & Syed Mohammad Akrama Ali Rizvi, Research Fellow, International Management Institute (IMI), New Delhi.

ABSTRACT

While there are several factors that contribute to stress, nothing impacts the life of a working individual more than the inadequacy of proper nutrition. This paper looks to address nutrition as a significant factor that can be intervened to address the vicious circle of stress leading to a decrease in efficiency, resulting in reduced work-life balance and contributing to more stress. This is a conceptual paper that focuses on implementing solutions to a problem that affects organizational sustainability in the long run.

KEYWORDS

Nutrition, Stress, Work life balance, Productivity

INTRODUCTION

One of the fundamental measures for employees at work is productivity. In the aftermath of COVID-19, the return to offices, and the macroeconomic scenario contributing to continuous layoffs, there has been a considerable increase in stress for employees. The continuous demand for performance and quality in work has resulted in a reduced work-life balance. It becomes important for senior management in organizations to devise mechanisms that mitigate stress and contribute towards an effective work-life balance for employees.

A lot of factors contribute to stress. In this paper, we focus on the role that nutrition plays in reducing stress, particularly its lack, which contributes to increasing stress and decreasing work-life balance. Lack of proper nutrition has been found to reduce the productivity of employees, leading to little being achieved in the given amount of time and resulting in greater stress. As employees continue to spend a significant amount of time in workplaces, their nutrition while at work contributes to both individual and organizational well-being and performance outcomes in the short and long term. However, the pressures of long working hours and addressing deadlines, which themselves lead to inadequate nutrition, in turn, contribute to more stress and health ailments, thus forming a vicious circle. In some cases, employees do not have the luxury of time to decide on and implement a proper diet, owing to pressures related to work. Over a period, the combined effect of inadequate nutrition and increased stress leads to physical and mental ailment, thereby causing organizations to lose man-hours of work and employees their rightful salaries.

This paper looks to address the factors that cause and contribute to this vicious circle of increased stress and decreasing work-life balance by keeping nutrition as a significant factor. The identification of an appropriate nutritional environment for employees will help senior management in organisations intervene in creating mechanisms for healthy employees with increased productivity, thereby contributing to organizational sustainability in the long run.

REVIEW OF LITERATURE

Stress has reached epidemic proportions in contemporary societies. The Harvard T Chan School of Public Health divides stress into three main types based on their occurrence: acute stress, for example, an employee having a heated argument with a co-worker; acute episodic stress, for example, the employee is under continuous pressure to achieve targets within specific deadlines; and chronic stress, for example, the employee suffering stress owing to conflict in the family (Harvard T. Chan School of Public Health, 2021). The macroeconomic situation in the post-COVID scenario does not paint a rosy picture in terms of economic growth and job scenarios across countries. With the Ukraine war causing havoc corresponding to oil prices, inflation has been on the rise in most countries across the last year. 2021 was marked as the year of resignation (Cook, 2021), which saw a record number of employees quitting jobs, citing overwork, extra responsibilities, and non-recognition in the organization as some of the significant factors leading to resignations. In the above scenario, people have been forced to work long hours during the day in multiple jobs to make ends meet, leading to an increase in stress.

A well-balanced diet and healthy living have been associated with reducing stress. There are two ways in which inadequate nutrition or unhealthy eating can cause a reduction in the productivity of the employee: absenteeism, which refers to the employee being absent owing to a certain illness or having a disability; and presenteeism, for example, an employee not having enough energy at the workplace to complete a given task (Burton et al., 1999; Schultz, Chen, & Edington, 2009). This loss in productivity leads to economic loss on the part of the organization. Nutrition is essential for maintaining optimum performance at work; a lack of it causes a decrease in productivity, lowers self-control, and causes exhaustion in daily life (Stahl, 2019).

Any kind of stress triggers a fight or flight response within the human body, which essentially causes certain physiological changes. While one can identify the causes leading to stress and try to reduce them, having a healthy and balanced diet addresses these physiological changes by stabilizing blood sugar levels in the body (Lewin, 2019). Blood sugar levels are affected by bouts of adrenaline, which supercharges during stress. Moreover, stress has also influenced the eating patterns of an individual (Harvard T. Chan School of Public Health, 2021). People experiencing stress are more likely to complete their meals with highly processed, ready-made foods, owing to a lack of motivation to create nutritious meals. Processed foods with IES's MCRC 13th International Conference February 28, 2023 Page 4: High sugar sometimes acts as a comforting mechanism in the face of stress—something referred to as stress eating, which happens as a result of cravings due to high levels of cortisol in the body. Stress causes disturbances in sleep and following a normal sleep schedule, which may lead one to ingest stimulants during the daytime, such as caffeine or energy drinks and snacks. Inadequacy in workplace nutrition, causing hindrances to workers' health and productivity, has been recognized by the International Labour Organisation as well (ILO, 2005). The report quantified a loss of around 20 percent in productivity owing to two contrasting reasons: malnutrition in developing countries owing to poor diets and weight gains, and obesity in industrialized nations owing to excessive diets. Thus, the nutrition problem is not in isolation; it is associated with economic and social conditions reflecting the influence of lifestyle on food intake.

This brings us to the question of work-life balance in contemporary times. From the human resources perspective, the expectations of the modern worker have changed over the years, from only being provided with monetary wages and salaries. One of the significant factors that influence prospective employees' joining an organization is the amount of work-life balance offered with the job. We should note that it is not only time management that contributes towards work-life balance, but a comprehensively healthy lifestyle with adequate nutrition leads towards it by supplying the necessary energy required for maintaining optimum efficiency (Krause, 2022). This is where the crux of our study lies. Any development in human life, whether positive or negative, is an outcome of daily repeated habits and behaviors over a long period of time. Thus, when employees focus on healthy and clean eating with a balanced, nutritious diet, despite the pressures of work, they are able to maintain a healthy body and mind, mitigating the challenges of work on an everyday basis. This also contributes to their healthy life as they approach midlife and later stages in life. Similarly, repeated iterations of neglecting diets and unhealthy lifestyles contribute to ailments and diseases in the long run.

When we place this in the context of long working hours and the continuous stress of meeting deadlines in contemporary organizations, adverse health consequences become inevitable (von Bonsdroff et al., 2017). This leads to the vicious cycle of stress leading to a decrease in efficiency, resulting in a reduced work-life balance and contributing to more stress. Nutrition is an effective intervening factor that can mitigate this cycle.

RESEARCH METHODOLOGY

As part of this conceptual paper, which highlights the vicious cycle of stress and work-life balance, we propose the following conceptual framework: From the above literature review, we propose stress as the independent construct, affecting the work-life balance of employees and their productivity as the dependent constructs. We identify nutrition to moderate the relationship between stress and work-life balance, as well as stress and employee productivity. The following propositions would test whether proper nutrition in an employee can mitigate the effects of stress on work-life balance and productivity and put an end to the continuous vicious cycle, thereby reducing the occurrence of more stress. The conceptual framework of the study is as follows:

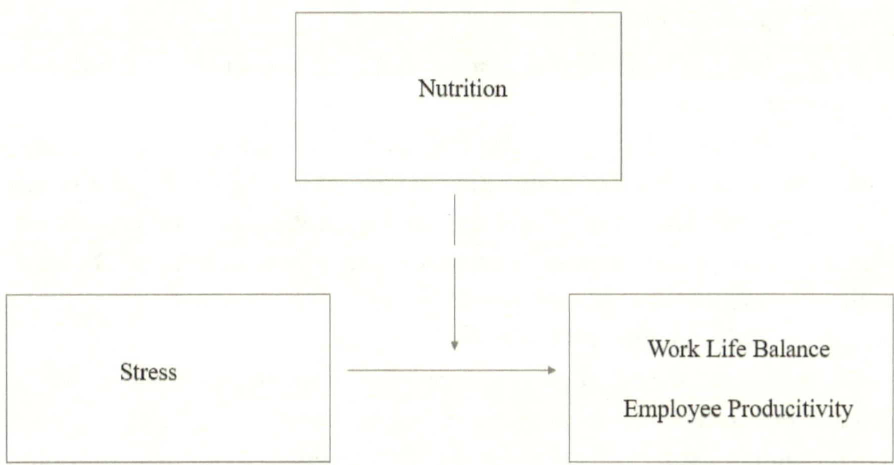

Figure: *Conceptual Framework of the Study*

Based on the conceptual framework, we introduce the following propositions among the different constructs used in the framework:

Proposition 1: There is a direct negative effect of stress on work-life balance. Proposition 2: There is a direct negative effect of stress on employee productivity.

Proposition 3: Nutrition moderates the direct effect of stress on work-life balance. Proposition 4: Nutrition moderates the direct effect of stress on employee productivity.

DISCUSSION

Nutrition has been identified to lead to a balanced body and mind, resulting in optimum employee productivity. In order to retain critical talent, organizations that focus on and invest in wellness and training programs for employees have to take into consideration the nutritional environment, which facilitates employees in creating good nutritional habits. Since the crux of the article lies in developments in human life in small portions over a long period of time, affecting organizations and economies, senior management in organizations needs to invest in the workplace nutrition of employees. Organizations can run wellness programs, weight management programs, health enhancement programs, and health promotion programs. Award systems can be started to promote better health and nutrition for employees, with the organization arranging for health checkups and maintaining the quality of nutrition provided to employees.

The economic fallout from absenteeism and presenteeism, as discussed above, owing to both a lack of nutrition as well as pushing employees towards readily processed foods and obesity, has been quantified, both in terms of lost working hours and a certain value amounting to billions of dollars. The long-term consequence is an unhealthy society with the potential to be a significant hindrance to the growth and prosperity of nations.

Organizations should focus on supplying their employees with whole grains, fruits, and vegetables to improve their serotonin levels, which helps one remain calm in the face of stress (Singh, 2016). Certain foods that contribute to reducing stress are oranges, spinach, chocolate, coffee, blueberries, broccoli, fish, bananas, walnuts, eggs, tea, flax seeds, whole grains, etc. (Singh, 2016). Practices such as encouraging employees to prepare their own food and checks and balances over skipping lunch employees will contribute a long way by not only improving employee productivity but also their morale, working as a defining characteristic for prospective employees. Organizations, as a microcosm of society, can lead towards effective stress mitigation by prioritizing the maintenance of proper nutrition and work-life balance for their employees. It will lead to substantive gains in subjective measures of business performance, such as improving employee commitment and their esprit de corps.

As a direction for future research, the constructs proposed in the conceptual framework above can be tested empirically by conducting a quantitative study using appropriate scales. The study can also be improved by testing the relationship between the constructs across different age groups to comprehensively explore the impact of nutrition on mitigating stress in human beings and contributing to a healthy lifestyle that ensures productivity at any age.

SUMMARY AND CONCLUSIONS

The creation and continuation of any new habit depend on the environment to a large extent. It is the responsibility of the organization to create a nutrition-conducive environment to mitigate both the challenges of malnutrition and excessive eating. Stress is an outcome of modern lifestyles and the work that employees do in organizations, but it is the onus of senior management to look at nutrition as an effective intervening factor in reducing the effects of the vicious loop of stress, work-life balance, and employee productivity, in turn contributing to organizational sustainability in the long run. The awareness and urgency for organizations, such that they actually create and nurture such an environment for employees, depends on their understanding of the quantifiable losses that stress and inadequate nutrition lead to. The existence of local laws and practices beyond organizational boundaries to provide proper nutrition goes a long way toward solving the crisis and is a welcome first step.

REFERENCES

Burton, W.N., Conti, D.J., Chen, C.Y., Schultz, A.B., Edington, D.W. (1999). The role of health risk factors and disease on worker productivity. Journal of Occupational and Environmental Medicine. 41(10), 863–877.

Cook, I. (2021, September 15). *Who is driving the great resignation?* Harvard Business Review. https://hbr.org/2021/09/who-is-driving-the-great-resignation

Harvard T Chan School of Public Health. (2021, October). *Stress and Health.* https://www.hsph.harvard.edu/nutritionsource/stress-and-health/

International Labour Organization. (2005, September 5). *Poor workplace nutrition hits workers' health and productivity, says new ILO report.* Press release, International Labour Organization. https://www.ilo.org/global/about-the- ilo/newsroom/news/WCMS_005175/lang--en/index.htm

Krause, J. (2022, August 1). *Better nutrition for a healthy work life balance.* Worklife. https://worklife.coloniallife.com/2022/08/better-nutrition-for-a-healthy-work-life- balance/

Lewin, J. (2019, January 30). *Stress relief: How diet and lifestyle can help.* BBC goodfood. https://www.bbcgoodfood.com/howto/guide/stress-diet-can-foods-help

Schultz, A.B., Chen, C.Y., Edington, D.W. (2009). The cost and impact of health conditions on presenteeism to employers: a review of the literature. *Pharmacoeconomics.* 27(5), 365– 378.

Singh, K. (2016). Nutrition and stress management. Journal of Nutrition and Food Sciences, 6(4), 1000528. doi:10.4172/2155-9600.1000528

Stahl, A. (2019, August 6). *3 ways your diet impacts work performance*. Forbes. https://www.forbes.com/sites/ashleystahl/2019/08/06/3-ways-your-diet-impacts-work- performance/?sh=3a4936d96eac

von Bonsdorff, M. B., Strandberg, A., von Bonsdorff, M., Törmäkangas, T., Pitkälä, K. H., & Strandberg, T. E. (2017). Working hours and sleep duration in midlife as determinants of health-related quality of life among older businessmen. *Age and ageing*, *46*(1), 108-112.

A Study on Cognizance of Paternity Leave in Service Sector

CHAPTER 09

Author – Komal Kaur Kataria, Apoorva Raut, Het Shah, Student & Prof. Falguni Mathews, Assistant Professor, SIES College of Commerce and Economics, Mumbai

ABSTRACT

Paternity leave refers to the time that fathers take off from work after the birth or adoption of a child in order to bond with and care for their newborn or adopted child. While the benefits of paternity leave for fathers, mothers, and children are well-established, access to paternity leave remains unequal across countries and within countries. Some fathers may feel pressure to return to work quickly in order to advance their careers, while others may face stigma or discrimination for taking paternity leave. Research conducted in service sector has shown that paternity leave can increase fathers' involvement in child care, lead to more equitable distribution of caregiving responsibilities within the family, and improve fathers' mental health and well-being. It can also reduce the burden of solo parenting for mothers and increase their ability to return to work after the birth or adoption of a child. However, unequal access to paternity leave can perpetuate gender inequality in the workforce and within families. Overall, the research suggests that paternity leave can have numerous benefits, but morework needs to be done to ensure that all fathers have access to and feel supported in taking paternity leave.

KEYWORDS

Paternity leave, Fathers, Service sector, Discrimination, Inequality

INTRODUCTION

Paternity leave is simply defined as a period of absence from work given to a father after or shortly before the birth of his child. In the literature, it is conceptualized as a process where employees get permission from their work to take time off for the reason of taking care of their pregnant wife, new-born baby and also in case of adoption. Due to a variety of factors, many who are in service sector are unaware that their 'parental leave' may include paternity, maternity, adoption leave; which leads to unfair working conditions for employees as he/she cannot work satisfactorily while handling their family. Therefore, it is clear that awareness of parental leave is an absolute necessity as it plays an important role in the lives of young parents. There are two types of paternity leave, paid and unpaid.

Many companies do not support such employee welfare schemes and many times even employees are unaware about their rights and about such welfare schemes as they are not promoted efficiently.

A Great environment by a father to his child brings goodness in children's life from the start, as in the first days, weeks, or months of a baby's life are sensitive and most important in shaping family dynamics. In spite of being such an important policy it hasn't been promoted in many companies, and even if its present its only provided for 15 days which in comparison to maternity leave is too short. This breaks or takes away many responsibilities and happy moments from once life as he cannot enjoy or relive that unreplaceable time of his life. Paternity leave also helps in many ways to build the foundation for a more equal distribution of responsibility in the future.

This research paper will be covering the Awareness of paternity leave among people. Since many people are unaware about their rights and about just how important this scheme is.

Paternity leave can help in building a strong relationship with a child over time, as time which is spent with the child by his father creates an inseparable bond and also commits to a fair relationship which is very necessary in this generation where both the parents are working parents and want to bring welfare for their family. But due to short or no paternity leave many fathers miss their precious time with their baby and how it feels to take care of their babies while they were newly born. Indeed, this research includes that paternity leave is necessary and longer periods of paternity leave creates fast development in a child's health as the first few months of children's lives is crucial and also creates stronger bond with his/her parents.

LITERATURE REVIEW

(DHANUKA & BANTHIA, 2021) in their study on "Paternity Benefit Leaves in India" published by "International Journal of Policy Sciences and Law" explain that not having a paternity leave for newly father affects the child care responsibilities and volunteer equally in the holistic development of new born child. And they concluded that having paternity leave breaks gender stereotypes from a multitude of dimensions.

(RAMASAYI GUMMADI, 2021) in their study on "Paternity Leave Policy in India: A Critical Analysis" published by "International Journal of Law Management & Humanities" the main goal of this research paper was to understand paternity leave policy in India and the loopholes on paternity leave policies. And also brought strong suggestion that the bill (The Paternity Benefit Bill, 2017) created unfair discrimination by not taking into consideration adoptive parents, homosexuals and the members of the trans community which are evolved by time and which gives rise to ambiguity.

(RISHI SARAF, 2021) in their research on "Paternity Leave – Amending Article 42" published by "International Journal of Law Management and Humanities, Volume 4, Issue 2" The paper argues for adding the concept of paternity leave in the constitution along with article 42 of the Indian constitution. Our constitution provides for maternity relief under the article 42 of directive principles of state policy. Concluded with that, in order to promote true gender equality, one should have permission to, expected to, and most important is needed to care for their small children, wife and his house for a few months.

(QI LI, CHRIS KNOESTER & RICHARD J. PETTS, 2022) A research on "Attitudes about Paid Parental Leave in the United States" published by "Sociological focus" this research spread the importance of rare and unequal paid parental leave offered in the United States. It also shows how paid leaves help and provide better and healthy growth in one's relationship.

STATEMENT OF PROBLEM

1. Lack of awareness about importance of paternity leave in service sector in India

2. Some companies in India don't have a policy regarding paternity leave.
3. Taking paternity leave is not normalized in India.

OBJECTIVES

1. To evaluate the prevalent HR welfare- measure of paternity leave in the service sector.
2. To build a case for paternity leave for better work life balance.

LIMITATION

1. Respondents working in the organised sector i.e. service sector are only considered for the study.
2. Study was conducted between the age group of 21-60
3. Employees of different working places from the metropolitan cities of India filled the questionnaire.
4. The number of responses recorded through the survey were limited.
5. The questionnaire was only in English so there was language barrier for certain people.
6. The study is limited to Service sector.
7. Certain employees didn't name their workplace as they wanted to keep it confidential.

RESEARCH METHODOLOGY

The driven study is wherein both primary and secondary data is collected. Secondary data is gathered from various websites, and survey data is consolidated based on data work. For collecting the primary data, people from the organised part of the service sector were interviewed. The respondents were from the age group of 21-60

SCOPE OF STUDY

The research was conducted to see the awareness of Paternity leave in service sector to get their opinions about paternity leave policy in India. Targeted audience for this study was the working population in service sector from the metropolitan cities of India. Our take away from this research was on the number of days expected by our sample for Paternity leave, whether fathers should be involved or not in the upbringing of the child, how they are satisfied with the Paternity leave policy in India.

DATA ANALYSIS & INTERPRETATION

The research was conducted in the service sector of 21-30 age group which was the largest of 73.3%, 6.7% of 31-40 age group, 11.1% of 41-50 age group, and 8.9% of which were from 51-60 age group.

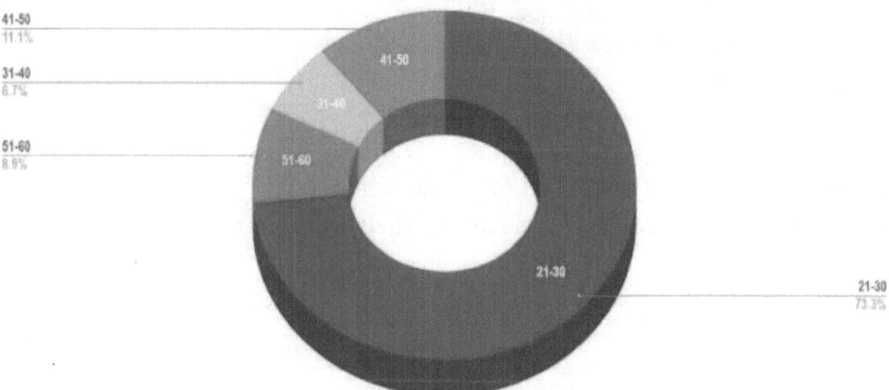

Out of which 35.6% were male respondents & 64.4% were female respondents.

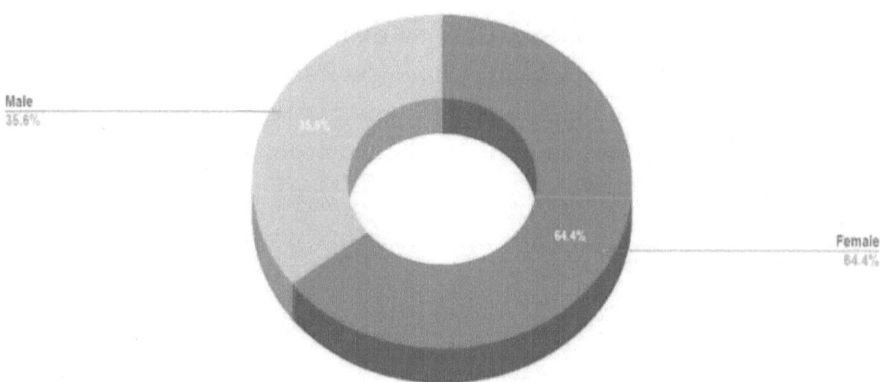

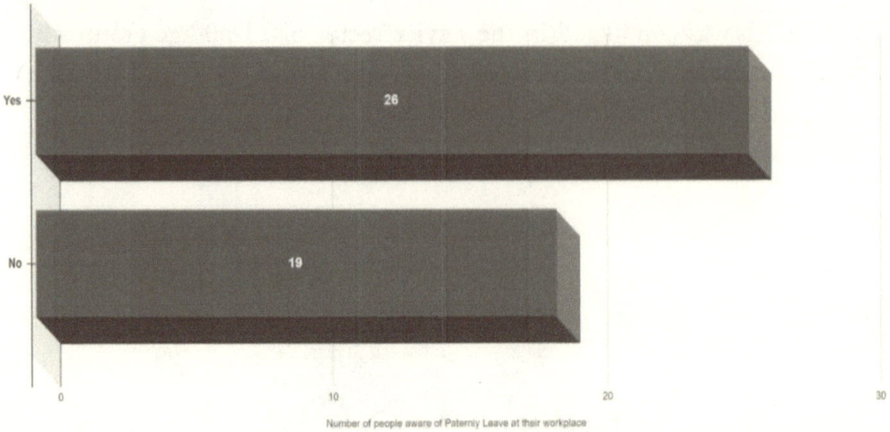

<u>Interpretation:</u> From the total respondents only 57.8% respondents were aware of the Paternity Leave available in their workplace,42.2% respondents were unaware.

Should the companies have Paternity Leave Policy?

<u>Interpretation:</u> 44.4% of surveyed people think that their company should have a Paternity Leave Policy, 42.2% people had Paternity Leave Policy in their Company, 4.4% people don't think their company should have a Paternity Leave Policy, 8.9 % are not sure whether their company should have the policy or not.

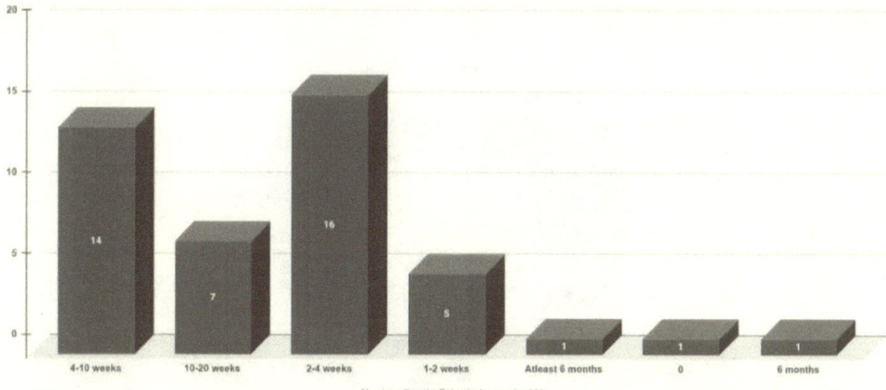

Interpretation: 16 respondents think that number of weeks Paternity Leave should be 2-4 weeks, 14 respondents think it should be 4-10 weeks, 7 think it should 10-20 weeks, 5 favour it to be 1-2 weeks, 1 were in favour of keeping the leave for 6 months and 1 respondent were in not having a Paternity Leave at all.

Should the Paternity Leave be equal to Maternity Leave

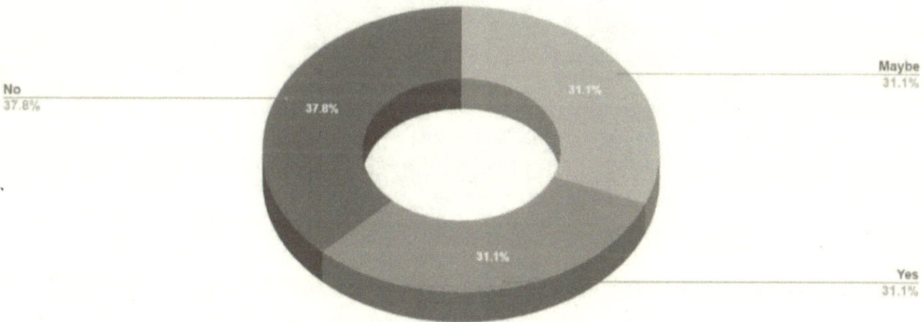

Interpretation: With the help of the survey, it is noticed that 37.8 % of people don't want Paternity Leave to be equal to Maternity Leave, 31.1 % want it to be equal and the rest 31.1% are not sure whether the leave for both of them should be equal or not.

Satisfied or not with the huge gap between the Paternity Leave & Maternity Leave

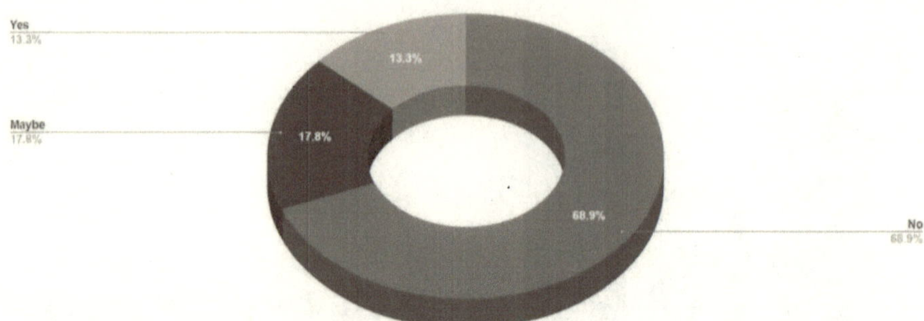

<u>Interpretation:</u> The above pie chart shows that 68.9% respondents out of 45 are not satisfied the huge gap between the number of leaves for both parents, 13.3 % seems to be satisfied and 17.8% are confused about their satisfaction of difference between the leave

Do you think paternity leave should be made available to parents with two or more kids?

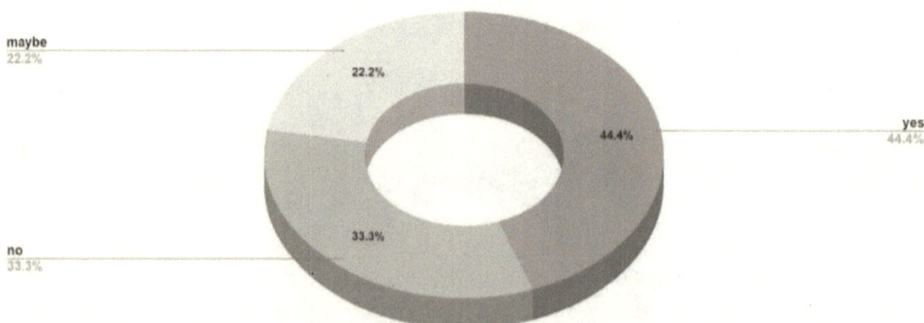

<u>Interpretation:</u> As the act says fathers with 2 or more kids are not entitled to the 15 days leave policy we asked the respondents that does this policy needs to change with respect to 2 or more kids. 44.4% agreed to the question, 33.3% said no and 22.2% were not sure about it.

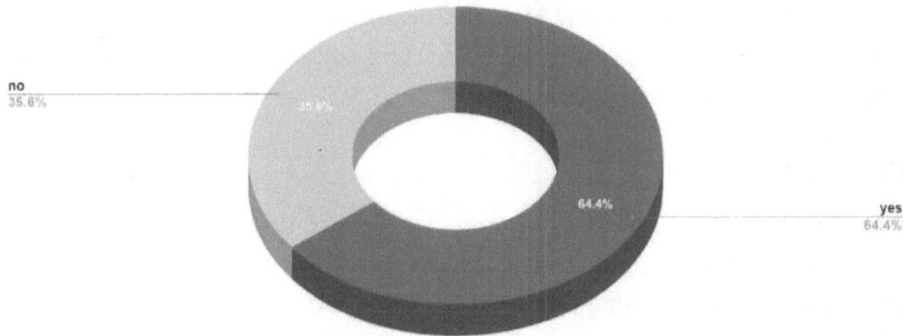

Interpretation: The pie chart represents the question about whether not having paternity leave affecting women's career. 64.4% of the respondents think yes not having paternity leave is affecting women's career. 35.6% of the respondents think it doesn't make any difference on women's career.

SUGGESTIONS/RECOMMENDATION

It is essential to consider a much clear and concise nationwide policy that incorporates paternity leave. A much clear comprehensive national policy is one that contains no unwanted exceptions, such as the Paternity Benefit Act of 2017, which offers little to no knowledge about the accessibility of paternity leave for adoptive parents, homosexuals, and members of the trans community. Not to mention that the bill generates unfair discrimination by neglecting to take into account the various sections of society which have evolved over time. Paternity Benefit

Bill, 2017 irrationally discriminates against the parent who has more than two children with no practical reasoning.

India and Indian companies should take some inspiration from other countries like Spain which has 30 days of paid Paternity Leave, Sweden has 16 months of 80% paid salary leave for both parents together and an additional 180 days leave if twins are born. Some companies like Microsoft provides 12 weeks of paid leave, Facebook having 17 weeks. India's law needs to change, the law can be changed with increase in number of days, different percentage of salary or companies can give work from home policy for a certain period.

It is pivotal that paternity and maternity leave should be equitable and reasonable for both genders while taking into account the various medical, social, and cultural factors that affect such a bond between the parent and the child. Having a paternity leave would also lead to work life balance in an employee's life. Moreover, any violation or misuse of the statutory principles governing paternity leave must be taken seriously, and appropriate redressal measures must be specified in the act.

CONCLUSION

The two primary objectives of paternity leave are to give the fathers a chance to bond with the offspring and to make it clear to the community at large that child care is something that needs to be viewed as an equal responsibility of both parents and that society cannot stigmatizesuch that men are the breadwinners of the house and women play a major role in nurturing and caring for the offspring. The entitlement to take paternity leave exists only in the form of gender equality conventions, and nothing has been specifically written concerning paternity leave benefits, making it ambiguous in nature. Not having an intact law about paternity leave affects women's career, they have to leave their jobs to take care of the baby. This is not fair to the women's because that age is also important for women's career. With mere existence of paternity leave the work life balance of employees is disrupted and this leads to an increase in stress.

People interpret the concept differently in various parts of the world. The paternity leave benefit will not only contribute to excellent child care, but it will also stimulate shared responsibility in the household, thereby breaking down gender stereotypes on the roles of men and women in society, requiring the effective implementation of such an updated, inclusive, and viable law in this sphere.

BIBLIOGRAPHY

https://www.mckinsey.com/capabilities/people-and-organizational-performance/our- insights/a-fresh-look-at-paternity-leave-why-the-benefits-extend-beyond-the-personal

https://www.ijlmh.com/paper/paternity-leave-amending-article-42/

https://judicialcompetitiontimes.in/Article/Details/24?Title=need-for-paternity-leave-in- india&Title=need-for-paternity-leave-in-india

https://www.mckinsey.com/capabilities/people-and-organizational-performance/our- insights/a-fresh-look-at-paternity-leave-why-the-benefits-extend-beyond-the-personal

https://ijpsl.in/wp-content/uploads/2021/06/Paternity-Benefit-Leaves-in-India-Need- Cost-and-Gender-Reform_Ananya-Dhanuka-Kashish-Banthia-1.pdf

https://blog.greenthumbs.in/paternity-leaves-in-india.php

Diversity & Inclusion Challenges – Hilton Vs. Marriott

CHAPTER 10

Author – Pranali Surlekar, Student & Dr. Dipaali Pulekar, Associate Professor, Amity Global Business School, Mumbai

ABSTRACT

Diversity in the workplace is no longer just a flag that businesses hoist to demonstrate their commitment to welcoming differences; it is becoming a need in today's modern, internationally linked society and economy. It is said that hospitality businesses should take the initiative to diversify their workforce if they desire new ideas, rapid development, a favourable corporate image, and an improved capacity to find competent employees. The paper investigates a comparative analysis of the D&I challenges between Hilton & Marriott International, which is elaborated in terms of inequitable inclusion, cultural misunderstandings, communication issues, stereotypes & prejudices and slower decision making.

The findings of this paper lay down suggestions to overcome the hurdles to D&I by developing a committee to manage inclusion, promoting diversity and individuality, inviting employee feedback, making meetings more efficient, setting specific objectives, and tracking success are a few of the areas of improvement to escalate the scope of D&I. The notion of LMX theory states that leaders are more intimate, amiable, inclusive, and communicative with subordinates who reports to them than others. The testimonials & interviews of HR Executives of the respective organisations is what adds value to this paper.

KEYWORDS

Diversity management, Challenges and hurdles, Inclusive workforce, Hospitality Sector, Diversity & inclusivity

INTRODUCTION

Understanding that each person has a unique set of life experiences, cultural backgrounds, and viewpoints is the cornerstone of diversity. Recognizing, appreciating, and utilising these distinctions in both your personnel and your clients is what diversity in hospitality entails to enhance the experience for everyone.

Because it depends on a complicated network of many firms, a diverse group of employees, and clients from a variety of backgrounds, the hospitality sector is a particularly diverse field. While there may be some difficulties, there are also many chances to develop a more inventive, creative, and productive workplace that serves all clients.

A diverse and inclusive environment is one in which everyone feels equally included in and supported in all parts of the workplace, irrespective of what they are or what they do for the company. The phrase "all places" is crucial.

Do the hiring processes, departments, and leadership all reflect diversity? Or is there a business where there are 50% female employees but none of the female managers? Do companies have a fair representation of individuals of diversity across all departments, though?

Numerous advantages of a multicultural and diverse workplace have been demonstrated through research.

- More rapid revenue growth
- Increased capacity for innovation
- Higher staff retention by 5.4 times

When it comes to the hospitality sector, there are various differences to be catered not only in terms of the internal stakeholders, but also the external stakeholders. Making sure to promote multiculturalism in this sector, is a lot more rigorous than expected. In order to broaden the roots of D&I in organisations and to bridge the discrepancies, leadership along with the core values of the company should be addressed.

DIVERSITY

Diversity acknowledges our shared intersectionality. Race, ethnicity, gender, sexual orientation, socioeconomic level, age, physical capabilities, religious beliefs, political opinions, and other ideologies are all welcomed in a varied culture. We embrace and value diversity, hire people from various backgrounds, and give funding to organisations that are frequently underrepresented.

EQUITY

Both an approach and a tool, equity. Equity fosters fairness and recognises the obstacles that result in unfair starting points and outcomes. Those who have a lower socioeconomic position, women, people of colour, LGBTQIA+ people, and those with disabilities are some of the categories that are most frequently disadvantaged.

INCLUSION

Through inclusion, everyone is made to feel welcome, at ease, and secure. An inclusive workplace recognises the inherent value and dignity of every individual and gives those who would otherwise be alienated or marginalised access to resources and possibilities.

LITERATURE REVIEW

(Ramani, 2023) Sean McGinley and Ravi S. Ramani (2023) state in their paper, everyone in the hospitality industry is familiar with the proverb "What gets evaluated is accomplished, and what gets rewarded, gets repeated." These principles have been utilised by the hospitality sector for a long time when dealing with operational, technological, or financial difficulties.

Their paper makes the case that the hotel and lodging sector may address the matter of diversity and inclusion, and particularly racial inclusivity, in managerial ranks by using this systematic approach to assessment and reward. Increased opportunities for promotion for people of colour can benefit organisations, as well as indirectly the academics, consultants, and executives who study this sector if hospitality companies adopt a gamified system that shifts promotion decisions away from excessive reliance on person-organization fit and towards more objective and transparent standards.

Additionally, by utilising the already varied human resources in the sector, implementing inclusive promotional practises at all levels of the organisation can assist hospitality enterprises in rebuilding workforces impacted by Covid-19. This article explains how organisations can enhance their promotional practises by developing more impartial metrics to direct decision-making and more diversified leadership teams across the board. Furthermore, we offer recommendations for scholars that can direct the academic discussion on racial disparity in the hospitality business.

(Hana Urbancová, 2020) Hana Urbancová, Monika Hudáková & et.al (2020) mention in their paper titled "Diversity Management as a Tool of Sustainability of Competitive Advantage" that diversity is a phenomenon that is becoming more prevalent in all fields of human endeavour and performance, including the labour market, and working teams, as a result of increased globalisation. Considering these developments, the purpose of this research paper is to identify and analyse the practise of diversity management as a factor of the long-term viability of competitive advantage in relation to the elements of diversity under consideration.

The data was gathered through primary examination of 549 Czech enterprises using a questionnaire poll. The findings show that there is a statistical relationship between the use of diversity management and the commercial sector in which the company works, as well as the size of the company.

This paper helped in cumulating the research objectives and for drafting the qualitative data.

(Ruchika Malik, 2017) Ruchika Malik, Tanavi Madappa and et.al (2017) summarize in their journal article "Diversity management in tourism and hospitality: an exploratory study", that the number of multinational organisations active in the hospitality and tourist sector has grown, bringing together people from various cultural backgrounds. The relevance of cross-cultural management, the multicultural challenges that an organisation faces, the best techniques for managing diversity, and the prospects of cultural diversity are all addressed in this article.

As a result, policies and initiatives designed to manage cultural diversity must be properly implemented and integrated, according to the researchers' findings. Additionally, managers must recognise the organization's present deficiencies in diversity management to take the required actions to create a positive working environment for both local employees and expats.

This journal article directed the formulation of the survey questionnaire, especially in terms of demographic implications and to investigate the future scope of this research.

(kim, 2008) Byeong Yeong Kim (2008) comply in his research article "Managing Workforce Diversity", that attracting, keeping, and efficiently using diverse employees have become priorities as hospitality companies' workforces become more and more varied. In today's volatile hospitality industries, diversity management is seen as essential to success. The current study investigates the definitions used to deal with diversity, explains diversity-related concepts, and evaluates the advantages of successful diversity management to offer techniques for managing diversity. It is said that hospitality businesses should take the initiative to diversify their workforce if they desire new ideas, rapid development, a favourable corporate image, and an improved capacity to find competent employees. This study also makes recommendations for efficient diversity management tactics, such as the creation of a learning organisation and the application of diversity management paradigms.

This article assisted in drafting the research objectives and also contributed to determining the qualitative approach of the research.

OBJECTIVES OF THE STUDY

- To understand the meaning of a diverse workforce
- To study the demographics of a diverse workforce
- To analyse the challenges of a diverse workforce
- To recommend solutions to manage the challenges of a diverse workforce

RESEARCH METHODOLOGY

Research Design, this paper had an amalgamation of various techniques. Hence, this paper followed a "Descriptive, Comparative Research Design."

The research includes data from existing resources (secondary source) and first-hand resources (primary source). The research questionnaire mainly focused on the descriptive aspects of the objectives of my study.

The secondary resources assisted me in analysing the comparative aspects of the challenges faced while managing a diverse workforce, while the primary resources made sure that all the objectives of the research were looked upon.

Data Collection, for the research, data was collected by both, primary and secondary techniques. The primary data has been collected via a well-structured survey questionnaire, to understand how the respondents define a diverse workforce, what all challenges do they face while recruiting an inclusive workforce, the hurdles faced while managing a diverse work environment & how to make sure to adapt a diverse & inclusive work environment.

The questionnaire consisted of close ended questions, open ended questions and 3 Likert scale based questions. The objective behind doing this survey was to comprehend from the HR executives itself their understanding of the entire cycle of diversity & inclusivity.

The secondary data has been collected mostly from journal articles, periodicals, blogs, and other documents available on the internet.

Population, the term "population" refers to the portion of the universe from which the study sample is drawn. The population for the study is all the HR Executives working in the hospitality sector.

Sample, it's a part of the population from which the data inferences are drawn. This paper, under the primary data had a sample size of 5 respondents. And the sample consisted of all the HR Executives working at Hilton & Marriott.

Sampling Technique, Purposive Sampling Technique - The reason behind selecting this sampling technique for the research was that they was a careful observation carried out and after going through the objectives and seeing that the research focuses on a comparative analysis the span of respondents was limited to eligible samplings.

Pilot Testing, for the pilot study, the research questionnaire was sent to HR Executives working in the Hospitality sector (apart from Hilton & Marriott).

- All the structures of the questions remained the same.
- The only modification required was to change the function of the open-ended questions. That is, instead of keeping them as a mandatory question, they could decide on their own whether they want to voluntarily respond to them or not. Respondents prefer survey questionnaires to be time efficient, which can be easily interpretated and filled. This way, there was flexibility for the respondents and the response rate was 30% higher than before.

FINDINGS AND DATA INTERPRETATIONS

The business was dedicated to creating an inclusive environment, with a multicultural and varied staff serving as its foundation. Diversity wasn't simply a buzzword at Hilton; it was a lifestyle. Its staff members spoke with over 40 languages and were from 90 different countries.

Thus, giving wonderful moments to the guests was at the centre of the hotel. So over ages, Hilton put in place a variety of programmes to promote diversity among its owners, suppliers, and community partners. The leadership team's main goal was to create a worldwide culture centred on its purpose, values, and vision.

Marriott has supported diversity and inclusion since 1927. Their success as the leading hospitality organisation with an ever-expanding worldwide portfolio depends on embracing differences since our firm is founded on the health and happiness of their workers. The foundation of their core principles and strategic business objectives is diversity and inclusiveness. People-first thinking is ingrained in their company's DNA and is part of their most priceless cultural legacy. "We all need to feel positive about oneself, the workplace, and the contribution that our firm makes to society", according to Marriott's main dimensions.

PARAMETERS	HILTON	MARRIOTT INTERNATIONAL
Core Foundations	Their vision, mission, and basic values are all based on diversity. They are dedicated to having a staff that is inclusive of all cultures, ethnicities, and opinions. Through the creation of gathering spots, our international brands foster connections between individuals from various backgrounds.	The foundation of their core principles & strategic business objectives is diversity and inclusiveness. People-first thinking is ingrained in their company's DNA and is part of their most priceless cultural legacy. "We all need to feel positive about oneself, the workplace, and the contribution that our firm makes to society", according to Marriott's main dimensions of associate wellness.
D&I Initiatives	The acceptance of a top down diversity strategy, the use of mentoring strategies to aid diversity training, and an intense focus on the procurement of knowledge and cultural competencies are among the conditions set for proper governance of a culturally diverse staff that are met by Hilton's Diversity Initiatives.	Marriott aimed to grow the number of diverse suppliers globally to more than 4,000 companies owned by people of colour each year. In order to support gender equality in the workplace, Marriott aims to raise the number of "woman owned open hotels" to 1000 or more by the year 2020.

PARAMETERS	HILTON	MARRIOTT INTERNATIONAL
Demographics	Among Hilton's over than 55,500 American workers, 69 percent are members of underrepresented racial or ethnic groups, while 53% are women, 5% define as LBGTQ, and 4% are disabled.	• People of color by level: - 21% (Executive), 35% (mid-level manager, 49% (entry – level manager) • Women by level: - 49% (Executive), 47% (mid- level manager, 49% (entry – level manager)
Rewards & Recognition	By ranking first among theTop 50 Companies for Diversity in 2021, DiversityInc has acknowledged Hilton for its dedication to diversity and inclusion. dedication to diversity and inclusion.	Marriott International, Inc. (NASDAQ), the first hospitality firm to join previously top-ranked corporations, was inducted into the DiversityInc Hall of Fame in 2020 after topping the DiversityInc Top 50 Companies for Diversity list.

1. **What according to you could be the possible Characteristics of Employees, working in a diverse workplace?**

- 75% of the total samplings believe that **Gender, Sexual orientation, Religion, Physical abilities/disabilities, Life experiences, Socioeconomic background** are the possible characteristics of the employees working in a diverse workplace.
- And the rest 50% of them presume that **Race** and **Ethnicity** is also a considered factor of a diverse workforce.

2. **When did the organization start a policy or take a step in recruiting diverse workforce?**

JW MARRIOTT EXECUTIVES	HILTON EXECUTIVES
Since 1927, Marriott has valueddiversity and inclusion. With our foundation built upon the wellbeingand happiness of our associates, embracing differences is critical to oursuccess as the largest hospitalitycompany with an ever growing global portfolio.	More focus on skilled workers.
The organization where I work believesin diversity. Many organizations believe in the same. When you are opening an organization that is the correct time to create these policies.	Many years ago.

3. How creatively does the HR team work, to source candidates from underrepresented communities?

JW MARRIOTT EXECUTIVES	HILTON EXECUTIVES
We encourage our diverse employees torefer their connections.	Jobs applied by diverse background workers and checking their fit to the organisation and stability.
We are having our company website and ofcourse there are many portals where you can post your openings with criteria.	Proactive scouting

4. Could you give any suggestions as to how you try to overcome diversity & inclusion challenges at the organisation?

JW MARRIOTT EXECUTIVES	HILTON EXECUTIVES
In order to create an inclusive workplace where all employees feel that their differences are recognised and valued for their unique abilities and ideas, it is crucialfor employers to go beyond diversity. By making concessions for workers' cultural needs, such as prayer times or religious holidays, a business may promote inclusiveness.	I believe travelling has given me unique perspective of different cultures and hencel find myself comfortable working withpeople from diverse backgrounds.
We believe in gender diversity. Womenworkforce is equally important for us. We believe in talent irrespective of anything else.	Role Modelling and setting examples.

CONCLUSION

D&I is a broader concept than headcounts, regulations, or initiatives. Equitable businesses outperform their opponents by valuing the unique requirements, perspectives, and skills of each team member. Individuals who are employed in inclusive and varied environments consequently exhibit greater loyalty and trust.

Although the concepts of diversity and inclusion are interrelated, they are not the same. Diversity is related to representation and the construction of anything. The degree to which the contributions, presence, and viewpoints of other groups of individuals are appreciated and included into a setting is referred to as inclusion. Even if an environment may be varied, it is not inclusive if it has people of many various genders, ethnicities, nations, sexual orientations, and identities but only values or privileges those viewpoints.

If we look at the foundation of Hilton & Marriott, the former was founded in 1919, whereas the latter was established in 1957. This interprets that the core values, goodwill, and business policies of Hilton would have a much stronger foundation, considering they've been in the business longer than Marriott.

OVERCOMING THIS CHALLENGE – SUGGESTIONS

A notion known as leader-member exchange theory allows leaders to effectively manage diverse teams (LMX). Instead, than focusing on the link between the leader and the entire team, the LMX theory is more interested in the interaction between the leader and each individual team member. The presence of in-groups and out-groups is stressed by LMX theory.

The LMX theory of leadership could have produced better results for a diverse workforce. When the team members are put together into an in-group team, the differences among them will be treated equally. The leaders will assign them comparable tasks so that the different team members may cooperate to accomplish the goals. Additionally, LMX theory has been shown to increase output levels, staff motivation, and work satisfaction. It will increase the motivation of out-group members, increasing their likelihood of joining the in-group.

LIMITATIONS OF THE STUDY

- This may percolate bias into my research as language was also a barrier. • Since the paper followed a purposive sampling technique, my respondents were out of my reach radius and hence positive response rate wasn't a full 100%.
- The secondary resources lacked some information as to how to provide solutions to the challenges faced and hence analyzing the holistic view of the problem was a minor issue.
- The primary questionnaire had a few open-ended questions which made the data interpretation subjective, and saturation wasn't attained. Additionally, quantitative tools should've been put into use to enhance the data and eliminate biases of any kind.

DETAILS OF FUTURE POSSIBILITIES OF RESEARCH

This research has a lot of scope in terms of advancement in D&I challenges not only pertaining to the hospitality sector, but also expanding in domains of Private & public organisations, MNCs and start-ups. The concept of aligning D&I initiatives with the organisational development, to merge it with the companies' larger vision & mission goals and how would organisations transform into a L.O, i.e., a learning organisation. To get effective outputs and data, quantitative tools should be utilized to infer validated propositions. Additionally, in depth research should be done in investigating transgender ratios in diverse organisations and whether an inclusive environment is created for them or not. The next research should widen the propositions of D&I, how Training and development is used as a tool to promote it, how organisations are making sure to eliminate biases, what are the various theories or paradigms which create an inclusive workspace, what sort of interventions & theories (TQM, BPR) can contribute to the long-term strategies of the VUCA world. And most importantly how corporate leadership plays a significant role in diversifying an organisation, with the concept of new age bosses.

REFERENCES

(n.d.). Retrieved from TalentLyft: https://www.talentlyft.com/en/resources/what-is-workplace diversity

BUSH, M. (2021, April 13). *Why Is Diversity & Inclusion in the Workplace Important?* Retrieved from great place to work: https://www.greatplacetowork.com/resources/blog/why-is-diversity inclusion-in-the-workplace-importantHana Urbancová, M. H. (2020). Diversity Management as a Tool of Sustainability of Competitive Advantage. *MDPI open access journals*, 12, 5020.

Hilton. (2021, May 10th). Retrieved from hospitalitynet: https://www.hospitalitynet.org/news/4104298.html

(2020). *Hilton Hotels : Diversity & Discrimination.* United States,United Kingdom: ICMR (IBS Center for Management Research).

kim, B. y. (2008). Managing Workforce Diversity. *Journal of Human Resources in Hospitality & Tourism* , 69-90.

Marriott International, Inc. (1996 – 2022). Retrieved from Global Diversity & Inclusion: https://www.marriott.com/diversity/cultural-diversity.mi

Ordorica, S. (2021, July 26). *The How And Why Of Building A Diverse Workforce.* Retrieved from Forbes: https://www.forbes.com/sites/forbesbusinesscouncil/2021/07/26/the-how-and-why- of building-a-diverse-workforce/?sh=5b6cfb4a4cb1

Ruchika Malik, T. M. (2017). Diversity management in tourism and hospitality: an exploratory study. *Emerald insight*, 323-336.

Widya, W. A. (2019, March 17). *THE CHALLENGE OF MANAGING DIVERSE TEAM.* Retrieved from WordPress: https://culcwaprillia.wordpress.com/2019/03/17/the-challenge-of-managing diverse-team/

Study On the Relation Between Selected Stock and Economic Indicators Using Linear Regression

Author – Manthan Mulveparab, Devasri Advani, Student & Dr. Maithili Dhuri (Finance), Assistant Professor, IES's Management College and Research Centre, Mumbai

ABSTRACT

Stock market participation by domestic investors has been increasing as the year passes. The number of demat accounts has also increased to nearly 10 crore. Since many people started investing, a study to gauge the risk in the market and its volatility caused by macro-economic factors became important. As we have seen, during COVID-19, many macro-economic decisions were taken by the government to keep the economy running, like decreasing the repo rate, making in-India projects, etc. Every economic factor has a direct or indirect impact on the stock market. In this globalized world, every economic factor is connected, and an absolute change in one factor can lead to an impact on another, either positively or negatively. This paper tries to study the relationship between stock market and economic factors and understand the impact of independent factors on Sensex.

The present paper investigates the relationship between the Sensex index and economic indicators such as forex reserves, exchange rate, inflation, and repo rate. Inflation and foreign exchange reserves are used to depict the economic situation of any country, so their impact on the BSE Sensex should be studied to understand the power of influence these indicators have. The data used for this study is secondary data taken from the BSE and RBI websites. Data is taken for 4 years, i.e., April 2018 to March 2022. In the course of analysis, linear regression is done by taking BSE Sensex as the dependent variable. Tests conducted show forex reserves have a strong correlation with the BSE Sensex as compared to other economic indicators.

KEYWORDS

BSE Sensex, Economical Indicator, Forex Reserves, Linear Regression

INTRODUCTION

Foreign reserves are deposits of foreign currencies kept by a central bank. Foreign reserves help governments maintain the stability of their currencies; they are a tool for monetary and exchange rate policy, help with the payment of foreign debt and liabilities, and serve as a buffer against unanticipated emergencies and economic shocks.

The BSE Sensex (also known as the S&P BSE Sensex) is a stock market index in India. It is one of the most widely followed equity indices in the country and is considered a barometer of the Indian stock market. The index is comprised of 30 of the largest and most actively traded companies listed on the Bombay Stock Exchange (BSE). The performance of the Sensex is used to represent the overall performance of the Indian stock market.

This exploratory research study is done to find out the impact of the foreign exchange reserves of India along with a few economic indicators like the repo rate, currency exchange rate, and inflation rate on the BSE Sensex. Data is taken from FY18-19 to FY21-22 (i.e., March 2018 to March 2022). Most studies suggest that the macroeconomic surroundings have a significant effect on the stock market capitalization rate, such as gross domestic product, exchange rates, interest rates, current account, and money supply (Kurihara, 2006; Ologunde et al., 2006).

REVIEW OF LITERATURE

Causal Relationship between Stock Market and Exchange Rate, Foreign Exchange Reserves, and Value of Trade Balance: A Case Study for India Bhattacharya et al. (2001) examined the "Causal Relationship between Stock Market and Exchange Rate, Foreign Exchange Reserves, and Value of Trade Balance." For the sample period from April 1990 to March 2001, they applied the Granger non-causality methodology that Toda and Yamamoto (1995) recently presented. The Bombay BSE Sensitive Index was used as a stand-in for the Indian stock market in this study.

The real effective exchange rate, foreign currency reserves, and trade balance are the three significant macroeconomic variables covered in the study. In relation to the Indian stock market, the study yields some intriguing findings, particularly when it comes to the currency rate, foreign exchange reserves, and trade balance. The results suggest that there is no causal linkage between stock prices and the three variables under consideration.

Co-Integration and Causal Relationship between Exchange Rates and Stock Returns: A Study on Indian Context by Radha K. V. and Batchu Satish (2015)

The present study investigates the relationship between sensex returns and Indian-USD exchange rates and the impact of the time series on each other. Exchange rate fluctuations will affect international trade and thus influence the stock market. The study is based on secondary sources obtained from the BSE and RBI databases for the period from January 1 to June 30, 2015. In the course of analysis, appropriate econometric tools are used. ADF and PP Unit root tests show stationarity at level. The Johansen cointegration test result indicates that there is a long-term relationship among the selected variables.

The correlation between exchange rates and stock rates was found to be negative. The Granger causality test highlighted a unidirectional relationship running from stock returns to exchange rates.

The principal conclusion of the empirical result is that the selected time series exhibit stationarity at level and provide an indication of a long-term cointegration relationship between exchange rates and stock returns. The coefficient of correlation between the two variables indicated a slight negative correlation between them. This made way for determining the direction of influence between the selected variables. Hence, the Granger causality test was applied, which proved unidirectional causality running from stock returns to exchange rates.

The Impact of Inflation on Stock Prices: Evidence from Pakistan by Ghulam Muhammad Qamri, Muhammad Abrar Ul Haq, and Farheen Akram

This empirical study aims to investigate the association between stock prices and inflation in Pakistan. Many previous studies around the globe examined the relationship between stock price and inflation and proposed different results; many of them found that there is a positive link between inflation and stock price. On the other hand, some studies have realized the negative relationship between these two terms. This research is based on the past ten years of data from the Karachi stock exchange (KSE 100), and the statistical results of this research show that there is a negative relationship between stock price and inflation.

Furthermore, when stock prices are low, firms avoid entering the capital market until the central bank provides an alternative to the firm's plan to invest in the capital market. Moreover, a firm's equity value is also hit by the startling inflation rate. Similarly, tightening monetary policy can reduce inflation and stock prices, as individuals will be left with less money to buy goods or stocks.

Securities exchanges are vital markers to gauge the financial state of any nation. Numerous elements are influencing securities exchanges (full-scale and small-scale components). Every element of the economic environment has an impact on the money markets, but the power is diverse. Here, the inflation rate is an imperative component that influences securities exchange. In addition, the inflation rate itself is a macroeconomic variable that relies on a wide range of elements, like oil costs, legislative arrangements, and so forth, whose effects are not quite the same as nation-to-nation and economy-to-economy.

Furthermore, in our economy, a low negative effect of the inflation rate has been found on stock costs, as we have concluded from our examination done above. We will acknowledge the substitute theory and reject invalid speculation based on the outcome we had in our examination. The pattern has demonstrated that the inflation rate and stock record have a specific relationship. Such association implies that when the government applies an expansionary money-related strategy to help the economy, the immediate effect is on the share trading system. As bringing down premium rates is ideal for the economy, the best time for new and small-scale financial specialists to put resources into money markets is when expansion and premium rates are casual.

Consequently, the impact of inflation on stock prices is not much stronger, so other factors like a company's performance, earnings per share, GDP growth, dividend policy, and other micro and macro factors can also be considered that influence or can influence the stock market. Therefore, investors should keep track of all these things while making investments. Furthermore, the government should come up with a strategy to find out the best fit between inflation rates and stock indices. so that it can control an unreasonable increase in inflation and encourage a bullish trend in a positive way to encourage local and international investors.

METHODOLOGY

The study investigates the impact of foreign exchange reserves on the BSE index in India. For this purpose, the study uses the monthly data for the period FY18–19 to FY2021-22, which includes 48 monthly observations. The two main variables of this study are the foreign exchange reserve and BSE Sensex, along with the exchange rate, repo rate, and inflation rate. All the requisite information regarding these two crucial variables for the sample was collected from the websites of the Reserve Bank of India and the Bombay Stock Exchange. The estimation methodology employed in this study is linear regression using SPSS.

OBJECTIVE:

1. To study the correlation between BSE Sensex and foreign exchange reserves between FY2018–19 and FY21–22.
2. Study the change in correlation pre- and post-COVID year, i.e., 2020.

HYPOTHESIS –

H0 = There is no significant relationship between forex reserves and BSE Sensex. H1: There is a significant relationship between forex reserves and the BSE Sensex.

DATA ANALYSIS

To study the correlation between the BSE Index (comprised of the top 30 companies by market capitalization) and economic indicators such as foreign exchange reserves, repo rate, exchange rate, and CPI with the help of SPSS software. The linear regression analysis has been done to study the correlation between variables.

Descriptive Statistics

	Mean	Std. Deviation	N
Index	4.2711E4	8620.11069	49
ForexReserves	5.04E5	89270.390	49
Reporate	.0497	.01016	49
CPI	.0496	.01578	49
USDINR	72.2339	2.70003	49

Correlations

		Index	Forex Reserves	Reporate	CPI	USDINR
Pearson Correlation	Index	1.000	.864	-.610	.223	.483
	ForexReserves	.864	1.000	-.906	.534	.708
	Reporate	-.610	-.906	1.000	-.691	-.771
	CPI	.223	.534	-.691	1.000	.502
	USDINR	.483	.708	-.771	.502	1.000

Pearson correlation suggests that among economic indicators like Forex Reserves, repo rate, CPI, exchange rate, etc. Forex reserves have a strong correlation with the price movement of BSE Sensex. A negative correlation between the BSE Sensex and repo rate indicates that there is a poor correlation between the two variables.

Model Summary

Model	R	R Square	Adjusted R Square	Std. Error of the Estimate
1	.957[a]	.915	.908	2617.34881

a. Predictors: (Constant), USDINR, CPI, ForexReserves, Reporate

ANOVA[b]

Model		Sum of Squares	df	Mean Square	F	Sig.
1	Regression	3.265E9	4	8.163E8	119.162	.000[a]
	Residual	3.014E8	44	6850514.786		
	Total	3.567E9	48			

a. Predictors: (Constant), USDINR, CPI, ForexReserves, Reporate

b. Dependent Variable: Index

R square, which provides information about how well our model fits. In this case, the **R square** value is **0.915,** which indicates that the model has 91.5% accuracy (good fit). Alternatively, in another language, information about the Y variable is explained 91.5% by the X variable. The SPSS analysis value of multiple R is 0.95, which indicates a good correlation between BSE Sensex and economic factors such as Forex reserves, exchange rate, repo rate, and inflation. The R square value of 0.90 indicates that the majority of points are on the line of the regression model.

The ANOVA table has given us a significance value of <0.05, so we can say that our model is significant. We can reject the null hypothesis, and H1 is accepted, stating that there is a relationship between stock market returns and economic indicators.

In the second half of the study, we have exploratory analysis for a short period of time (2018 -2022).2 years of data from before COVID years (2018–2020) as well as during COVID years (2020–2022). Data analysis was performed separately to study the correlation between the factors of the BSE Sensex and Economic indicators.

a. Before COVID

Descriptive Statistics

	Mean	Std. Deviation	N
Index	3.7246E4	2697.92868	25
ForexReserves	4.25E5	25495.585	25
Reporate	.0586	.00590	25
USDINR	70.1920	2.17709	25
CPI	.0411	.01542	25

Correlations

		Index	Forex Reserves	Reporate	USDINR	CPI
Pearson Correlation	Index	1.000	.204	-.132	.013	.178
	ForexReserves	.204	1.000	-.925	.240	.850
	Reporate	-.132	-.925	1.000	-.315	-.701
	USDINR	.013	.240	-.315	1.000	.077
	CPI	.178	.850	-.701	.077	1.000

Model Summary

Model	R	R Square	Adjusted R Square	Std. Error of the Estimate	Change Statistics				
					R Square Change	F Change	df1	df2	Sig. F Change
1	.260[a]	.067	-.119	2854.07189	.067	.361	4	20	.833

a. Predictors: (Constant), CPI, USDINR, Reporate, ForexReserves

ANOVA[b]

Model		Sum of Squares	df	Mean Square	F	Sig.
1	Regression	1.178E7	4	2944283.347	.361	.833[a]
	Residual	1.629E8	20	8145726.346		
	Total	1.747E8	24			

a. Predictors: (Constant), CPI, USDINR, Reporate, ForexReserves

b. Dependent Variable: Index

In this part, we have taken a data frame from April 2018 to March 2020 (2 years before COVID's 20). It is a small exploratory study performed to understand the impact of economic factors on stock market returns before and after the COVID-19 pandemic.

Multiple R indicates the correlation coefficient that measures the strength of linear relations. The SPSS analysis value of multiple R is 0.260, which indicates a very poor correlation between BSE Sensex and Economic factors such as Forex reserves, exchange rate, repo rate, and inflation.

The ANOVA table has given us a significance value of 0.8, i.e., >0.05, so we can say that our model is insignificant. In addition, there is absolutely no correlation between the BSE Sensex and Economic factors.

a. During and After COVID

Descriptive Statistics

	Mean	Std. Deviation	N
Index	4.8403E4	9.01074464E3	24
ForexReserves	5.85E5	48258.880	24
Reporate	.0403	.00113	24
USDINR	74.361	1.0080	24
CPI	.0585	.01050	24

Correlations

		Index	Forex Reserves	Reporate	USDINR	CPI
Pearson Correlation	Index	1.000	.972	-.077	-.154	-.504
	ForexReserves	.972	1.000	-.235	-.259	-.509
	Reporate	-.077	-.235	1.000	.564	.368
	USDINR	-.154	-.259	.564	1.000	.317
	CPI	-.504	-.509	.368	.317	1.000

Pearson correlation suggests that among economic indicators like Forex Reserves, repo rate, CPI, exchange rate, etc., Forex reserves have a strong correlation with the price movement of the BSE Sensex. A value of 0.972 showed a strong correlation between forex reserves and the BSE Sensex.

Model Summary

					Change Statistics				
Model	R	R Square	Adjusted R Square	Std. Error of the Estimate	R Square Change	F Change	df1	df2	Sig. F Change
1	.986[a]	.973	.967	1.62725539E3	.973	171.560	4	19	.000

a. Predictors: (Constant), CPI, USDINR, ForexReserves, Reporate

ANOVA[b]

Model		Sum of Squares	df	Mean Square	F	Sig.
1	Regression	1.817E9	4	4.543E8	171.560	.000[a]
	Residual	5.031E7	19	2647960.127		
	Total	1.867E9	23			

a. Predictors: (Constant), CPI, USDINR, ForexReserves, Reporate

b. Dependent Variable: Index

In this part, we have taken a data frame from April 2020 to March 2022 (2 years of COVID's 20). It is a small exploratory study performed to understand the impact of economic factors on stock market returns during the COVID-19 pandemic.

Multiple R indicates the correlation coefficient that measures the strength of linear relations. The SPSS analysis value of multiple R is 0.97, which indicates a very strong correlation between BSE Sensex and economic factors such as forex reserves, exchange rate, repo rate, and inflation. The R square value of

0.97 indicates that the majority of points are on the line of the regression model.

The ANOVA table has given us a significance value of 0.0, i.e., >0.05, so we can say that our model is insignificant. In addition, there is absolutely no correlation between the BSE Sensex and economic factors.

CONCLUSION

This study tries to assess the impact of economic factors such as foreign exchange reserves, exchange rate, repo rate, and CPI on the BSE Sensex, covering a period of March 2018 to March 2022. The result shows that there is a significant positive impact of economic factors on the BSE Sensex. Linear regression performed on the data indicates a strong relationship between dependent and independent variables.

The purpose of this research is to examine the trend of India's foreign exchange reserves in order to provide essential information that will assist stockbrokers, agents, planners, and government policymakers in making decisions about the stocks and stock markets of India, particularly about the BSE. Additionally, the study will attempt to advance knowledge of India's foreign reserves and stock markets for executives, directors, researchers, and other students.

BIBLIOGRAPHY

1. Ghulam Muhammad Qamri, Muhammad Abrar Ul Haq, Farheen Akram, The Impact of Inflation on Stock Prices: Evidence from Pakistan, Microeconomics and Macroeconomics, Vol. 3 No. 4, 2015, pp. 83-88. doi: 10.5923/j.m2economics.20150304.01.
2. Foreign Exchange Reserve and its Impact on Stock Market Capitalization: Evidence from India by Sarbapriya Ray Research on Humanities and Social Sciences www.iiste.org ISSN 2224-5766(Paper) ISSN 2225-0484(Online) Vol.2, No.2, 2012
3. Radha K V And Batchu Satish (2015).Cointegration And Causal Relationship Between Exchange Rates And Stock Returns: A Study On Indian Context.
4. Aggarwal, R. (1981). Exchange rates and stock prices: A study of U.S. capital markets under floating exchange rates. Akron Business and Economics Review, 22(2), 7-12.

A Study on Transit Time from Dispatches to Delivery in Steel Industry

CHAPTER 12

Author – Sajeevan Sayujya, Student, IES's Management College and Research Centre, Mumbai

ABSTRACT

The report here by briefs about the vast steel industry followed by Indian steel industry. There are various steel companies in Indian market each of them have different market share and stand in the market. This report talks about the delay in delivery of products due to unexpected problems that arise during dispatch of goods. Time or no of days are added to the process, because of issues tied to manufacturing malfunctions, supply shortages, human errors, weather conditions and other issues that are having variable abilities to control them. However, measures can be taken to minimize losses, along with their financial impact, through proper planning that is what is mentioned in this report. To deal with the loss in time or delay of delivery, first and foremost thing is to know about the minimum no of days taken to deliver a product from location to another. Then is the step to make a chart with estimation of no of days to take from dispatch location till delivery location. Then gathering all the information regarding the invoice data and then further creating lorry receipt. Restructuring the data as per my requirement for analysis and interpretations. Also finding the root cause for transit delay of goods. While working on the project I got deep insights on how a steel manufacturing company operates. The process of raw materials till finished goods ready for dispatch was shown to us in the factory. India's steel industry is one of India's most important industries. India overtook Japan as the second largest steel producer in January 2019. India's steel industry can be divided into three categories: major producers, major producers and secondary producers.

KEYWORDS

Inco terms, transit time, liquidated damage, dispatch, turnaround time Paper

INTRODUCTION

Since India began its economic liberalisation process, considerable changes have been made to the Indian Steel Industry's organisational structure. SAIL, a state-owned corporation, had previously played a highly important essential and crucial part in the expansion and development of India's steel industry. The Indian government enacted a sizable number of economic reforms in 1991. The steel sector in India, in particular, saw a boost in development as a result of these changes, and it has since expanded rather quickly. India consistently sets astronomical growth benchmarks for its steel industry. India produced 1.59 million tonnes of pig iron and 14.33 million tonnes of finished carbon steel in 1992. Additionally, since 1991, the nation's capacity for producing steel has grown quickly.

Steel is a commodity that we utilise on a daily basis. It is utilised in the construction of our homes, automobiles, and eating utensils, among other things. Steel is used in a variety of industries, including building and infrastructure, engineering, cars, and so on. It is a vital engineering and building material. Steel is widely utilised all over the world due to its strength, and it can be recycled indefinitely without losing its properties. With an output of 10.14 MT as of April 2022, India was the second-largest producer of crude steel worldwide. A total of 133.596 MT of crude steel and 120.01 MT of finished steel were produced in FY22, respectively.

The production of crude steel and finished steel in April to October 2022 was 71.56 MT and 68.17 MT, respectively. The domestic accessibility of raw materials like iron ore and the affordability of labour have been the main drivers of growth in the Indian steel industry. As a result, the steel industry has been crucial to India's manufacturing output. India's steel industry has grown tremendously over the last 10–12 years. While domestic steel demand has surged by roughly 80% since 2008, production has increased by 75%. Parallel to this growth, the ability to produce steel has increased, and this growth has primarily been organic.

In the past several months, the Modi government has launched numerous FDI policy reforms in industries like defence, rail infrastructure, building development, insurance, pensions, and medical equipment. With the introduction of drastic reforms to FDI standards to increase demand for steel, cement, and economic activity with the ultimate goal of contributing to the construction of 50 million affordable homes for the poor, the struggling construction sector will benefit greatly.

LITERATURE REVIEW

India is credited as being a pioneer in the production and use of iron and steel, which dates back more than three thousand years. Following independence, the Indian government assumed control and limited capacity creation to the public sector. The government built four integrated steel factories between the 1950s and 1960s at Durgapur, Bhilai, Rourkella, and Bokaro. For technological assistance at the time, the Indian steel industry worked with the former USSR, the Federal Republic of Germany, and the United Kingdom.

For the purpose of reviving the industry, the Indian government adopted a three-pronged strategy in the 1980s. This strategy included the expansion of existing steel plants, the establishment of new capacities, and the modernization and upgrading of technologies in existing plants. However, a difficult period for the Indian steel sector occurred between 1997 and 2001 as a result of weak demand and falling steel prices globally. Many steel companies were compelled to withdraw from the race. However, because to a rebound in American demand and the recovery of Asian economies, the steel sector overcame this challenging scenario. India's industrial recovery truly got going in 2002–2003, stabilised in 2003–2004, picked up steam in 2004–2005, and reached a new high from 2005 to 2007.

Due to the high demand for steel from the infrastructure, building, automotive, and power sectors, the Indian steel industry experienced phenomenal expansion in both crude and finished steel output during that time. But the 2008 global recession had a severe impact on the sector. Indian steel companies were compelled to reduce their output in order to maintain the steel price's stability. The steel market's demand-supply imbalance and the high cost of raw materials have a significant negative impact on the profit margin.

Steel Tycoon **Mr. Lakshmi Nivas Mittal (2001)** advised to securing land and iron ore mining locations are issues that need to be solved by the state governments in India for further growth. He also suggested that the Indian government should not lift the qualitative and quantitative restrictions on iron ore exports.

According to **B. K. Tripathy (2003),** the deregulation of the Indian steel industry and the dismantling of the four fundamental state regulations on capacity growth, imports and exports, price, and distribution for the major producers paved the way for a market-centric industry. By expanding investment in industrial and economic infrastructure, demand must be stimulated.

Although Indian steel policy has been liberalised, **Mr. Nitish SenGupta (2005)** emphasised that domestic firms could no longer disregard the global steel market. He believed that the Indian steel industry needed to modernise and that it should make being competitive in the global market a requirement.

According to **Dr. Ghosh, Sajal (2006),** the health of the steel industry is directly related to the strength of the Indian economy and the rapid development in demand for goods in industries like real estate, infrastructure, and cars. Evidently, India has now become a preferred place for international players to manufacture steel. The global steel sector seems to be rushing to make investments in countries with rapid economic growth, like India. Through 102 Memorandums of Understanding signed by various state governments, the industry has secured investments totaling US$5,994 million to increase its ability to produce 103 million tonnes of steel.

High grade iron ore from the nation should not be exported, according to **Mr. J. J. Irani (2007).** He believed that, taking into account their growth plans, the country's current steel factories should receive a guaranteed supply of iron ore for the ensuing 20–25 years.

According to **Mr. S.K.Roongta and Mr. Muthurman (2008)**, the two biggest corporations in India have started undertaking significant capacity expansions in order to increase production capacities. At a cost of more than Rs. 50,000 crore, they want to increase production to 26 million tonnes.

According to **K. S. Kavitha and Dr. P. Palanivelu (2014)**, the iron and steel industry is crucial for a nation's economic growth in terms of foreign exchange, job creation, the development of infrastructure, and technology. They are among the Indian economy's most energy-intensive sectors. A crucial industry for national development is the steel industry. According to the study's findings, the amount of steel consumed per person in a given country is regarded as a key indicator of its level of socioeconomic development and inhabitants' standard of life. The report also comes to the conclusion that the

Indian iron and steel industry has benefited from the strong demand for iron and steel from industries like infrastructure, automobiles, and real estate.

The financial performance of selected units in the Indian steel sector was analysed by **Rooh Ollah Arab, Seyed Saadat Masoumi, and Azadeh Barati (2015)** using financial parameters like Liquidity, Solvency, Activity, and Profitability position. The following steel companies have been chosen for this study: Tata Steel Ltd., Jindal Steel & Power Ltd., J. S. W. Steel Ltd., Essar Steel, Steel Authority of India Ltd.

OBJECTIVES

- To reduce the extra time taken by the transporters to deliver the product.
- To dispatch the products within 3 days of receipt of dispatch.
- To create a standardized process to understand and track the reasons deliveries are late.

RESEARCH METHODOLOGY

Applied research aims to find solutions to specific problems or to find answers to specific questions. Research should provide applicable and practical knowledge. This is the research most appropriate for my project.

There are three main types of research design:

- Data collection – past records from April 2021 – March 2022.
- Measurement – the standard days set for each location.
- Analysis – with the help of various data converted into pivot tables.
- Sample size is 2750 no of items and the data is from April 2021 to March 2022.

DATA ANALYSIS

The goal of data gathering and interpretation is to gather meaningful information and make the most informed judgments possible. Data gathering and interpretation provides endless benefits for a wide range of institutions and individuals, from enterprises to newlyweds looking for their first house. At first, I took all the data of their prime customers and created an excel table to analyse and calculate no of days, on time delivery, status etc.

Invoice No	Invoice Date	Name of Customer	Address	LR Date	Transporter	Delivery Status	Date of Delivery	Dispatch TAT	Delivery TAT	TAT
2022000103	15-04-2021	Jindal Steel & Power Ltd.	Ramgarh Balkudra, Patratu 829143	20-04-2021	Transolution Pvt Ltd	Delivered on 30th April	30-04-2021	5	10	ON TIME

Above, is an example of how data was aligned to start with the 1st step of data analysis. The data was segregated into the following no of columns and were all filtered out to differentiate easily.

- Given items were:

  Invoice No, Invoice date, Name of customer, Address, LR Date (Lorry receipt date), Transporter, Delivery Status, Delivery Date

- Found with the help of excel:

  Dispatch TAT = LR date – Invoice Date Delivery TAT = Delivery date – LR date

TAT is concluded as on time/ delay on the basis of the following parameters addressed below.

Parameters for concluding delays & on time delivery of products for various regions are as follows:

Transit Time (In Days)	Full Truck	Part Load	By Train
Jamshedpur (Jharkhand)	8 to 10	10 to 12	3 to 4
Bokaro (Jharkhand)	8 to 10	10 to 12	4 to 5
Patratu/Ramgarh (Jharkhand)	8 to 10	10 to 12	3 to 4
Bellary (Karnataka)	3 to 4	5 to 6	3 to 4
Hazira (Gujarat)	2 to 3	3 TO 4	2 to 3
Jajpur/Angul (Rajasthan/Odisha)	8 to 10	10 to 12	4 to 5
Wardha (Maharashtra)	3 to 4	4 to 5	2 to 3
Vizag (Andra Pradesh)	4 to 5	6 to 7	2 to 3
Hospet (Karnataka)	5 to 6	7 to 8	3 to 4
Burnpur/Durgapur (West Bengal)	8 to 10	10 to 12	3 to 4
Tarapur/Dolvi (Maharashtra)	1 to 2	1 to 2	1 to 2
Mettur (Tamil Nadu)	5 to 6	7 to 8	4 to 5
Boisar (Maharashtra)	3 to 4	4 to 5	2 to 3
Raigarh (Chhattisgarh)	5 to 6	8 to 10	2 to 3

THE TOTAL NUMBER OF INVOICES ARE AS FOLLOWS

JINDAL	831
JSW	535
TATA	966
SAIL	207
Electro steel	202

TATA STEEL LTD

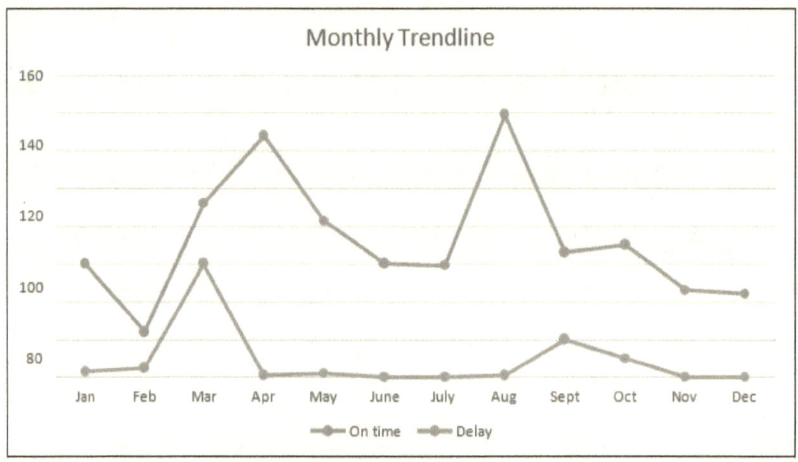

- The average number of delays is 9 days.
- The deviation noticed in the line chart trend is of 32 days.
- Mode of delayed delivery is 0, which means most of the months have 0-5 number of days delayed.

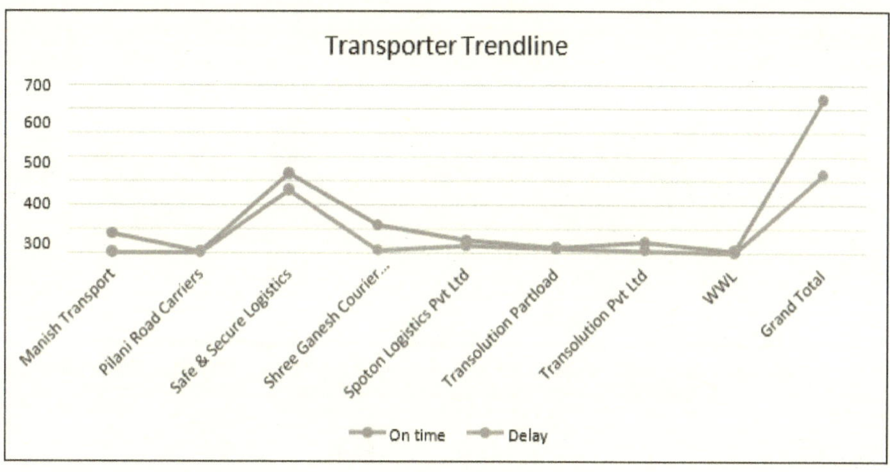

- Average number of days for delay in delivery of goods were of 40 days.
- The standard deviation of On time delivery of goods were of 100 days.
- The mode is 0, which means most of the transporters have fulfilled their duties of delivering goods on time.

JINDAL STEEL & POWER LTD

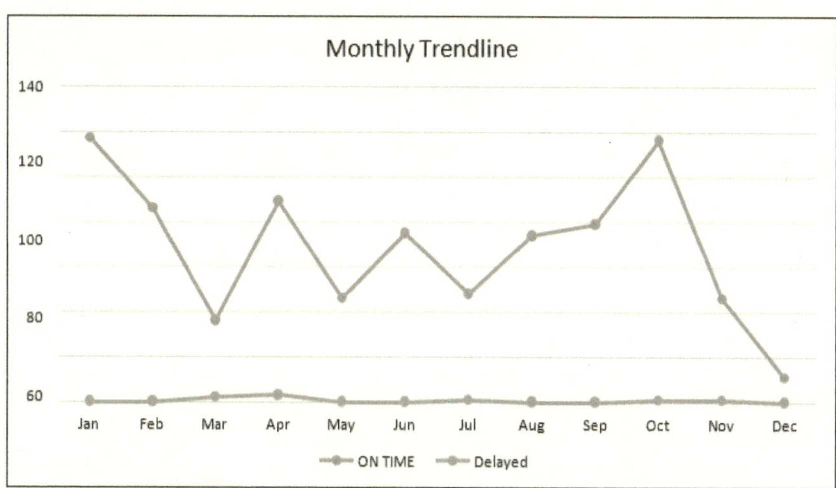

- Through statistics I found out that average delay is approximate to 1 day.
- While, the deviation in On time delivery was found to be of 31 days.
- The mode was found to be 0, concluding most of the months had on time delivery.

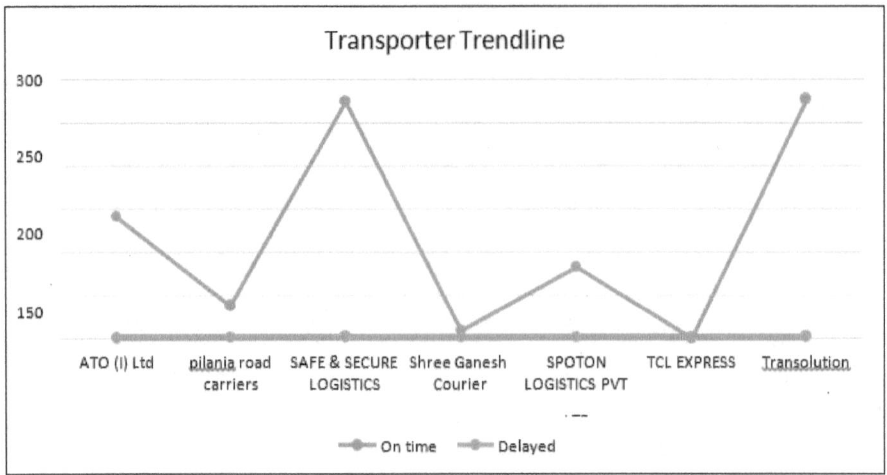

- The no of delays in lying on the X axis which is almost counted to be as nil.
- The mean of delayed deliveries is by 2 days
- The standard deviation for no of on time deliveries are 109 days.
- Mode is 1, which means most of them had delays for 1 or more number of days.

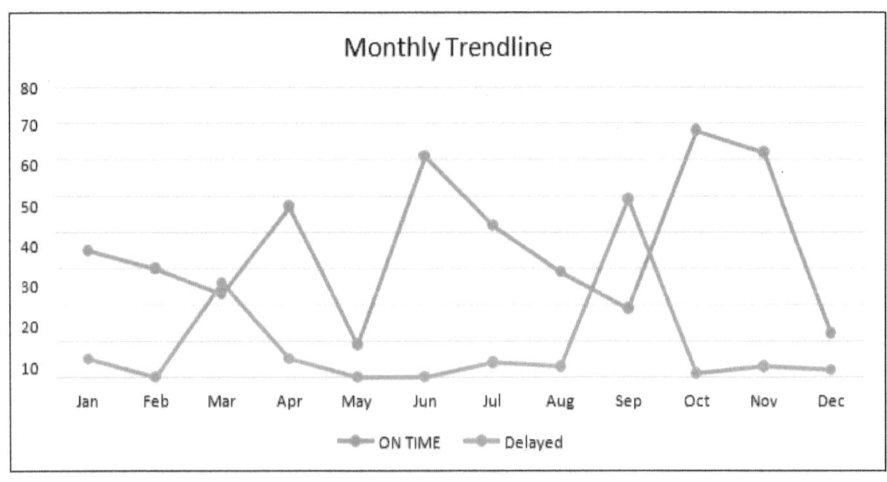

JSW STEEL LTD

- The average number of days of delay were 8days.
- The standard deviations in the chart above is of 19 days.

- The mode calculated was 0 for the number of delays, which means most of months had no delays.

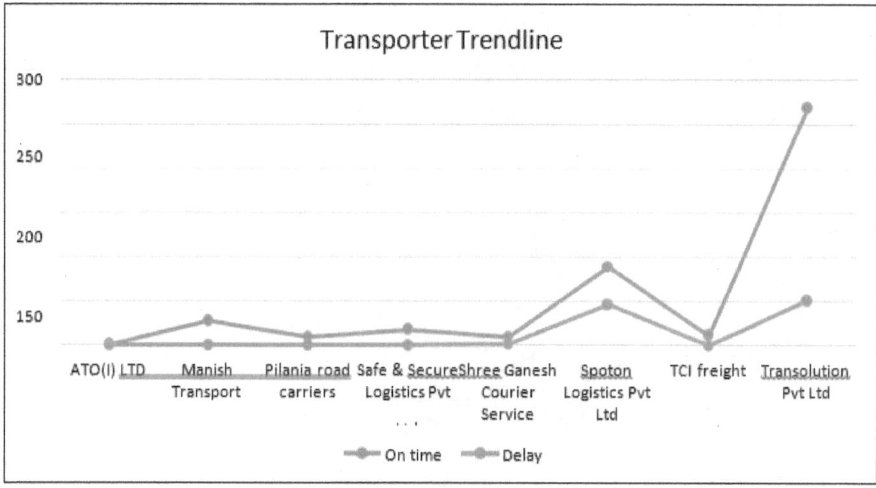

- The average delay was of 12 days.
- The standard deviation noted were of 85 days for On time delivery.
- The mode was calculated as 0, which shows that most of the transporters were successful in delivering goods on time.

STEEL AUTHORITY OF INDIA LTD

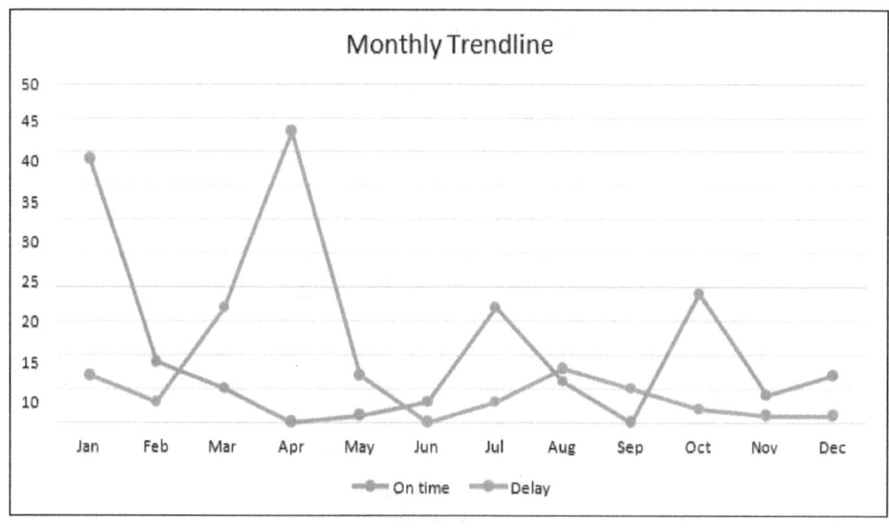

- I can observe that the average delays were by 8 days.
- Standard deviation of On time delivery in the chart is by 11 days.
- The mode was found out to be 7, which means there were multiple delays in delivering a product.

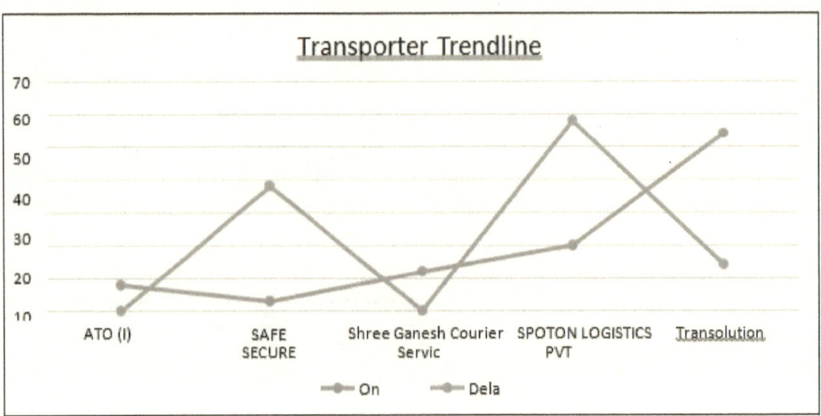

- The average number of days delayed is around 22 days.
- While, standard deviation is noticed to be by 18 days.
- Mode is 0 but from the chart we can make out that there were many delays in the delivery of goods.

ELECTROSTEEL LTD

- Average no of delays is by 1 day.
- While, the deviation of On time delivery is by 17 days.

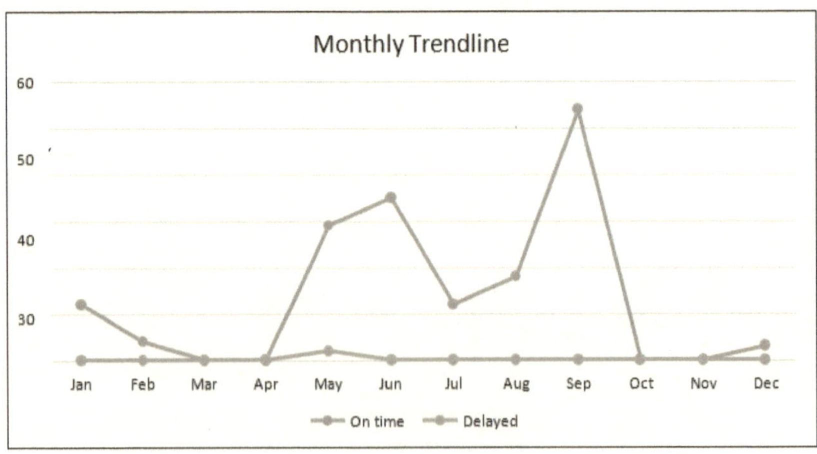

- The mode is 0 here which means most of the months had on time delivery.

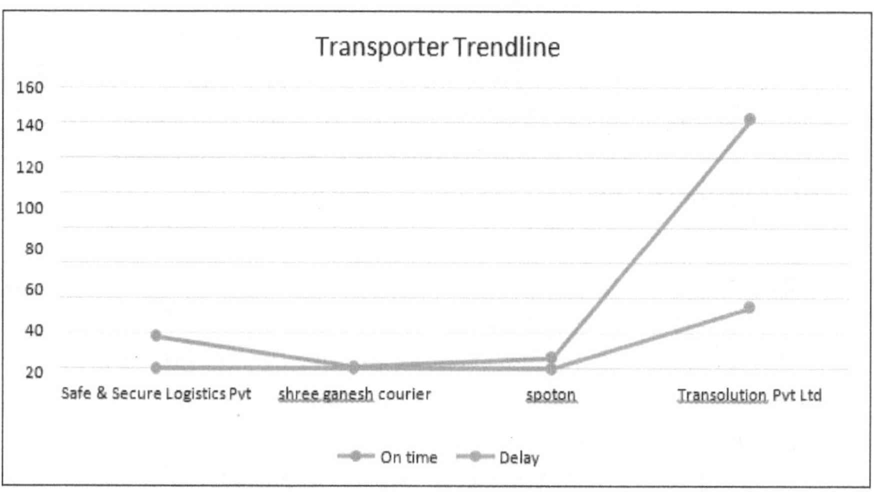

- Average delay is by 9 days.
- The deviation of on time delivery were of 58 days.
- The mode here is 0, majority of the transporters tried to deliver the goods on time.

CONCLUSIONS

Late delivery is part of the most serious constraint on business operations. Good planning and experience is considered important for managing shipping delays, but it is advisable to add at least one week to the expected transit time as a backup for unexpected delays. Delayed delivery impacts business through production delays because the raw materials needed for the process do not arrive on time. Delays in production mean that businesses are unable to meet consumer demand, and consumers may source products from alternative sources. Decreased demand and loss of customers can lead to lower sales and higher levels of operation as factories struggle to meet deadlines, negatively impacting the company's profitability. Some products lose value due to longer shipping times. For example, perishables quickly spoil and lose value unless care is taken to speed up the delivery process and avoid delays.

- Monthly average delays were experienced more by TATA, JSW & SAIL, while most deviations were seen by TATA & Jindal.

- Transporters average delays were maximum for TATA, while most deviations were seen by Jindal.
- Most of the customers had delays in the month of March, April and September. There may be many reasons for delays it could be due to year ending, climatic changes, festivities or due to consolidation.

RECOMMENDATIONS

Few important days to be take into consideration:

1. Ship Date: The shipping date definition is the date the order is shipped from the seller or warehouse to the customer.
2. Invoice creation date: The invoice creation date does not always match the invoice date, but it is the invoice creation time and may be the number of days before the order is processed.
3. Delivery date: This is the actual date the shipment will be delivered to the customer. The delivery date does not always match the delivery date for various reasons.
4. Return date: The return period is the total time a customer must initiate a return and return the item to the seller. This is also different from the return deadline, which is the last day a customer must make an e-commerce return.

Opportunities and Challenges of Digitalization in Healthcare

CHAPTER 13

Author – Aishwarya Jagushte, Soundarya Katare & Riya Patel, Student, IES's Management College and Research Centre, Mumbai

ABSTRACT

Digital technology has led to a global revolution. The urgent need for cutting edge technical tools and platforms in the fields of public health, medicine, and wellness has been highlighted by the COVID-19 pandemic. During COVID-19, digital health tools were utilized to support communications, monitoring and surveillance, the delivery of healthcare services, and the dissemination of vaccines. The COVID-19 provided a platform for beneficial changes including the adoption of digital technologies in India's healthcare industry. The greatest digital and telephone working industries in India were able to keep health activity at 70% to 80% in the early 2020s.For the purposes of promoting health and preventing disease, the healthcare industry is separated into primary, secondary, and tertiary level health centres, which correspond to marginalized populations, rural areas, and urban regions, respectively. The world is becoming increasingly more connected and is able to solve more and more complex societal problems Global digital revolution through increased collaboration and information sharing.

Keywords - Digitalization, Post-Covid, Business opportunities, Healthcare.

Objectives 1.To study the implications of digitalization on the post-Covid healthcare business in India. 2.To assess data quality and access barriers in post Covid healthcare. 3.To study various challenges faced during digital inclusion in India, with a specific focus on rural India.

INTRODUCTION

An interdisciplinary field called "digital health" seeks to improve the effectiveness of patient monitoring, diagnosis, management, prevention, rehabilitation, and long-term care delivery. The emergence of digital health did not happen immediately. When health telematics first appeared in the 1970s, the history of digital health began. Through the use of health telematics, telecommunications provide the health-care systems with a fantastic potential to improve health, health education, and follow-ups. At the time, health telematics sought to concentrate on diseases and advancements in the diagnosis and Opportunities and Challenges of digitalization in healthcare treatment of disorders. One of the most well-known areas of digital health today is health telematics, or telemedicine.

The health care systems discovered that the Internet is an excellent infrastructure for health promotion with the dawn of the 21st century and widespread usage of desktop personal computers and the Internet. eHealth was developing at this period. eHealth places a greater emphasis on health than disease, in contrast to health telematics.

Another technological change and the advent of mobile phones in the 2010s create the possibility for the emergence of a new industry, mobile health (mHealth). Adherence is one of the key distinctions between eHealth and mHealth. The community is able to get healthcare services whenever and wherever they need them thanks to having a device that is constantly with them.

The general interest in digital marketing, which has been increasing over the past ten years, served as the inspiration for this master's thesis. We are curious to learn about the effects of COVID-19 on the medicines sector during this pandemic. most of the news and articles.

Early discussions focused mostly on the technology, concept, and application of digital marketing to everyday business. Less research has been done with the pandemic in mind. The most popular issue in the world right now is COVID-19, and as a result, digital marketing has developed into a crucial component of any company's marketing plan.

To investigate the effects of COVID-19 on the pharmaceutical industry and how the sector is utilising digital marketing as a marketing strategy, we have chosen to collaborate with a pharmaceutical company in the developing nation of India. The qualitative method used in the empirical study is designed. We conducted interviews with the marketing department staff and used principles from many works on digital marketing in our research. Additionally, we discussed the methodology that was used to address our study questions.

Our study has revealed that, for practically all firms during this period, digital marketing is the most successful marketing strategy. The business for which we worked thinks that digital marketing will eventually produce results. We talked about the marketing difficulties faced by pharmaceutical firms during the pandemic, difficulties in embracing digital transformation, and techniques used by the business to maintain client loyalty by implementing relationship marketing principles. In addition, we looked into ways to help pharmaceutical businesses deal with problems they were having.

LITERATURE REVIEW

According to the Indian Economic Survey 2021, the domestic market is expected to grow 3x in the next decade. India's domestic pharmaceutical market stood at US$ 42 billion in 2021 and is likely to reach US$ 65 billion by 2024 and further expand to reach US$ 120-130 billion by 2030. India's biotechnology industry comprises biopharmaceuticals, bio-services, bio-agriculture, bio-industry, and bioinformatics. The Indian biotechnology industry was valued at US$ 70.2 billion in 2020 and is expected to reach US$ 150 billion by 2025. India's medical devices market stood at US$ 10.36 billion in FY20. The market is expected to increase at a CAGR of 37% from 2020 to 2025 to reach US$ 50 billion. As of August 2021, CARE Ratings expect India's pharmaceutical business to develop at an annual rate of ~11% over the next two years to reach more than US$ 60 billion in value.

In the global pharmaceuticals sector, India is a significant and rising player. India is the world's largest supplier of generic medications, accounting for 20% of the worldwide supply by volume and supplying about 60% of the global vaccination demand. The Indian pharmaceutical sector is worth US$ 42 billion worldwide. In August 2021, the Indian pharmaceutical market increased at 17.7% annually, up from 13.7% in July 2020. According to India Ratings & Research, the Indian pharmaceutical market revenue is expected to be over 12% Y-o-Y in FY22.

SEVERNESS IN GLOBE –

In the most recent memory, no event has ever tested the healthcare industry like the 2020 pandemic, and like any other test, it has left 'n' number of questions in its wake – it has changed the stakeholders' perspectives on some key aspects and functions, specifically within the digital transformation framework. As per the Accenture survey, 93 percent of healthcare providers reported that they are innovating with a sense of urgency in the change demanded.

As per customer experience came to the forefront, in services across business and industry, it made a delayed-yet-determined entry into the healthcare sector. The commercialization of healthcare has also played into this development. These days patient experience is the keystone of the sector, as it gears up for increased digitalisation across its value chain. In terms of a better approach, the healthcare Opportunities and Challenges of digitalization in healthcare industry is witnessing large investments in remote clinical capabilities which includes telemedicine, virtual consultations, online lab testing etc.

Research suggests that digital health solutions in conditions such as chronic heart disease can support patients in health-promoting behaviours, improve their medication compliance, empower them and enhance their communication with healthcare professionals. This might reduce the number of hospital stays.

The continual advance toward this accessible, functional smart data healthcare environment is propelled by centralized, intraoperative system- and vendorneutral solutions. In implementation of such solutions, healthcare providers can minimize the isolating effects of data depot and achieve the goal of comprehensive decisionmaking to benefit patients and improve the efficiency of healthcare services.

IN MAHARASHTRA –

On 15th August 2020, Hon'ble Prime Minister Shri Narendra Modi announced the launch of the National Digital Health Mission as a part of his Independence Day address. This unprecedented digital initiative is being seen as the first major step towards Universal Health Coverage in India. The move augurs well since healthcare record management in India is as inefficient and disconnected as the sector itself. There are also vast technological and procedural variations across private and public sector facilities.

Currently, a standard government hospital or local healthcare facility is unable to uniformly document all records for services. Although such facilities exist to certain extent in urban area hospitals, there is a great lack of uniform standards of record keeping. This creates issues such as requirement of repeated diagnostic tests and consultations, delayed treatments, concealment or ignorance of medical history etc. All these can often lead to wrong diagnosis and treatment as well as increased costs of treatment. Even in hospitals where digital records are maintained, there is no provision of electronic transfer of patient records from one service provider to another. This lack of access leads to either the patient carrying the medical records in paper format or not having access to them at all. Through the National Digital Health Mission (NDHM), the government is endeavouring to leverage the existing digital infrastructure such as the frameworks related to Aadhar, UPI and the pan India coverage of internet-enabled smartphones to create a cohesive digital system. This is expected to be rolled out soon. However, there are also other components that must be integrated into this ecosystem to make it all-inclusive.

IN INDIA –

Digital transformation in the pharmaceutical industry is crucial for improved patient care, cost-effectiveness, greater transparency, improved production, and drug development.

Verdict has conducted a poll to assess by how much time the COVID-19 pandemic has accelerated the digital transformation of the pharmaceutical industry.

COVID-19 accelerated digital transformation of the pharma industry by five years

Analysis of the poll results shows that COVID-19 has fast-forwarded digital transformation of the pharma industry by more than five years, as opined by a majority 35% of the respondents.

While 30% of the respondents voted that the pandemic accelerated digital transformation by more than six years, 5% voted that digital transformation was accelerated by five to six years.

Digital transformation of the pharma industry has been accelerated by two to three years and three to four years, according to 9% and 8% of the respondents, respectively.

Further, 8% of the respondents voted that digital transformation of the pharma industry has been accelerated by four to five years.

Approximately 27% of the respondents opined that COVID-19 has accelerated the digital transformation of the pharma sector by less than one year.

Impact of COVID-19 on digital transformation of the pharma industry –

The COVID-19 pandemic impacted the pharmaceutical industry in many ways by delaying routine treatments, straining healthcare budgets, derailing drug development for non-COVID related diseases, and causing supply chain disruptions. The pharmaceutical industry was forced to adopt various digital technologies to overcome the challenges posed by the pandemic.

Technologies such as cloud computing and cybersecurity helped the industry adopt remote working and perform decentralised clinical trials, according to Global Data. Companies need to adopt digital technologies according to the business needs and develop a robust digital transformation strategy before investing in new technologies, adds Global Data.

Extending care beyond hospital walls is a top priority for healthcare leaders[1]

Expanding out-of-hospital care could improve outcomes, reduce costs, and offer patients more convenience:

40%

of hospitals are expected to have shifted 20% of their beds to the patient's home by 2025[2]

60%

of patients find virtual care more convenient than in-person care[3]

80%

of patients are willing to seek care for minor illnesses at retail clinics[4]

1. Ranked as the second-highest priority after staff retention and satisfaction in the 2022 Philips Future Health Index report
2. Gartner 2022
3. McKinsey survey 2022
4. McKinsey survey 2019

Source – Healthcare redefined article

Healthcare has become one of India's largest sectors, both in terms of revenue and employment. Healthcare comprises hospitals, medical devices, clinical trials, outsourcing, telemedicine, medical tourism, health insurance and medical equipment. The Indian healthcare sector is growing at a brisk pace due to its strengthening coverage, services, and increasing expenditure by public as well private players.

India's healthcare delivery system is categorised into two major components - public and private. The government, i.e. public healthcare system, comprises limited secondary and tertiary care institutions in key cities and focuses on providing basic healthcare facilities in the form of primary healthcare centres (PHCs) in rural areas. The private sector provides majority of secondary, tertiary, and quaternary care institutions with major concentration in metros, tier-I and tierII cities.

India's competitive advantage lies in its large pool of well-trained medical professionals. India is also cost competitive compared to its peers in Asia and western countries. The cost of surgery in India is about one-tenth of that in the US or Western Europe. The low cost of medical services has resulted in a rise in the country's medical tourism, attracting patients from across the world. Moreover, India has emerged as a hub for R&D activities for international players due to its relatively low cost of clinical research.

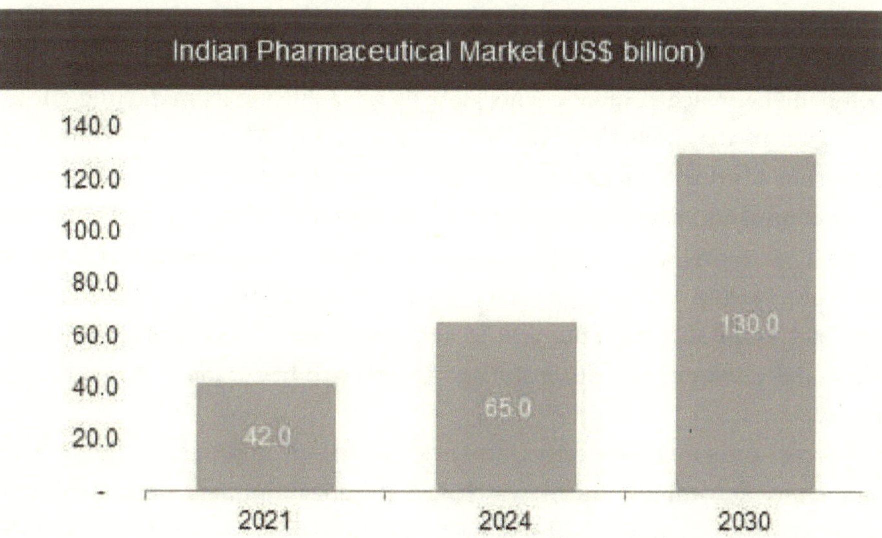

Source – Indian brand equity foundation (Market Size)

RESEARCH METHODOLOGY

A mixed research research design. Secondary research was conducted to understand the current environment in the digital space and there after understand the need as well as the scope of digitalization in pharmaceutical industry.

The analysis is based on 482 responses received from the readers of Pharmaceutical Technology, a Verdict network site, between 20 January and 01 March. The collected data was formatted with excel and then analysed for results.

ANALYSIS

By comparing the research results to the information available from prior literature reviews, we were able to examine the data we collected from participating companies.

Due to the Pandemic, everyone has started using the Internet to pass the time during lockdowns, thus the company has created deals for its clients who place orders through the official Med Manor website. Since YouTube and Fitube have paid them more, we can determine that the video adverts are more effective at reaching consumers' thoughts than the standard marketing banners.

Modern marketing strategies offer a quick and inexpensive way to reach millions of consumers. When compared to traditional marketing, the company has reached more clients globally after shifting its marketing efforts to digital media, including YouTube videos, blogs, WhatsApp banners, and television ads. Especially for businesses where customers can read reviews and leave comments about their personal experiences, digital marketing has had an impact on raising sales income. Customers began leaving comments beneath YouTube video advertisements and on product-related blogs not just to solicit feedback and boost sales, but also to help the business understand the needs, likes, and preferences of its customers in order to better tailor its upcoming items.

People are more concerned about their health and safety during this pandemic. According to our research and empirical findings, businesses have adopted digital marketing throughout the pandemic, and this is the only way to conduct business in order to sustain sales and customers after social estrangement. According to the literature mentioned above, several businesses have begun to produce products connected to health and safety that were helpful during the Pandemic. Even after the epidemic, according to the company, digital marketing will be a long-term economic strategy.

Face-to-face pharmaceutical marketing has fallen out of favour during COVID19, and internet marketing is now more often used.

According to this literature, due to the nature of Pandemic, corporations were unable to conduct their conventional pharmaceutical marketing operations through distributors and marketing personnel. We discovered that even these companies' staff members have COVID-19 while performing their marketing activities. Therefore, they began to train the staff on how to do marketing via digital means, specifically through WhatsApp status updates and sharing ad films to friends and family.

We also discovered that businesses have begun to provide discounts if customers buy their products from the company's official website, demonstrating the shift from traditional pharmaceutical marketing to digital transformation. We also learned that in order to keep customers loyal, the business must be able to serve them around-the-clock and without interruption.

We also found that firms have started to give offers if the customer purchases it products through company official website which shows the pharma marketing has thrown out of the gear and moved to digital transformation. We also learnt the company should manage to be available to the consumers 24/7 without taking the holidays to maintain customer Loyalty.

India is the third largest drug producer in the world according to Business World India, and which contributes to the 60% vaccines globally and maintain high regulatory standards of market like US and European countries said according to Hannah Ellis, P. (2020). Corona virus has shown effect on Indian pharmaceutical market. Due to this, key representatives of pharma market, NITI Aayogh an Indian government health policy are trying for the promotion and development of pharma hubs in India for the benefit of society. Indian government has taken initiative package of 13.6 billion Indian rupees for the domestic manufacturing of the drug materials and Intermediates to avoid the delay of raw materials from China during this pandemic period (Diksha, 2020).

The increase in the prices of vitamins and penicillin in India is in a fear that if the pandemic is going to be the same then the country might face the shortage of medicines (Arushi, 2020). Effects of pandemic on Indian Pharma sector may be as such deficiency of active pharmaceutical ingredients (API) and finished drug products, increasing price of essential drugs, inter-state transport challenge, increase is packing cost, labour supply and so on (Diksha 2020).

CONCLUSION

Digital health will support the future needs of medicine by analysing the massive amounts of recorded patient's data that generate by high-tech devices from multiple sources. Digital care can transform disease-centred services toward patient-centred services. Many of the digital health solutions are still in their infancy and need to be improved. Furthermore, they need extensive and successful validation in human testing and improved clinical reliability. Medical professionals also need to be familiarized and adapt themselves with these advances for better health-care delivery to the patients. Along with digital care growth, researchers, scientists, clinicians, payers, and regulators must accompany technology developers to reach the ultimate goal, which is to help patients live longer and feel better.

In the future, a powerful combination of data science and technology will not only offer the required resilience but will also help to redefine the industry and enable better experiences for patients and doctors. Pharma and healthcare have experienced a seismic upheaval in the industry during the pandemic, making them one of the most sought-after job destinations with a wealth of opportunities awaiting talented personnel. According to experts, initiatives should be developed to provide flexible organisational support systems for workers and other stakeholders in order to capitalise on the momentum gained during this time.

By analysing the vast amounts of patient data generated by high-tech gadgets from many sources, digital health will help meet the medical field's future needs. Digital care can change patient-centred services from services focused on the condition. Numerous digital health solutions still require development and are in their early stages. They also require enhanced clinical dependability and thorough and effective human testing validation. To provide patients with improved healthcare, medical practitioners must become familiar with and adapt to these advancements. To achieve the ultimate aim of assisting patients in living longer and feeling better, researchers, scientists, physicians, payers, and regulators must collaborate with technology developers.

But it is what is needed for today! Accelerating the entire treatment development process will define the ecosystem that pharmaceutical technology must serve, going beyond merely the equipment and technology used in the laboratory. The enterprise-wide adoption of digitization will pave the road for the pharmaceutical industry's successful transformation.

REFERENCE

1. https://www.ncbi.nlm.nih.gov/pmc/articles/PMC8103966/
2. https://www.ibef.org/industry/healthcare-india
3. https://www.ibef.org/industry/pharmaceutical-india
4. Ansuman, T. (2018). India Emerges As Top Five Pharmaceuticals Markets Of The World.
5. Arushi, J. (2020). [Covid -19] Impact on Pharma Retail Sector.
6. Ayati, N, Saiyarsarai, P &Nikfar, S. (2020). Short and long term impacts of
7. COVID-19 on the pharmaceutical sector. DARU Journal of Pharmaceutical Sciences, 28(2), pp.799-805.
8. Busca, L. & Bertrandias, L. (2020). A Framework for Digital Marketing Research: Investigating the Four Cultural Eras of Digital Marketing. Journal of Interactive Marketing, 49, pp.1-19

Covid 19's Effects on Stock Returns of Pharmaceutical Industry & Healthcare Sectors

CHAPTER 14

Author – Vinayak Vijay Sagvekar, Student, IES's Management College and Research Centre, Mumbai

ABSTRACT

In Wuhan, China, the contagious COVID-19 disease was first identified in late 2019. In March 2020, the World Health Organization (WHO) declared it a global pandemic and the biggest disaster of the century. For all nations, whether the world's superpower, the United States of America, or the contender for the title, China, COVID-19 is a game-changing moment. Discovered statistical evidence of China's volatility spreading to all other markets during the initial wave of the COVID- 19 pandemic. These events included stock market crashes and instances of rather explosive dynamics in 18 major countries. The problem has had extensive effects that extend beyond health. Locking down or closing nations has a greater financial cost. Even though the COVID-19 initially had a greater impact on industrialized economies, the second wave of the pandemic had a much greater impact on emerging economies like India, Brazil, Peru, and Mexico. Due to partial lockdowns and consequently on the financial markets, the developing countries saw significant effects on their economic activity. In several nations, it was also seen that some industries, such pharmaceuticals and healthcare services, were operating improbably better than other adversely affected industries An investor's primary objective is to make money, and they put money in a variety of financial instruments with the hope that their investments will increase daily. The stock market, unlike any other kind of investment, is expensive but payout much greater, but the market's unpredictable volatility is a huge source of danger. India's largest industry now in terms of both employment and income is healthcare. By volume, India is the third-largest pharmaceutical market in the world. With 20% of all generic exports, India is the leading exporter of generic drugs worldwide. Attractive destination for establishing generic R&D centers, because of its low operating costs and high-quality products. India exports goods to more than 200 nations. Increased COVID-19 cases had a substantial impact on economic growth in India as well as on people's health and daily lives. Several businesses' stock returns might indicate a country's poor development, but the healthcare and pharmaceutical industry stands out. The purpose of this is to study "how this pandemic had impacted on the healthcare and pharma stocks". To compare various sectors with our test sector (pharmaceutical and healthcare sector), on the basis of several parameters, daily closing prices of sector-specific indices will be studied.

INTRODUCTION

In Wuhan, China, the contagious COVID-19 disease was first identified in late 2019. In March 2020, the World Health Organization (WHO) declared it a global pandemic and the biggest disaster of the century. For all nations, whether the world's superpower, the United States of America, or the contender for the title, China, COVID-19 was a game-changing moment. Statistical evidence was discovered of China's volatility spread to all other markets during the initial wave of the COVID-19 pandemic. These events included stock market crashes and instances of rather explosive dynamics in 18 major countries. The problem had extensive effects that extend beyond health. Lock down or closure of nations had a greater financial cost. Even though the COVID-19 initially had a greater impact on industrialized economies, the second wave of the pandemic had a much greater impact on emerging economies like India, Brazil, Peru, and Mexico. Due to partial lockdowns and consequently on the financial markets, the developing countries saw significant effects on their economic activity. In several nations, it was also seen that some industries, such pharmaceuticals and healthcare services, were operated improbably better than other adversely affected industries. An investor's primary objective is to make money, and they put money in a variety of financial instruments with the hope that their investments will increase daily. The stock market, unlike any other kind of investment, is expensive but payout much greater, but the market's unpredictable volatility is a huge source of danger. India's largest industry now in terms of both employment and income is healthcare. By volume, India has been third-largest pharmaceutical market in the world. With 20% of all generic exports, India was the leading exporter of generic drugs worldwide. Attractive destination for establishing generic R&D centers, because of its low operating costs and high-quality products. India exports goods to more than 200 nations. Increased COVID-19 cases had a substantial impact on economic growth in India as well as on people's health and daily lives. Several businesses' stock returns might indicate a country's poor development, but the healthcare and pharmaceutical industry stands out. The purpose of this is to study "how this pandemic had impacted on the healthcare and pharma stocks". To compare various sectors with our test sector (pharmaceutical and healthcare sector), on the basis of several parameters, lowest as well as highest closing prices of sector-specific indices will be studied.

KEYWORDS

India, Healthcare and pharmaceutical sector, Abnormal returns, COVID- 19, stock performance, Nifty Pharma, Pharmaceutical Company.

OBJECTIVE

The primary aim of study is to examine the relationship between this pandemic and performance of Indian healthcare and pharmaceutical stocks. The secondary aim of the study is to find out how this pandemic has impacted the healthcare and pharma stocks in India. The other objectives are to observe the performance of selective firms (Cipla, Divi's Laboratories, Sun Pharmaceutical Industries, Torrent Pharma, Zydus Lifesciences, Abbott India, Alkem lab, Lupin, Aurobindo Pharma, IPCA Labs, Dr. Reddy.) and to analyse short-term and long- term impacts of the pandemic on the pharmaceutical sector.

LITERATURE REVIEW

Since COVID-19 has infiltrated every country in such a short period of time, numerous studies had been conducted regarding the effects of the pandemic on both established economies and emerging economies. According to Daube (2020) and Dev and Sengupta (2020), the financial markets were already unstable when COVID-19 entered the market, which accelerated price declines and caused stock market crashes in a number of different countries. A crisis-like event like this one might cause unanticipated swings in the stock market, which puts the traditional correlations between variables in risk. This encourages us to research how the epidemic affects market volume and return.

Research has looked at how COVID-19 and stock markets are related, as well as how the industry is responding to the pandemic. Prior to the COVID-19 pandemic, NIFTY Pharma and NIFTY50 were discovered to be the two indices with the most volatility by Batra & Taneja (2020). The stock market reflects the current situation of the economy and it reacts to major events. Past literature has shown the same from time to time, for example, how news affects the stock market (Li, 2018) or how stock market responded to foot-and-mouth disease (FMD) outbreaks in Korea (Pendell D. et al., 2013).

HYPOTHESIS

This research aims to examine the effects of COVID-19 on the share prices of particular pharmaceutical companies and to compare price volatility before and after COVID 19.

H0: There is no significant impact of COVID-19 before and after on pharmaceutical companies and healthcare sectors.

H1: There is significant impact of COVID-19 before and after on pharmaceutical companies and healthcare sectors.

RESEARCH METHODOLOGY

This study is based on secondary data. The data will be collected from the Bombay Stock Exchange SENSEX (BSE SENSEX), National Stock Exchange SENSEX (NSE SENSEX), Nifty Pharma and other published sources. The analysis is based on fundamental analysis and technical analysis.

MARKET OVERVIEW

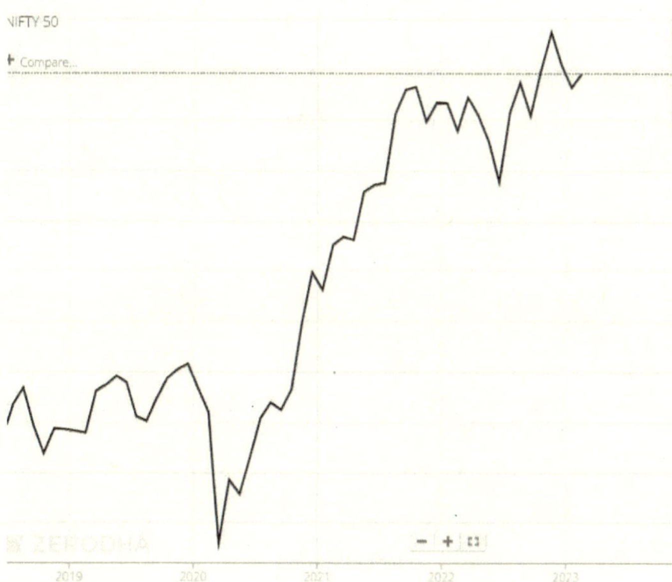

Nifty Chart: -

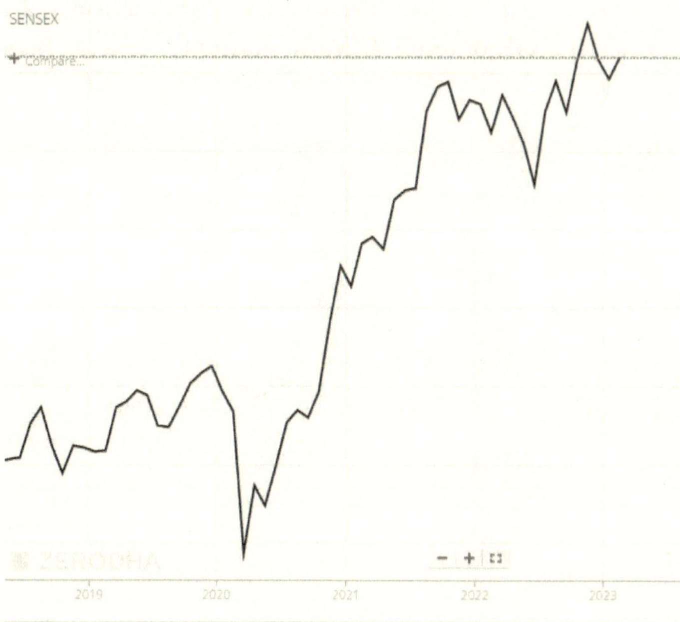

Sensex Chart

Nifty Pharma

ANALYSIS

The Indian pharmaceutical market was valued at **$20.0 billion** in 2019 which has increased at a CAGR of more than 6% during the forecast period 2020-2025.

2019-20	**Cr. 2,89,998**
2020-21	$ 55 Billion
2021-22	$ 42 Billion
2022-current	$ 50 Billion
2024	$ 65 Billion
2030	$ 130 Billion

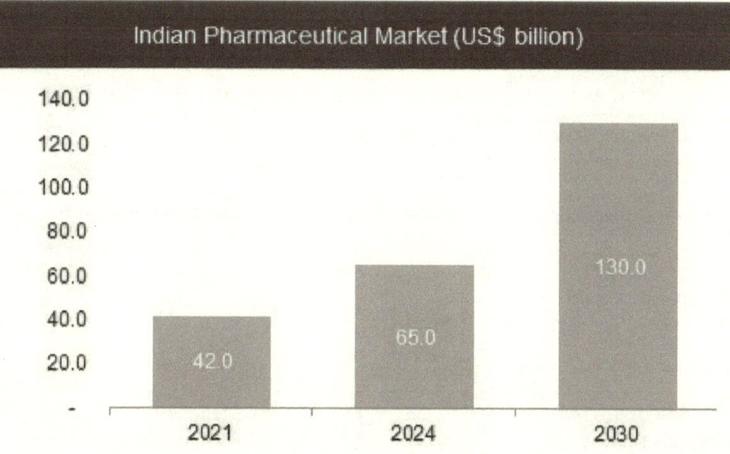

No.	Top 10 Indian P'ceutical company	MP/ per Share Jan 2020	CMP/per share Jan 2023 (in rupees)	Highest price with Month and Year		Fundamental Analysis			
						PE Rat io	Sect or PE	PB Rat io	Sect or PB
1	Sun Pharmaceutical Industries	375	1070	1070	Jan-23	73.87	33.63	4.73	4.12
2	Divi's Laboratories	1817	3500	5420	Oct-21	29.3	33.63	7.39	4.12
3	Cipla	445	1090	1180	Nov-22	32.88	33.63	3.92	4.12
4	Dr. Reddy Laboratories	2860	4400	5600	July-21	33.26	33.63	3.78	4.12
5	Torrent Pharma	925	1630	1750	Nov-22	67.11	33.63	8.76	4.12
6	Zydus Lifesciences	253	455	670	May-21	9.76	33.63	2.3	4.12
7	Abbott India	12500	22500	23925	Oct-21	54.49	33.63	15.43	4.12
8	Alkem lab	2015	3775	4060	Sep-21	22.35	33.63	4.16	4.12
9	Lupin	550	780	1260	Jun-21	-22.09	33.63	2.76	4.12
10	Aurobindo Pharma	445	455	1060	May-21	9.07	33.63	0.98	4.12

According to the above mentioned statistics, the stock price of pharmaceutical companies increased throughout the Pandemic. Some companies saw a decline to their potential price, while others were unable to reach their previous price due to their weak fundamental qualities.

No.	Indian P'ceutical company	MP/ per Share Jan 2020	CMP/per share Jan 2023 (in rupees)
1	Sun Pharmaceutical Industries	375	1070
2	Divi's Laboratories	1817	3500
3	Cipla	445	1090
4	Dr. Reddy Laboratories	2860	4400
5	Torrent Pharma	925	1630
6	Zydus Lifesciences	253	455
7	Abbott India	12500	22500
8	Alkem lab	2015	3775
9	Lupin	550	780
10	Aurobindo Pharma	445	455
11	IPCA Labs	390	880
12	GlaxoSmithKline	1600	1330
13	Laurus Labs	72	385
14	Pfizer	3950	4490
15	JB chemicals	425	2040
16	Ajanta Pharma	650	1220
17	Sanofi India	6550	5950
18	Glenmark	310	440
19	Alembic	545	580
20	Natco Pharma	600	570
21	Eris Life	475	670
22	AstraZeneca	2500	3600
23	Procter&Gamble	4200	4140
24	Granules India	123	330
25	Caplin Labs	280	755
26	Jubilant Pharmo	250	375
27	Hikal	115	427
28	Indoco Remedies	175	422
29	Marksans Pharma	17	69
30	Wockhardt	140	235

PAIRED SAMPLES STATISTICS

		Mean	N	Std. Deviation	Std. Error Mean
Pair 1	Pre_Covid	1518.40	30	2568.361	468.916
	Post_Covid	2285.43	30	4143.854	756.561

PAIRED SAMPLES CORRELATIONS

		N	Correlation	Sig.
Pair 1	Pre_Covid & Post_Covid	30	.958	.000

PAIRED SAMPLES TEST

		Paired Differences							
					95% Confidence Interval of the Difference				
		Mean	Std. Deviation	Std. Error Mean	Lower	Upper	t	df	Sig. (2-tailed)
Pair 1	Pre_ Covid - Post_ Covid	- 767.033	1836.994	335.388	-1452.978	-81.088	-2.287	29	.030

Here the p-value is 0.03 which is less than 0.05.

1. **H0:** There is no significant impact of COVID-19 before and after on pharmaceutical companies and healthcare sectors.
   H1: There is a significant impact of COVID-19 before and after on pharmaceutical companies and healthcare sectors.
2. Level **of significance** = 0.05
3. **Test statistic:** Paired t test
4. **Decision Rule:** $p<0.05$, then accept H1, reject H0.
   $p > 0.05$, then accept H0 and reject H1.
5. From the table, the **p value is 0.03.**
6. Hence, we

Accept H1: There is a significant impact of COVID-19 before and after on pharmaceutical companies and healthcare sectors. &

Reject H0: There is no significant impact of COVID-19 before and after on pharmaceutical companies and healthcare sectors.

CONCLUSION

The COVID-19 outbreak has significantly increased the demand for generic and branded generic drugs due to the fact that the pharmaceutical industry and healthcare sector rose in response to the pandemic. Many companies continued with that uptrend due to their strong fundamentals, while some companies left that uptrend after the pandemic due to their weak fundamentals.

POLICY IMPLICATIONS AND FUTURE STUDY

In the present study, SPSS was used to analyze the volatility and return of NSE stock indices in the pharmaceutical and healthcare sectors before and after the COVID period. These study results will benefit the healthcare and pharmaceutical sectors, which are represented by stock market indices and have responded to the COVID-19 shock. Markets respond throughout time to a company's expansion, cash flow generation, and competitive advantage. As a result, investors have both opportunities and risks due to the tremendous volatility of the equity markets. The COVID pandemic has affected stock prices and increased volatility in the Indian financial sector and stock markets. Stocks with bad fundamentals can aid investors in reducing their exposure to ongoing uncertainty by being included in their portfolios. This sector analysis of the global stock market, based on statistical analysis, identifies which country's stock market is most impacted. It also offers insight into future directions.

REFERENCE

- https://ro.uow.edu.au/aabfj/vol15/iss1/2/
- https://www.nseindia.com/
- https://www.bseindia.com/
- https://kite.zerodha.com/
- https://www.moneycontrol.com/

- https://www.technoarete.org/common_abstract/pdf/IJSEM/v9/i9/Ext_57120.pdf
- https://economictimes.indiatimes.com/markets/stocks/news/
- Batra, L., & Taneja, H.C. (2020). Evaluating volatile stock markets using information theoretic measures. Physica A: Statistical Mechanics and its Applications, 537, 122711.
- Daube, C. H. (2020). The Corona Virus Stock Exchange Crash. Leibniz Information Centre for Economics, Kiel, Hamburg

A Study on Impact of Covid-19 on Digital Payment in Maharashtra

CHAPTER 15

Author – Nayan Asati, Anthony Kelvin, Student, IES MCRC & Dr. Namrata Acharya (Finance), Assistant Professor, IES's Management College and Research Centre, Mumbai

ABSTRACT

Coronavirus disease (COVID-19) is a contagious disease caused by the virus SARS-CoV-2. It was first identified in December 2019, in Wuhan, China. The disease soon spread worldwide, resulting in the COVID-19 pandemic.

In cashless transactions, digital payments are made or accepted in lieu of real money. This covers any online payment method that eliminates the need for currency, such as credit/debit cards, cheques, DDs, NEFT, RTGS, and e-wallets. During the pandemic, digital transactions in Maharashtra had per capita transaction rate of 6.9.

Globally, two-thirds of individuals currently send or receive digital payments, with emerging economies accounting for an increasing proportion from 35% in 2014 to 57% in 2021.The pandemic accelerated the transition to digital payments. Digital payment systems continue to have a high level of public trust because they have demonstrated that they are reliable and sustainable. This research focuses on the value of digital payments during pandemic, various digital payment systems, and the development of digital payments during the last three years and additionally, the future of digital payments.

OBJECTIVE

Digital payments began to take off in our nation during the pandemic. Maharashtra, the commercial centre, was our primary goal.

- To understand the role that digital payments played in pandemic

- To study various online payment methods
- To compare and analyse current digital payment data with data from the prior year
- To understand how digital payments are used
- To draw attention to the problems associated with digital payment methods

The current study has both primary and secondary sources as its foundation. The purpose of the study is to examine how Covid 19 has affected digital payments in Maharashtra. A thorough online survey will be carried out. Moreover, data will be acquired from MCA and IBEF.

INTRODUCTION

Demonetization and COVID-19 were two words that played a crucial part in India's road to becoming a paperless economy. One created the groundwork for digital payments, while another became the primary source for expanding the digital payments ecosystem.

According to a recent Accenture prediction issued on November 24, 2020, around 66.6 billion transactions worth USD 270.7 billion are predicted to transition from cash to cards and digital payments in India by 2023, increasing to USD 856.6 billion by 2030. According to the survey, the Indian payment gateway aggregator business is presently valued at Rs 9.5 trillion.

COVID-19 appears to be another demonetization-like industry trigger.

In terms of reacting to this scenario, digital payment providers have been fairly hands-on, delivering greater assistance on items such as food, masks, sanitizers, COVID-19 insurance, integration with contributions to the PM CARES fund, and other critical products and services.

DIGITAL PAYMENT

Digital payment is a way of payment which is made through digital modes. In digital payments, payer and payee both use digital modes to send and receive money. It is also called electronic payment. No hard cash (currency notes) is involved in the digital payments. All the transactions in digital payments are completed online. These transfers could be done through means of cards (debit/credit), mobile wallets, mobile apps, net banking, Electronic Clearing Service (ECS), National Electronic Fund Transfer (NEFT), Immediate Payment Service (IMPS), pre-paid instruments or other similar means.

DIGITAL PAYMENT MODES IN MAHARASHTRA

1. **Banking Cards**: Banking cards provide consumers with the most security, convenience, and control of any payment option. The range of cards available, including credit, debit, and prepaid, provides further flexibility. These cards offer two-factor authentication for safe payments, such as a secure PIN and an OTP.
   Some examples of card payment systems are RuPay, Visa, and MasterCard. Payment cards enable customers to make purchases in shops, online, through mail-order catalogues, and over the phone. They save both customers and businesses time and money, making transactions easier.
2. **USSD:** The revolutionary payment service *99# operates via the Unstructured Supplementary Service Data (USSD) channel. This service enables mobile banking transactions with a simple feature phone. It is not necessary to have mobile internet data to use USSD-based mobile banking. It is envisioned that it would provide financial depth and inclusion of the underbanked society in mainstream banking services.
3. **AEPS:** Aadhaar Enabled Payment System (AEPS) is a bank-led architecture that facilitates online interoperable financial transactions at PoS (Point of Sale / Micro ATM) utilising Aadhaar verification through any bank's Business Correspondent (BC)/Bank Mitra.
4. **UPI:** Unified Payments Interface (UPI) is a technology that integrates several bank accounts into a single mobile app (of any participating bank), combining many banking services and smooth money routing merchant payments under one umbrella. It also handles "Peer to Peer" collect requests, which may be scheduled and paid according to need and convenience. Each bank has its own UPI app available for the Android, Windows, and iOS mobile platforms (s).
5. **MOBILE WALLETS:** A mobile wallet is a method of carrying currency in digital form. You may link your mobile device's credit card or debit card details to the mobile wallet application, or you can transfer money online to the mobile wallet. You may use your Smartphone, iPad, or smart watch to make purchases instead of your traditional credit card. To load money into a digital wallet, an individual's account must be linked to it. Most banks and some private firms offer e-wallets. Paytm,

Freecharge, Mobikwik, Oxigen, mRupee, Airtel Money, Jio Money, SBI Buddy, itz Cash, Citrus Pay, Vodafone M-Pesa, Axis Bank Lime, ICICI Pockets, SpeedPay, and other similar services are available.

6. **INTERNET BANKING:** Internet banking, often known as online banking, e-banking, or virtual banking, is an electronic payment system that allows bank or other financial institution clients to execute a variety of financial transactions via the financial institution's website. National Electronic Fund Transfer (NEFT), Real Time Gross Settlement (RTGS), Electronic Clearing System (ECS), and Quick Payment Service are all part of it (IMPS).
7. **MOBILE BANKING:** Mobile banking is a service offered by a bank or other financial institution that allows its clients to execute various sorts of financial transactions remotely using a mobile device such as a phone or tablet. It does so by utilising software, sometimes referred to as an app, given by banks or financial institutions. Each bank has its own mobile banking app for the Android, Windows, and iOS platforms (s).
8. **MICRO ATMs**: A micro ATM is a gadget that provides basic banking services to a million Business Correspondents (BC). The platform allows Business Correspondents (for example, a local kirana shop owner who will operate as a "micro ATM") to make quick transactions.

EVOLUTION OF DIGITAL PAYMENT IN MAHARASHTRA

The Indian banking sector has grown effectively by inventing and attempting to adapt and apply electronic payments to improve the banking system. Since the advent of e-payments in India, the banking sector has grown like never before. The ratio of e-payments to paper-based transactions has grown significantly as a consequence of technological advancements and greater consumer awareness of the simplicity and efficiency of internet and mobile transactions. India's payments framework, particularly the digital payments system, has advanced rapidly in recent years, propelled by advancements in data and communication technology and promoted and in accordance with RBI's vision. With the availability of the internet in the 1990s, the era of online banking began. Internet banking transformed the financial services industry. The Reserve Bank of India (RBI) piloted the progress of digital payments in India, which was described in the Payment Systems in India report issued in 1998. The Payment and Settlement Act of 2007 defines Digital Payments as any "electronic funds transfer," which includes point-of-sale transfers, ATM transactions, direct deposits or withdrawals of funds, transfers initiated by phone or internet, and card payments.

The introduction of MICR (Magnetic ink character recognition code) clearing in the early 1980s, Electronic Clearing Service and Electronic Funds Transfer in the 1990s, and the issuance of credit and debit cards by banks in the 1990s are all critical achievements in the overall development of the payments framework. Banks began issuing credit and debit cards in the 1990s, followed by the National Financial Switch in 2003, which enabled interconnectivity of ATMs across the country, the RTGS and NEFT in 2004, the Cheque Truncation System (CTS) in 2008, second factor authentication for 'card not present' transactions in 2009, and the new RTGS with upgraded features in 2013.

In 2008, the National Payments Corporation of India (NPCI) was founded. It has been at the forefront of the development of the retail payment mechanism. Moreover, non-bank organisations have been involved in the issuing of prepaid instruments (PPI), including mobile and digital wallets. These efforts have been supplemented by notable NPCI projects such as the implementation of grid-based CTS operations, interoperability on NACH (National Automated Clearing House), IMPS, NFS, RuPay, APBS and AEPS, National Unified USSD Platform (NUUP), UPI and BHIM application.

These developments reflect the progress of the country's Digital Payments framework. This was followed by a notable move by the Indian government, which established the Committee of Digital Payments in August 2016 under the Chairmanship of Ratan P. Watal, Principal Adviser of NITI Aayog. With demonetisation in November 2016, India saw a significant increase in the use of digital payment methods. Demonetisation prompted Indians to convert to cashless techniques, which come with a slew of hidden charges, but once the weight was lifted, Indians returned to using cash.

ADVANTAGES OF DIGITAL PAYMENT

1. **EASE AND SPEED:** The most basic argument for going digital is the ease of use it provides. Various types of digital payments have made it more easy - paying bills online or on your smartphone, purchasing a public transportation ticket with an e-wallet, or making a transaction with a tap-and-pay card - all have been reduced to a matter of seconds.

You can pay for anything digitally down to the precise paisa as opposed to scrambling for exact change.

2. **SECURIY:** Payment rules in India are overseen by a foresighted, yet cautious, authority concerned with the protection of its population. It has implemented and continues to use different safeguards to protect transactions. The initial few stages were additional factor authentication (AFA) and real-time transaction notifications. Biometric/Aadhaar-based authentication and comprehensive fraud prevention features were added to this.
3. **CONSUMER SAFETY AND PROTECTION:** In addition to preventive measures, there are redressal systems in place to protect customers in the event of a breach. When you lose your wallet or cash, you know it's all gone. It is simpler with digital payment instruments - you lose it, you block it, lowering your financial risk. You may also file chargebacks and disputes for transactions that were incorrectly charged ·to you. If you are a victim of fraud and report it in a timely manner, you may be held liable for restitution.
4. **FINANCIAL ADVANTAGES:** The government and payment instrument issuers are rewarding clients through cash back programmes and discounts in order to popularise digital payments. Some provide loyalty schemes based on instrument usage. Payment service providers have also begun to provide payment and fraud insurance, therefore mitigating risk.

GOVERNMENT INITIATIVE FOR ONLINE PAYMENT

1. **DigiVaarta:** DigiVaarta is launched to spread the awareness of a DIGIDhan and also on the usage of BHIM app.
2. **DIGI shala:** It is launched on DD channel to promote digital payments.
3. **DigiDhan Abhiyan campaign:** It is organized to promote cashless transactions.
4. **Vittiya Saksarta Abhiyam:** It is an initiative by MHRD to engage youth to use a digitally enabled cashless economy.
5. **Lucky Grahak Yojana and DigiDhan Vyapa rYojana offer** cash awards to consumers and merchants who utilize payment instruments for personal consumption expenditures.

6. **TDS Deduction at Source:** In order to discourage the practice of making business payment in cash, 2% tax deducted at source (TDS) will be levied on cash withdrawals exceeding Rs. 1 crore in a year from a bank account.
7. **Use of Low-Cost Digital Modes:** Any business entity with annual turnover more than 50 crore shall offer low cost digital modes of payments to their customers and no charges shall be imposed on customers as well as merchants. BHIM UPI, Aadhaar Pay, NEFT and RTGS can be used to promote less cash economy.
8. **Digital Smart Cards:** Government officials made social security pension payments through digital smart cards which led to reduction in bribe. Go Digital and get discounts on Insurance, petrol and Diesel: 0.75% discount is give on petrol and diesel purchase if digital payment is made by e-wallets or debit cards or credit cards.
9. **Discount on Rail Tickets:** People travelling by train by purchasing monthly tickets will enjoy a discount of 0.5% if tickets are purchased digitally.
10. **INR 10 lakhs of Insurance:** People travelling long distances using Indian Railways will get travel insurance of Rs 10 lakhs on unforeseen happening if tickets are purchased digitally.
11. **Rupay Card from NABARD:** Those people who have kisan credit card can get Rupay cards from NABARD.
12. **10% discounts for highway tolls:** It can be availed when payments are made using digital payment mode.

DISADVANTAGES OF DIGITAL PAYMENT

1. **FRAUD AND SECURITY:** Consumers are most concerned about security breaches and data security issues, which can be viewed as a major barrier to the adoption of digital payments. Creating a safer path for transactions is a must, not an option, because hacking and security breaches can result in financial and reputational losses for the firm.
2. **AWARNESS AND ADAPTION:** Maharashtra is a cash-based society. Despite the increasing growth of digital payment options, there is still a lack of understanding among individuals about security, data privacy, and other issues, leading many to feel that making purchases via cards or cash is preferable to mobile applications. Customers still do not

regard mobile wallets as a secure form of payment, and the mobile wallet sector must commit significant time and effort to change this.

LITERATURE REVIEW

1. Sudha, G., Sornaganesh, V., Thangajesu, Satish, M., Chellama, A.V., August 2020. Based on primary data gathered from 220 respondents, this paper discusses the various digital payment mechanisms used in the event of a pandemic. The Digital India initiative is an Indian government flagship programme whose vision is to transform India into a digital society and an information economy. All purchases in this futuristic society can be done via contactless cards, smart phone applications, and other technological ways. The Central Bank of India declared last year that it intended to increase digital transactions to 15% of GDP by 2021. As the world's fastest-growing mobile industry, the government aims for a billion digital transactions every day.
2. Rajeshwari M. May through June 2019. This article explains how Digital Banking has considerably reduced bank operational costs. This has made it simpler for banks to charge reduced service costs while also offering greater interest rates to depositors. The banks benefited more from the lower operational expenses. Traditional banking is being transformed into a digital environment through digital transformation. This article discusses the importance of digitization in Indian banking, variables influencing the breadth of digital banking in India, and digital banking trends in India.

   Data were gathered from a variety of sources, including academic articles, Indian government publications, and several RBI databases. The survey also revealed that the ease of use of digital banking will encourage integration.
3. July 2019, Jayalakshmi. S. and Parvathi. S. This article demonstrated that digital payment is an efficient way for businesses of all sizes to reach out to prospective customers and to investigate the concepts of digital banking, digital payment, and digital payment methods. Digital payments have several advantages over cash, including ease, security, and clarity. Poor internet connectivity and additional charges for digital transactions are major impediments to the implementation of this

digital payment system in India. In the next years, there will be a whole new method of transmitting capital in the Indian economy.

RESEARCH METHODOLOGY

The study relies on both primary and secondary data. Secondary data was gathered from numerous sources such as research articles, authenticated websites, RBI bulletins, and daily newspapers, while primary data was gathered via a structured questionnaire.

OBJECTIVES

1. Understanding the Significance of Digital Payment in a Pandemic.
2. Research online payment methods.
3. To compare and analyse current and prior year digital payment data.
4. Understanding the applications of digital payments.
5. To draw attention to the problems with digital payment methods.

PRIMARY RESEARCH

Conclusive Studies

Sampling Method: The Non-Probability Convenience sampling approach was used to choose the samples in order to acquire the necessary information from them.

The sample size is 150.

Respondents Individuals who use digital payment apps

Structured Questionnaire as a Data Collecting Technique

SECONDARY RESEARCH

Cumulative Payment Transactions in the Last 12 Months/table and chart

Diffusion of Digital Payment Transactions by State/table and chart

Monthly Increase (LAKHS) of BHIM - UPI Transactions/table and chart

DATA ANALYSIS AND INTERPRETATION

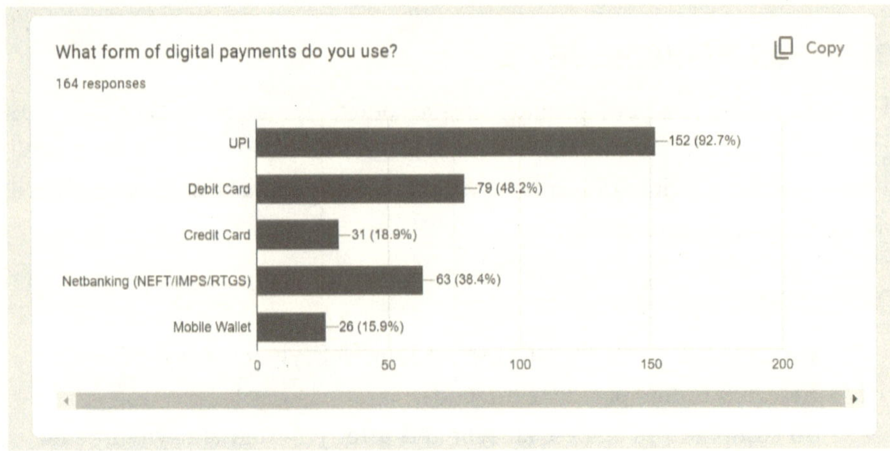

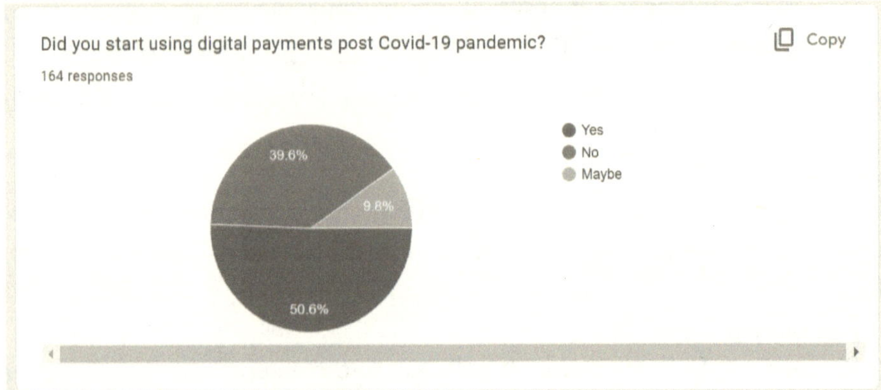

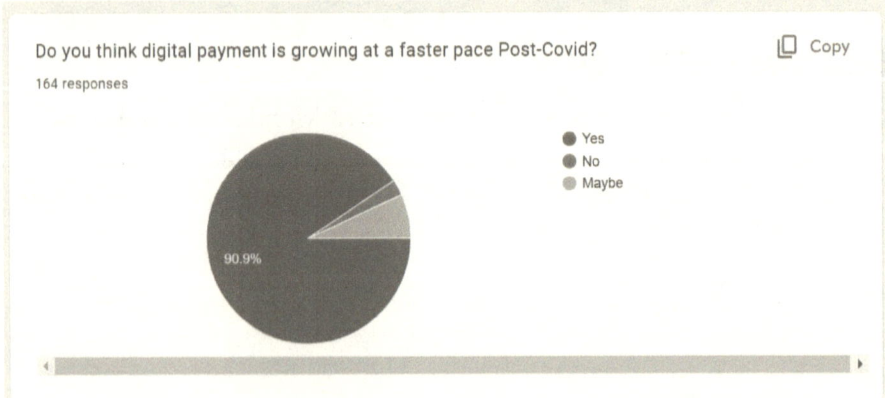

The poll survey findings indicate a significant shift towards digital payment methods and reduced reliance on cash during the COVID-19 pandemic and subsequent lockdowns. The majority of respondents reported increased usage of digital payments compared to cash, driven by factors such as convenience, safety, security, and the need for physical distancing. Some participants even expressed willingness to exclusively use digital payment methods. However, cash still remains relevant for small transactions and in situations where acceptance infrastructure for digital payments is limited, particularly with small-scale vendors. Approximately 90.9% of the participants believe that digital payment usage has grown at a faster pace after the pandemic. This growing inclination towards digital payments highlights the potential to expand the digital payment ecosystem with the right infrastructure in place.

The survey also revealed that 85% of people prefer using digital payment methods, while 15% do not. Among the digital payment options, UPI (Unified Payments Interface) was the most preferred method, with a majority of users opting for Google Pay. Debit cards ranked second in popularity, while mobile wallets were used by a smaller percentage of respondents.

Regarding frequency of use, 72% of respondents reported using payment apps 1-5 times a day, while 18.9% used them 5-10 times a day. Additionally, the survey found a significant increase in digital payment adoption, with 97.6% of respondents currently using digital payments compared to only 25.6% before the pandemic.

SECONDARY RESEARCH

However, digital payments are on the rise in India. As in most other areas of the world, digital purchases have hit a record high this year in the country with nearly 1.5 billion people. As stated for the first time by the local outlet, all channels from the unified payment interface (UPI) to the Aadhar- Enabled Payment System (AEPS) registered dramatic growth. In comparison to the gloom created by the Covid-19 pandemic and the lockdown across the economy, digital payments and fintech were one industry that saw record highs in 2020 when a vast number of people opted to stay at home and retain social distances. With fears over catching new coronavirus infections from visiting bank branches and using currency notes, many people—not only in metros but even in smaller towns—began to use their smartphones to make purchases and even take loans for smooth banking services. As the COVID-19 lockdown and ensuing constraints pushed more and more people to opt for digital transactions, Uttar Pradesh reported a huge 126 percent leap in digital transactions in 2020 compared to the previous year. In September, the Card spends between 60-70 percent of the January average at the point of sale of terminals in shops. This means that people use digital payments in physical modes like shopping. The value of transactions on the Unified Payment Interface, a portal built by India's Largest Banks in 2016, hit an all-time high last month as people worried, they would treat bank notes in the midst of the pandemic. Transfers of electric funds from banks, which had declined in April as economic growth slowed by almost half, have also recovered. Digital payments reached a record high in 2020 with all platforms from the Unified Payments App to the Aadhar-enabled Payment System (AePS) recording stellar progress.

CONCLUSION

Despite the challenges, digital payment systems continue to attract people due to their convenience, time-saving nature, cashless transactions, and availability outside of banking hours. The COVID-19 pandemic further accelerated the adoption of digital payments as people sought touchless and socially distant alternatives. In response, both businesses and the government have embraced digital payment systems, encouraging their use and ensuring the safety of critical services. This shift towards digital payments is not limited to online transactions, as merchants are exploring hybrid solutions that blend physical and digital experiences. The ongoing focus on safety precautions during the post-lockdown period necessitates the development of innovative solutions to meet the needs of the public, retailers, and businesses. The government, along with regulatory bodies like the RBI and NPCI, has actively promoted digital payments through various channels and platforms. The digitization of the banking sector, facilitated by smartphone usage, is meeting the increasing expectations of the population by reducing errors and improving convenience. Digital banking has also freed businesses from the constraints of traditional banking hours, enabling transactions at any time. It's important to note that the study's findings are subjective and limited to the knowledge and preferences of the respondents in Maharashtra.

Profitability Analysis of Dabur India (2018-2022)

CHAPTER 16

Authors – Deepika Devadas & Yuti Keni, Student, IES's Management College and Research Centre, Mumbai

ABSTRACT

Dabur Ltd is an Indian multinational consumer goods company, founded by **S. K. Burman** and headquartered in **Ghaziabad**. It manufactures Ayurvedic medicine and natural consumer products, and is one of the largest fast-moving consumer goods companies in India. Dabur derives around 60% of its revenue from the consumer care business, 11% from the food business and remaining from the international business unit. This qualitative research paper is based on secondary data which is obtained from the research papers published in various journals, newspapers, articles, annual reports of the company, and articles related to this study. Nowadays, as we know that people are becoming more conscious about their health. So people demand more natural and Ayurvedic products than other products. Dabur is one of those company which gives best Ayurvedic product. It is found that customers do shift from one brand to another but in case Dabur customers are more brand loyal due to the permanent curing nature of the herbal products which encourages consumers to buy more and more herbal products. This study will help to evaluate the performance of the herbal products of Dabur India Ltd in terms of revenue, EPS, return on Equity, Return on Total Assets, etc.

KEYWORDS

Ayurveda, ayurvedic products, profitability ratio analysis, performance evaluation, Dabur India Ltd.

INTRODUCTION

Dabur India LTD. which was started as a family business, turned to be the world's largest ayurvedic and health care company of India. It was incorporated on September 16 1975 for manufacture of high-grade edible & industrial guar gum powder and its sophisticated derivatives. In the year 1978 the company launched **Hajmola tablet** an ayurvedic medicine used as a digestive aid.

It has been observed that India's consumer behaviour has changed dramatically during the last two decades. Consumers are becoming more aware of the impact of products on the environment while making purchases. It now enjoys the distinction of being the largest Indian F.M.C.G. Company and is poised to become a true Indian multinational.

Ayurveda goods can be found in our traditional ayurvedic system. This traditional medical technique has evolved after several years of tests, studies, and meditations by natural scientists. Ayurveda is a health-promoting science that aims to improve one's well-being and happiness. These goods are environmentally friendly and are thought to be safe for human health.

Table 1: Dabur is famous for Products like

Segments	Products
Health Supplements	• Dabur Chyawanprash • Dabur Honey • Dabur Glucose D • Dabur Amla Juice
Oral care	• Dabur Red Paste • Dabur Meswak • Dabur Lal Dant Manjan • Dabur Babool • Dabur Red Gel • Dabur Herbal
Foods	• Real Fruit Power Juice • Dabur Pickle
Hair Care	• Almond Hair Oil • Almond Shampoo • Amla Hair Oil • Vatika Enriched Coconut Hair Oil • Vatika Health Shampoo
Skin Care	• Dabur Sanitize Germ Protection Soap • Vatika Dermoviva Neem Soap
Cold & Cough	• Honitus Cough Syrup

Segments	Products
Digestives	• Dabur Pudin Hara • Dabur Hajmola
Home Care	• Odomos • Odonil • Sanifresh

Source: Compiled by Author

Dabur has a distribution network spread across five continents and over fifty countries with offices in Europe, America and Africa and production units in Nepal, Egypt, UK and UAE.

VISION

Dedicated to the Health and well-bring of every Household.

MISSION

Ghar Ghar Ayurveda- Contemporise Ayurveda and make it relevant for the new generation.

Ratio related to finance are used to evaluate a company's financial performance as well as we can see the future success of the company. Liquidity ratios, Solvency ratio, and Profitability ratios are used to analyse the company's performance.

LITERATURE REVIEW

Ayurveda literally means life wisdom. It's a blend of science and the art of living a healthy lifestyle. It is well known for its natural methods of treating illness in the human body and psyche.

Ayurveda, which is a natural system of medicine, originated in India more than 3000 years ago. It is derived from the Sanskrit words ayur (life) and veda (science or knowledge). In other words, it means knowledge of life. It's a mix of science and the art of living a healthy lifestyle.

Ratio analysis is a technique utilized to assess the company from a different angle. Among the various ratios, the performance ratio is also one that is used to evaluate the performance of the company. Through this we can find various further plans on the company and also certain recommendation.

Table 2: The review of the various literature on profit analysis and Ayurveda

Sr. No.	Area	Learning	Author
1.	Profitability Ratio Analysis	Consumers nowadays prefer ayurvedic products instead of chemical products as they are becoming more health conscious. This study will help to understand the performance of Dabur India Ltd in terms of revenue, return on equity, return on total assets, etc.	Bharathi & Suresh Ramana Mayya (May 2022)
2.	Sustaining Competitive Advantage	This study focuses on the decisions and strategies that Dabur uses to gain a competitive advantage among the top FMCG companies in the Indian market.	Thomas Mathew (19/04/2016)
3.	Consumer perception regarding Dabur India Ltd.	This study focuses on understanding the consumer perception regarding Dabur, their motivation to buy the products and their level of satisfaction after the consumption of the products.	AMIT KUMAR DUBEY (January – 2016)
4.	A study on influence of digitalization in marketing mix of Dabur India ltd.	This study explains the efforts of Dabur India Ltd. To digitalize their system to maintain their position in the market.	Bindu Tiwari and Dr. Naveen Kumar
5.	Ratio analysis	This paper explains how financial statement analysis is important for equity evaluation. The operating and financing activities are differentiated from each other. The difficulty of upcoming ratios that indicate equity encouragement is thus considered a problem in the present financial accounting statement analysis.	Nissim & Penman (2001)
6.	Financial Ratio Analysis	This study tries to understand the relative effectiveness of 11 major Chinese ports using a creative and widely used kind of Data Envelopment Analysis (DEA). DEA is a non-parametric method for calculating the relative productivity of managerial units by weighing inputs and outputs. The DEA results show that a port's efficiency ratio is higher when it is compared to the corresponding ratio of another port.	Ablanedo- Rosas, et al., (2010)
7.	Understanding profitability	This study evaluates the drivers of desirableness of listed commercial banks in developing countries using internal and external (market)-based profitability indicators, with a focus on Malawi from 2009 to 2012. The study focussed on correlation and multivariate regression analysis.	Lipunga, A. M. (2014)

Source: Compiled by Author

Accordingly, we can find that Ayurveda plays an important role in human life as it is healthier option to live. On basis of present ratios, ratio analysis techniques are used to forecast the future. The profit analysis ratio are used to find out the financial success of the company.

Here in this research paper we are concentrating more on profitability ratio of the company rather than computing all ratios like liquidity ratio, valuation ratio etc. We are also taking Ayurveda as one of the important element to live life healthy. Here we are very specific about the topic rather than taking more topics.

RESEARCH METHODOLOGY

The necessary information required for making this research paper is collected from various magazines, journals, financial report of the company and from the website. This paper is based Quantitative data. The quantitative data is collected from secondary data. We have taken the values from the annual report of the company:

- To analyse various profitability component of Dabur India Ltd.
- To study the performance of the company through ratio analysis.
- To know about the importance of Ayurvedic product made by the company.
- To know about the effects of various profitability ratios on the company's success.
- To know about revenue earned by the company from various segments.

FINDINGS & DISCUSSION

The purpose of every business is to earn maximum profit. The company need to properly analyse the profit, to know about the growth of the company. Through this ratio we can be able to compare the various changes in the profit in current year compared to past year. Which will help the company to take future decision regarding the growth, development etc. It can also help us to achieve our vision and mission effectively.

Table 3: Input of Dabur data to analyse the profitability ratio (2018-2022) (In crores)

Year	Turnover (Sale)	Gross Profit (GP)	Operating Profit (OP)	Earning After Share (EAT)	Total shareholder's equity	Total asset	No. of shares outstanding
2021-22	8179.50	2056.70	2075.37	1432.93	5863.87	8593.00	1767063892
2020-21	7184.73	1826.71	1835.85	1381.89	5391.22	7504.16	1767425349
2019-20	6309.80	1538.40	1557.67	1170.35	4574.23	6100.11	1767063892
2018-19	6273.19	1612.18	1641.98	1264.29	3968.82	5578.78	1766291141
2017-18	5592.29	1475.63	1497.52	1072.05	4226.86	5812.7	1761520510

Source: Compiled by Author

After analysing the data of Dabur India we can say that:

i. The sale of the company is increasing from 2017-18 to 20121-22. The major increase we can see is in the year 2020-21 to 2021-22 that is 7184.73 crores to 8179.50 crores. The company is continuously working to make their brand powerful. The company's maximum profit is from food products but still theirs other products like beauty and personal care products are also demanded by the consumer and earning good profit. The maximum demand for the dabur product id from south Asian Consumer as well as consumer from all background as E-commerce has evolved.

ii. Gross profit of the company is also increasing every year. The major increase in the year is from 2019-20 i.e.1538.40 crores to 2020-21 i.e. 1826.71 crores. It is because there is increase in sale. We can also see that from year 2018-19 to 2019-20 the gross profit is decreasing to 1538.40 crores from 1612.18 crores due to Covid-19 pandemic in 2020.

iii. The operating profit of the company is also increasing year to year. More increase observed in the year 2020-21compare to all year. This is also because of the increase in sale. We can also see that from year 2018-19 to 2019-20 there is decrease in operational profit due to Covid-19 pandemic.

iv. Earning after taxation is also increasing every year but due covid-19 pandemic the EAT was decreased in 2019-20. But in later few years the EAT tends to increase continuously.

v. Shareholders' Equity is showing an upward trend from year to year except during the year 2018-19. The increase is due to continuous increase in profit, but decrease may be due to ore appropriations.

vi. Total assets are increasing continuously year after the year from 2017-18 to 2021-22.

Table 4: Profit from various segments.

Particular	2017-18	2018-19	2019-20	2020-21	2021-22
Consumer care business	4550.66	5157.60	5256.05	6185.23	6719.70
Food business	947.38	1006.25	944.66	889.61	1312.80
Other segment	97.03	89.28	90.15	94.43	123.36

Source: Compiled by Author

After analysing the various segments of Dabur India we can see that:

i. Dabur earns maximum revenue from consumer care business sector, and every years its increasing at same pace.

ii. We can see that food business is also growing very well year to years.

iii. From above table we can also see that there was slight decrease in 2018-19 in the revenue of other segments, but later in 2019-20 its increasing.

Table 5: Profitability ratio of Dabur

Year	Gross profit (GP) (%)	Operating profit Margin Ratio (OPMR)(%)	Net Profit Margin Ratio (NPMR)(%)	Earnings per share (EPS)(Rs)	Return On Total Asset (ROTA)(%)	Return on Equity (ROE)
2021-22	25.14456874	25.37282	17.51855	8.11	16.67	24.23
2020-21	25.42489419	25.55211	19.23371	7.82	18.41	25.63
2019-20	24.38112143	24.68652	18.5 813	6.62	19.18	25.58
2018-19	25.69952448	26.17456	20.15386	7.16	22.66	37.75
2017-18	26.38686477	26.7783	19.17014	6.09	18.44	23.41
Average	25.40739472	25.712862	96.821168	7.16	19.072	27.32

Source: Compiled by Author

After computing the profitability ratios, we can analyse that there are certain changes in it year to years that are as follows:

i. From 5592.29 crores in 2017-18 to 8179.50 crores in 2021-22, the company's sales have grown. As a result, the gross profit ratio has fluctuated from a high 26.38686477% in 2017-18 to a lowest of 24.38112143% in 2019-20 The average sales of last five years is 25.40739472%.

ii. The operating profit of the margin ratio is unadulterated profit. As per the study, there is increase in operating profit in the year 2017-18 to 26.7783% and is decreasing in the year 2019-20 to 24.68652%. In 2018-19 and 2019-20 thr ratio was decreasing but further it climbed to 25.55211%. in the year 2020-21 this says that the company is trying to perform very well with proper plans.

iii. We can say that the Net profit ratio is been increasing to 19.17014% in 2017-18 to 20.15386% in 2018.19, but later the net profit margin is decreasing. This indicates how much the company is profitable after deducting all expenses, interest, taxes, etc. Even if the net profit is fluctuating it did not fluctuate much.

iv. Earnings per share is one of the most important to attract public attention, which is the key measure of company performance. We can see that Dabur's eps is increasing from 6.09 in 2017-18 to 7.16 in 2018-19. But there is decrease in EPS in year 2019-20 to 6.62 and increase in 2020-21 and 2021-22. Which is the most positive factors for company as well as shareholders.

v. Total return on asset is increasing from 18.44% to 22.66% but later the it is decreasing in the year 2019-20, 2020-21 and 2021-22 to 19.18, 18.41 and 16.67 respectively. This show that the company is generating profits with available assets.

vi. Dabur ROE (Return on Equity), which denotes the return earn on the investment of stockholders in the firm. The ROE is increasing from 2017-18 to 2018-19 but there is decrease in ROE 2019-20 and 2021-22. It indicates that as average performance of the company's management on the invested financial resources.

SUMMARY AND CONCLUSION

Dabur Ltd. is a company that manufactures ayurvedic products. It is consistently making profit year after year which shows that there is an increased demand of ayurvedic products as consumers are becoming more and more health conscious. Health supplements such as Chyawanprash are doing good in terms of profitability. Since it is immune booster, it was in high demand during the Covid pandemic. Thus, it may be finally concluded that Dabur, an ayurvedic company is earning good profits.

We can provide certain recommendations which are as follows:

- Dabur can concentrate more on the promotional activities of its herbal products to increase the awareness among the consumers.
- It should also target the rural market as there is less market growth of the products manufactured by Dabur India Ltd.
- It should increase the number of outlets so that all its products are available under one roof.
- There should be continuous supply of products so that it is available whenever demanded by the customers to avoid any non- availability of products.
- All dabur products must be available at every retail store whenever consumer demand it.
- Dabur should make their application available with good service were consumer can buy their product online from any dabur product safely.
- They should take customer feedback constantly, to meet customer needs.

Table 6: SWOT analysis of Dabur India Ltd.

Strengths	Weakness
• Lower prices • High market share • Wider ratio chain • Large National presence • Healthy • Well-functioning website and E- commerce	• Duplicate products • Strict rules and regulations • International competitors • Effect of Cola market • Selling less merchandise to local retailers
Opportunities	**Threats**
• Increase product line • Increased demand in foreign market • Introduction of Ayurvedic beverages • Recent Health trends • Practice of Yoga and Ayurveda all over the world	• Competition from MNC's • Entrance of local brands • Variety of products

Source: Compiled by Author

Thus, to conclude, we can say that Dabur is one of the largest FMCG providers and ayurvedic products and consumers agree that Dabur offers a hundred per cent herbal merchandise. Consumers are changing their purchasing patterns when it comes to buying intake items. They prefer ayurvedic products instead of chemical products. Fewer side effects, the permanent curing nature of the ayurvedic products made the consumers buy more and more ayurvedic products due to which Dabur is earning good revenue and is able to face the competition in the market.

REFERENCE

1) Website - https://www.dabur.com
2) Annual report of Dabur of last 5 years - https://www.dabur.com/investor/financial-information/reports/1289/Annual-Reports
3) Wikipedia - https://en.wikipedia.org/wiki/Dabur
4) Bharathi & Suresh Ramana Mayya (16/05/2022) - Performance Evaluation of Dabur India Ltd through Profitability Ratio Analysis: A Case Study from https://doi.org/10.5281/zenodo.6546944
5) Thomas Mathew (19/04/2016) - Dabur India Limited – The World Leader in Ayurvedic Products - Sustaining Competitive Advantage from https://docplayer.net/60140433-Dabur-india-limited-the-world-leader-in-ayurvedic-products-sustaining-competitive-advantage.html

6) AMITKUMARDUBEY(January–2016)-ASTUDYONCONSUMER PERCEPTION WITH RESPECT TO DABUR HONEY from https://e-research.siam.edu/wp-content/uploads/2020/11/IMBA-2016-IS-A-STUDY-ON-CONSUMER-PERCEPTION-WITH-RESPECT-TO-DABUR-HONEY-compressed.pdf
7) Bindu Tiwari and Dr Naveen Kumar (July 2020) - A STUDY ON INFLUENCE OF DIGITALISATION IN MARKETING MIX OF DABUR INDIA LTD from Profitability Analysis Of Dabur India.docx
8) https://www.moneycontrol.com/financials/daburindia/balance-sheetVI/DI
9) https://www.capitalmarket.com/Company-Information/Financials/Profit-and-Loss/Dabur-India-Ltd/3392
10) Dabur India Ltd. 2021 Management Discussion and Analysis retrieved on 17/02/2022 from https://www.dabur.com/digital-annual-report/reports/management-discussion-analysis.pdf
11) Nissim, D., & Penman, S. H. (2001). Ratio analysis and equity valuation: From research to practice. Review of accounting studies, 6(1), 109-154. Google Scholar⊕
12) Ablanedo-Rosas, J. H., Gao, H., Zheng, X., Alidaee, B., & Wang, H. (2010). A study of the relative efficiency of Chinese ports: a financial ratio-based data envelopment analysis approach. Expert systems, 27(5), 349-362. Google Scholar⊕
13) Lipunga, A. M. (2014). Determinants of profitability of listed commercial banks in developing countries: Evidence from Malawi. Research Journal of Finance and Accounting, 5(6), 41-49. i. Research Journal of Finance and Accounting, 5(6), 41-49. Google Scholar⊕

Post Covid Changing Pattern of Diabetes: A Case Analysis in Mumbai

CHAPTER 17

Author – Snehal Kale & Vijay Kumar Jaiswal, Student, IES's Management College and Research Centre, Mumbai

ABSTRACT

COVID-19 was havng pandemic effect which is also known as coronavirus pandemic which cause severe respiratory problems. first identify at Wuhan, China in December 2019. Adults with some underlying medical conditions, such as cancer, heart conditions, chronic lung diseases, and diabetes, are more likely than others to become severely ill if infected with COVID-19.29 As a result, they are more likely to need hospitalization, be admitted into an intensive care unit, need a ventilator to help them breathe, or die. Among patients hospitalized with severe COVID-19 complications, 39.7% also had diabetes as an underlying medical condition. The percentage increased to 46.5% for patients 50 to 64.11. People younger than 18 with COVID-19 were up to 2.5 times more likely to be newly diagnosed with diabetes in the months after infection than those without COVID-19 and those who had other respiratory infections before the pandemic.

KEYWORDS

Lifestyle ;Diabetes; Chronic diseases; Diet ;Exercise; Health; Risk reduction; Well-being Management; Prevention

INTRODUCTION

Diabetes is chronic condition which is emerging in day to today lifestyle which leads to decrease life competency and increasing expense for the treatment. Diabetes is a chronic metabolic disorder that has become a major public health concern globally. An individual lifestyle is characterized by various factors such as daily physical activities, diet, nutrition, stress, alcohol consumption, drug abuse, smoking, sleep, etc with the outbreak of COVID-19, the healthcare system has faced significant challenges, including managing and preventing the spread of the virus and addressing the health needs of individuals with pre-existing conditions. Mumbai, a densely populated metropolitan city in India, has been significantly affected by the COVID-19 pandemic, and there have been reports of changing patterns of diabetes in the city. This case analysis aims to explore the post-COVID changing pattern of diabetes in Mumbai, India. The study will investigate the impact of the pandemic on the prevalence of diabetes, the management of diabetes during the pandemic, and the challenges faced by healthcare providers and patients. The analysis will also examine the changes in lifestyle, dietary habits, and physical activity levels of people with diabetes in Mumbai in response to the pandemic. This case analysis is essential as it can provide insights into the changing patterns of diabetes in the post-COVID era and can help healthcare providers and policymakers develop effective strategies to manage diabetes and other chronic conditions during pandemics. Additionally, this study can provide valuable information for individuals with diabetes in Mumbai to adapt to the changing environment and make necessary adjustments to their lifestyle to manage their condition better. The COVID-19 pandemic has affected the health and wellbeing of people worldwide, and it has been reported that people with underlying health conditions, such as diabetes, are more susceptible to severe illness and mortality from COVID-19. In Mumbai, where diabetes is already a significant health concern, the pandemic has brought about new challenges and changes in diabetes management and care. According to a study conducted by the Indian Council of Medical Research (ICMR) in Mumbai, the prevalence of diabetes among COVID-19 patients was found to be higher than that in the general population. The study also highlighted the challenges faced by healthcare providers in managing diabetes during the pandemic, such as limited access to healthcare facilities, shortage of diabetes medication, and disruptions in regular check-ups and follow-ups. Moreover, the COVID-19 pandemic has also led to changes in lifestyle and dietary habits, which can have significant implications for diabetes management. The lockdowns and restrictions on movement and travel have led to reduced physical activity levels and changes in eating patterns, which can result in weight gain, insulin resistance, and poor glycemic control Therefore, this case analysis will provide a comprehensive understanding of the post-COVID changing pattern of diabetes in Mumbai and its impact on diabetes management and care. The study will use both qualitative and quantitative data analysis to identify the challenges faced by healthcare providers and patients, changes in lifestyle and dietary habits, and the effectiveness of the measures taken to manage diabetes during the pandemic. The findings of this case analysis can provide crucial insights into the changing pattern of diabetes in the post-COVID era, and can help healthcare providers and policymakers develop targeted interventions to prevent and manage diabetes during pandemics. The study can also help individuals with diabetes in Mumbai make informed decisions regarding their lifestyle and diabetes management. Lifestyle choices play a significant role in the development of chronic diseases such as diabetes. According to the World Health Organization, diabetes is a leading cause of death and disability worldwide, and the number of people living with diabetes is expected to rise to 4.9 million by 2030. The positive aspect is that by making simple lifestyle changes, such as maintaining a healthy diet and exercise routine, individuals can significantly reduce their risk of developing diabetes and other chronic diseases. In this study, we will explore the link between lifestyle and diabetes, and provide practical strategies for managing diabetes through lifestyle changes. By implementing these changes, individuals can take control of their health and improve their overall well-being.

OBJECTIVE

Objectives of the study are as follows:

- To analyze the statistics of diabetes in the globe
- To encourage readers to take control of their health and make positive changes to reduce their risk of developing chronic diseases.
- To provide practical strategies for managing diabetes through lifestyle changes, such as diet and exercise.

To study the link between lifestyle choices and the development of chronic diseases such as diabetes

METHODOLOGY

The research methodology for this study involves a combination of several methods, including Literature review: A thorough review of existing research on the link between lifestyle and diabetes, as well as strategies for managing diabetes through lifestyle changes. Analysis of data from government and health organizations to understand the statistics of diabetes, its impact and its increasing rate.

ANALYSIS

RANGE	INTERPRETATION
99 mg/dL or lower	normal
100 to 125 mg/dL	prediabetes
126 mg/dL or higher	diabetes

REPORTS AND ANALYSIS OF INDIA, MAHARSHTRA, MUMBAI (2019-2021)

(2019-2021)	INDIA	MAHARASHTRA	MUMBAI
WOMEN			
high (141-160 mg/dl)(%)	6.1	5.7	9.2
very high (>160 mg/dl)(%)	6.3	5.4	6.3
high or very high (>140 mg/dl) or taking medicine to control blood sugar level(%)	13.5	12.4	17.5
MEN			
high (141-160 mg/dl)(%)	7.3	6.5	11.4
very high (>160 mg/dl)(%)	7.2	5.9	6.1
high or very high (>140 mg/dl) or taking medicine to control blood sugar level(%)	15.6	13.6	18.2

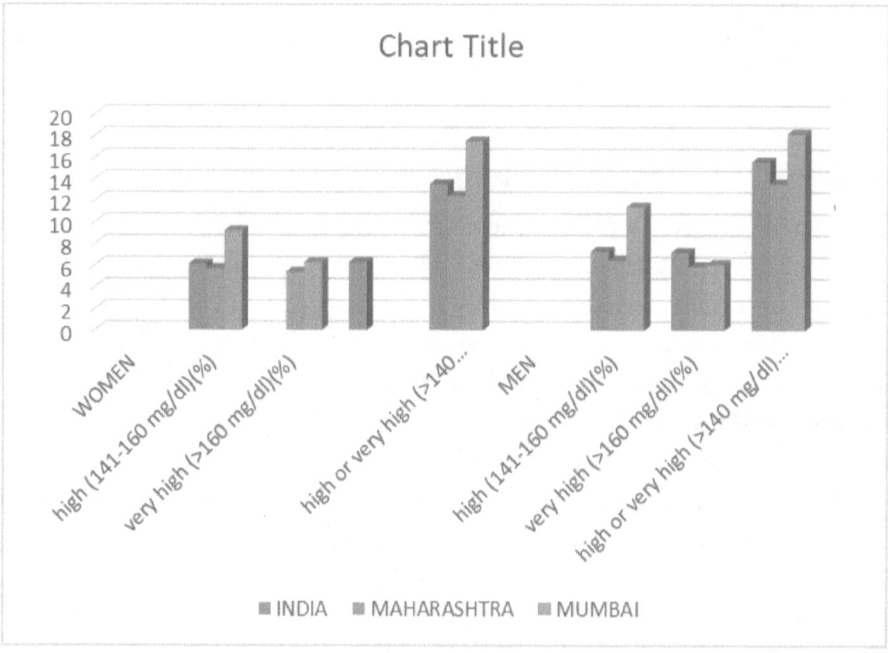

The COVID-19 pandemic highlighted the persistent problem of health disparities for some populations.38 For example, some racial and ethnic minority groups are at higher risk of severe complications from COVID-19 because of higher rates of diabetes, heart disease, and other underlying conditions. Hospitalization rates associated with COVID-19 are highest among American Indian, non-Hispanic Black, and Hispanic populations.

Figure highlights post COVID-19 scenario since the pandemic started. These groups also have higher rates of obesity, which is a primary risk factor for type 2 diabetes. lifestyle has been changes after pandemic covid-19 including a non-disease person along with the diabetic patient having diet control, regular monitoring of glucose.

LITERATURE REVIEW

1. Kimberly McKenzie, Rulla Alsaedi JULY 27 2021

the purpose of this literature review was to identify educational approaches addressing low health literacy for people with type 2 diabetes. Low health literacy can lead to poor management of diabetes, low engagement with health care providers, increased hospitalization rates, and higher health care costs.

These challenges can be even more profound among minority populations and non-English speakers in the United State

2. Manish Kumar Maurya, Rajeev Kumar Varma, Ishwar Chandra chaurasia, Ravikant Vishwakarma,Nitin Yadav JUNE 2019

The type-1 diabetes which is most occurring in children. About 90% of incidence of type-2 diabetes mellitus. It is mainly occurring after the age 40s. In this case insulin secreted but only in low amount and it is co-related of our life style such as overeating, physical activity etc Hyperglycemia, usually a consequence of insulin resistance and pancreatic beta cell failure. The term diabetes mellitus includes several different metabolic disorder. The type 1 diabetes mellitus occurs due to the destroyed the beta cell and thus it does not produce the sufficient amount of insulin to control the blood sugar level. Type [2] diabetes is occurring due to the insulin resistance, life style such as excessive body weight and insufficient exercise. The main goal of diabetes management is, as far as possible, to restore carbohydrate metabolism to normal state. The treatment of diabetes is required insulin replacement therapy, which is given through injection or tablets. Diabetes can be also control by the dietary modification, and exercise metformin play a vital role in the treatment of diabetes which help to lower the production of glucose level. The world-wide incidence of diabetes mostly occurring in United states other than India, Brazil, china

3. Charles AK Yesudian, Mari Grepstad, Alessandra Ferrario 02 December 2014

Diabetes and its complications are a major cause of morbidity and mortality in India, and the prevalence of type 2 diabetes is on the rise. This calls for an assessment of the economic burden of the diseases. The body of literature on the costs of diabetes and its complications in India provides a fragmented picture that has mostly concentrated on the direct costs borne by individuals rather than the healthcare system. There is a need to develop a robust methodology to perform methodologically rigorous and transparent cost of illness studies to inform policy decisions.

CONCLUSION

Increased risk and severity: Studies have indicated that individuals with pre-existing diabetes have a higher risk of severe illness and complications if they contract COVID-19. This includes a greater likelihood of hospitalization, intensive care unit admissions, and mortality.

New-onset diabetes: COVID-19 has been associated with the development of new-onset diabetes in some cases. Researchers have observed cases of transient hyperglycemia during the acute phase of infection, as well as instances of new diabetes diagnoses following recovery from COVID-19. The exact mechanisms behind this phenomenon are not yet fully understood.

Impact on glycemic control: The pandemic has presented unique challenges to individuals with diabetes, including disruptions in access to healthcare services, limited physical activity opportunities, changes in dietary habits, and increased psychological stress. These factors can contribute to suboptimal glycemic control, making it more challenging for people with diabetes to manage their blood sugar levels effectively.

Telemedicine and remote monitoring: To mitigate the risks associated with in-person visits, healthcare providers have increasingly turned to telemedicine and remote monitoring technologies for diabetes management. This shift has allowed for continued patient care, including virtual consultations, remote glucose monitoring, and telehealth education.

Focus on lifestyle interventions: The pandemic has underscored the importance of lifestyle modifications in diabetes management. With increased attention on maintaining overall health and building resilience, individuals with diabetes are encouraged to prioritize regular exercise, healthy eating habits, stress management, and adequate sleep.

Health disparities and vulnerable populations: COVID-19 has highlighted existing health disparities, with certain populations experiencing a disproportionate burden of both the virus and diabetes. This includes racial and ethnic minorities, individuals with low socioeconomic status, and those with limited access to healthcare resources. Addressing these disparities and ensuring equitable care for all remains a critical concern.

In conclusion, the COVID-19 pandemic has influenced the patterns of diabetes in several ways, from increased risks and new-onset cases to challenges in glycemic control and changes in healthcare delivery. Moving forward, ongoing research, public health interventions, and individual efforts are crucial to understanding and effectively managing diabetes in the post-COVID-19 era.

REFERENCE

National family heahttp://rchiips.org

http://www.who.int/en/news-room/fact-sheets/detail/the-top-10-causes-of-death

https://www.nmanet.org

Sugar Industry in the State of Maharashtra

CHAPTER 18

Author – Shubhangi Patil, Student & Prof. Beena Narayan (Economics), Professor, IES's Management College and Research Centre, Mumbai

ABSTRACT

Maharashtra sugar industry is one of the most notable and large scale sugar manufacturing sector in the country. The Maharashtra sugar industry has been contributing nearly 40% of India's, total sugar production. The pace of growth of sugar manufacturing has been massive over the past few years. The latest sugar statistics of sugar production in Maharashtra indicates that this state is doing better than the other states in the country. The sugar industry in Maharashtra is highly popular in the co-operative sector, as farmers own a portion in the sugar factories. These co-operative sugar factories are backbone of the sugar industry of Maharashtra. The Maharashtra sugar industry has been a spectacular growth owing to the different conductive in the state. One of the chief crops manufactured in Maharashtra is sugarcane with most of sugar industries been setup over the years.

KEYWORDS

Sugar Industry, Farmers, Economy of Maharashtra, National Federation Co-Operative Sugar Factories Ltd. (NFCSF)

REVIEW OF LITERATURE

Hussain et al reported that to analyze the agricultural land use pattern at micro level in Kolhapur District. This study is based on secondary data collected from secondary records. Agriculture production is influenced by physical, climatological, socio-economic, technological and organization factors. This is normal year for agriculture phenomenon in this district. The crop data has been computed with the help of Weaver's technique of crop combination. Sugarcane is one of the most important commercial crops is being grown in an area of around 3.06 lakhs hectare in Tamilnadu with a productivity of 106 Mt ha-1. Farmers cultivating sugarcane are facing multiple problems. Water is one of the major constraints and it is affecting the productivity and profitability of sugarcane growers and millers. The problem is going to further deteriorate due to variability of rainfall influenced by climate change. So, unless sugarcane farmers are provided with options of high yields with much less water, they will find it difficult to meet its growing demand for sugar.

INTRODUCTION

Sugar Industry in India is well maintained and is growing at a steady pace, boasting of a consumer base of over billions of people. The sugar industry is the 2nd largest agricultural industry followed after the textile industry. Maharashtra Sugar Industry is one of the most notable and large-scale sugar manufacturing sector in the country. The pace of growth of sugar manufacturing has been massive over the past few years. The largest statistics of sugar production in Maharashtra indicates that this state is doing better than the other states in the country. The Sugar Industry in Maharashtra is highly popular in the cooperative sector, as farmers own a portion in sugar factories. The Maharashtra Sugar Industry has seen a spectacular growth owing to the different conductive in the state. One of the chief crops manufactured in Maharashtra is sugarcane, with a host of sugar industries been set up over the years.

OBJECTIVES

Researcher has conducted research work on the basis of set of objectives for knowing the growth and development of sugarcane industries and their ancillaries. It will also emphasis on the production of sugar in the state of Maharashtra, also research will more speak about how it is affecting the Economy of Maharashtra. The research will be focusing on the subject of sugar cane Industries affecting the farmers of Marathwada. Also will speak about the reason that the sugarcane Industries is on the verge of extinction and the over production in the State of Maharashtra. To examine the financial position of the co-operative sugar factories and it's departments of by-products. To study the functional areas like production, marketing, finance and human resource of by-products production in the sample units. To draw conclusion and suggest appropriate suggestion, if necessary.

RESEARCH METHODOLOGY

The concern study is based on secondary data. The data has been collected through journals, magazines, articles published in various types of conference proceeding, ph.d thesis, websites, Maharashtra Rajya Sahakari Sakhar Karkhana Sangh, report of National Federation Co-operative Sugar Factories Ltd. (NFCSF). The interpretation and analysis of data will be based on statistical tools and techniques.

OVERVIEW OF MAHARASHTRA

Maharashtra ranks second in the list of largest sugarcane producing state in India in 2021-22 which accounts for more than one third of the country's sugar production. Maharashtra has been pioneering state with respect of setting up co-operative sugar factory and the first such factory was set up in 1948. The successful establishment and operation of this factory initiated a trend in co-operative development with rapid multiplication of co-operative factory in the state. Based on joint consideration of sugar recovery, yield and different cultural practices adopted to suit the environmental conditions the areas can be grouped into distinct zones.

The Maharashtra Sugar industry has been contributing nearly 40% of India's total sugar production. In 2001-02, sugar industry in Maharashtra produced an approximate 138 lakh tonns of sugar, the per ton price touching Rs 290 with innovative technologies being implemented in the Maharashtra Sugar industry, the potential can be fully realized. The total sugar production of the state last year (2020-2021) was 106.40 lakh tonnes.This year (2021-22) nine additional sugar mills (199) were involved in the process. 190 was the previous year sugar mills.

LIMITATIONS OF THE STUDY

The main factor affecting the sugar production is the availability of raw material i.e sugarcane for crushing. And another main factor is the increased diversion of sugar for ethanol production. Production of sugarcane and sugar in the country has shown wide fluctuations from year to year. These fluctuations are due to variations in the area under sugarcane, mainly sugarcane production depends on pattern of rainfall, incidence of disease and pests on crop, availability of seeds material, irrigation facility and availability of fertilizer as per recommendation, climatic condition, water availability during the crop growth period and most important government policy on sugarcane grown.

There are some features of technical performance such as duration of season, crushing capacity and it's utilization, lost hour percentage to availability hours, cane quality, fiber, purity, sugar recovery, milling performance, biogas, reduced mill extraction, boiling house efficiency, total sugar losses, consumption of chemicals.

Finding of the study

Distribution

DISTRICT WISE SUGAR CONTRIBUTION % IN TOTAL SUGAR PRODUCTION OF MAHARASHTRA

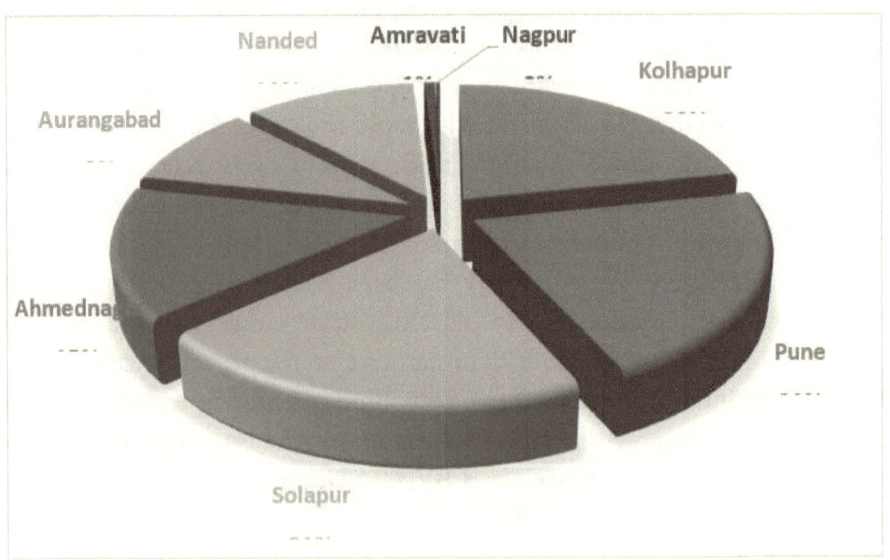

Some of the towns of Maharashtra which have sugar factories :

Navapura, Nityanandnagar, kurunda, Mohagaon, Sipora, Varud, pimpalgaon, Sonawade, khuldabad, halgaon, Indapur, Karandwadi, Mankeshwar, Pawarwadi, kadepur, Devdaithan, Sujatapur, Sheshnagar, Radhanagri, patoda.

Kolhapur is the leading district in the production of sugar in Maharashtra with 30.04% followed by pune (29.12%) Solapur (28.43%) Ahmednagar (20.07%) Aurangabad (12.92%) Nanded (15.32%) Amravati (

0.96 %) and Nagpur (0.38%). The distribution is ranged across the State of Maharashtra.

CONCLUSION

It can be concluded that south and central Maharashtra has adequate irrigation facilities and other complementary inputs therefore maximum sugar factories are located in this area whereas Marathwada, Vidarbha and Khandesh followed suit, lack of irrigation facilities, despite the fact that they are not gifted with the necessary factor endowments so that these are facing financial problems as compare to south and central Maharashtra. Lower yield of sugarcane per acre due to erratic monsoon and more diversion of sugar for ethanol production cut sugar production.

In 2021-22 around 200 sugar mills were involved in crushing sugarcane across the State with the crushing capacity of 8 lakh tonnes a day, these mills crushed 1320.31 lakh tonnes of sugarcane. Last year (2020- 21) this figure stood at 1013.64 lakh tonnes. So this year, the mills crushed nearly 306.67 lakh tonnes more sugarcane than previous year.

The crushing season of Maharashtra lasted longer in 2021-22 i.e the sugarcane crushing season which used to be around 90-120 days, went upto 240 days in some parts of the state this year. The average crushing season went upto 173 days, which was140 the previous year.

From the study of sugar production in Maharashtra we got following data:

Total sugar mills in operation 200 (101- cooperative & 99 private) Total daily crushing capacity 801300 MT.

Total cane crushed 1320.31 LMT (Lakh Metric tonnes) Total sugar produced 137.28 LMT.

In order to utilize it's capacity fully and run efficiently, the sugar mills within the industry should get uninterrupted supply of raw sugar cane uniformly throughout the seasons and government should ensure the supply of raw inputs. There is a need of coordinated and concerted effort for appreciation and consolidation of the needs of the consumer. There is an urgent need to improve in productivity both in terms of yield as well as sugar contents and recovery by adopting better harvesting practices and close coordination of sugar mills with farmers.

REFERENCES

1. https://m.economictimes.com/news/economy/agriculture/sugar-production-of-maharashtra
2. https://m.economictimes.com/news/economy/agriculture/at-137-lakh-tonnes-maharashtra
3. www.business.mapsofindia.com
4. WWW.Wikipedia.org
5. WWW.livemint.com

A Comparative Study on Electric Scooter and the Traditional Scooters in Mumbai Suburban Region

Author – Khushi Vijan, Drishti Joshi, Bhumi Gori, Student & Prof. Falguni Mathews, Assistant Professor, SIES College of Commerce and Economics, Mumbai

ABSTRACT

This abstract understands the slow rising demand of E scooters in contrast to traditional (normal) scooters in the Suburban region of Mumbai which is understood in terms of pricing, economical cost, impact on environment, charging facilities and sustainability. The issue of Electric scooter arises on its maintenance options and charging limitations. This paper gets us an overview of what consumers think about its performance and durability in the long run as compared to an traditional scooter and also to comprehend the response on the burn down of Electric scooters and thus to get a grasp of consumers whether they find it as a future threat or not. This analysis will help us find out whether Electric scooters are entirely fool proof replacements to Traditional scooters. Although, the problems arising are capable of being reconciled over a period of time. To know the insights of consumers on both the types of scooters a research was conducted by primary method of data collection through Google forms. The questioning done was on the basis of its durability, environmental impact, performance, appearance, the retail price.

The implication of the study reveals that consumers in case of buying an electric scooter will have to bear a high initial cost, they find it less reliable due to its charging facility, repair charges, and the taxes levied on it. Inspire of, all these limitations a majority of people are content with the fact that Electric scooters are an incredible alternative to traditional scooters due to zero emissions and also on the fact of use of renewable energy.

KEYWORDS

Electric – Scooter, Traditional scooter, Environment, Batteries, Charging Facility, Performance.

INTRODUCTION

Scooters are one of the most preferred types of vehicles among the residents of Mumbai. There are various factors involved for the huge popularity of scooters within the suburban areas of Mumbai which amounts to over 39 lakh users of two wheeled vehicles. With the stressing concerns of climate change with increasing CO_2 (carbon dioxide) emission by the traditional vehicles using combustible engines (petrol, diesel and CNG) electric scooters have proved themselves as great alternatives. Even though the basic structure of these 2 types of mobiles is similar, the differentiation can be made through the environmental effects, economic sustainability and consumer behaviour. This paper also observes the reluctance of people in Mumbai towards adopting Electric scooters over traditional scooters.

E-Vehicles have been very popular in past few years with rising fuel price many people are switching to more eco-friendly option over past 3 years there was 1,360% rise in sale of EVs in Mumbai. Even with that rise in number of sales, people are still hesitant to buy E-Scooters; one of the major drawbacks of electric scooter is the initial cost of buying. One of the top selling inexpensive E-Scooter Okinawa Praise Pro retails at Rs. 84,000 with over 10,000 units sold whereas one of the latest big budget traditional scooter Honda Active 6G trades at Rest. 90,000. It is difficult to adopt this futuristic technology since many areas in Mumbai suburban region experience heavy electricity cut-offs. No proper charging stations infrastructure has proved to be hurdle in way of acceptance of electric scooter on roads of Mumbai.

REVIEW OF LITERATURE

The literature is based on 2 search engines (Research Gate, Google Scholar) to find few different papers on the research topic. To find the following papers words such as electric scooters, electric vehicles were used.

While electric scooters are not the most driven vehicle on the roads of India, Sandeep Singh et al. (Singh) concluded in there study of electric scooter in Tiruchirappalli city that electronic vehicles can be used by large population in rural and urban regions by introducing new low cost E-Scooters, less of operating cost, skilled technicians, better charging infrastructure. All these add-ons can help in popularization of electric scooter.

Roche et al. (roche, 2010)measured the negative impact on individual preferences after the real-life experience with electric vehicles through stated choices as there was long panel survey conducted to measure attitudinal effects of before and after using of electric vehicle.

Putri et al (Putri, 2021) analysed various methods to raise consumer intention to an electric vehicle and made its customer familiar with it. They also initiated programmes about electric vehicles. They launched long term development programmes to reach many clients with correct object served to them so that it can built a good perception among the electric scooter buyers.

India accounts for 18% of the carbon emissions which can be controlled by using an environment friendly alternative like electric vehicle. Using electric vehicles is good for the environment and country as it helps reduce pollution. Masurali et al. (Masurali A., 2018) concluded that the government should create measures to make people aware of such a vehicle which is effective for the environment.

Pritam K. (Pritam K. Gujarathi, 2018)concludes that with increasing carbon emission there is need to search and find out obstacles in way of more sustainable and cleaner alternatives to fossil fuel using vehicles as most vehicles in India still rely on petrol, diesel etc.

OBJECTIVES OF THE RESEARCH

- To study attitude of people towards electric scooters.
- To analyse if electric scooters are considered as an eco-friendly alternative with respect to traditional scooters (petrol, diesel, CNG).
- To conduct a detailed comparison of electric scooters and traditional scooters.

STATEMENT OF PROBLEM

The present specifications of an electric scooter are useful to the potential users but also has some faults in it. The electric scooter launched in India has faced many burndowns in its past this was due the charging difficulties, inefficiency in its system, high tax levied, high maintenance cost, lack of skilled labour, and other such reasons. The purpose of this research is to find those reasons, understand the market situation and know the comparison with the traditional scooters.

RESEARCH METHODOLOGY

The present study is conducted is based on the primary and secondary data. The primary data is collected from the Google form which was circulated to the reviewers. This form had close ended questions. The secondary data was collected from, newspaper, research paper and online articles.

The data obtained for the study is also collected from internet, websites, electric scooters company's website, and with help of other research papers related to electric vehicles. The qualitative data and analysis were achieved from websites which had shown detailed Bar graph study.

LIMITATIONS

The main focused limitation faced by the electric scooter is the lack of charging options available as most of them can be charged in conventional outlets but for a full charge 7-10 hours are required. The fast-charging option is not available yet.

SCOPE OF STUDY

The scope of study of this research paper includes the charging facility of E scooter, rates, eco friendly alternative, appearance, attitude of people towards Electric scooter, and shows a detailed comparision with Traditional scooters. This study was conducted through a questionnaire. 39 responses were collected in total.

DATA ANALYSIS AND INTERPRETATION

To know in-depth perception of people towards electric scooter a Google form was circulated among friends, classmates and relatives about the following topics to gain their insights towards electric scooter as compared to traditional scooters. The age group covered was from 18-25, 26-35, 36-45, 46-55 years.

Preference- The preference here is more on the side of traditional scooter which is because of the simple reason that most of them already own one

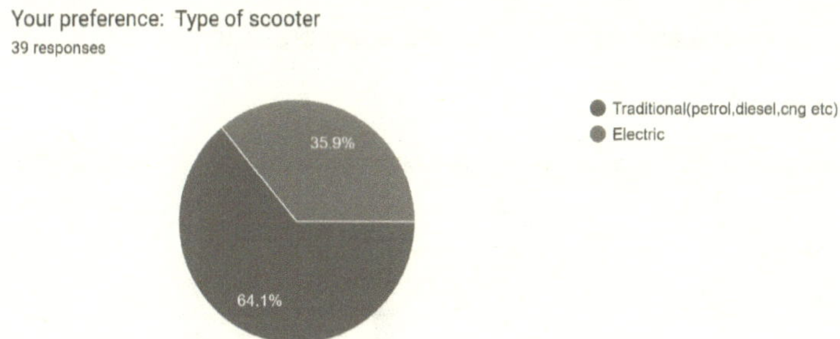

Impact on environment- The data informs that around 64% of people find electric scooter environment friendly and the other 28% people are still left in a dilemma. According, to the reports published by the Office of Energy Efficiency and Renewable Energy of United States Department of Energy which says electric scooter has a conversion efficiency of 85%-90% which contributes greater to environment.

Interpretation: Here, it can be interpreted that majority of sample population has voted to Traditional scooter which might be because of the fact that traditional scoters are more known and cheaper as compared to Electric scooter.

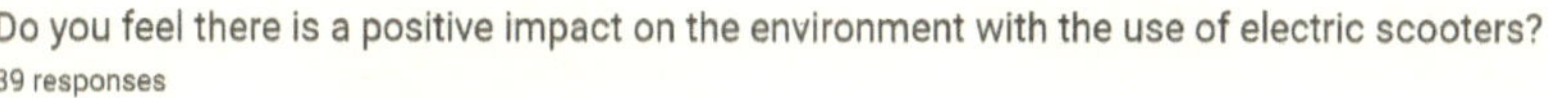

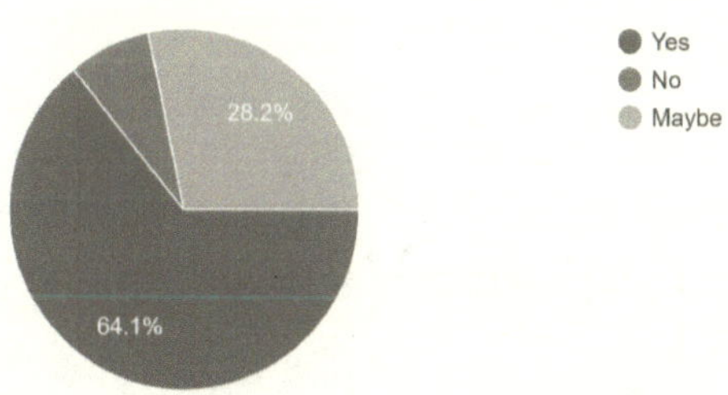

Interpretation: Here, the majority of population believes that Electric scooters are more environment friendly as using them they do not pollute the air during a ride because of their rechargeable battery, which means zero emissions. E- Scooters also prove to reduce noise pollution in cities.

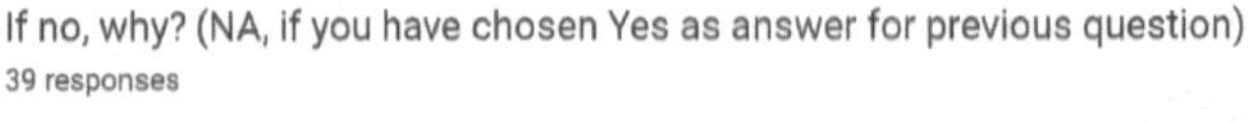

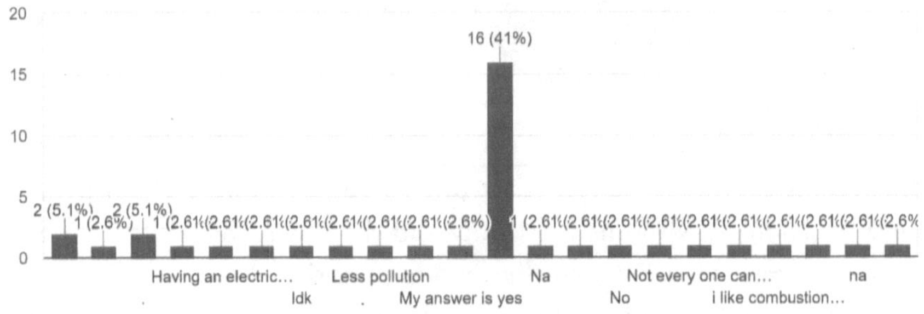

Do you feel it is expensive to own an electric scooter as compared to a traditional scooter?
39 responses

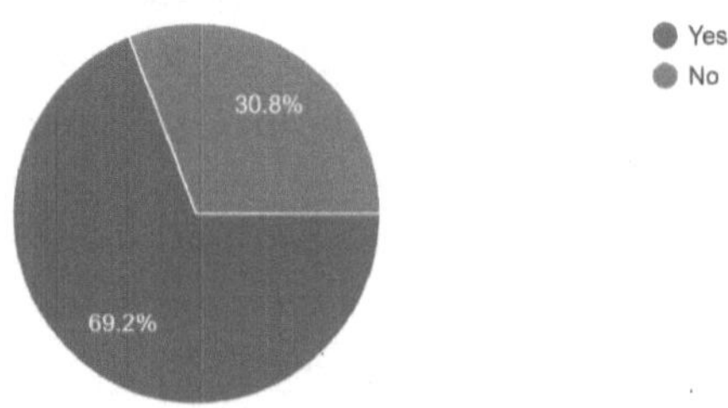

Interpretation: The electric scooter has outperformed the number for its appearance as many of the users and public in general have liked it. Along with this its users have claimed a high number for its comfort to ride the e- scooter.

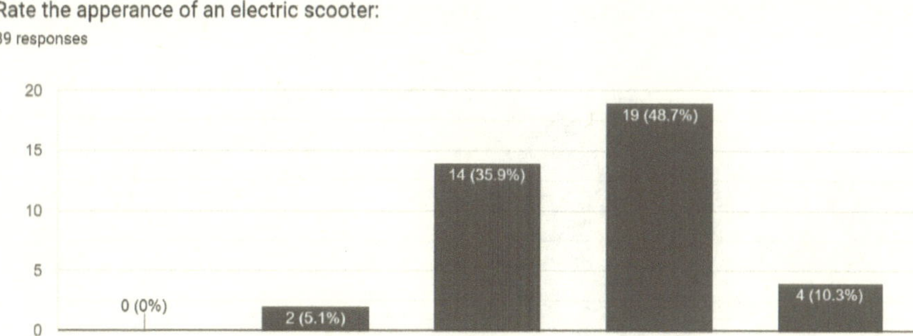

Interpretation - The people in the analysis agree with its inconvenient charging facility. As per a published report in Brazil the users exchanged the discharged battery with a charged battery as the charging can take up to 7-10 hours.

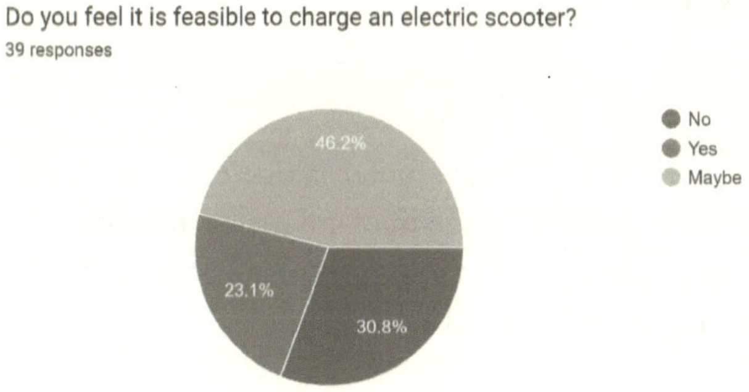

Interpretation - The analysis tells us that around 77% of people are aware of the burn down of electric scooter which may create a sense of fear among the masses that same could happen to their scooter as well. Hence, the use of a traditional scooter is much preferred.

Are you aware about the recent burn down of the Ola Scooters?
39 responses

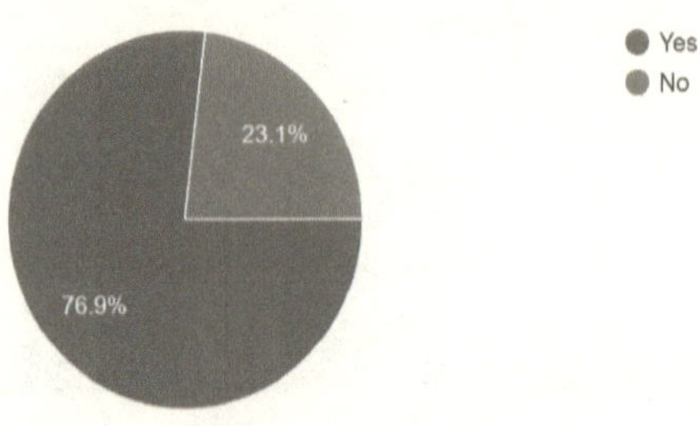

Are you afraid that something like this could happen to your scooter?
39 responses

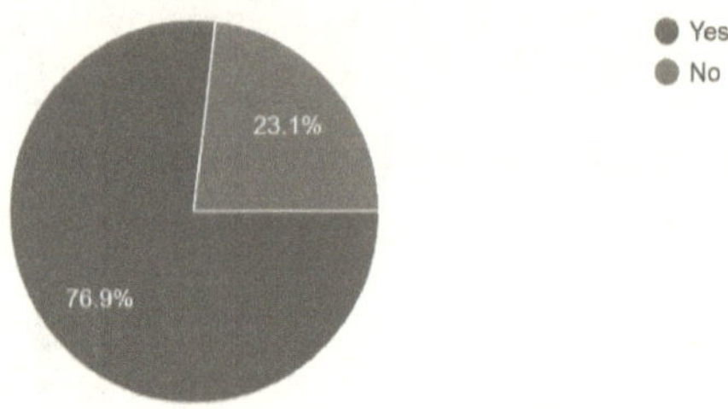

Interpretation: The burndown of Electric scooter is due to main reason of battery and charging facility whereas sometimes might be because of the simple reason of the functioning parts of the scooter. Many burndown cases faced were because of unmonitored overnight charging.

SUGGESTIONS & RECOMMENDATIONS

a. First, we can start with the charging station of an electronic vehicle (EV). Easy access to charging stations will defiantly make people switch to electric scooters.
b. Government should try focusing on the awareness of electric scooters by giving articles, sessions, subsidizing electric scooters.
c. There is also harmful waste that is produced by batteries used batteries that are harmful; it needs to find an alternative for the harmful waste.

d. In electric scooters, there are chances of getting malfunctioned or frauds. Government should be careful and introduce new policies protect the consumers assuring them of new this new technology.
e. Government should adopt various new strategies to popularize and increase the sales of electronic scooter.

CONCLUSION

Looking at the responses we got from the google forms we can say that one of many reasons people prefer electric scooters is the sustainability it promises. Even though people still prefer to continue using the traditional scooters the hesitation arises because of the high initial cost of the electric scooter. People also find the appearance of electric scooters attractive and believe it is comfortable to drive. More than 76.9% people are aware of the recent burndowns of the Ola Scooters. Due to the expensive pricing of the electric scooters, people still find the traditional Scooters to be the best. From the responses we can say that 64.1% people feel that there is a positive impact in the environment with the age of electric scooter. Thus, at the end we can conclude that electric scooter is great environment friendly option to traditional scooters, there should be subsides provided by the government to manufactures to cut down cost of the vehicle so that an average consumer can be able to afford it.

BIBLIOGRAPHY

Masurali A., S. P. (2018). *Perception and Awarness level of Potential Customers towards Electric Cars.* INTERNATIONAL JOURNAL FOR RESEARCH IN APPLIED SCIENCE AND ENGINEERING TECHNOLOGY.

Pritam K. Gujarathi, V. A. (2018). *Electric Vehicles in India: Market Analysis with Consumer Perspective,.* Surat: River Publishers.

Putri, B. &. (2021). *Factors Affecting E-Scooter Sharing Purchase Intention: An Analysis Using Unified Theory of Acceptance and Use of Technology 2.* International Journal of Creative Business and Management.

roche, M. M. (2010). *Public attitude towards demand for hydrogen fuel cell vehicles: a review of the evidence and methodological implications.*

Singh, S. (n.d.). *Investigating the Characteristics and Choice of Electric Scooter Users.* Tiruchirappalli .

https://gemopai.com/blog/electric-scooter-vs-petrol-scooter-which-is-the-future-choice-of-scooters#:~:text=It%20is%20more%20economical%20to,which%20is%200.25%20rs%2Fkm

https://www.businessinsider.in/business/auto/news/best-selling-electric-scooters-in-india/slidelist/93948816.cms

https://www.bikewale.com/honda-bikes/activa-6g/#:~:text=Honda%20Activa%206G%20is%20a,a%20torque%20of%208.79%20Nm

https://www.bikewale.com/best-scooters-in-india/#:~:text=Honda%20Activa%206G%2C%20Suzuki%20Access,in%20the%20two%20wheeler%20market

https://www.bikewale.com/okinawa-bikes/praise/

Money Market:- A Publication on Indian Money Market

CHAPTER 20

Author – Gayatri Singh, Student, IES's Management College and Research Centre, Mumbai IES's Management College and Research Centre, Mumbai

ABSTRACT

In India, the development of the economy is greatly influenced by the money market. However, in contrast to the American and London money markets, it is not very developed. In this market, players who are approved by the RBI borrow and lend short-term funds to one another.

Institutions with surplus cash are guaranteed to receive a certain return thanks to the money market. If not, the institutions will have these funds sitting idle. Similar to this, the money market guarantees funds for the poor at fair interest rates. Money market operations ensure liquidity position in this way.

Now let's talk about the different money market instruments used in India. The RBI oversees the money market in India. As a result, both the trading instruments and the market participants need RBI approval.

Long-standing institutions in India provide foreign investors with a transparent setting that ensures the security of their long-term investments. These include a free and active press, a court system that has the power to overrule the executive branch and actually does so, an advanced legal and accounting system, and an accessible intellectual infrastructure. India's vibrant and fiercely competitive private sector has long served as the engine driving its economy. It generates more than 75% of its GDP and has a large opportunity for partnerships and joint ventures.

India is currently one of the most attractive emerging financial markets worldwide. India has a strong competitive advantage in the global marketplace thanks to skilled managerial and technical labour that is on par with the best in the world and a middle class that is larger than either the United States or the European Union in terms of population.

Over 40,000 crores of rupees are traded on average each day in the Indian money market. This amounts to 6% of the overall amount of money that commercial banks have disbursed to the system and more than 3% of the total amount of money in circulation in the Indian economy. This suggests that in only one day, the money market trades 2% of India's annual GDP.

INTRODUCTION

A financial system's money market is a crucial component. In the money market, short-term financial assets and financial assets that are close replacements for money are traded. The characteristics of money market instruments include liquidity (rapid conversion into money), low transaction costs, and no decrease in worth. The money market is used to deploy surplus funds, which are then used to cover short-term cash needs and other obligations. Short-term fund providers and consumers can access the money market to meet their borrowing and investing needs, respectively, at a competitive market clearing price. It plays a critical function in supplying an equilibrating mechanism to balance out short-term liquidity, surpluses, and deficits, and in the process, it makes it easier to implement monetary policy. One of the main ways the Central Bank affects liquidity and the general level of interest rates in an economy is through the money market. The Bank's interventions to affect liquidity act as a signalling tool for other financial system components. The money market serves as a wholesale debt market for very liquid, short-term products with no risk.

In this market, funds are offered for terms ranging from one day to one year. This market is dominated mostly by the government, banks, and financial organisations. Short-term fund management is done on a formal financial market. Although there are a few different categories of players on the money market, each type's role and degree of participation vary significantly.

Government has a significant role in most economies and the money market, where it is the largest borrower. Both Treasury bills and Government securities (G-secs) are securities that the Reserve Bank of India (RBI) issues on behalf of the Government of India in order to finance that government's borrowing needs. The Central Bank (RBI), in addition to serving as the government's banker, controls the money market and provides rules governing its activities.

The banking sector is another important participant in the money market. Banks use savers' savings to fund loans to investors in the economy. Credit creation is the name given to this procedure. Banks are not permitted to lend the full amount when giving loans for investments, nevertheless. Most industrialised economies require all commercial banks to maintain minimum liquid and cash reserves in the form of Statutory Liquidity Ratio (SLR) and Cash Reserve Ratio (CRR) defined under the policies of Central Banks in order to encourage specific prudential rules for good banking activities. Before allocating deposits towards their credit plans, the banks are obligated to make sure that these reserve criteria are satisfied. Banks may use the money market to raise the shortfall amount if they fall short of the statutory reserve requirements.

To meet their various shortfalls and deficits in short-term financing, other institutional actors including financial institutions, corporations, mutual funds (MFs), foreign institutional investors (FIIs), etc. also engage in money market transactions.

However, the extent of these parties' involvement is mostly determined by the rules set forth by the governing bodies of an economy. For instance, FII involvement in the Indian money market is limited to government securities investment exclusively.

FEATURES OF MONEY MARKET

The money market is a wholesale market with daily settlements and very high transaction volumes. Trading in the money market is done over the phone, with written confirmation coming from the borrowers and lenders in the form of emails and messages. Commercial banks, mutual funds, investment institutions, financial institutions, and lastly the Reserve Bank of India are just a few of the numerous players in the money market. Through its operations, the bank makes sure that short-term interest rates and liquidity are kept at levels that support the goal of preserving price and exchange rate stability. In the money market, the Central Bank holds a vital position. The money market has two ways to get money from the central bank: by borrowing or by selling securities. By controlling access to its facilities and through open market operations, REPO transactions, changes in bank rate, and cash reserve requirements, the bank can affect liquidity and interest rates. An efficient implementation of monetary policy depends on a healthy money market. It provides:

1. A balancing mechanism for short-term surpluses and deficiencies.
2. A focal point of Central Bank intervention for influencing liquidity in the economy, and
3. A reasonable access to the users of short-term funds to meet their requirements at realistic/reasonable price or cost.

GROWTH OF MONEY MARKET

The Indian money markets have experienced phenomenal growth in the years after reforms. The increasing demands of major sectors including the economy, services, and agriculture for short-term funding have been met by banks and other financial institutions. The Indian money markets, which are governed and overseen by the Reserve Bank of India (RBI), have over time also demonstrated the necessary maturity and resiliency. The organization and structure of the money market has undergone a sea change in the last decade in India. This was accompanied by a growth in quantitative terms also.

Up to 1987, the money market consist of 6 facts

1. Call Money Market;
2. Inter Bank Term Deposit/Loan Market;
3. Participation Certificate Market;
4. Commercial Bills Market;
5. Treasury Bills Market;
6. Inter-corporate Market

The market had 3 main deficiencies:

1. It had a very small basis, with just the RBI, Banks, LIC, and UTI giving money to the many borrowers.
2. There were very few money market products.
3. The Indian Banks Association, RBI, or a voluntary agreement between the parties controlled the interest rates, which were not market-determined (IBA).

LIMITATION OF THE STUDY

1- It is not possible to capture the whole market.

2- Scope is very limited

STUDY OBJECTIVES

1- To study about Indian money market and its related aspects like types and the instruments.

2- To study about participants and organizational structure of Indian money market.

3- To find out the investors saving preferences.

LITERATURE REVIEW

1- Money Market Integration in India: A Time Series, by Rastogi Nikhil, 2008 Study claims that despite being heavily regulated prior to deregulation, Indian financial markets had made significant progress. He implies that achieving efficiency, which is the hallmark of any established financial market, is the key goal. This study examines the effectiveness and degree of financial market integration seen at the low end of the market.

2- The Narasimham Committee II (1998) agreed with the Vaghul Committee's view that the call/notice/term money market in India, like in most other developed markets, should be exclusively limited to banks in its articles on the call/money/term money market.

3- Market efficiency and financial market integration in India were explored by Rusty Sadananda and colleagues in their work between March 2006 and March 2012 using time series methods. They looked at how economic changes affected the integration of different financial market segments.

RESEARCH METHODOLOGY

Data Collection: Data for the study was collected from the primary as well as secondary sources.

PRIMARY SOURCE OF DATA COLLECTION: -

The survey approach was used as the primary data collection method. The survey data was gathered using a Structured Questionnaire. The questionnaire was created with the study's objectives and elements in mind. The questionnaire was designed in such a way that it could be simply comprehended by the respondents. To minimise responders' time, the questionnaire was designed in a single format.

SECONDARY SOURCE OF DATA COLLECTION :-

Secondary data is gathered from selected websites as well as online publications by some scholars. Secondary data was relevant for the Review of Literature investigation. We were able to investigate various parts of numerous researchers, which provided us an idea about the factors previously described as well as the conclusions derived from them. It also gave us an idea of what else could be researched to tackle the research challenge.

RESPONSES

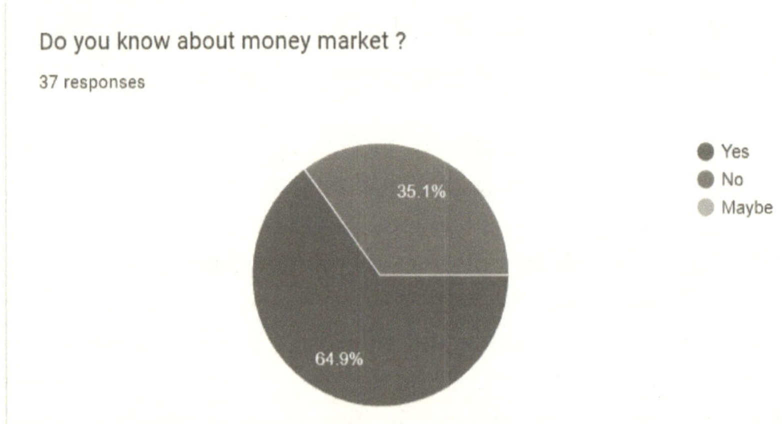

From the above data, 64.9% of respondents know about money market and 35.1% don't know about it. We can say that a good number of population is aware about money market.

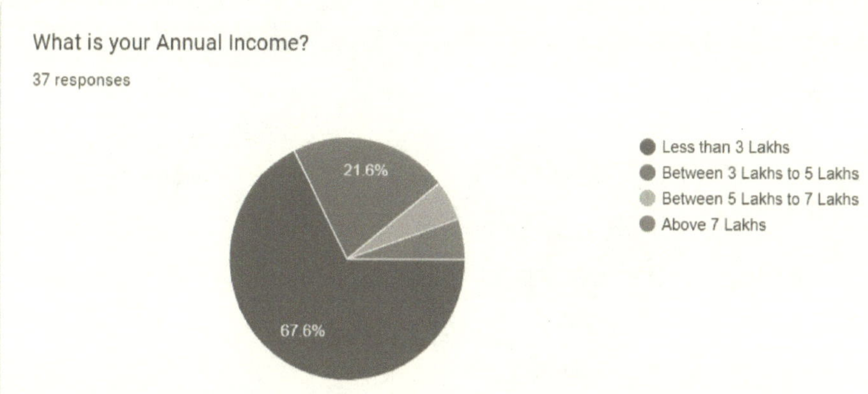

From the above data we can see that 67.6% respondents have the annual income of less than 3 lakhs, 21.6% respondents have the income between 3 lakhs to 5 lakhs, 5.4% respondents have annual income between 5 lakhs to 7 lakhs and 5.4% respondents have the annual income above 7 lakhs.

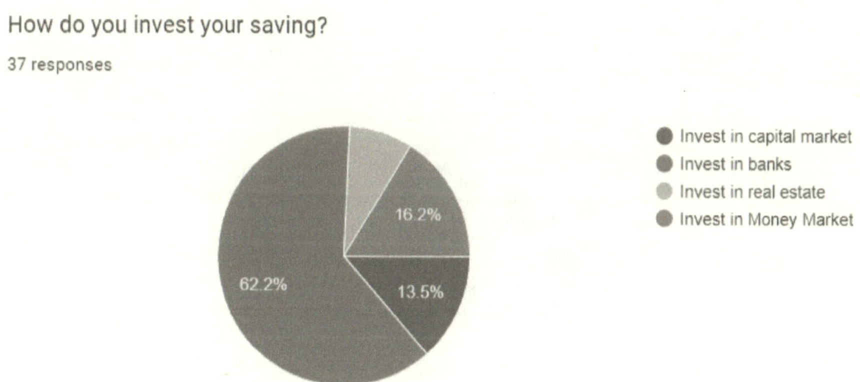

From the above data we see that 62.2% respondents invest in banks, 16.2% invest in money market, 13.5% invest in capital market and 8.1% respondents invest in real estate.

How long do you like to hold your money market Instruments?

37 responses

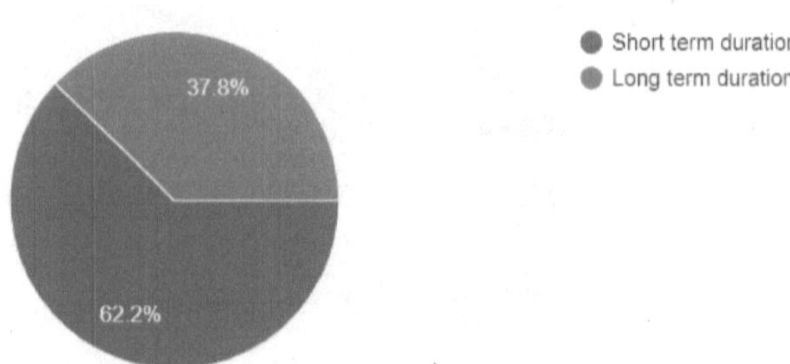

From the above data we can see that 62.2% respondents hold the money market instrument for short term duration and 37.8% respondents hold for long term duration.

For fixed income what type of investment would you prefer?

37 responses

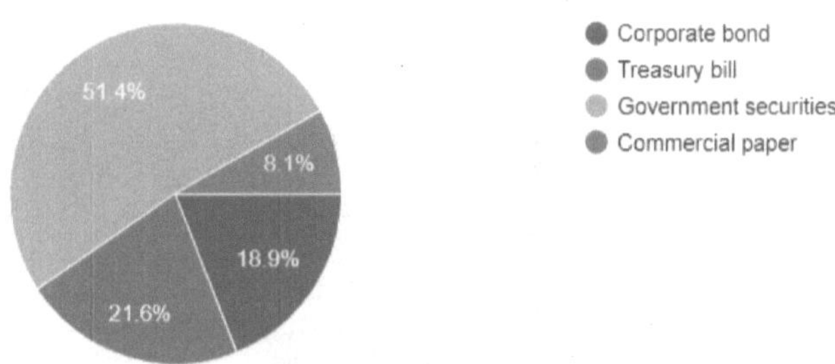

From the above data we see that 51.4% respondents invest in government securities, 21.6% invest in treasury bill, 18.9% corporate bond and 8.1% invest in commercial Paper. We can clearly see that majority of population prefer investing in government Securities.

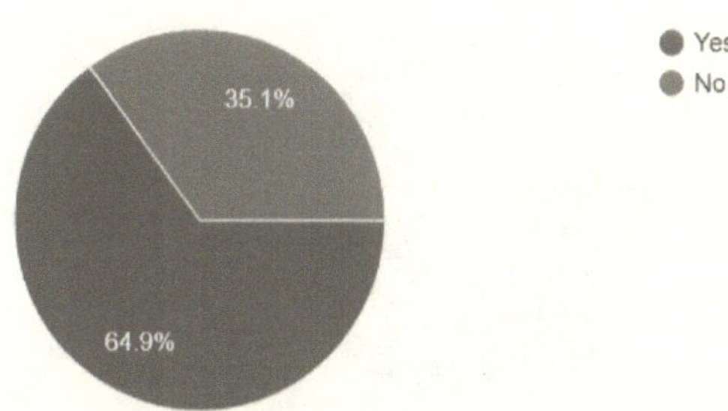

From the above data we can see that 64.9% respondents have been affected by recession for their investment decisions whereas 35.1% respondents are not affected by it.

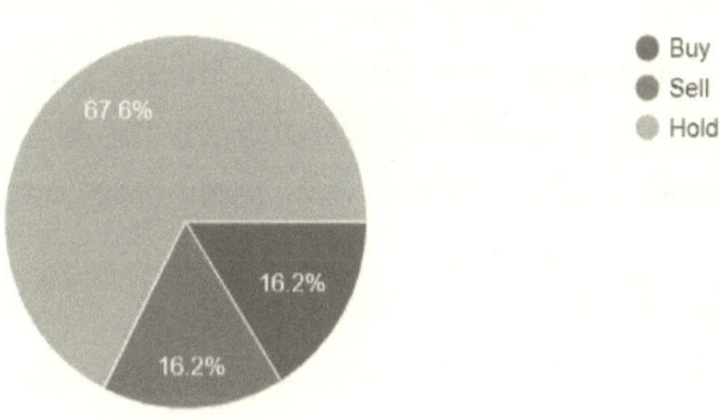

From the above data we have found out that during recession 67.6% respondents prefer holding the instrument, 16.2% prefer selling it and 16.2% prefer buying it. Which means that majority of population is towards holding the instrument during recession.

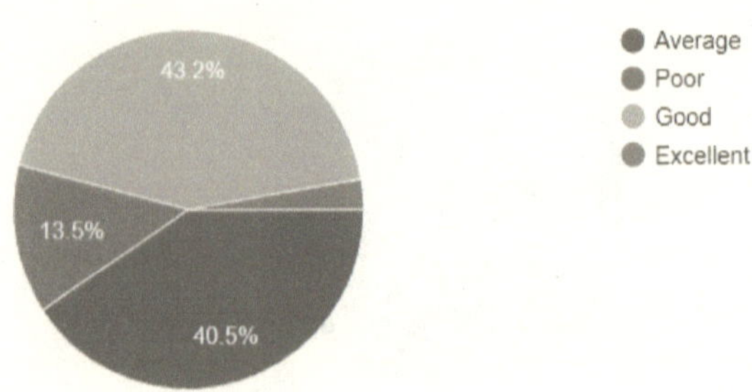

From the above data we see that 13.5% respondents have had poor experience with the Indian money market, 40.5% have average experience, 43.2% have good experience and 2.7% have rated excellent experience with the Indian money market.

FINDINGS

1) Is past price affect the present price?

- - Prices may fluctuate as a result of shifting economic conditions or shifting consumer demand. Prices may go up or down in response to shifting demand, or they may stay the same despite shifting demand.

2) Is there any change in economic growth?

- - Yes, the state of the economy can vary since, as stated above, it tends to affect prices. As a result, there may be positive, negative, or no change in the rate of economic expansion.
- - Recession may have positive or negative impact on economy

3) How can one manage the short-term deficit?

- - One can overcome the short-term deficit by managing the funds
- - Managing the funds means there can be issue of money market securities

4) Does recession tend to liquidate the money market instruments?

- \- In response to the aforementioned query, an investor during a recession may sell their stock, buy the instrument, or take no action (hold).
- \- Recession have an impact on the liquidity.

5) Is there a risk in money market instruments?

- \- As they are for a shorter length of time, i.e., money market instruments are considered low risk or no risk products in the market (a year or less than one year). Its market offers low- or no-risk instruments.
- \- The instrument is divided in various risk categories elevated risk, minimal risk, or no risk instruments.

SUGGESTION

Few suggestions relevant to the development of money market in India are enumerated below:

> To eliminate ambiguity and provide bankers confidence when lending or borrowing, there should be a way to make the call range bound. In this regard, it is stressed that RBI's repos and reverse repos could determine the call money market's floor and ceiling.

Additionally, Open Market Operation must be added to the Repo mechanism and call money market (OMO). OMO has the potential to affect both market volumes and interest rates.

In order to create a level playing field, the non-bank component should be subject to the same regulation as the banks as soon as practicable.

Money market transactions should be transparent. For any money market product, screen-based trading with two-way quotes is required.

The CD and CP lock-in period should be totally eliminated in stages.

Government paper retailing ought to be promoted. In this situation, the major dealers may be involved.

FIIs are currently permitted to purchase government-dated assets in both the primary and secondary markets. The involvement of FIIs could be boosted.

CONCLUSION

Our daily lives are impacted by the money market, which is a thriving business. Money exchanges hands quickly in the short-term market, thus participants must be aware of changes, current on news, and creative with their plans and offerings.

The development of settlement solutions is related to non-bank companies leaving the interbank call money market. Any schedule for the development of a pure interbank call/notice money market would be useless until the fundamental problem of settlements was resolved.

In short, the Reserve Bank's numerous policy actions have aided in the creation of a larger range of instruments, including market repo, interest rate swaps, CDs, and CPs.

The money market specializes in debt securities that mature in less than one year

Money market securities are very liquid, and are considered very safe. As a result, they offer a lower return than other securities.

The easiest way for individuals to gain access to the money market is through a money market mutual fund.

A Study of Investing Behavior of Retail Investors Towards Indian Mutual Funds with Respect to Investors in Mumbai

CHAPTER 21

Author – Shreya Kambli & Akash Birwadkar Student, IES's Management College and Research Centre, Mumbai

ABSTRACT

This study examines the awareness & attitude of India retail investors in mutual funds. The paper describes the journey of mutual fund industry in India and its growth phases. This study also looks after the failure of mutual funds in particular section of the society and also examines the investors decisions towards mutual funds. The total no. mutual fund investors as on 31st December, 2022 was 141.1 million, there is almost more than fivefold increase in a span of 10 years. Referring to India contest related to investors behavior there are various parameters which average investors thinks of before investing, major parameters are return and safety, most of the Indian household more tend to be extremely conservative with their saving and tend to invest in 'safe assets' such as tangible assets such as gold, jewelry, real estate or fixed deposits in bank and perceives mutual funds mutual funds as a risky investment. This is all due to lack of financial literacy among the Indian investors. Using questionnaire method of survey, data will be collected from individuals within Mumbai region to understand the reason of conservative buying behavior of Indian retail investors towards mutual funds.

KEYWORDS

Mutual Funds, Retails Investors, Preferred Investment, Behavior of Investors, AMC's.

INTRODUCTION

India is country with huge number of retail investors, A retail investor is a non-professional, individual investor who invest certain amount of their savings in the capital market. The Indian capital market has been developing hugely with the changes in modern strategy. Recently Mutual funds have emerged as an important investment avenue for retail investors. A mutual fund is a company that pools money from many investors and invests the money in securities such as stocks, bonds, and short-term debt. The combined holdings of the mutual fund are known as its portfolio. Mutual funds in India was introduced in 1963 with the formation of Unit Trust of India. MFs have changed during the past 15 years to become a product. The term "product" is used because MF schemes are "tailor made" to meet the demands of investors, regardless of their age, financial situation, risk tolerance, and return expectations. Average Assets Under Management (AAUM) of Indian Mutual Fund Industry for the month of January 2023 stood at ₹ 40,80,311 crore. Assets Under Management (AUM) of Indian Mutual Fund Industry as on January 31, 2023 stood at ₹ 39,62,406 crore. The AUM of the Indian MF Industry has grown from ₹ 8.26 trillion as on January 31, 2013 to ₹39.62 trillion as on January 31, 2023 around 5 fold increase in a span of 10 years. The MF Industry's AUM has grown from ₹ 22.41 trillion as on January 31, 2018 to ₹39.62 trillion as on January 31, 2023, around 2 fold increase in a span of 5 years. This study has been conducted as an eye opener not just for marketers of mutual funds, but also it was necessary to determine the preference, awareness, and investors' perceptions of mutual funds in Mumbai.

TYPES OF MUTUAL FUNDS

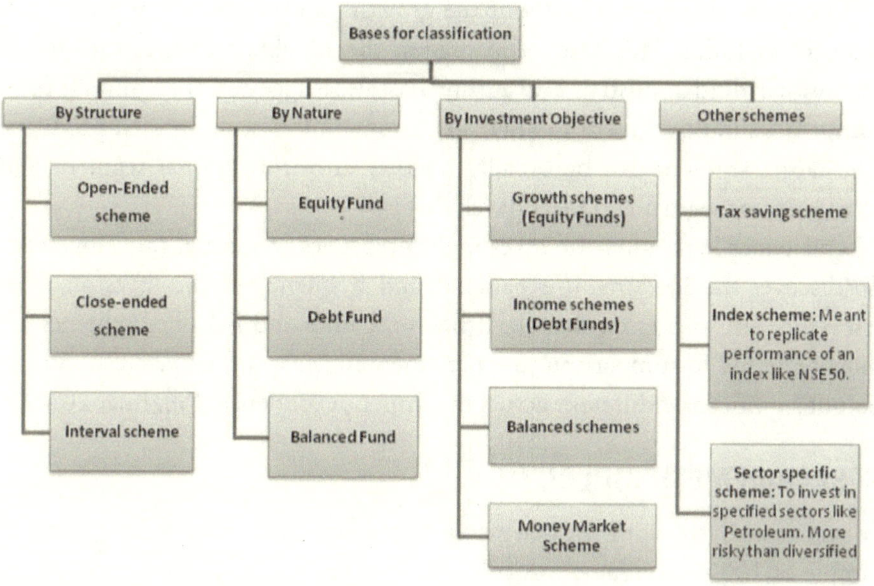

LITERATURE REVIEW

The author studies the saving objectives of individual investors. Mutual Fund investment preference in future. Factors influencing fund/scheme selection by investors, the author have also provided some principal suggestions and interpretations such as the employer can influence the employee's decisions by providing the financial education. (Ranganathan, 2006)

The author studies the behavior of selected mutual fund investors in Thiruvarur district of Tamil Nadu. The author concludes that India need just proper structure and strong regulatory framework for the protection of small and retail investors. (Dr.S.Suresh, 2019).

The competition in the industry of mutual funds as many new AMC compete by launching new schemes also author suggest that The target market of salaried class individual has a lot of scope to gain business, as they are more fascinated to Mutual Funds than the self-employed. (Islam, 2016)

The researcher has conducted to study the perception of Indian Individual investors towards the investment in mutual fund author also suggests that older mutual schemes must be wind up or a thorough review of strategy is needed. (Goel, 2013).

This research paper talks about the growth and progress of mutual funds industry in India. This study also suggest the suitable measures for growth for mutual fund industry. The author has also suggested that mutual fund companies should segment their target customers and position their products. The target segment can be broadly divided into institutional segment and retail investor segment. (D.Kandavel, 2011).

This paper locks after the investment objectives of mutual fund investors. To discover the investment experience and frequency of the investors. The researcher also suggested that the growth schemes and balanced schemes are most preferred in comparison to other schemes. Male and female respondents do not significantly different across investment experience. (Sharma, 2015).

RESEARCH METHODOLOGY

For data analysis, both primary and secondary data have been used. A sample of 100 respondents was collected for the analysis in this work, which used the descriptive research method. The study was carried out in relation to retail investors in Mumbai, Maharashtra. The study makes extensive use of original data. Using a standardised questionnaire, the main data was gathered. Based on the study's goals, this questionnaire was developed. Journals, research papers, publications, and pertinent websites served as the sources for the secondary data. Respondents were screened, and their inclusion was solely determined by the depth of their understanding of financial markets, namely MFs. This was required since the questionnaire assumed that the respondent was familiar with some fundamental mutual fund terminology.

RESEARCH OBJECTIVE

The overall aim is to conduct a study on behaviour of retail investors towards mutual funds selection. It can be further sub-divided in to the following objectives:

1. To discover the investment Motive of mutual fund investors
2. To identify the types of mutual fund schemes preference by elected mutual fund investors.

FINDINGS & DISCUSSION

A survey was being conducted to understand the thoughts of retail investors on mutual funds schemes in India. The findings and discussion depends on the responses of approx. 100 respondents.

Table – 01(a): Age and Awareness level

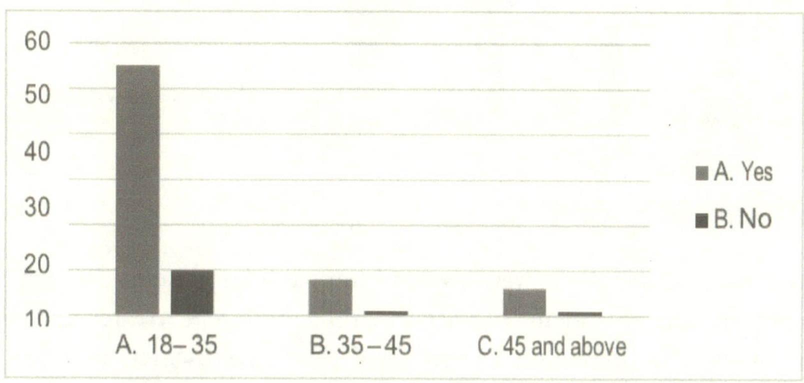

From the collected data it has been analyzed that 67.90% of awareness level was between the age group of 18-35. And only 7.41% from the age group of 45 and above were aware of mutual funds schemes in Mumbai.

Table – 01 (b): Age and Investment

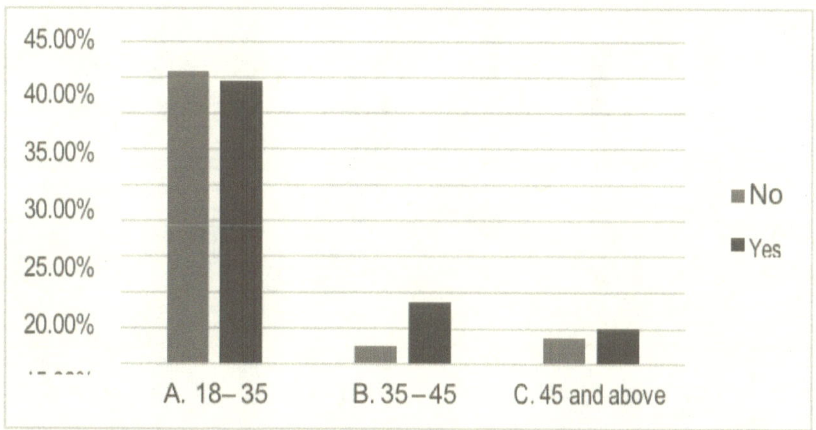

From age group of 18-35 39.51% do invest in mutual funds. and from total respondents 53.09% invests in mutual funds.

Table – 02: Occupation and Medium of awareness to invest

Count of How you got aware of mutual funds you invested in?

18.00%
16.00%
14.00%
12.00%
10.00%
8.00%
6.00%
4.00%
2.00%
0.00%

A. Professional
B. Business
C. Service
F. Student

How you got aware of mutual...
A. Self – research
B. Advised family member/ friends/ colleague's
C. Through your education
D. Advertisement

What is your Occupation?

Most of the respondent were aware of mutual funds scheme through Self-research. In cases of students it is been seen that both self- research and advise from family/friends/colleague's is preferred. Also advertisement as a medium of awareness was only seen between service sector and students i.e. 2.33%.

Table 03: Occupation and Preferred platform for investment

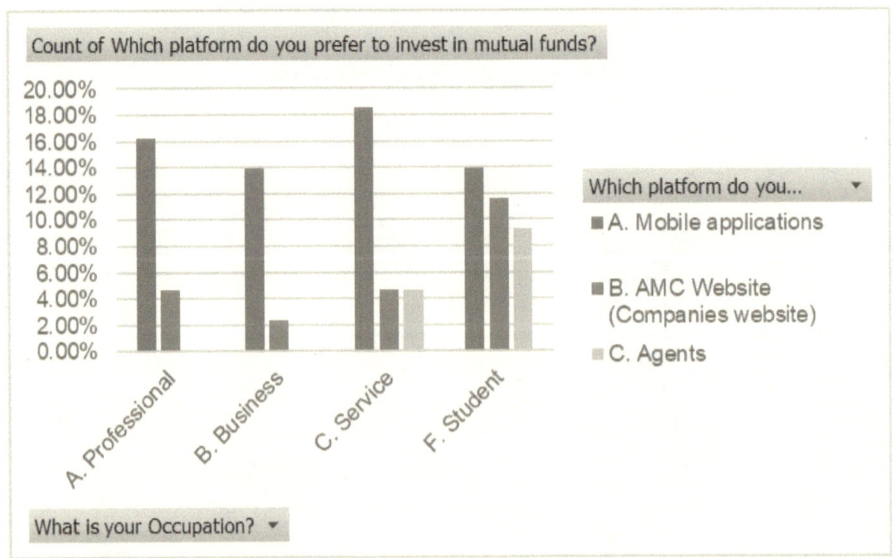

Mobile application as a mode of investment has been the most preferred by all the occupations (62.79%) and 13.95% of people prefer to invest through agents

Table 04: Preferred mutual fund schemes.

Scheme	Count (%)
A. Regular Income	22 (51.2%)
B. Growth	28 (65.1%)
C. Money Market	11 (25.6%)
D. Open ended	6 (14%)
E. Close ended	3 (7%)
F. Pension Funds	3 (7%)
G. Fixed Maturity Funds	11 (25.6%)
H. Tax-Saving Funds	13 (30.2%)
I. Equity Funds	24 (55.8%)
J. Debt Funds	11 (25.6%)

Top 3 preferred mutual funds schemes are Growth (65%), Equity funds (55.8%), Regular income (51.2%) and least preferred are close ended and pension funds

Table 05: Age and investment frequency

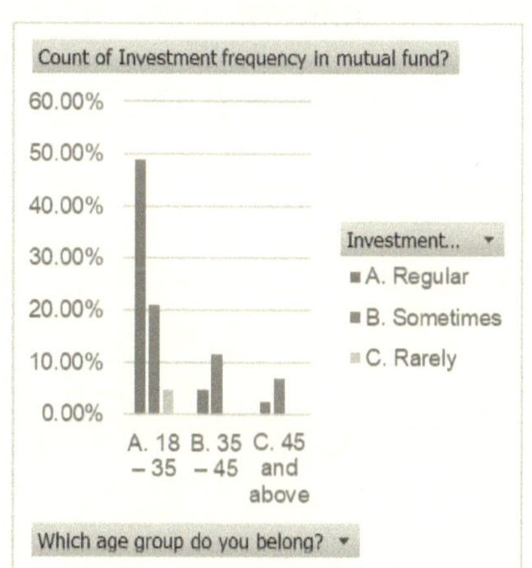

Age group of 18-35 invests regularly in the mutual funds

Table 06: Satisfaction Level

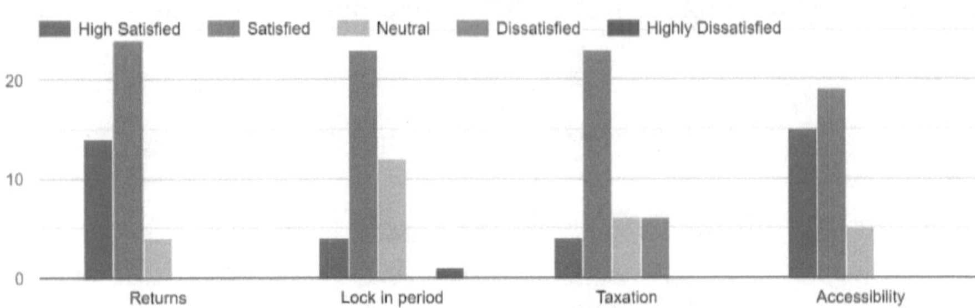

People have more satisfaction level in terms of returns, lock in period and taxation

Table 07: Mutual Funds company awareness

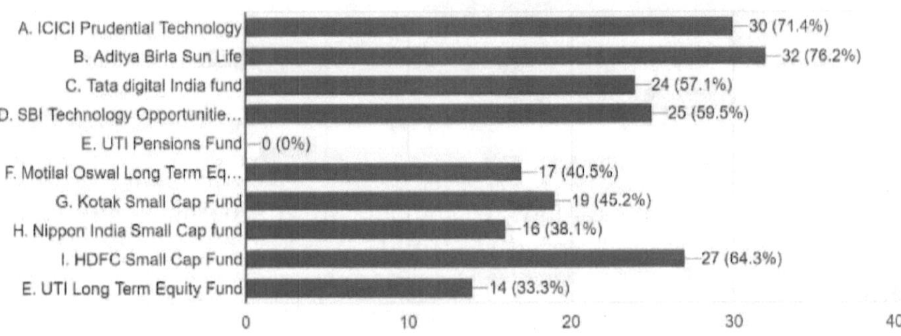

Most of the respondents are aware of Aditya Birla Sun Life, ICICI Prudential Technology and HDFC small cap funds.

Table 08: Occupation and Mutual Funds Preference

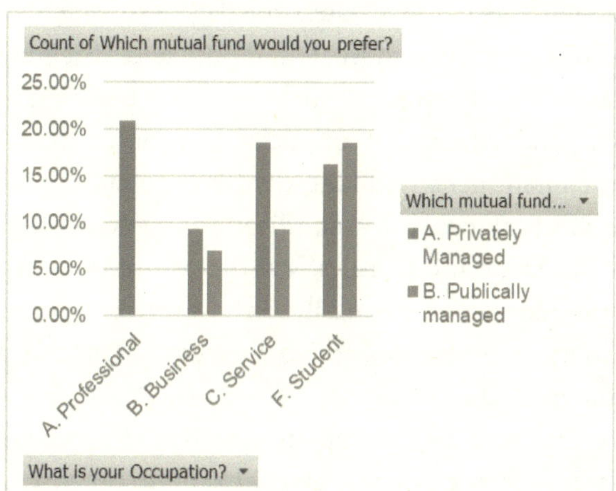

65.12% of the respondents prefer privately managed mutual funds. Out of which Professional are the one who prefer the most.

CONCLUSION/ SUMMARY

According to our findings it is been observed that 49.3% respondents invest in mutual funds schemes. Out of which most prefers growth and equity schemes and 76.2% of respondents are aware of Aditya Birla Sun Life mutual fund company who invest in equity market. So according to the findings we can infer that other companies providing mutual funds should focus on growth and equity schemes. UTI mutual funds are not known more to people as they also provide pensions mutual fund scheme which people do not prefer. Most of the responses use mobile applications to invest in mutual funds which get less foot falls on AMC websites (Companies website). So mutual fund companies can give certain benefits to the investors who invest through their websites. If you look at the Awareness of the mutual fund in Table 02. It is seen that awareness through advertisement is low compared to others so the companies should invest more on the advertisement part. So more people will get aware and they will invest in mutual fund. Most of the homemakers are used to watching televisions and they are less active on social media. Increasing television advertisement will increase the awareness of mutual fund in homemakers and it will encourage them to invest. This research helped us to some extent to understand the behavior of investors towards mutual funds schemes.

SCOPE OF FURTHER RESEARCH TO BE HIGHLIGHTED

Investor Satisfaction and Loyalty: Assess the degree to which Mumbai's retail investors are satisfied with their mutual fund purchases. Examine the elements that affect shareholder happiness, such as fund performance, openness, customer support, and redemption simplicity. Look at the connection between investor loyalty, contentment, and long-term investment behavior.

Examine the effects of regulatory modifications, such as the SEBI (Securities and Exchange Board of India) rules, on the attitudes of Mumbai's retail investors towards mutual funds. Analyze the impact of regulatory actions on enhancing investor protection, increasing transparency, and encouraging confidence in the mutual fund sector.

Comparative Analysis: Make a comparison between Mumbai's retail investors and those in other Indian cities or regions. Examine the investment to see if there are any noticeable differences Investor Satisfaction and Loyalty: Assess the degree to which Mumbai's retail investors are satisfied with their mutual fund purchases. Examine the elements that affect shareholder happiness, such as fund performance, openness, customer support, and redemption simplicity. Look at the connection between investor loyalty, contentment, and long-term investment behavior.

Examine the effects of regulatory modifications, such as the SEBI (Securities and Exchange Board of India) rules, on the attitudes of Mumbai's retail investors towards mutual funds. Analyse the impact of regulatory actions on enhancing investor protection, increasing transparency, and encouraging confidence in the mutual fund sector.

Comparative Analysis: Make a comparison between Mumbai's retail investors and those in other Indian cities or regions. Examine the investment to see if there are any noticeable differences.

REFERENCE

Ranganathan, K. (2006). A Study of Fund Selection Behaviour of Individual Investors Towards Mutual Funds - with Reference to Mumbai City. SSRN Electronic Journal. https://doi.org/10.2139/ssrn.876874 In-Text Citation: (Ranganathan, 2006)

Islam, M. (2016, September 1). Customer Behavior towards Purchasing Mutual Fund- A Study of Dehradun City. International Journal of

Computer Engineering in Research Trends, 3(9), 521. https://doi.org/10.22362/ijcert/2016/v3/i9/48902 In-Text Citation: (Islam, 2016)

Goel, S. (2013). Performance Of Mutual Funds And Investors' Behavior. Jaypee Institute Of Information Technology, Noida.

Dr.S.Suresh (2019). A study on the fund selection behaviour of mutual fund investors of thiruvarur district in tamilnadu, Department of Business Administration, Annai Vailankanni Arts and Science College, Thanjavur.

D.Kandavel (2011). Factors influencing the retail investors to prefer investment in mutual funds in puducherry: an emprical study, Annamalai University, Annamalai Nagar, Tamil Nadu, India.

Sharma, R. (2015). Behaviour of mutual fund investors towards investment option: Mutual fund. Journal of Management Research and Analysis, 2(2), 162-168.

A Study on Consumer Behavior Towards Amul Products

CHAPTER 22

Author – Rishabh Khatri, Sanil Kinjawadekar & Vishal Shah, Student, IES's Management College and Research Centre, Mumbai

ABSTRACT

Consumer buying behavior is the sum total of a consumer's attitudes, preferences, intentions, and decisions regarding the consumer's behavior in the market place when purchasing a product or service. The study of consumer behavior draws upon social science disciplines of anthropology, psychology, sociology, and economics It lets the companies understand how consumer decides about buying their product or acquiring services. Marketing managers are always interested to know more about consumers' behavior so they can prepare better communication and advertising campaigns and messages about their products and services. This thesis is about studying which factors of social, cultural, personal or psychological characteristics has the most effect on consumer decision making process when selecting home cleaning service company. The research work is carried out to highlight the important elements for customers in the household and let the service provider understand overall picture of customer behavior towards the AMUL company with the help of understanding the factors affecting consumer behavior for choosing a certain service provider. Better understanding of consumer behavior would let the marketers make the service structure as desired and attractive for the household customer and maintain business activities according to customer demands. This research work would let the customer record their voice in understanding the companies what kind of service do they want which can improve their life quality with the tailored services by the service provider.

KEYWORDS

"Availability", "Brand trust", "Consumer behavior", "Satisfaction"

*Corresponding Author

INTRODUCTION

In this paper we will the study the consumer buying behavior towards AMUL products. So, what is Consumer buying behavior? It is a psychologic reaction of a customer towards brand image, offerings, influence and appearances. By studying consumers buying behavior of their consumers a company can find out the key factors which a consumer likes or dislikes and on which they can work to provide better products experiences to the consumers. Consumer buying behaviour is the sum total of a consumer's attitudes, preferences, intentions, and decisions regarding the consumer's behaviour in the market place when purchasing a product or service.

The study of consumer behaviour draws upon social science disciplines of anthropology, psychology, sociology, and economics. Consumer behaviour is broadly studied field. It lets the companies understand how consumer decides about buying their product or acquiring services. Marketing managers are always interested to know more about consumers' behaviour so they can prepare better communication and advertising campaigns and messages about their products and services. Consumer makes buying decision every day and many people don't even know the factors which derive them to this decision. Usually the factors affecting consumer buying behaviour include psychological, social, cultural and Buying the new home cleaning service involves consumers' research for the best option available and it might take various factors in account in its decision-making process. This thesis is about studying which factors of social, cultural, personal or psychological characteristics has the most effect on consumer decision making process when selecting home cleaning service company. The research work is carried out to highlight the important elements for customers in the household and let the service provider understand overall picture of customer behaviour towards the Amul company with the help of understanding the factors affecting consumer behaviour for choosing a certain service provider. Better understanding of consumer behaviour would let the marketers make the service structure as desired and attractive for the household customer and maintain business activities according to customer demands. This research work would let the customer record their voice in understanding the companies what kind of service do they want which can improve their life quality with the tailored services by the service provider

LITERATURE REVIEW

Dr. Swati Bisht, Ms Shikha Saraswat (2021)

There are a number of strategies and media options available to the marketers of today. Each strategy poses some advantages and some disadvantages. Topical advertising and brand mascots also comes packed with strategic advantages with lesser disadvantages. Topical advertisement leads to better customer engagement by reinforcing the relation between the brand and the customer, provokes thoughts, gives ease of remembrance because of leveraging the current news item. Because of these strategic advantages one can use this approach. Topical advertisement or copy content in combination with brand mascot could lead to better memorability, relatability and brand differentiation.

Mr. Abhishek Singh & Dr. Ajay Singh (2020)

The authors found out that Amul has a strong brand value in the market and it increases rapidly through its advertising. Amul focuses on advertising, quality and customer service which makes it a chief brand in the dairy industry. Competitors like Mother Dairy focus on availability, thus they attract only existing customers and narrow their captured markets. Amul should provide doorstep facility which is preferred from survey. The demand of Amul products is higher than its supply which impose customers to buy competitor's products.

Pooja A Patel, Nikita R Khatwate & Saptarshi Mukherjee (2020)

This paper gives an insight about importance of consumers buying behavior in marketing Amul milk in Ahmedabad city. From the research, it can be concluded that the consumer behavior survey results are some where important to the company for their professional as well as personal growth and development. After understanding about what the consumers actually think about their work and the company, the management can take necessary measures to have a satisfactory and motivated workforce. The overall experience of the respondents towards Amul milk was found to be satisfactory because of its good quality, reputation, easy availabilities.

However, some consumers are not satisfied with high price etc. 33 therefore if slight modification are done then definitely company can be as a monopoly and strong market leader.

Amul has also to take care of its competitors into consideration and more importantly its customers before making any move.

RESEARCH METHODOLOGY

The research methodology is the basic procedures or techniques used to classify, select, process and evaluate information on the subject. It includes following terms: Research Problem:

OBJECTIVE

- To study consumer behavior towards AMUL products.

SUB-OBJECTIVES

- Seek the general perception of consumer towards AMUL Milk.
- To know the consumer psyche and their behavior towards AMUL Milk.
- To know the relationship of sales with the advertisement.
- To know awareness of people towards AMUL Milk.
- To know which advertisement tool is mostly preferred by people.
- To know the preference of AMUL Milk with comparison to Other competitive brands.
- To know the factors which affects consumer's buying behavior to purchase milk.

Research Design: Descriptive research (A Research design specifies the methods and procedures for conducting a particular study. It is a map (or) blue print to which the research is to be conducted. Descriptive research design has been considered as a suitable methodology for present study and for data analysis).

Sampling Design: Convenience sampling (The sampling design used was Convenience sampling, which is a nonprobability sampling method. The convenience factors were the availability and approachability of the respondents).

Population: A population is usually a broad number of individuals or artefacts that is the main subject of a scientific inquiry. In this research, population are those who uses dairy products.

Tools used: Pie and Bar-Graph Chart Sampling size :70

Method: Interview through questionnaire; Scale: Continuous and Likert scale.

FINDINGS

1. All the respondents were well aware about AMUL products, hence awareness level among consumers is high.

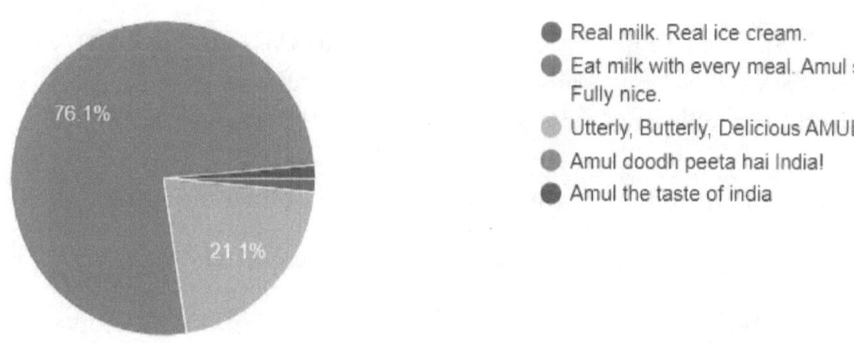

Brand recall value is quite high with respect to AMUL milk slogan "AMUL doodh peeta h India".

- 76.1% of the respondents were able to recall AMUL by the slogan "AMUL doodh peeta h India".
- 21.1% knows AMUL by the slogan "Utterly butterly delicious AMUL".
- The remaining people were those who remember slogans of other dairy products.

2. Television plays an important role in communicating the brand AMUL to the audience.

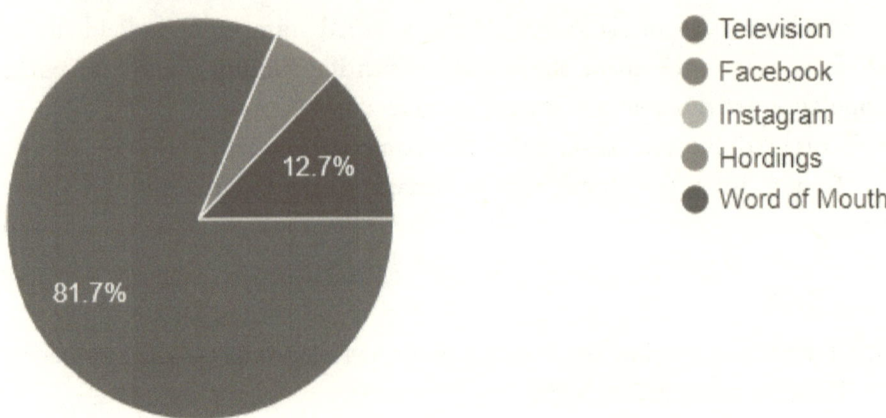

- 81.7% of the respondents came to know about AMUL through TV AD's.
- 12.7% were aware of AMUL by other person's reviews.

The other people have come to know about AMUL through hoardings.

3. Amongst all the product people consume AMUL butter the most.

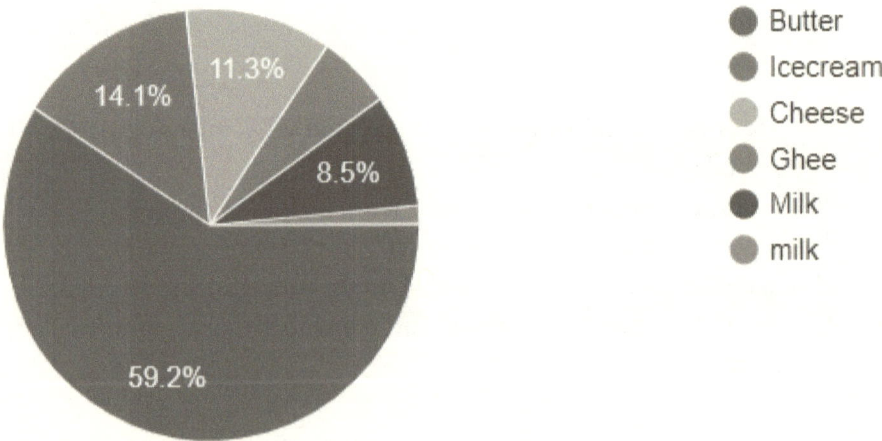

- 50.2% of the respondent consumes AMUL butter.
- 14.1% of the respondents consumes AMUL ice-cream.
- 11.3% of the respondents consumes AMUL cheese.
- 8.5% of the respondents consumes AMUL milk.
- The rest of the population are of AMUL ghee.

4. Most of the people buy AMUL products on every week and every month.

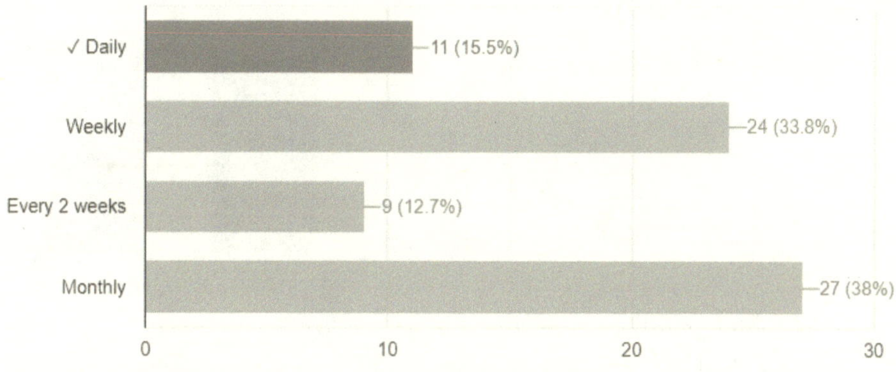

- 15.5% of the respondents were the daily consumers of these products.
- 33.8% of the respondents are the weekly consumers.
- 12.7% of the respondents consumes these products every two weeks.
- 38% of the respondents are the monthly consumers of this products.

5. Most of the people buy AMUL products for their quality and the price at which they are available.

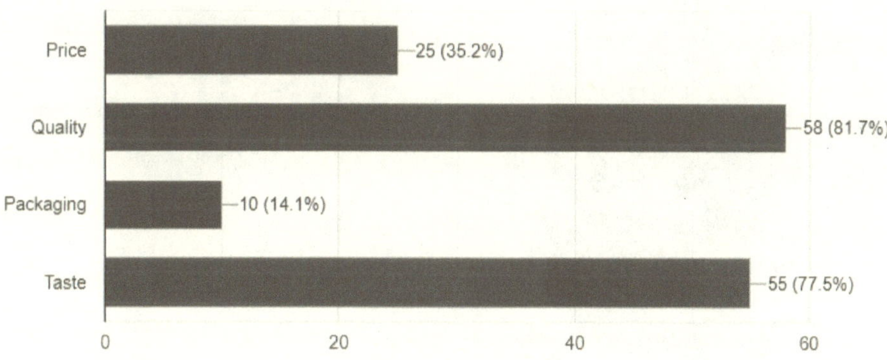

- 35.2% of the respondents liked the price of AMUL products.
- 81.7% of the respondent liked the quality of the AMUL.
- Only 14.1% of the respondents buys AMUL products for their packaging.
- 77.5% of the respondents like the taste of AMUL products.

6. The satisfaction level of the consumers towards their products is very high.

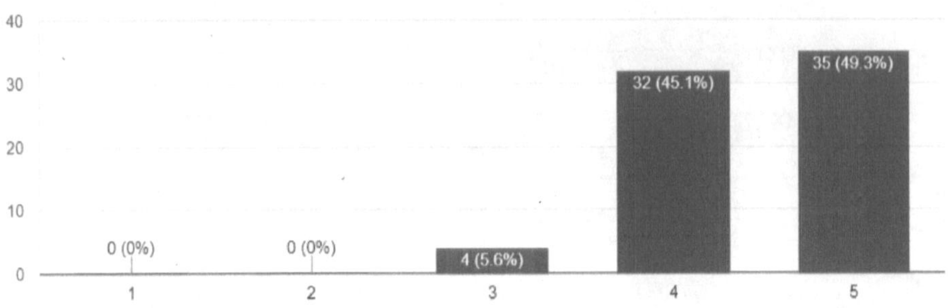

- 5: Very high: 49.3%
- 4: High: 45.1%
- 3: Neutral: 5.6%
- 2: Low: 0%
- 1: Very Low: 0%

7. People prefer either supermarket or retail market to buy AMUL products they generally don't buy them online.

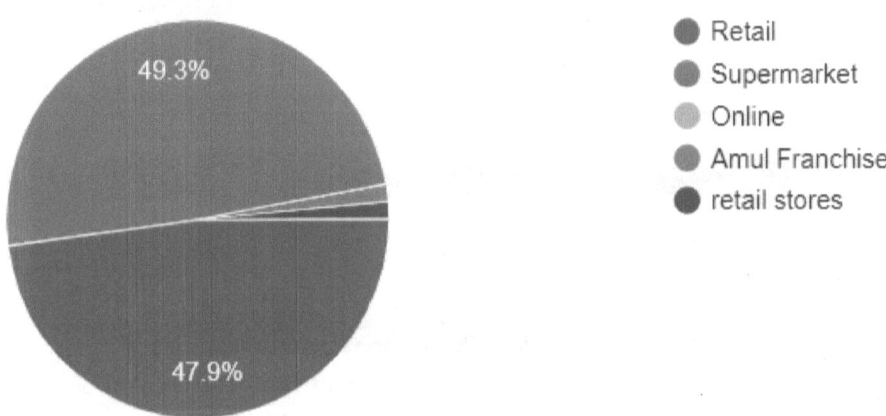

- 49.3% of the respondents buys AMUL products from the Supermarket.
- 47.9% of the respondents buys from retail stores.
- The other buys from online or AMUL franchise.

8. AMUL pro and AMUL cool are two products which are not well received by the consumers.

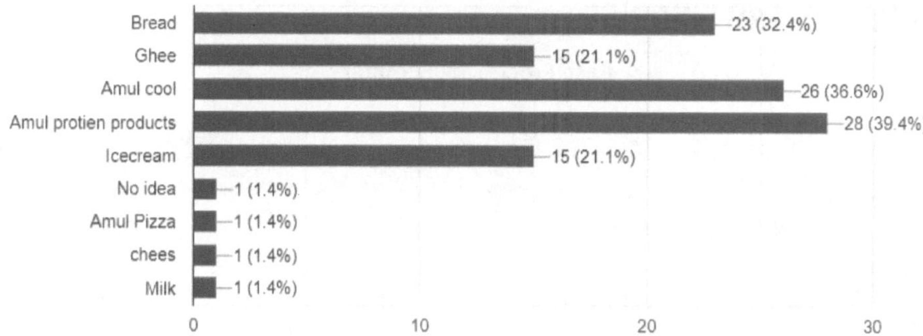

Amongst all the products people are less satisfied with these products and these products are AMUL bread (32.4%), AMUL ghee (21.1%), AMUL cool (36.6%), AMUL Pro (39.4%), AMUL ice-cream (21.1%), AMUL pizza (1.4%), AMUL cheese (1.4%), AMUL milk (1.4%).

9. The packaging of AMUL products is good and sturdy.

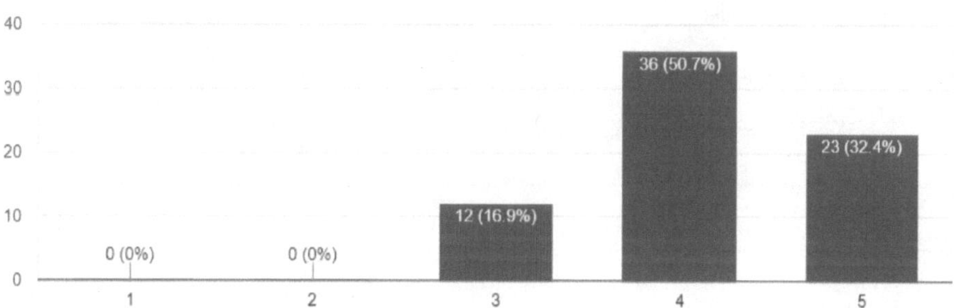

- 5: Very secure and attractive: 32.4%
- 4: Secure: 50.7%
- 3: Neutral: 16.9%
- 2: Bad: 0%
- 1: Very Bad: 0%

Most of the consumers from the sample refers AMUL to others.

ANALYSIS AND FINDINGS

Case Processing Summary

	Cases					
	Valid		Missing		Total	
	N	Percent	N	Percent	N	Percent
Gender * How often do you purchase these products ?	72	100.0%	0	.0%	72	100.0%

Gender * How often do you purchase these products ? Crosstabulation

Weekly Daily			How often do you purchase these products ?				Total
			Monthly	Every 2 weeks			
Gender	Female	Count	12	10	12	6	40
		% within Gender	25.0%	30.0%	15.0%	100.0%	
			62.5%	60.0%	30.0%	55.6%	
		% within How often do you purchase these products ? % of Total 30.0% 75.0% 16.7%	13.9%	16.7%	8.3%	55.6%	
	Male	Count	4	6	8	14	32
		% within Gender	18.8%	25.0%	43.8%	100.0%	
			37.5%	40.0%	70.0%	44.4%	
		% within How often do you purchase these products ? % of Total 12.5% 25.0% 5.6%	8.3%	11.1%	19.4%	44.4%	
Total		Count	16	16	20	20	72
		% within Gender	22.2%	22.2%	27.8%	27.8%	100.0%
		% within How often do you purchase these products ?	100.0%	100.0%	100.0%	100.0%	100.0%
		% of Total	22.2%	22.2%	27.8%	27.8%	100.0%

According to the above analysis, it can be inferred that majority of females(30% each) are buying Amul products on Weekly and Monthly basis

Among Males, it can be seen that 43.8% males are buying Amul products twice a week hence it can be inferred that females are frequent buyers of Amul products than Males.

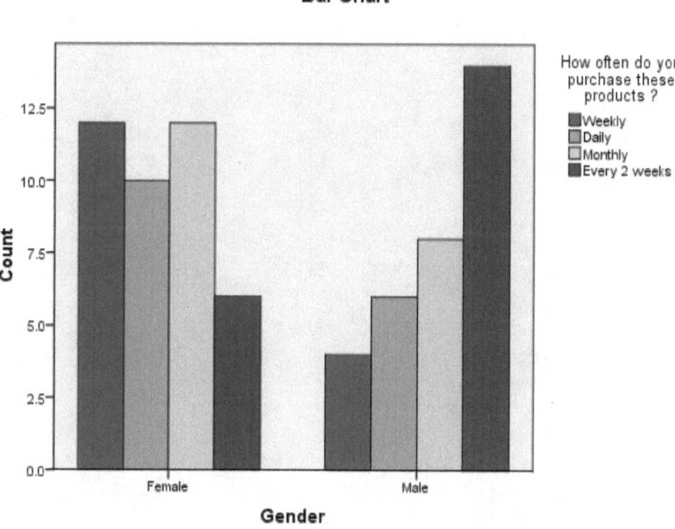

Chi- Square Test

Hypothesis

H0- Slogan Recall is independent of age H1- Slogan Recall is dependent on age

Age * Which slogan comes to your mind first when you hear AMUL? Crosstabulation

Real milk. Real ice cream Eat milk with every meal. Amul slice. Fully nice.	Which slogan comes to your mind first when you hear AMUL?				
	Utterly, Butterly, Delicious AMUL!	Amul doodh peeta hai India!			Total

Age	Above 60 Count		0	0	2	2	4
	% within Age		.0%	50.0%	50.0%	100.0%	
	% within Which slogan comes to your mind first when you hear AMUL?		.0%	12.5%	5.0%	5.6%	
	% of Total		.0%	2.8%	2.8%	5.6%	
	.0%						
	.0%						
	.0%						
	51-60	Count	2	3	1	6	12
		% within Age	16.7%	25.0%	8.3%	50.0%	100.0%
		% within Which slogan comes to your mind first when you hear AMUL?	50.0%	25.0%	6.2%	15.0%	16.7%
		% of Total	2.8%	4.2%	1.4%	8.3%	16.7%
	36-50	Count	1	4	7	12	24
		% within Age	4.2%	16.7%	29.2%	50.0%	100.0%
		% within Which slogan comes to your mind first when you hear AMUL?	25.0%	33.3%	43.8%	30.0%	33.3%
		% of Total	1.4%	5.6%	9.7%	16.7%	33.3%

	18-35	Count	1	5	6	20	32
		% within Age	3.1%	15.6%	18.8%	62.5%	100.0%
		% within Which slogan comes to your mind first when you hear AMUL?	25.0%	41.7%	37.5%	50.0%	44.4%
		% of Total	1.4%	6.9%	8.3%	27.8%	44.4%
Total		Count	4	12	16	40	72
		% within Age	5.6%	16.7%	22.2%	55.6%	100.0%
		% within Which slogan comes to your mind first when you hear AMUL?	100.0%	100.0%	100.0%	100.0%	100.0%
		% of Total	5.6%	16.7%	22.2%	55.6%	100.0%

CHI-SQUARE TESTS

	Value	df	Asymp. Sig. (2- sided)
Pearson Chi-Square	8.125[a]	9	.522
Likelihood Ratio	8.003	9	.534
Linear-by-Linear Association	.871	1	.351
N of Valid Cases	72		

a. 10 cells (62.5%) have expected count less than 5. The minimum expected count is.22.

Pearson Chi-Square value is 0.522 > 0.05. Hence H0 rejected, H1 accepted Hence we can say that slogan recall Is dependent on age.

DISCUSSION

Consumer behaviour towards AMUL products has been very positive. This is attributed to the fact that AMUL is a highly trusted brand in India, with a strong customer base. Consumers are willing to pay premium prices for AMUL products as they are known to be of high quality and consistent. Moreover, the wide range of products offered by AMUL, coupled with its wide distribution network, makes it a preferred choice for many. AMUL's customer-centric approach also helps it to maintain its leading position in the market. The company takes the time to understand consumer preferences and tastes, and constantly innovates in order to meet their needs. It also provides customers with attractive discounts and offers, which further increase customer loyalty. In addition, AMUL's commitment to sustainability and ethical practices has helped to build a positive image in the minds of consumers. Consumers appreciate the fact that AMUL is engaged in activities that are beneficial to the environment and society. This has further increased customer loyalty and trust in the brand.

SUMMARY AND CONCLUSIONS

The research is really important for the company or any type of business to know about what a customer actually needs in order to fulfil customer's needs and solve their problems. By doing this company can run its business in the long run and possibility of growth can be achieved.

After doing this research, we can say that people are very well aware about the different products of AMUL such as milk, curd, butter, etc. And many such milk related products. Most of the people have the brand image of AMUL in their mind whenever they think to buy any milk related products. This indicates that how this company has attracted the customers and retained those in the long run by making regular advertisements through different medias.

This also indicates that how the company was giving the importance to creative and attractive advertisements, just to grab the attention of the people and make them aware about the products. Even people are aware about the slogans used by AMUL such as "AMUL doodh pita hai India", "AMUL The taste of India". This implies that how the company made the use of different slogans by creating unique advertisements just to hold the attention of the people and which is a very difficult task to do, but AMUL company even made it look easy by creating such unique slogans which have entered into the minds of the people and thus it helped a lot to gain the market share in the long run. Thus AMUL company achieved tremendous growth in the long run by attracting the new customers as well as retaining them by providing good quality products and making attractive ads regularly, and hence it won the faith of their customers due to which it became successful in increasing the turnover.

REFERENCES

1. Kumar, S. R., & Advani, J. Y. (2005). Factors Affecting Brand Loyalty: A study in an emerging market on fast moving consumer goods. Journal of Customer Behavior, 4(2), 251-275. Doi:10.1362/1475392054797223
2. Strategies Adopted by FMCG Companies for Making Their Brands Outstanding. (2014, March 12). December 8, 2017
3. Retrieved from: https://www.yourarticlelibrary.com/marketing/product/strategies- adopted-by-fmcg-companies-for-making-their-brands-outstanding/29858
4. Swaroopa Moses; Charles Ambrose; A Study on Impact of Marketing Strategies on Consumer Behavior towards FMCG sector with reference to Nestle [St. Joseph's Evening College, Bangalore.]; Vol.7, No.2, April-June 2018

A Study on Financial Performance Analysis of Bajaj Auto Limited

CHAPTER 23

Author – Riya Kansara & Rishi Acharya, Student, IES's Management College and Research Centre, Mumbai

ABSTRACT

Finance is the management of money. However, this process of management includes activities such as forecasting, saving, lending, borrowing, and investing. Finance is but a lead within which lies a conglomerate of other activities associated with investments, money, capital markets, credit, debit or leverage, and banking. Financial performance helps to know the overall performance of the company. This research paper is based on Bajaj auto limited. Bajaj auto ltd is one of the foremost automobile companies in the automobile industry in India founded on 29th November 1945 by Jamnalal Bajaj. The company produces two-wheelers and three-wheelers and had tremendous goodwill among the customers. It is the world's third-largest manufacturer of motorcycles and the second-largest in India. It is the world's largest three-wheeler manufacturer. From investors point of view, it has a strong and positive mindset. This study is about the financial performance of Bajaj auto ltd necessary to attract new investors and easy to make additional on Bajaj Auto ltd by using Liquidity ratio, Profitability ratio, Leverage ratio, Turnover ratio of the company. The study to analyze the financial performance of the company was conducted using financial data from company's annual report of last three years.

KEYWORDS

Automobile Industry, Bajaj Auto, Financial Performance, Investment and Ratio Analysis

INTRODUCTION

FINANCIAL PERFORMANCE

Financial performance is a subjective measure of how well a firm can use assets from its primary mode of business and generate revenues. The term is also used as a general measure of a firm's overall financial health over a given period. Analysts and investors use financial performance to compare similar firms across the same industry or to compare industries or sectors in aggregate There are many stakeholders in a company, including trade creditors, bondholders, investors, employees, and management. Each group has an interest in tracking the financial performance of a company. The financial performance identifies how well a company generates revenues and manages its assets, liabilities, and the financial interests of its stakeholders and stockholders. A company's financial performance tells investors about its general well-being. It's a snapshot of its economic health and the job its management is doing—providing insight into the future: whether its operations and profits are on track to grow and the outlook for its stock The most widely used financial performance indicators include: Gross profit margin, Net profit/net profit margin, Working capital, Operating cash flow, Current ratio, Debt-to-equity ratio,Quick ratio, Inventory turnover, Return on equity.

BAJAJ AUTO LTD.

Bajaj auto ltd is one of the foremost automobile companies in the automobile industry in India. It produced more two-wheelers and three-wheelers in a year and also had tremendous goodwill among the customers. And another investor's point of view it had a strong and positive mind set. And therefore, a new study about its financial performance is necessary to attract new investors and easy to make additional on Bajaj Auto ltd by existing investors. The present Report will be focused on the analysis of the financial performance of Bajaj auto ltd from 2020-2023. In this regard liquidity ratio, Profitability ratio, Turnover ratio, and Earning ratio were used in the study for accurate results and to plan based upon these results. Bajaj Auto is the world's third-largest manufacturer of motorcycles and the second-largest in Indian. It is the world's largest three-wheeler manufacturer. In December 2020, Bajaj Auto crossed a market capitalisation of ₹1 trillion (US$13 billion), making it the world's most valuable two-wheeler company. Bajaj Auto Ltd (BAL) any of the two and three assembling producers in India. The employer is known for its L and D item development and assembling capabilities. The agency is the biggest exporter of and 3 wheels inside the empire Bajaj Auto Limited is an Indian multinational automotive manufacturing company based in Pune. It manufactures motorcycles, scooters and auto rickshaws. Bajaj Auto is a part of the Bajaj Group. It was founded by Jamnalal Bajaj (1889–1942) in Rajasthan in the 1940s. On November 29, 1945, M/s Bachraj Trading Corporation Private Limited was founded. It began by importing and offering two- and three-wheelers for sale in India. In 1959, it received authorization from the Indian government to produce two- and three-wheelers, as well as authorization from Piaggio to produce Vespa Brand Scooters in India. In 1960, it converted to a public limited company. The company altered its branding from a scooter maker to a two-wheeler manufacturer with the introduction of motorcycles in 1986. Bajaj Auto and Kawasaki inked a technical assistance agreement in 1984 to work together to increase motorcycle production and sales in the local market Automobiles, auto-rickshaws, motorcycles, and scooters are all produced and sold by Bajaj. In 2004, Bajaj Auto was India's top motorbike exporter. For the Indian market, 4-stroke commuter motorcycles with sporty performance are being introduced for the first time by Bajaj.

This was accomplished by Bajaj using the 150cc and 180cc Pulsar. The CT 100 Platina, Discover, Pulsar, Avenger, and Dominar are some of the bikes made by Bajaj. It sold about 37.6 lakh (3.76 million) motorcycles in FY 2012–13, accounting for 31% of the Indian market. About 24.6 lakh (2.46 million) of these motorcycles were sold in India, accounting for 66% of the total, while 34% were exported. The decision to make those physical games three was made after seeing the improvement opportunities within the safety and financial a part of power-saving breeze energy businesses. Unique aspects that can each engage fitness and deal with intermediate enterprise. As a result, PT Bajaj Auto Indonesia and a few merchant firms have transferred the whole enterprise with all benefits and liabilities to Bajaj Investment and Holding Ltd. (BHIL). Moreover, Bajaj Investment and Holding Ltd. receives a transfer of Rs. 15,000,000,000 in real cash and money reciprocals. Changing to Bajaj Auto Ltd was a key component of the Bajaj Holdings and Investment Ltd plan (BAL).

LITERATURE REVIEW

The automotive industry is of particular importance in this study because it is currently one of the one of the biggest markets in the world. being a pioneer in both processes and products technology, which have been acknowledged as one of the drivers of the manufacturing industry of economic expansion. For businesses competing, innovation has proven to be a leveraging factor. To distinguish between product features and attributes in this competitive climate, in this essay, quality, consumer satisfaction, and business are examined in relation to Bajaj Auto Ltd. feeling of happiness or disappointment brought on by comparing a product's performance or result to their expectations. All organization must pay attention to its stakeholders and external customers. Many readings have revealed believe a company's long-term success is intimately related to its capacity to develop and sustain loyal and satisfied customers. Satisfaction refers to a person's emotions of liking or disliking that result from comparing a product's Comparison of actual performance (or result) versus anticipated performance. When a performance falls short of expectations, the Customer is not pleased. The buyer or consumer is satisfied if the performance meets expectations.

RESEARCH METHODOLOGY

Sources: ProQuest, Resource gate, Academia and Google scholarly

Key Words: Automobile Industry, Market Segmentation, Bajaj Auto Ltd., Financial Performance, Ratio Analysis and Investments.

The gathered data is a secondary data from various articles, research papers and annual report.

FINDINGS

Ratio Analysis of the Company

The contribution of the automobile industry to Indian economic development is very high. In India's GDP, automobile industry involvement is prominent. And also India is a developing country and its nature and environment are more suitable for starting a new business. So, that year by year the number of manufacturing and other industries increased. Bajaj Auto Limited, Maruti Suzuki, Hyundai, Tata Motors, Mahindra and Mahindra, Honda Motor Company, and Ashok Leyland are the leading automobile companies doing automobile business in India. Our study is conducted on Bajaj Auto Limited.

ABOUT THE COMPANY

Particulars	Amount
Market Capitalization	109,010 Cr
52 Week High	4131.75
52 Week Low	3125.00
Equity capital	289.37 Cr
Face Value	10.00

Bajaj auto ltd is one of the foremost automobile companies in the automobile industry in India. It produced more two-wheelers and three-wheelers in a year and also had tremendous goodwill among the customers. And another investor's point of view it had a strong and positive mind set. And therefore a new study about its financial performance is necessary to attract new investors and easy to make additional on Bajaj Auto ltd by existing investors. The present Report will be focused on the analysis of the financial performance of Bajaj auto ltd from 2020-2023. In this regard liquidity ratio, Profitability ratio, Turnover ratio, and Earning ratio were used in the study for accurate results and to make a decision based upon these results

PRICE CHART (LAST 3 YEARS)

Liquidity Ratio: Liquidity ratios are a measure of the ability of a company to pay off its short-term liabilities. Liquidity ratios determine how quickly a company can convert the assets and use them for meeting the dues that arise. The higher the ratio, the easier is the ability to clear the debts and avoid defaulting on payments.

Ratios	As on 31st March, 2022	As on 31st March, 2021
Current Ratio = Current asset / Current liabilities	9994.47/ 4689.44 = **2.13**	14175.13/ 5643.21 = **2.51**
Acid Test Ratio (Quick Ratio)	(9994.47 - 1230.51) / 4689.44 = **0.44**	(14175.13 - 1493.89)/5643.21 = **2.24**
Cash Ratio	(563.97 + NA)/4689.44 = **0.120**	(505.13 + NA)/5643.21 = **0.089**

- The current ratio measures the ability of a company to cover its short-term obligations with its short-term assets. A higher current ratio indicates a stronger ability to meet short-term liabilities. Comparing the two periods, the current ratio decreased from 2.51 to 2.13, suggesting a slight decrease in the company's liquidity or ability to cover its short-term liabilities.
- The acid test ratio, also known as the quick ratio, measures a company's ability to pay off its current liabilities using only its most liquid assets (excluding inventory). A higher quick ratio indicates a stronger ability to meet short-term obligations. Comparing the two periods, the acid test ratio decreased from 2.24 to 0.44, indicating a significant decrease in the company's ability to cover short-term liabilities using its most liquid assets.
- The cash ratio measures the ability of a company to pay off its current liabilities using only cash and cash equivalents. A higher cash ratio indicates a stronger ability to meet short-term obligations using cash. Comparing the two periods, the cash ratio increased from 0.089 to 0.120, suggesting an improvement in the company's ability to cover short-term liabilities using cash and cash equivalents.

CAPITAL STRUCTURE RATIOS –

Ratios	As on 31st March, 2022	As on 31st March, 2021
Debt – Equity Ratio = Long term debt / Net worth	123.07/26668.80 = **0.00**	121.96/25202.26 = **0.00**
Total outside liabilities to net worth = Total Outside Liabilities / Net Worth		

- The Debt-Equity Ratio indicates the proportion of long-term debt relative to the net worth of a company. A ratio of 0.00 suggests that the company has no long-term debt in both periods. This implies that the company's long-term obligations are relatively low compared to its net worth.

- Without the specific values for total outside liabilities, it is not possible to interpret the ratio or make any comparisons between the two periods. The information provided for this ratio is incomplete.

WORKING CAPITAL RATIOS –

Ratios	As on 31st March, 2022	As on 31st March, 2021
Current Asset Turnover Ratio = Sales/Average Current Assets	= 32135.98/ (9994.47+141475.13/2) **= 2.66:1**	= 27132.90/ (14175.13 + 6596.96/2) **= 2.61:1**
Current Assets Holding Period = 365 Days / Current asset turnover Ratio	= 365/2.66 **137 Days**	= 365/2.61 **= 139 Days**
Inventory Turnover Ratio = COGS/Average Inventory	=33144.7/ (1230.51+1493.89/2) **= 24.33:1**	= 27274.1/ (1493.89+1063.50/2) **= 21.32:1**
Inventory Holding Period = 365 Days / Inventory turnover Ratio	= 365/24.33 **= 15 Days**	= 365/21.32 **= 17 Days**
Debtors Turnover Ratio = Sales/ Average Debtors	= 32135.98/ (2716.85+1516.38/2) **= 15.18%**	= 27132.90/ (2716.85+1725.10/2) **= 12.21%**
Average Collection Period = 365 Days / Debtors Turnover Ratio	= 365 / 15.18% **= 24 Days**	= 365 / 12.21% **= 29 Days**
Creditors Turnover Ratio = Purchases/Creditors	= 22169.88/3633.18 **= 6.10%**	= 18308.09/4573.81 **= 4%**
Average Credit Availed = 365 days / Creditors turnover ratio	= 365/6.10% **= 60 Days**	= 365/4 **= 91 Days**

- The Current Asset Turnover Ratio measures a company's ability to generate sales from its average current assets. Comparing the two periods, the ratio increased slightly from 2.61:1 to 2.66:1, indicating a slightly more efficient utilization of current assets to generate sales.
- The Current Assets Holding Period represents the average number of days it takes for a company to convert its current assets into sales. Comparing the two periods, the holding period decreased slightly from 139 days to 137 days, suggesting a slight improvement in the efficiency of converting current assets into sales.
- The Inventory Turnover Ratio measures how efficiently a company manages its inventory by indicating how many times the inventory is sold and replaced during a period. Comparing the two periods, the ratio increased from 21.32:1 to 24.33:1, suggesting an improvement in inventory management and faster turnover of inventory.

- The Inventory Holding Period represents the average number of days it takes for a company to sell its inventory

Profitability ratio: Profitability ratios are a type of accounting ratio that helps in determining the financial performance of business at the end of an accounting period. Profitability ratios show how well a company is able to make profits from its operations.

PROFITABILITY RATIOS	2022	2021
PBIT Margin (%)	18.7	21.43
PBT Margin (%)	19.62	21.4
Net Profit Margin (%)	15.14	16.41
Return on Net worth / Equity (%)	18.81	18.07
Return on Capital Employed (%)	22.76	22.96
Return on Assets (%)	15.72	14.44
Total Debt/Equity (X)	0	0
Asset Turnover Ratio (%)	1.04	0.99

Ratios	As on 31st March, 2022	As on 31st March, 2021
Contribution Margin (%) = Sales – Variable Cost/Sales X 100	= 33144.71 – 24329.81/33144*100 **= 26.59%**	= 27741.08 – 19609.65/ 277471.08*100 **= 29.31%**
Gross Profit Margin (%) = Sales – COGS / Sales x 100	= 33144.71 – 24329.81/33144*100 **= 26.59%**	= 27741.08 – 19609.65/ 277471.08*100 **= 29.31%**
Net Profit Margin (%) = PAT /Sales x 100	= 5018.87/33144.71*100 = 15.14%	= 4554.59/27741.08*100 **=16.41%**
Return on Capital Employed (%) = EBIT/ Net Asset x 100	=6513.99/ 27232.5 * 100 **= 23.91%**	= 5945.66/ 25886.99*100 **= 22.96%**
ROE (%) = PAT/Net Worth x 100	= 5018.87/27232.5*100 **= 18.42%**	= 4554.59/11711.86*100 **= 38.88%**

VALUATION RATIOS	2022	2021
EV/Net Operating Revenue (X)	3.17	3.81
EV/EBITDA (X)	16.25	17.04
Net Operating Revenue (X)	3.19	3.83
Price/Net Operating Revenue	3.19	3.83
Earnings Yield	0.05	0.04

Valuation Ratio: Valuation is the financial process of determining what a company is worth. Valuation ratios put that insight into the context of a company's share price, where they serve as useful tools for evaluating investment potential.

Basic EPS (Rs.)	173.6	157.5

- The EV/Net Operating Revenue ratio compares the enterprise value (which includes both equity and debt) to the net operating revenue. It indicates the market's valuation of the company relative to its operating revenue. A lower ratio suggests a relatively lower valuation. Comparing the two years, the ratio decreased from 3.81 to 3.17, indicating a relatively lower valuation in 2022 compared to 2021.
- The EV/EBITDA ratio compares the enterprise value to the earnings before interest, taxes, depreciation, and amortization (EBITDA). It is a measure of a company's valuation relative to its operating profitability. A lower ratio generally suggests a relatively lower valuation. Comparing the two years, the ratio decreased from 17.04 to 16.25, indicating a relatively lower valuation in 2022 compared to 2021.
- The Net Operating Revenue ratio represents the ratio of net operating revenue to a specific variable (not specified in the provided chart). Without the specific variable, it is challenging to provide a detailed interpretation. However, comparing the two years, the ratio decreased from 3.83 to 3.19, indicating a decrease in net operating revenue relative to the unspecified variable.

SUMMARY AND CONCLUSIONS

On the basis of the financial ratios in the financial statements, ageing and expected dates of realization of financial assets and payment of financial liabilities, other information accompanying the financial statements, our knowledge of the Board of Directors and Management plans and based on our examination of the evidence supporting the assumptions, nothing has come to our attention, which causes us to believe that any material uncertainty exists as on the date of the audit report that the Company is not capable of meeting its liabilities existing at the date of balance sheet as and when they fall due within a period of one year from the balance sheet date. We, however, state that this is not an assurance as to the future viability of the Company. We further state that our reporting is based on the facts up to the date of the audit report and we neither give any guarantee nor any assurance that all liabilities falling due within a period of one year from the balance sheet date, will get discharged by the Company as and when they fall due.

REFERENCES

1. Swadin Kumar Mohanthy (2018) A Study on Customer Satisfaction at Bajaj Auto Ltd. Malla Reddy Engineering College (A) Maisammaguda, Dhulapally, Secunderabad.
2. Mello. S., Lasser, R., Mackey, W. and Tait, R. (2006), Value Innovation Portfolio Management, Achieving double-digit growth by customer value, J.Ross Publications.
3. Surry, D.W. and Ely, P.D. (2001), Adoption, Diffusion, Implementation, and Institutionalization of Educational Technology, Boston, Blackwell Publishing Ltd.

Behavioral Finance and Its Role in Investment Decision Making

CHAPTER 24

Authors: Rajsee Warang and Siddhesh Kadam, students, IES's Management College and Research Centre, Mumbai

ABSTRACT

Behavioral finance is a field of study that combines psychology and economics to understand the decision-making processes of individuals and institutions in financial markets. It seeks to explain why individuals may deviate from traditional financial theory in making investment decisions and how these deviations can impact financial markets.

In investment decision-making, behavioral finance highlights how psychological biases, such as overconfidence, framing effects, and loss aversion, can affect investment choices. For example, overconfidence can lead to excessive trading and poor portfolio performance, while loss aversion can cause individuals to hold onto losing investments for too long.

Behavioral finance can inform investment strategies by incorporating insights from psychology into investment decision-making processes. By understanding the psychological factors that influence investment decisions, investors can make better-informed choices and potentially achieve better investment outcomes.

Overall, the role of behavioral finance in investment decision-making is to provide a more comprehensive understanding of how individual behavior affects financial markets and to help investors make more informed investment decisions.

KEYWORDS

Behavioural finance, Behaviour, Finance, Psychology, Investment, Decision Making

INTRODUCTION

Behavioral finance is a branch of economics that studies how investors make financial decisions by combining insights from psychology, sociology, and economics. It acknowledges that investors are not always rational and that psychological biases, emotions, and social factors frequently influence their decisions.

Behavioral finance has a significant impact on investment decision-making. Investors who are aware of their own biases and tendencies are better able to make sound decisions and avoid common pitfalls. Investors, for example, may be overly optimistic about the prospects of a specific stock or investment, causing them to buy when prices are high and sell when prices are low. They may also be overly influenced by recent market trends, causing them to make rash decisions based on short-term market fluctuations.

Investors can learn to identify and control their biases by understanding the principles of behavioral finance. They can, for example, use a disciplined approach to investment decision-making based on a long-term strategy and a diversified portfolio. They can also use risk management tools like stop-loss orders and asset allocation to avoid making emotional decisions.

Furthermore, behavioral finance has resulted in the development of new investment strategies that account for the psychological factors that influence investor behavior. Some investors, for example, employ momentum investing, which entails purchasing stocks that have recently performed well and selling those that have recently performed poorly. Others employ value investing, which entails purchasing undervalued stocks and holding them for the long term.

Overall, behavioral finance has a significant impact on investment decision-making, which helps investors make better decisions and achieve their financial goals.

OBJECTIVES OF THE STUDY:

1. To investigate the influence of various cognitive and emotional biases on investment decision-making and their consequences for investment performance.
2. To analyze the role of investor sentiment and market sentiment indicators in understanding and predicting market trends and their impact on investment decisions.

FACTORS RESPONSIBLE FOR PSYCHOLOGICAL BIASES OF INVESTORS

Several factors can contribute to investors' psychological biases, which include:
A. Cognitive Biases: Cognitive biases are thinking errors that occur when people process information.

a. Confirmation Bias: Confirmation bias is the tendency of people to pay close attention to information that confirms their belief and ignore information that contradicts it. This bias may lead investors to focus only on information that reinforces their opinions about an investment. Selectively choosing which information to use can lead to a lack of diversification and investments that are too risky.
b. Anchoring Bias: The tendency to rely too heavily on the first piece of information encountered when making decisions. Regardless of the accuracy of that information, people use it as a reference point, or anchor, to make subsequent judgments. An anchoring bias can cause an investor to make an incorrect financial decision, such as buying an overvalued investment or selling an undervalued investment.
c. Overconfidence Bas: Overconfidence bias is a behavioral principle that can be used to describe overestimating one's financial acumen. Investors may be tricked into thinking they can beat the market or may suffer higher trading costs as a result.

B. Emotional biases

Emotional biases can influence an investor's decision-making process. Fear, for example, can cause irrational decisions, such as selling investments too soon during a downturn. Greed, on the other hand, can lead to an investor taking excessive risks in trying to achieve greater returns.

C. Social biases

An investor's biases can be influenced by social factors. An investor, for example, may feel pressure to conform to the opinions or actions of others in their social or professional circles, even if this goes against their better judgment.

D. Experiential biases

Previous experiences as an investor can influence their decision-making process. For example, if an investor has previously suffered a significant financial loss, they may be more risk-averse in the future.

E. Personality traits

Personality traits, such as impulsivity or overconfidence, can all contribute to an investor's biases.

It is important for investors to be aware of these biases, as that can help them take steps to mitigate them, such as taking into consideration a diverse perspective, taking a more analytical approach to decision-making, and sticking to a long-term investment strategy.

REVIEW OF LITERATURE

SR NO.	TITLE OF RESEARCH PAPER	RESEARCHER AND YEAR	OBJECTIVES	FINDINGS
1.	Influence of Behavioural Factors on the Adoption of Digital Finance An Empirical S	Jain, Niyati (2022)	-To understand the perception of risk and its dimension while explaining the adoption of digital finance. -To understand the benefits and dimensions of the adoption of digital finance faced by individuals.	-Perceived risk is associated with the adoption intention of digital finance -Perceived benefit is associated with the adoption intention of digital finance
2.	Influence of behavioral traits on investment decisions	M C, Minimol (2018)	-To determine various components of investment decisions -To study whether components of investment decisions of individual investors vary significantly due to demographic factors. -To study the difference in behavioural traits of individual investors due to demographic factors	-This study shows that the attitude of investors has a significant impact on investors decision making -The next part of the analysis statistically proved that the investment patterns of individual investors vary significantly due to their behavioral traits.

INFERENCES BASED ON THE RESPONSES RECEIVED FROM THE PARTICIPANTS

Table 1. TABLE ON BEHAVIORAL BIASES THAT HAVE INFLUENCED YOUR INVESTMENT DECISIONS IN THE PAST

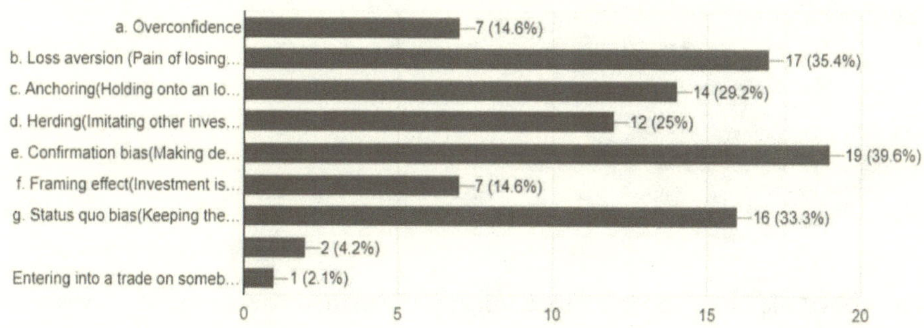

From the above chart, we get to know that a lot of people feel Confirmation biases (making decisions based on one's belief) and Loss aversion (the pain of losing is greater than gaining) are the major factors responsible for behavioral biases. People tend to base their decisions on their prior beliefs, ignoring other news, and loss aversion, which causes people to hold onto losing investments in the hopes that they will eventually turn profitable. For example, if someone believes that a particular stock is good, they will ignore any negative news that may be released about the company.

Table 2. TABLE ON WHICH OF THE INVESTMENT STRATEGIES RESPONDENTS FOLLOW

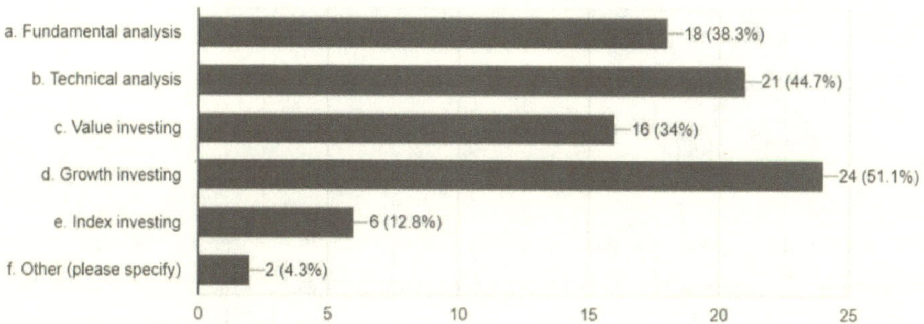

From the above chart, we get to know that most people prefer Growth investing, Technical Analysis, and Fundamental Analysis as strategies for investing. Other analysis is not much preferred by the respondents.

Table 3. TABLE ON WHICH OF THE FOLLOWING FACTORS HAS THE GREATEST IMPACT ON INVESTMENT DECISION-MAKING

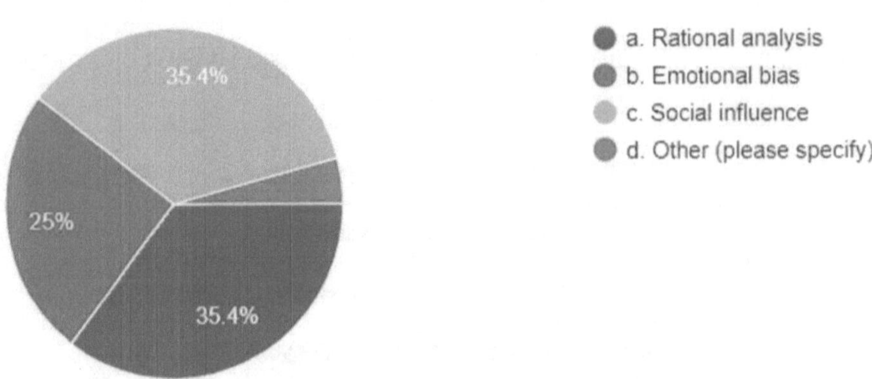

The above pie chart explains that, mostly investment decisions are impacted by Rational Analysis and Social Influence rather than Emotional or other factors. Many investors do their research and due diligence before investing in a particular stock but at the same time, there are people who invest based on social influence.

Table 4. TABLE ON HAVE THE RESPONDENTS EVER REGRETTED AN INVESTMENT DECISION THEY MADE IN THE PAST AND REASON FOR THE SAME

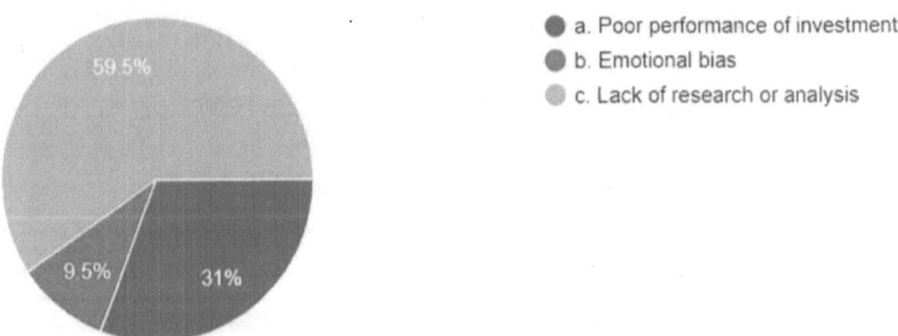

People think lack of research or analysis of stock is the reason behind them regretting their decision to invest in a particular stock. The major reason is a lack of awareness about the topic and not having in-depth knowledge about the same.

Table 5. TABLE ON REASON FOR THEIR IMPULSIVE DECISION

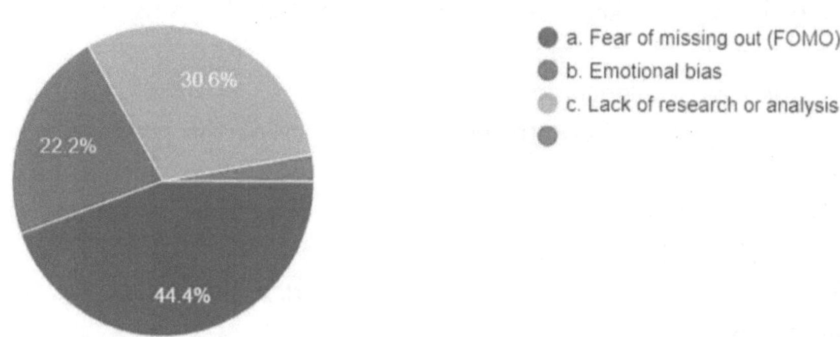

Most people invest in the stock market because of FOMO i.e. Fear of Missing Out and just because their friends are also investing. They lack the knowledge and experience one needs while investing and thus the decisions taken there turn out to be non-favourable to them.

CONCLUSION

This research was undertaken with the purpose of understanding the preferences of investors towards investment. With this project, the aim was to understand how consumers' minds get influenced, or what their mindsets are while making investments. This research report concentrated on the population of Mumbai, which comprised our 100 respondents. It can be concluded that a lot of people might be ignorant about investments, while a lot of people are keen on investing in different asset classes. The research was conducted keeping in mind all the age groups, which were the 100 responses.

Through the questionnaire conducted, we learned that a lot of people feel confirmation biases (making decisions based on one's beliefs) and loss aversion (the pain of losing is greater than the pain of gaining) are the major factors responsible for behavioral biases. While most people prefer growth investing, technical analysis, and fundamental analysis as strategies for investing, it explains that, mostly, investment decisions are impacted by rational analysis and social influence rather than emotional or other factors. At times, people have regretted investment decisions and felt that a lack of research or analysis of stocks was the reason behind their regretting their decision to invest in a particular stock.

While a lot of people have indulged in impulsive decisions, most people invest in the stock market because of FOMO, i.e., fear of missing out, and just because their friends are also investing.

Summarizing the conclusion:

The most preferred investment asset class among the participants was equity.

Most people evaluate the performance of their portfolio by comparing it with their personal financial goals.

It was found that most people review their portfolio once a month, while others review it every quarter.

LIMITATIONS

Due to time and resource constraints, this study suffers from the following limitations:

- The study has been conducted only between a few people, and the sample size is limited to 102 customers.
- The study is based on a primary survey that has been conducted through a structured questionnaire. The respondents might have deliberately given responses that they did not actually experience, and hence, subjectivity might be present in their responses.
- Only behavioral investment is studied. Other aspects are not covered in this study.
- In spite of all due and diligent efforts to explore the correct possible solution regarding the investment behavior and strategies of respondents, the data may not be fully reliable. Moreover, the data are dependent on time and may change with the changing preferences and mindsets of respondents.
- Due to time constraints, we were not able to do an in-depth study of the topic. There are topics that can be further studied in detail by researchers.

FURTHER SCOPE FOR STUDIES

The study covers how behavioral biases can influence the decision-making of an individual; it also examines which investment strategies individuals use; it also studies what impacts decisions, when respondents regret decisions, and how people make impulsive decisions.

All the other factors are not covered in this study, which is the scope of the study for researchers.

Researchers can examine the biases of respondents while making decisions; they can also examine investment choices based on income; and they can study the factors responsible for making investments with regard to age.

BIBLIOGRAPHY

https://shodhganga.inflibnet.ac.in/handle/10603/426717

https://shodhganga.inflibnet.ac.in/bitstream/10603/426717/5/05_chapter1.pdf

https://shodhganga.inflibnet.ac.in/bitstream/10603/426717/9/09_chapter5.pdf

https://shodhganga.inflibnet.ac.in/handle/10603/429645

https://shodhganga.inflibnet.ac.in/bitstream/10603/429645/5/05_chapter%201.pdf

https://shodhganga.inflibnet.ac.in/bitstream/10603/429645/9/09_chapter%205.pdf

https://shodhganga.inflibnet.ac.in/handle/10603/429645 https://www.investopedia.com/articles/02/112502.asp

"Value Investing and Behavioral Finance" a book by Parag Parikh

A Study on Indian Foreign Trade

CHAPTER 25

Author – Deepika Jaiswar & Shaunak Nande, *Student, IES's Management College and Research Centre, Mumbai*

ABSTRACT

India is the most important player in the global economy. Trade plays very strong role in the country's economy and growth. As the trade increases, the business and the employment will also increase, by that the country will also grow. The Indian trade and external sector have a high impact on the GDP growth and expansion in per capita income. In 2022, foreign exchange reserves in India stood at 524.52 US billion dollar. India's merchandise export in January 2022 was USD 34.06 billion, an increase of 23.69% over USD 27.54 billion in January 2021 and an increase of 31.75% over USD 25.85 billion in January 2020. India's overall exports (Merchandise and Services combined) in April-November 2022 is estimated to exhibit a positive growth of 17.72% over the same period last year. India's overall export in December 2022 is estimated to be USD61.82 billons, exhibiting a negative growth of -5.26% over the same period. The total export is 421.894US billion-dollar, total import is 612.608 US billion dollar. US is the largest exporter of India; and China is the largest importer of India; but in year 2020 it witnessed the largest reduction in trade since World War II due to COVID-19 and it has impacted the economy of the country. The export of goods and services accounted for 19.74% and import accounted for 23.64% of Gross Domestic Production of India During the pre-COVID-19 era but it has so much of impact on trade in India is estimated to be 348 million dollar and India falls under the category of 15 most affected economies. Now again India has witnessed the sharpest rise with the sixth position jump from 43rd to 37th rank. This paper highlights the performance of Indian foreign trade with another country, state wise import and export of the product, it focuses on the performance of the industries and Indian merchandise trade. It tries to focus on meaning and definition of foreign trade and various economic policies related to foreign trade which contributes to its growth.

KEYWORDS

Indian Trade, International Trade, COVID-19 era, Export, Import, GDP.

INTRODUCTION

Trade is an exchange of goods and services from the different economic sector. The parties are not in any obligation to trade, the transaction will only happen if both the parties are considered it beneficial to their interests. There is no country in the world today which produces all the commodities it needs. Every country tries to produce those commodities in which it has a comparative advantage. It exchanges part of those commodities with the commodities produced by other countries relatively more efficiently. The relative difference in factor endowments, technology, tastes etc., among the nations of the world has greatly widened the basis of international trade. Trade plays very strong role in the country's economy and growth. As the trade increases, the business and the employment will also increase, through that the country will also grow. India is from agriculture economy but from few decades it has been shifted to service economy, foreign trade has been the source of multiple growth. It has not pushed the India economy towards greater per capita income but also pushed towards manufacturing excellence, India economy apart from the challenges from rising imports has controlled over several other issues.

OBJECTIVES OF THE STUDY

The following are the main objectives of the study:

1. To know the meaning and definition of the foreign trade
2. To study the types of foreign trade & foreign trade regulation in India
3. To understand new foreign trade policy
4. To know role of foreign trade in economic development
5. To study the India's import, export and GDP in last five years
6. T study export and import of the commodities
7. To state wise export of the product
8. To study the trade of India with another countries
9. To study overall Performance of State Trading Corporation of India

LITERATURE REVIEW

Dr. Pramod R. Botre (2018)- A researcher has taken the data from 2005-06 to 2015-16 of foreign trade, and it classified in two parts as export and import of oil and non-oil with trade balance. it concludes that liberalization, privatisation and globalization changes in the business environment for improving the foreign trade relation with other countries is very important.

Nazaquat Hussain (2017)- The paper examines the latest trend of foreign trade performance in India and its impact on Indian economy and society. It concluded that strong policy is require to push the export and import.

Prof. A.R. Dubay (2011)- A researcher examine the emerging trend and patterns of India's foreign trade in lite of trade reforms the data has been taken 2006-07 to 2008-09 and conclude that composition of trade which traditional product now change to non-traditional items, the direction of trade shows that EU, USA and OPEC countries to be the major destination of Indian export and import.

RESEARCH METHODOLOGY

The present research paper is based on secondary source of data. The secondary information has been collected from published books, articles published in different journals, various reports and websites.

FOREIGN TRADE

Meaning:

Foreign Trade is the exchange of goods and services between two countries in the international market. It helps in the availability of raw material/finished product in a country that either does not have it or has it in scarcity. No country is self-sufficient in terms of natural or man-made resources, so it is prudent to approach other countries that have them in abundance. Foreign trade in India includes all import and exports to and from India. Central Government is the administered by the Ministry of Commerce and Industry.

TYPES OF FOREIGN TRADE

Foreign trade can be classified into following groups:

- **Import Trade:** It is the purchase of goods and services from one country to another country. The flow of goods is from a foreign land to the home nation. Countries import goods and services when they need raw materials for producing goods or when they need a finished product for domestic consumption.

- **Export trade:** It is the selling of goods and services from one country to another country. The flow of goods is from the home nation to a foreign land. Countries export goods and services to another nation when they have that particular commodity in abundance.
- **Entrepot trade:** This process is also called re-export. In this form of trade, a business purchases goods or services from one country, reprocesses those products, and then sells them to another country.

FOREIGN TRADE REGULATION IN INDIA

The foreign policy of India is governed and regulated by the Foreign Trade (Development and Regulation) Act, 1992. This Act was established on the 7th of August in the year 1992. The Act hasn't been originated as a separate act to regulate the foreign policy, but the same came into existence as a replacement to the Import and Exports (Control) Act, 1947. The entire scenario of exports and imports in India is regulated and managed by the Foreign Trade (Development and Regulation) Act, 1992. This act has eliminated all the existing nuances of the previously introduced act and has given the Government of India some of the most enormous powers to control it. This act is considered to be a supreme legislation in accomplishment of the foreign trade taking place in the country. The Act has been incorporated with a major intention to provide a proper framework as to the development as well as standardization of the foreign trade by the way of facilitating imports and enhancing the exports in the country and all the other matters related to the same.

FOREIGN TRADE POLICY

The session was conducted on 12 January 2021 on the topic "New Foreign Trade Strategy for the year 2021-26." According to the committee, the main purpose of the policy would be to position India as a leader in global trade within the next five years.

The Ministry of Commerce and Industry was briefed on a few of the following proposals for the new policy as discussed with the committee, and the government appears committed to making considerable progress toward realizing its $5 trillion dream.

ROLE OF FOREIGN TRADE IN ECONOMIC DEVELOPMENT

The role of foreign trade in economic development are:

- **Foreign trade and economic development:** Foreign trade plays a very important role in the economic development of any country.
- **Foreign exchange earnings:** Foreign trade provides foreign exchange which can be used to remove poverty and other productive purposes.
- **Market expansion:** The demand factor plays a very important role in increasing the production of any country.
- **Foreign investment:** Foreign trade provides incentives for foreign investors to invest in those countries where there is a shortage of investment.
- **Increase in national income:** Foreign trade increases the scale of production and national income of the country.
- **Price stability:** Foreign trade helps to bring stability to the price level. All those goods which are short and prices are increasing can be imported and those goods which are surplus can be exported. Thereby stopping fluctuation in prices.
- **Specialization:** There is a difference in the quality and quantity of various factors of production in different countries. Each country adopts the specialization in the production of those commodities, in which it has a comparative advantage. So, all trading countries enjoy profit through international trade.

FINDINGS

India's Import

Imports of goods and services represent the value of all goods and other market services received from the rest of the world. They include the value of merchandise, freight, insurance, transport, travel, royalties, license fees, and other services, such as communication, construction, financial, information, business, personal, and government services. They exclude compensation of employees and investment income and transfer payments. Data are in current U.S. dollars.

India Imports - Historical Data		
Year	**Billions of US $**	**% of GDP**
2021	$758.87B	23.89%
2020	$509.43B	19.10%
2019	$602.31B	21.27%
2018	$640.30B	23.69%
2017	$582.02B	21.95%

From: 2017 To: 2023 Zoom: 5Y 10Y 20Y 30Y All

INDIA'S EXPORT

Exports of goods and services represent the value of all goods and other market services provided to the rest of the world. They include the value of merchandise, freight, insurance, transport, travel, royalties, license fees, and other services, such as communication, construction, financial, information, business, personal, and government services. They exclude compensation of employees and investment income and transfer payments. Data are in current U.S. dollars.

India Exports - Historical Data		
Year	**Billions of US $**	**% of GDP**
2021	$679.68B	21.40%
2020	$499.10B	18.71%
2019	$529.24B	18.69%
2018	$538.64B	19.93%
2017	$498.26B	18.79%

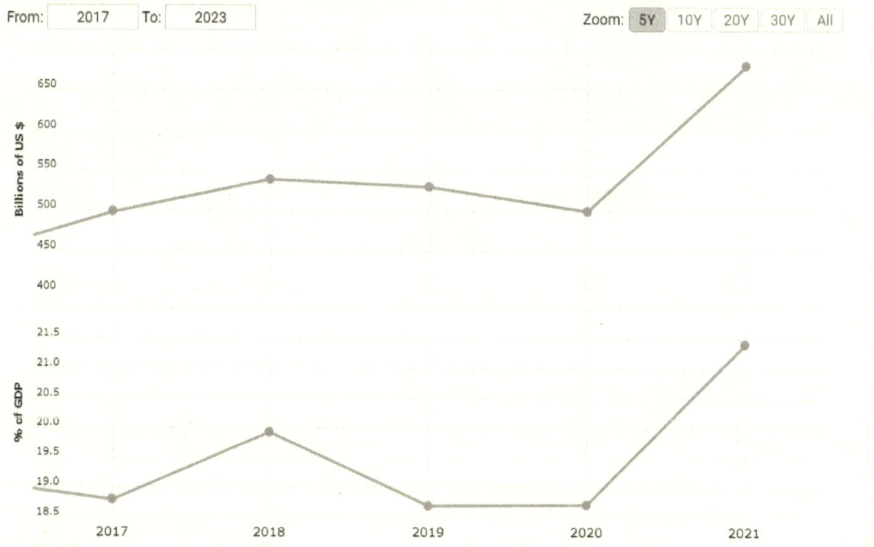

TRADE TO GDP RATIO

Trade is the sum of exports and imports of goods and services measured as a share of gross domestic product.

India Trade to GDP Ratio - Historical Data		
Year	**Trade (% of GDP)**	**Annual Change**
2021	45.29%	7.48%
2020	37.81%	-2.16%
2019	39.96%	-3.65%
2018	43.62%	2.87%
2017	40.74%	0.66%

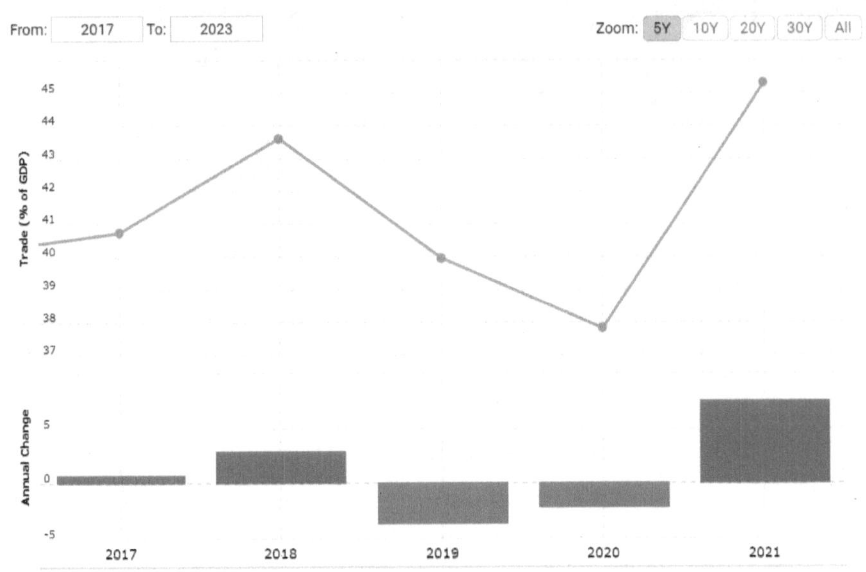

TRADE PERFORMANCE IN INDIA

Foreign trade performance in India deals with export, import and trade balance of foreign trade.

Table 1: Export of Principal Commodities

Export of Principal Commodities (In Rs.) from India						
(2017-2018 to 2022-2023-upto December 2022)						
(Rs. in Crore)						
Commodities	2017-2018	2018-2019	2019-2020	2020-2021	2021-2022	2022-2023[1] (P)
1. Plantation	11731.69	11627.59	11242.31	11066.44	13261.32	11841.82
2. Agriculture and Allied Products	179070.1	199825	185897.5	240728.8	282457.6	244146.4
3. Marine Products	47646.41	47664.94	47618.1	44175.75	57910.36	50157.93
4. Ores and Minerals	21308.34	25191.32	32605.4	52069.59	45068.9	24548.68
5. Leather and Leather Manufactures	35091.46	37049.86	34046.2	25782.63	34734.89	30886.77

Export of Principal Commodities (In Rs.) from India						
6. Gems and Jewellery	267832.9	281408.1	254114.2	191928.1	291481.1	230725.2
7. Sports Goods	1500.23	2195.06	1972.39	1987.98	2801.35	2448.88
8. Chemicals and Related Products	242114.4	306130.7	319029.8	357786.3	419784.7	344180.8
9. Plastic and Rubber Articles	48814	66059.14	58340.75	59800.31	79172.78	57198.09
10. Articles of Stone, Plaster, Cement, Asbestos, Mica or Similar Materials; Ceramic Products; Glass and Glassware	29136.54	35792.81	37365.86	41863.35	48040.84	37559.21
11. Paper and Related Products	17085.42	24420.9	23901.71	25222.32	39264.46	29558.74
12. Base Metals	181858.3	177767.4	169499.9	204875.4	351755.9	219206.7
13. Optical, Medical and Surgical Instruments	14657.06	16244.07	16766.74	16464.79	21642.28	22059.19
14. Electronics Items	39148.04	58858.07	79567.83	78639.05	111667	127847.2
15. Machinery	158792.4	203532.1	202556.9	195526.2	268327	232463
16. Office Equipment	506.85	1013.86	1356.37	1117	1562.56	1744.39
17.Transport Equipment	151383.3	185574.9	167875.3	149965.7	193559.2	164242.8

Export of Principal Commodities (In Rs.) from India						
18.Project Goods	142.05	112.58	217.84	16.81	28.13	14.33
19.Textiles and Allied Products	232307.6	257651.8	238928.4	224224.2	320006.7	207583.9
20.Petroleum Crude and Products	241434.5	325929.1	292340	190896.3	503820.4	586178.9
21.Others	34952.96	43676.91	44610.67	44906.02	59838.82	53000.36
Total	**1956515**	**2307726**	**2219854**	**2159043**	**3146186**	**2677593**

Table 1 explained India's exports of primary commodities from 2017-18 to 2022-23; in this period, three are significant commodities, namely Engineering goods, Gems & Jewelry, and petroleum products, which shared the highest contribution in total exports. From 2017-18 to 2022-23 total exports observed in up and down situation, like from 2017-18 to 2018-19 it has been increased drastically, then from 2018-19 to 2019-20 slightly decreased and then again decreases and then it starts to increase from 2021-22, so from this researcher can say that during research period exports are not constantly either increased or decreased and more volatility observed in exports.

Table 2: Import of Principal Commodities

Import of Principal Commodities (In Rs.) by India						
(2017-2018 to 2022-2023-upto December 2022)						
(Rs. in Crore)						
Commodities	2017-2018	2018-2019	2019-2020	2020-2021	2021-2022	2022-2023[1] (P)
1. Plantation	6697.22	7504.21	6299.84	6179.19	9232.67	7973.59
2. Agri & Allied Products	143230.2	129751.1	134823	147974.8	223669.2	197842.7
3. Marine Products	793.3	1088.13	1290.17	1668.85	1667.69	1531.62
4.Ores & Minerals	204632.1	234972.5	193534.8	154452.7	304811.5	378081.5
5.Leather & Leather Manufactures	6809.61	7645.32	7396.61	4418.97	6341.25	6683.59

Import of Principal Commodities (In Rs.) by India						
6. Gems & Jewellery	481433.7	451215	384857	405898.8	608665.5	473292
7. Sports Goods	1882.37	2324.98	1953.68	1957.72	2495.1	1978.88
8. Chemicals & Related Products	260368.6	334084.1	313495.7	332757.3	504257.5	461912.9
9. Plastic & Rubber Articles	109822.1	129132.5	120924.3	117067.9	174054.4	162375.5
10. Articles of Stone, Plaster, Cement, Asbestos, Mica or Similar Materials; Ceramic Products; Glass and Glassware	17498.27	19520.05	18353.41	16323.68	21989.49	21693.84
11. Paper & Related Products	53350.56	61307.51	55141.03	43225.82	62385.23	62166.99
12. Base Metals	176790.4	226534.7	201649.3	175673.9	260216.9	251863.7
13. Optical, Medical & Surgical Instruments	34426.31	41226.12	40580.3	37648.62	54486.26	46425.31
14. Electronics Items	332201.1	388118.1	371809.5	388812.2	528176.3	442491.5
15. Machinery	252340	321888	319905	266708.1	359410.8	326962.8
16. Office Equipment	302.09	369.16	625.66	602.18	426.43	474.9
17. Transport Equipment	123576.8	145019.1	154369.9	113621.8	122685.5	135897.6
18. Project Goods	13392.28	16617.76	14354.61	11106.88	10108.68	6078.46
19. Textiles & Allied Products	41257.71	47277.91	53082.51	39149.17	57159.18	62673.63
20. Petroleum Crude & Products	700320.8	986275.1	925167.5	611353.1	1207782	1306605
21. Others	39907.76	42803.33	41340.5	39355.98	49420.67	41639.36
Total	**3001033**	**3594675**	**3360954**	**2915958**	**4569443**	**4396646**

It is observed from Table 2 that India imports of major commodities from 2017-18 to 2022-23, in this period three are major commodities, namely Petroleum Crude & products, electronic goods and Machinery Electrical & Non-Electrical shared the highest contribution in total imports. From 2017-18 to 2022-23 total imports observed in up and down situation, like from 2017-18 to 2018-19 it has been increased, then from 2018-19 to 2019-20 slightly decreased and then decreased drastically and from year 2020-21 to 2021-22 it has suddenly increased, so from this researcher can say that during research period imports are not constantly either increased or decreased and more volatility observed in imports.

Table 3: Foreign Trade of Services by Services Export Promotional Council of India

Foreign Trade of Services by Services Export Promotion Council of India									
(2018-2019 to 2020-2021)									
(US$ in Million)									
Services	**2018-2019**			**2019-2020**			**2020-2021**		
	Export	**Import**	**Net**	**Export**	**Import**	**Net**	**Export**	**Import**	**Net**
Charges for the use of Intellectual Property n.i.e.	692	8028	-7335	934	7705	-6771	1310	7707	-6397
Construction	3388	2527	861	3096	2746	351	2620	2606	14
Financial Services	4858	3486	1372	4734	2919	1814	4338	4763	-424
Government Goods and Services n.i.e.	610	1114	-504	659	1107	-448	630	1021	-392
Insurance and Pension Services	2661	1790	871	2431	1738	692	2376	2058	318
Maintenance and Repair Services n.i.e.	189	1201	-1012	194	1182	-988	159	834	-675
Manufacturing Services on Physical Inputs Owned by Others	260	42	219	232	68	164	296	28	268
Other Business Services	39112	40413	-1301	45716	46881	-1165	49161	49522	-361
Personal, Cultural and Recreational Services	1853	2571	-719	2207	3131	-924	2336	2810	-474
Telecommunications, Computer and Information Services	86344	7409	78935	96110	10212	85899	103078	12278	90800
Transport	19464	20529	-1065	20988	24285	-3297	21854	19755	2099
Travel	28441	21704	6737	29998	22011	7987	8483	11507	-3024
Others n.i.e.	20128	15246	4882	5892	4284	1608	9447	2633	6814
Total Services	**208000**	**126060**	**81941**	**213191**	**128269**	**84922**	**206090**	**117524**	**88565**

It is observed from Table 3 that India imports of major commodities from 2018-19 to 2021-22, in this period three are major commodities, namely are charges for the use of intellectual properties, construction, Financial services and telecommunications, computer and information services. Trade doesn't mean the export and import of goods but it also means that export and import of services also. The exports of the services are increasing by the years from 2018-19 to 2020-21. The import of services remains almost constant in year 2018-19 to 2019-20 and then the import of the services decreases from year 2019-20 to 2020-21.

Table 4: State-wise Export of Principal Commodities

Selected State-wise Export of Principal Commodities (In Rs.) from India						
(2021-2022)						
(Rs. in Crore)						
States/UTs	**AC, Refrigeration Machinery etc.**	**Accumulators and Batteries**	**Agro Chemicals**	**Aircraft, Spacecraft and Parts**	**Alcoholic Beverages**	**Aluminium, Products of Aluminm**
Andhra Pradesh	6.8	95.57	28.43	649.49	2.77	2712.76
Assam	6.97	2.23	0.19	-	0	3.33
Bihar	256.43	149.21	192.37	0	19.95	368.29
Delhi	896.78	86.57	22.45	2313.85	15.05	325.63
Goa	-	-	115.87	18.44	45.76	-
Gujarat	838.01	271.08	11495.96	11.43	221.38	3541.01
Haryana	570.42	230.84	175.55	359.34	43.78	1429.72
Jharkhand	0.15	-	-	-	-	32.46
Karnataka	774.04	36.45	12.03	2645.84	49.01	947.09
Kerala	74.44	48.77	0.34	125.6	46.98	40.22
Madhya Pradesh	1056.79	-	-	-	7.2	101.8
Maharashtra	3618.91	1052.58	19091.05	1533.23	1153.71	12025.87
Odisha	-	-	-	-	-	36337.76
Punjab	18.47	300.35	62.29	-	203.54	352.14
Rajasthan	300.37	30.21	154.55	0.58	0.51	892.94
Tamil Nadu	1143.05	1299.42	2969.25	349.77	124.13	12249.61
Telangana	94.28	195.64	1094.69	490.4	0.02	515.93
Uttar Pradesh	406.31	332.5	850.78	2.89	197.54	1835.22
Uttarakhand	4.39	0.04	0.78	-	-	0.26
West Bengal	840.68	673.97	245.54	23.6	1.13	5159.2

Selected State-wise Export of Principal Commodities (In Rs.) from India						
Nepalganj	24.95	12.66	8.54	0.23	0.22	41.36
Other Ports	0.01	0.1	0.02	-	-	-
India	**10932.5**	**4818.19**	**36520.64**	**8524.67**	**2132.68**	**78912.61**

On the basis of Table 4 following observation can be made.

All states do some product export for the growth of their states and for which they are famous for. In this table we have observed that the export of the commodities is AC, Refrigeration Machinery etc., Accumulators and Batteries, Agro Chemicals, Aircraft, Spacecraft and Parts, Alcoholic Beverages and Aluminum, Product of Aluminm.The highest export of the commodities is Aluminum, Product of Aluminm. These are the states all of the commodities export has been done, these states are Andhar Pradesh, Delhi, Gujarat, Haryana, Karnataka, Kerala, Maharashtra,Rajashthan, Tamil Nadu, Telangana, Uttar Pradesh, West Bengal. The highest amount of export has been done in Maharashtra.

Table 5: Direction of Foreign Trade Export and Import of India

Direction of Foreign Trade Export and Import (In Rs.) of India								
(2018-2019 to 2021-2022)								
Country	2018-2019		2019-2020		2020-2021		2021-2022	
	Export	Import	Export	Import	Export	Import	Export	Import
1. Belgium	47008	73002	41165	62831	38684	51247	75226	74177
2. France	36594	46598	36132	43661	35358	32161	49626	43053
3. Germany	62214	106170	58725	96928	60123	101105	73727	111548
4. Italy	39092	37003	35264	31778	34995	28592	60962	37630
5. Netherlands	61575	28504	59213	23995	47871	24544	93746	33386
6. United Kingdom	65251	52744	62088	47496	60605	36613	78272	52288
7. Canada	19936	24656	20215	27423	21913	19959	28071	23350
8. United States of America	366628	248559	376306	253369	381917	213725	567601	323033
9. Australia	24574	91638	20205	69183	29936	60975	61841	125030
10. Japan	34012	89278	32005	88034	32821	80819	46050	107297
11. Switzerland	8292	126172	8505	119239	9343	133868	10059	174295
12. Iran	24461	94113	23855	9762	13213	2448	10832	3463
13. Iraq	12506	156601	13287	168354	11105	105655	17970	238418
14. Kuwait	9319	51949	9112	67932	7797	38525	9264	82115
15. Saudi Arabia	38854	199395	44267	190245	43359	119759	65310	254678

Direction of Foreign Trade Export and Import (In Rs.) of India								
16. United Arab Emirates	210213	208564	204239	214513	123334	196362	209158	334473
17. Indonesia	36891	111180	29302	106764	37159	92330	63211	132049
19. Russia	16728	40817	21400	50291	19652	40632	24234	73655
20. Afghanistan	4992	3078	7085	3766	6106	3753	4129	3806
21. South Africa	28334	45522	29114	49507	29075	55766	45353	81823
22. Benin	2987	2604	2297	2534	4102	2440	5348	2984
23. Egypt Arab Republic	20154	11698	17724	14391	16761	14019	27922	26236
24. Kenya	14441	961	14937	633	14031	961	19623	1083
25. Sudan	6435	5195	7791	2800	7566	2712	8028	960
26. Tanzania	11925	6281	12327	7288	10644	6888	17224	17011
27. Zambia	2238	3567	1754	5986	1987	944	2540	878
28. People's Republic of China	117293	492079	117684	461525	157213	482496	158196	705123
29. Bangladesh	64393	7339	58177	8975	71510	8053	120337	14750
30. Hong Kong	91117	125972	77752	119999	75201	112218	81835	142401
31. Bhutan	4591	2590	5235	2871	5193	3214	6538	4054
32. South Korea	32881	117255	34341	110883	34699	94476	60353	130299
33. Malaysia	45104	75492	45107	69167	44971	61791	52124	92631
34. Maldives	1557	147	1608	42	1452	181	4983	517
35. Nepal	54301	3558	50713	5045	50466	4975	71852	10208
36. Singapore	80943	113919	63027	104394	64383	98220	83013	141574
37. Pakistan	14427	3476	5718	98	2415	18	3831	19
38. Thailand	31106	51980	30451	48048	31301	42002	42898	69622
39. Sri Lanka	32996	10376	26935	6407	25858	4752	43334	7530
40. S A A R C	177258	30565	155471	27203	163000	24947	255004	40883

On the basis of Table 5 following observation can be made.

In this table we have observed that Total 40 countries are participating in export and import. The most of the countries do not produce the commodities what they are needing, so they import and the most of the countries which they produce and are famous for they export to gain the income of the country and make the country and to provide employment in the country. The most common destination for the exports of India is United States, China, United Arab Emirates, Hong Kong, and Germany. The most common destination for the import of India are China, United States, United Arab Emirates Saudi Arabia and Switzerland. The import has been increased from year 2017-18 to 2018-19. But in year 2018-19 and 2019-20 the import has suddenly starts fall because of COVID-19. COVID-19 has also impacted the trade of the India. The lockdown which has happened in the country had made the impact every business but it has also impacted the trade of the country. But after the COVID-19 the market has again came to its pace and started working than the previous years.

Table 6: Overall Performance of State Trading Corporation of India

Overall Performance of State Trading Corporation of India				
(2017-2018 to 2020-2021)				
Description	**2017-2018 (A)**	**2018-2019 (A)**	**2019-2020 (A)**	**2020-2021 (A)**
Exports	266	11	11	Nil
Imports	10216	8437	2536	12
Domestic Sales	343	445	383	235
Total Turnover Tax	10825	8893	2930	247
Profit Before Rax	32.25	-897.12	-113.63	-51.23
Profit After Tax	38	-	-	-

On the basis of Table 6 following observation can be made.

In the table 6 we have observed that due to COVID-19 all the type of business was affected and trade market was also affected as well. From year 2018-19 to 2020-21 the trade of import and export had been decreased and and after COVID-19 the trade market has started to perform well. The profit before tax has been constantly decreasing -897.12 in year 2018-19, -113.63 in year 2019-20 and -51.23 in year 2020-21 as market is performing better.

CONCLUSIONS

The present research study concludes that, With the Liberalization, Privatization and Globalization of the Indian economy and following liberal foreign trade, there had been changes in the business environment. The traders face more difficulties for selling of goods and services. Process of import and export are difficult one for every developing country. For the fast and stable development of the country, the commercial relations of the country with the other countries all over the world are very important. This is possible when a country allows imports as well as exports of goods and services. The trade transactions are to be monitored for which framing of the foreign trade policies is very much essential. Government has encouraged exporters to improve production of various commodities. The exports and imports of a country give rise to monetary transactions with other countries. The various new initiatives undertaken are the move towards promoting exports, promoting use of technology, and reduction in the transaction cost.

References

1. https://www.indiastat.com/
2. https://edurev.in/t/113989/Role--Importance-of-Foreign-Trade-in-India-Sector-#:~:text=Foreign%20trade%20has%20played%20a,spirit%20of%20development%20in%20them.
3. https://www.investopedia.com/terms/t/trade.asp
4. https://www.macrotrends.net/countries/IND/india/imports
5. https://vakilsearch.com/blog/new-foreign-trade-policy-2021-2026/#:~:text=The%20government%20launched%20the%20Foreign,the%20industrial%20and%20production%20industries.
6. https://blog.ipleaders.in/foreign-trade-policy/#:~:text=The%20Foreign%20Trade%20(Development%20and%20Regulation)%20Act%2C%201992&text=This%20Act%20was%20established%20on,(-Control)%20Act%2C%201947.

Impact of Instagram on Emotional Well-being of Gen-Z

CHAPTER 26

Author – Shreya Bangera, Shweta Rane & Drushti Parab, Student, IES's Management College and Research Centre, Mumbai

ABSTRACT

Generation Z (Gen -Z) refers to the generation of individuals born from 1997 to 2012. These are individuals who are digitally active as compared to the previous generations. When it comes to social media they prefer Instagram over other applications. The frequency of the usage is high on daily basis because of better user experience, engaging content, current trends and networking. In this paper we will be studying Gen Z's use of social media and its effects on individuals and society as a whole. It describes how they use social media and the generational differences that result from both personal and environmental factors. Personal factors consist steady and driving factors. It also makes an effort to present analysis of emotional well-being. Instagram usage is related with several negative psychological effects including poor sleep quality, bullying, body image, FOMO, sets unrealistic expectations, feelings of inadequacy and low self-esteem, which might further lead to higher levels of anxiety, stress, depression and can also promote a 'compare and despair' attitude amongst the Gen-Z. Its intensity appeared to influence the emotional well-being of individuals who spent more time on the application. Mixed analysis will be supported to find significant implications for all the users.

KEYWORDS

'emotional well-being', 'Gen-Z', 'Instagram', 'social media', 'stress', 'virtual presence', 'well-being'

INTRODUCTION

Gen-Z:

Generation Z, commonly referred to as Gen-Z (people born between 1996 and 2014), is so far the most progressive generation as compared to generations before it. They are the new wave of the modern world. It has led to advances in many areas, including technology, work, interpersonal relationships, emotional well-being, etc. Technological advancements and social media play a vital role in the development of Gen-Z because they give them access to unlimited knowledge and provide the opportunity to connect with people and organizations around the globe. Because of their concepts and desires to make the world a better place, they are regarded as a revolutionary generation. They prefer transparency, flexibility, self-reliance, and personal freedom as non-negotiable factors, and overlooking them could lead to dissatisfaction among peers, low morale, decreased productivity, and lack of employee engagement.

INSTAGRAM

Instagram is one of the most preferred social media platforms today. It primarily focuses on sharing photos and videos that can be edited by filters and organized by hashtags and geographical tagging. It lets user interact with other users by following them, letting others follow you, sharing stories, commenting, liking, tagging, saving photos and private messaging features. Instagram has turned into a multifaceted app that combines elements from YouTube (live streams, IGTV), Snapchat (Insta-Stories), Twitter (political statements) and Facebook (sharing photos) into one platform. The stats from a Business Insider survey states the fact that 65% of Gen-Z checks Instagram on a daily basis, given its versatility. This indicates proves that Gen-Z prefers Instagram in great numbers.

EMOTIONAL WELL-BEING

When we think about wellness, we see averting disease, maintaining good health, and eventually enhancing the quality of life. Emotional wellness, on the other hand, refers to the knowledge, comprehension, and acceptance of our feelings as well as our capacity for efficient problem-solving under pressure. This is a frequently disregarded yet vital aspect of wellness. Emotional well-being is important because it can impact how people function and lead their daily lives, during overwhelming experiences, people lose a sense of control because what was familiar is no longer the same. In addition, it may have an impact on your relationships, career, and general mental and physical health. The state of one's physical health might be affected by emotional problems.

LITERATURE REVIEW

Research proves that there is correlation between Instagram usage and psychological well-being (anxiety, stress, and depression). Instagram usage appeared to influence psychological well-being, with participants who spent more time on Instagram reporting poorer psychological well-being. Whereas higher levels of self-compassion are associated with lower levels of reported depression, anxiety, and stress. Possible explanations and future directions are discussed as to what could explain the positive association between self-compassion and Instagram usage Invalid source specified..

The authors explore persuasive issues such as Social Comparison, Mental Health, Colourism and their relationship with Instagram use, focusing on young adults living in India. Social comparison has been linked to colourism and mental health problems, according to research. However, gender was found to have insignificant relation. Discussions revealed the need to raise awareness regarding these issues to enjoy social media while safeguarding the user's well-being Invalid source specified..

The research explores the effect of online technologies on youth's mental well-being. The benefits of using online technologies were reported as increased perceived social support, self-esteem, increased opportunity for self-disclosure, increased social capital, and safe identity experimentation. Adverse consequences were reported as increased exposure to harm, social isolation, cyber-bullying, and depression. The majority of studies reported either mixed or no effect of online social technologies on youth's wellbeing Invalid source specified..

Research examines the awareness of how the present Gen-Z is using social media as well as to review its repercussion on them as an individual, organizations, and society as a whole. The paper distinguishes Gen-Z's systematized differentiation in the behaviour, principles, and choices which are constant over the time. It describes how their use of Instagram is influenced by both personal and environmental factors Invalid source specified..

RESEARCH METHODOLOGY

Objectives:

- To analyse Gen Z's use of Instagram and its effects on their emotional well-being.

SUB-OBJECTIVES

- To understand the effects of Sharing, learning and interacting model of Instagram on Gen-Z.
- To analyse the virtual presence of Gen-Z on Instagram.
- To understand the emotional experience that Gen-Z goes through while using Instagram.
- To understand the impact of Instagram on Gen-Z's personal and environmental factors.

DATA COLLECTION

Primary data is collected through a questionnaire from Gen-Z (people born from the year 1996-2014). Secondary data is collected through websites, books, articles, and research papers.

SAMPLE SIZE

The Sample size consists of 210 respondents residing in India.

LIMITATIONS OF THE STUDY

1. Neutral responses by respondents did not give us a correct view of Instagram's impact on their emotional well-being
2. Since the knowledge of emotional well-being amongst Gen-Z is relatively low, the responses were not adequate to get a deeper understanding of the concept.
3. There was limited data collected through online questionnaires and, the respondents do not represent the entire population of India.
4. Though the study is based on an individual's perception there could be a difference in the opinions shared, hence conclusions and suggestions cannot be generalized.

FINDINGS AND DISCUSSIONS

A survey was conducted amongst Gen-Z (individuals born from the year 1996-2014). The aim was to consolidate a list of responses to understand the impact of Instagram usage on the emotional well-being of Gen-Z. From the sample size of 210 respondents, 44.8% were female and 55.2% were male.

What is your average usage time on Instagram per day?

205 responses

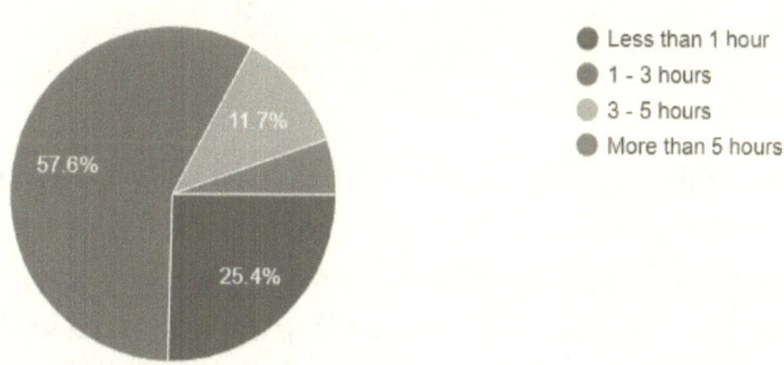

From the responses collected, we could find that 57.6% and 11.7% of Gen-Z spend 1-3 hours and 3-5 hours respectively of their day on Instagram. This indicates that Instagram's user interface is appealing and its Sharing, Learning, and Interacting, model is effective for its users.

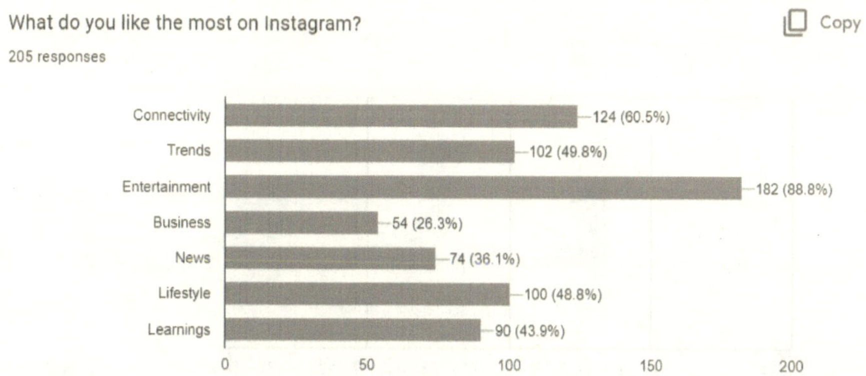

Out of 210 respondents, 88.8% choose Instagram for entertainment and 26.3% for Business, which is relatively low. From this data, we can infer that Gen-Z prefers Instagram for entertainment.

Does the content on Instagram affect your mood ?

205 responses

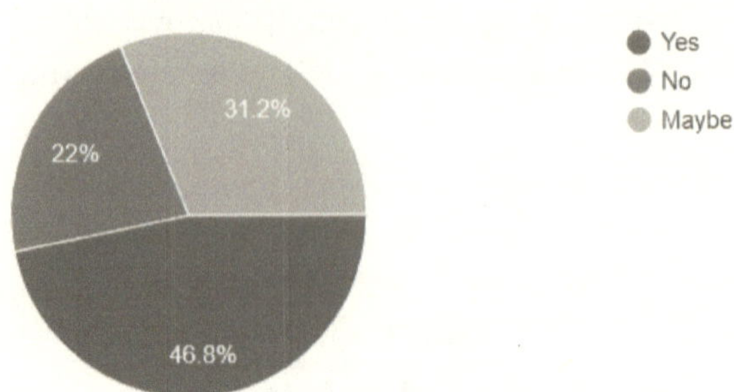

From this question, we can infer that 46.8% have accepted that Instagram affects their mood and 31.2% are undecided. This means a majority of the respondents feel Instagram's content directly affects their mood.

Our study focuses on understanding the emotional well-being of Instagram users in order to study this effectively we classified it into two groups which were further subdivided into 5 factors. Group A speaks about the positive experience while using Instagram and group B showcases the negative experience.

Have you faced any of these positive experiences while using Instagram?

Copy

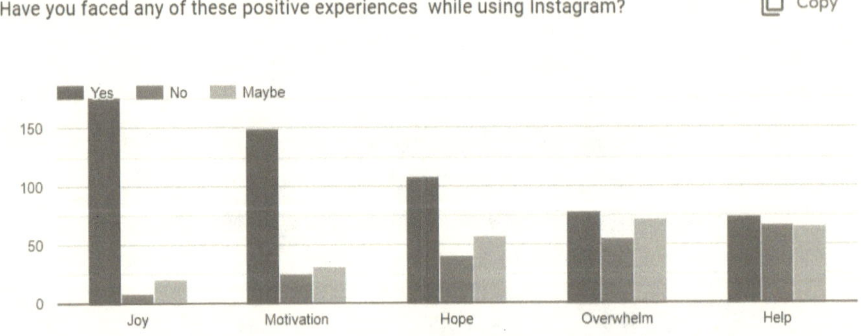

In Group A, the majority of users claimed that they experienced joy, motivation, and hope whereas there was a lower percentage of users who felt overwhelmed and help while using Instagram.

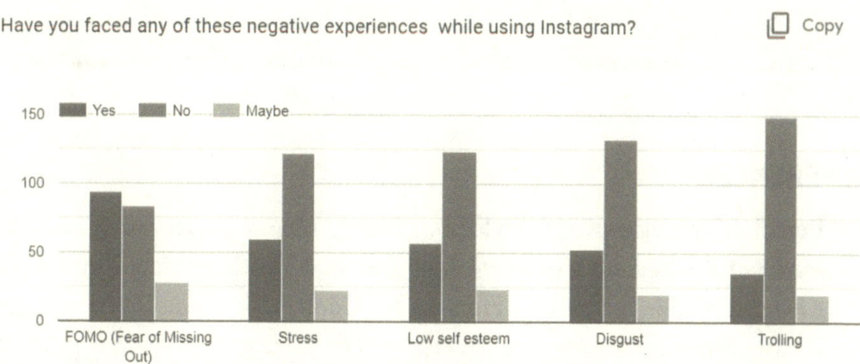

In group B, majority of the users claimed that they faced FOMO and majority of the users have not faced trolling while using Instagram.

CONCLUSION

In this digitally transforming world, our study is focused on understanding the impact that Instagram has on the emotional well-being of Gen Z. Emotional well-being is a growing yet crucial concept in today's world, and we attempted to understand the awareness level of this concept amongst them. From this study, we conclude that Instagram is highly popular and does impact their emotional well-being. The study was further broken down into understanding Gen-Z's personal and environmental factors. They tend to mindlessly scroll on Instagram as a temporary solution to either procrastinate or avoid stressful situations. It also showcased Instagram may have its advantages such as easy connectivity with people anywhere and anytime. However, when it came to understanding if online conversation were favoured over face-to-face conversations majority of individuals denied it. Considering virtual presence, Gen-Z claimed that they felt good about themselves when they got higher number of likes and comments on their posts. Our findings show that Instagram alone cannot be the only factor affecting the emotional well-being of Gen-Z.

SUGGESTIONS

Further research should be continued to investigate the impact of Instagram on emotional well-being and create awareness about how it would affect the intellectual and physical well-being of an individual. Once awareness is attained, one can choose from a variety of options, including mental yoga, mental coaching and life coaching, as these techniques may be useful in helping Gen-Z's overcome any challenges pertaining to their emotional well-being.

REFERENCES

- Best.P, Manktelow.R, & Taylor.B. (2014). *Online communication, social media and adolescent well-being.* Children and Youth Services Review, 10.
- Keyte.R, Mullis.L, Egan.H, Hussain.M, Cook.A, & Mantzios.M. (August 2020). *Self Compassion and Instagram Use Is Explained by the Relation.* Journal of Technology in Behavioral Science, 6.
- Sharma.A, Sanghvi.K, & Churi.P. (2022). *The impact of Instagram on young Adult's social comparison, colourism.* The impact of Instagram on young Adult's social comparison, colourism, 16.
- Yadav.G, & Rai.J. (2017). *The Generation Z and their Social Media Usage: A Review and a Research Outline.* Global Journal of Enterprise Information System, 7.

Analysing the Importance of Style and Dressing in the Business World

CHAPTER 27

Author – Ruchi Jagada, Yugandhara Lanjekar & Simran Pawar, Student, IES's Management College and Research Centre, Mumbai

ABSTRACT

In a modern business work place, the term "Business Dress Code" would mean anything from a formal suit and tie to jeans and t-shirt. Dress codes speak for the employees and what an organization considers as appropriate work attire. The purpose of this research paper is to examine the importance of style and dress code in the business world. The paper emphasizes on the three types of dress codes - formal, business casual and casual, different perception of employees, clients and employers. It will showcase the impact that different dress code may have on their productivity, the significance of different dress code at different work place. Adding to this, this research paper will highlight the outcome of adapting different dress codes at workplace, it will ascertain the determinants of following a dress code at work place. Additionally, new dress codes will be explored and recommended to inbuilt confidence while working. This paper will also survey on probable different styles to promote gender equality at work place. In the end, this paper will also distinguish between the environment of the organizations that lack a dress code and follow a dress code. Sources from books, journals and questionnaires will be used to derive at a conclusion.

KEYWORDS

"Business styling", "Casual", "Dress code", "Formal", "Workplace attire"

INTRODUCTION

Dress is clearly a significant means of self-identification and role definition. Personal styles have great psychological implications for both the wearer and the person interacting with the wearer" (Bowman & Hooper, 1991).

The level of formality in a dress code establishes the atmosphere the business wants to foster. If a firm places a high importance on teamwork and togetherness, eliminating status gaps among employees by establishing a uniform dress code will support these objectives. For example, all employees at Toyota Corporation wear polo shirts and khakis as a way of expressing a unified, team-oriented culture. Also, a casual dress code can help communicate a fun and friendly organizational culture. This may result in employees feeling empowered to deliver exceptional customer service which, in turn, strengthens the company's fundamental value of providing service excellence (Peluchette & Karl, 2007).

Over the last 20 years, dress codes throughout corporations in India has undergone drastic changes. In the workplace, change has been most prominently seen in the areas of formal, business casual and casual. In todays' business world, "style" is usually correspondent for "personal style," or the way an individual speaks of themselves through aesthetic choices such as their clothing and the way they put an outfit together in their professional entity. Research study provides varying results as to whether business work attire has a negative or positive impact on employees and their working. Employees' opinions on the calibre of their performance are influenced by the dress code of the company. Additionally, how someone dresses affect how higher management, clients, and co-workers view them. The goal of this paper is to demonstrate a link between business attire standards, productivity and morale. To demonstrate how each company's dress code is believed to effect employee performance and morale.

LITERATURE REVIEW

THE IMPACT OF WORK ATTIRE ON EMPLOYEE BEHAVIOUR

This qualitative study's main objective was to examine how formal workplace clothes affected people's identity, behaviour, and views. The findings of this study revealed that employee beliefs and experiences led them to believe that professional dress has neutral effect on attitude, behaviour, productivity, or performance in non-consumer facing jobs. The findings of this study add to our understanding of how workplace dress affects productivity and organisational behaviour.

DRESS CODES IN THE WORKPLACE: EFFECTS ON ORGANIZATIONAL CULTURE

The United States is a global manufacturing leader, and to stay competitive, Americans spend billions of dollars on things like professional attire, hairstyles, plastic surgery, and physical preparation. Over the past 30 years, there has been a dramatic shift in styles due to both economic growth and decline. As America became the world's economic leader, many cultural changes were occurring, which had an impact on people's perceptions of what constitutes acceptable work attire. Businesses started to realise the drawbacks of a casual dress code once the electronic era arrived. Managers became aware of the benefits of a formal, business-casual clothing code. This notion permeated the modern world economy.

AN EXPLORATORY STUDY OF BUSINESS ATTIRE: FORMAL OR CASUAL

Every element of life has been significantly impacted by global climate change, from consumer shopping habits to corporate business practises. Consumers today are becoming more knowledgeable about sustainability problems that could help to mitigate the crisis of global warming. They are using less fossil fuels, purchasing more fuel-efficient cars, and using solar or wind energy to power their homes. A Deloitte & Touche survey conducted in 2007 found that nearly one-fifth of the consumers surveyed were open to buying more environmentally friendly goods in the future.

A STUDY TO DETERMINE HOW CASUAL DRESS IN THE WORKPLACE AFFECTS EMPLOYEE MORALE AND PRODUCTIVITY

This study evaluated the effect of casual dress on employee morale and productivity, two important factors that influence the bottom line. Its goal was to give managers and other key decision makers insight into how casual dress work environments compare to conventional corporate cultures.

Overall, this study's findings suggest that as dress standards become laxer, employee morale does rise. Overall, it appears that as dress codes loosen, productivity may be slightly reduced, though results vary based on the size of the business.

IMPORTANCE OF STYLE AND DRESS CODE IN THE BUSINESS WORLD

Every business has a dress code that employees must adhere to in order to appear professional. Workers need to be conscious that how they choose to dress plays a big part in how others perceive them as professionals. Additionally, you promote your employer as an employee. One needs to dress appropriately if they want to make a good first impact at work. First perceptions are crucial, in fact. If you don't conduct yourself professionally, it might be challenging to be hired by a reputable business. You would struggle to win others' respect and admiration, even if you were selected. Credentials are crucial, but looks are also significant.

3.1 RESEARCH METHODOLOGY

Primary data is collected through questionnaire from various consumers and secondary data is through websites, books, articles etc. sample size being primary data was collected from 100 consumers from Mumbai from all types of age groups.

3.2 OBJECTIVES OF THE STUDY

The objectives of this paper are to understand the role of style and dressing in the business world, to know about the impact of dressing on the employees, to evaluate the outcome of adapting different dress codes at workplace and to provide recommendations/suggestions.

3.3 LIMITATIONS OF THE STUDY

- Random answers by respondents do not give a correct view of their change in behaviour
- The data was collected through online questionnaires; however, internet users are not a representative of the population as a whole

- Sample size is low as compared to the population so the results will be based on the chosen respondents only and cannot be applied for the whole population
- Though the study is based on the preferences provided by corporate employees, we all know that human behaviour is ever changing and hence conclusions and recommendations cannot be applicable for a long period.

FINDINGS AND DATA ANALYSIS

A survey was sued to conduct this research and was distributed among various employees and students across India. The goal of this survey was to compile a list of responses to understand better how employees and students feel about the workplace attire and how it affects the Business world's culture. Out of them 60.5% respondents were female and 39.5% were male.

1) Do you like following particular dress code in the office?

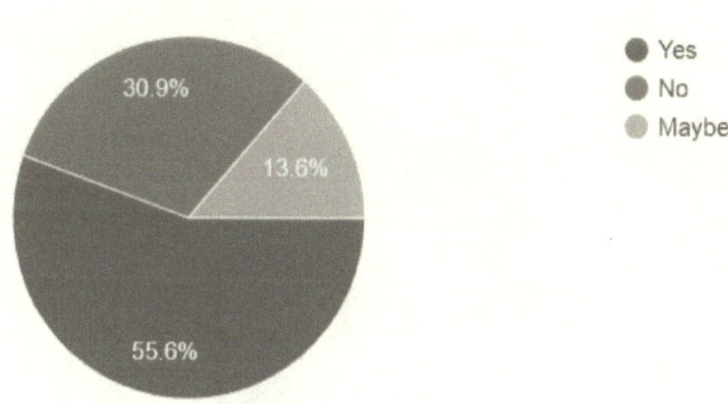

First, respondents were asked do they like following a particular dress code in office. Majority of the respondents answered yes (55.6%). 25 respondents said no (30.9%) and 25 respondents answered no (30.9%)

2) How does dressing casually reflect your personality?

81 responses

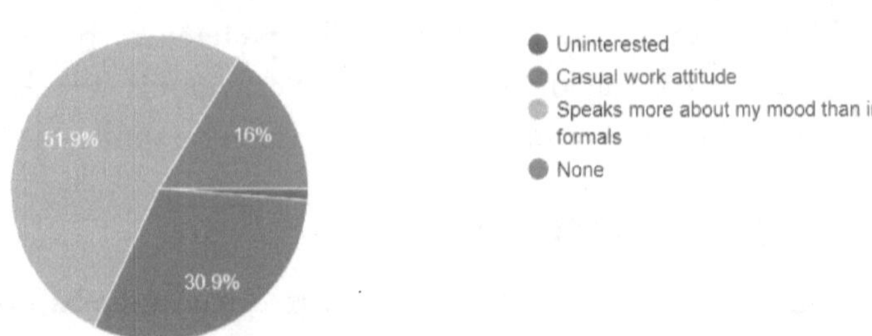

Next, respondents were asked if their casual dressing reflect their personality. Majority of respondents answered that it speaks about their mood than in formals (51.9%). 30.9% of respondents answered that they have a casual work attitude and 16% responded that their personality doesn't get affected.

3) What kind of impression are you looking to make?

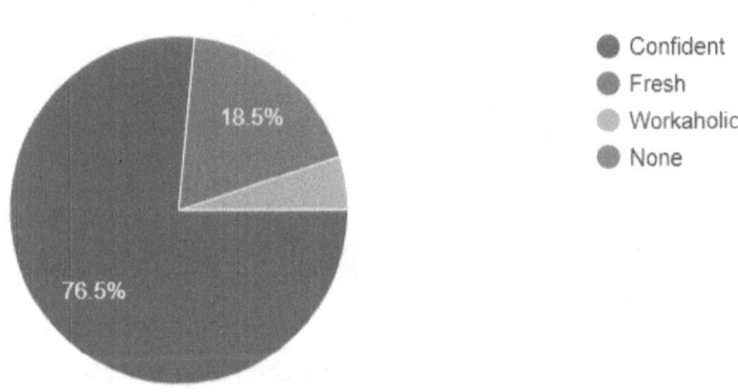

The next question that was asked was what kind of impression respondents are looking to make. 76.5% of them answered to look confident. 18.5% of respondents responded that they look fresh and 4.9% of respondents answered that they dress to look workaholic.

4) Did anyone look at you differently because of wearing formal attire?

81 responses

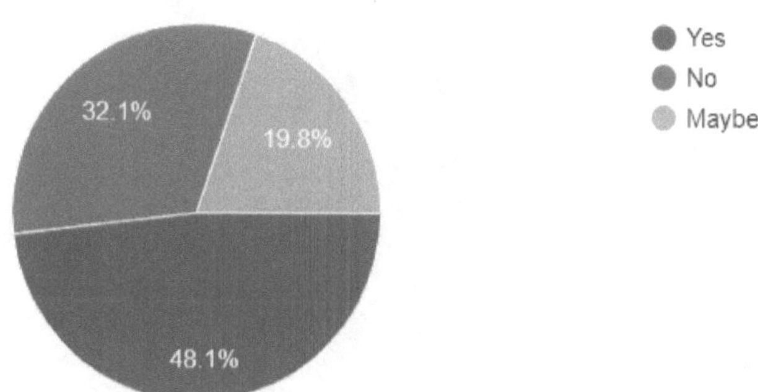

Respondents were then asked that does anyone look at them because of wearing formal attire. 48.1% of respondents answered yes, 32.1% answered no and 19.8% answered maybe for this question.

5) Could our dress code be considered discriminatory?

81 responses

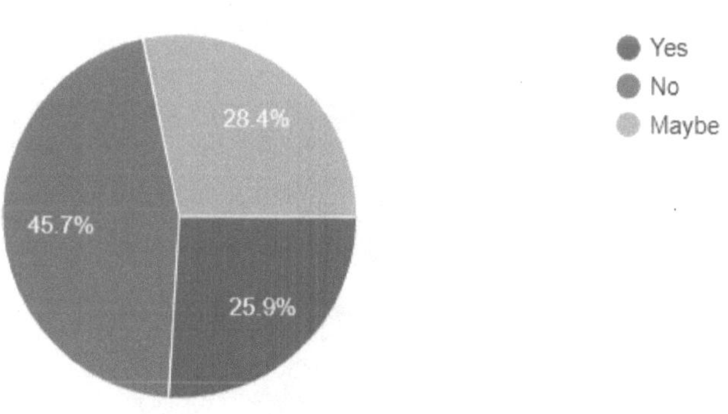

6) Does your attire reflect on your performance like building up your confidence?

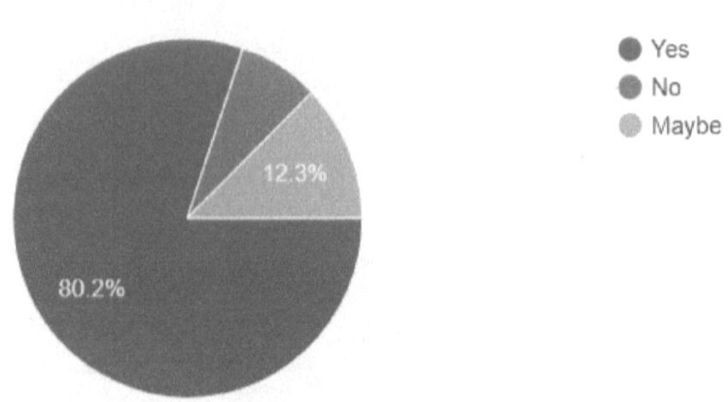

Next question was asked whether the dress code is considered discriminatory. 45.7% answered no, 28.4% respondents answered maybe and 25.9% answered yes for this question.

Next, respondents were asked that does their attire reflect on their performance like building up their confidence. 80.2% responded with a yes, 12.3% with maybe and 7.4% responded with a no for this question.

7) Given a choice, would you prefer wearing pajamas and t-shirts to work?

81 responses

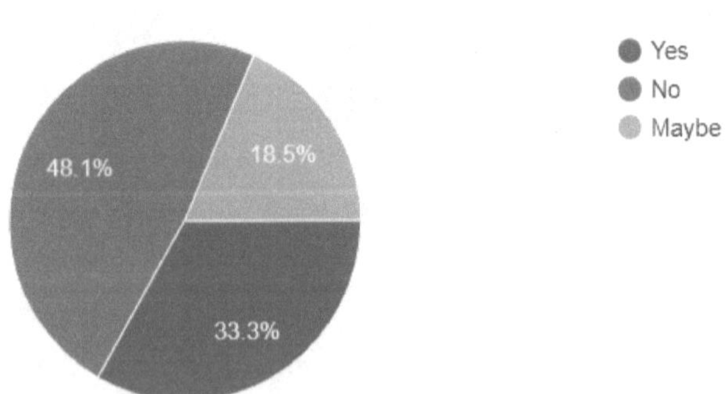

The final question asked was if given a choice, would respondents prefer wearing pyjamas and t-shirts to work. 48.1% responded with a no, 33.3% answered with a yes and 18.55 answered with a yes.

CONCLUSION

Overall, it was anticipated that the majority of survey participants would say that their workplace dress influences the culture and how they perceive themselves and other people. The study's findings confirmed these predictions. Job position, clothing choices, and respondents' perceptions that their appearance at work affects how others see them all tended to have a greater impact on how respondents felt that workplace apparel affected the company. Last but not least, the survey results demonstrate that the majority of participants believe that professional apparel increases their level of confidence and benefits the company.

Companies were especially worried when workers arrived at work sporting significant alterations to their look, such as piercings, damaged clothing, and an untidy appearance due to improper grooming. As a result, some businesses reinstated their suit and tie policy. According to a study from the Society for Human Resource Management, the percentage of casual dress policies dropped from 53 % in 2002 to 38 % in 2006 The current trend is to dress for success, but the current styles permit various colours and have a more tailored, modern look. "Natural fibres, multiple buttons, and bolder ties and shirts are new trends f(Feingold, 2001)

A more relaxed attitude may increase employee comfort and morale, but it may have a negative impact on performance. Professional appearance at work encourages self-assurance and competence. Top managers and company clients have a more favourable impression of you when you are dressed formally. Employees tend to feel more valued in companies that are committed to their personal growth (Hanley, 2009). Organizations might think about periodically having casual days as a motivation to boost performance and productivity while maintaining a balance between professionalism and employee morale. There is a system where each industry identifies trends to encourage maximum efficiency, despite the fact that there is no universal dress code, according to research. Organizations must take into account its mission statement and values while developing and executing a dress code.

SUGGESTIONS & RECOMMENDATIONS

- Dressing neatly and in tidy clothes that fits properly and exudes personality
- Be shrewd and simple in your outfit selections
- Instead than dressing to impress, wear comfortable, functional clothing

REFERENCES

- Angie Shinn, Ali Swig art, Ashley Gritters and Matt Schmailzl (2011) Dress Codes In The Workplace: Effects On Organizational Culture
- Hamsikaa Narayanan (2019) A Brief Study on the Corporate Dressing in Chennai, Tamil Nadu, India Using Primary Data. University of Madras, India
- Sana Mahmoud Abbasi (2013) Power Dressing and its influence on Business Performance. Director of the Fashion Design Program, College of Fine Arts & Design, American University in the Emirates, Dubai
- Sarah Maloney Hughes (2001) The Effect of Casual Dress on Performance in the Workplace. The Master's College.
- Mazharul Islam Kiron (2023) Importance of Style and Dress Code in the Business World, Aditya Birla Fashion and Retail Limited, Bangalore, India
- https://app.myloft.xyz/browse/home

Thesis

- Ethan Surrett (2021) How Workplace Attire Affects Employee Perceptions and Organizational Culture. The University of Southern Mississippi in Partial Fulfillment of Honors Requirements
- Marisa Avallone Sharkey (2000) A study to determine how casual dress in the workplace affects employee morale and productivity. Rowan University

Gen-z's Perception on Financial Influencers and How It Affects Their Financial Decisions

CHAPTER 28

Author – Akhileshwaran Bharatarajan, Abhishek Aji, Sahil Chavan, Jeetu Kunder, Student & Prof. Falguni Mathews, Assistant Professor, SIES College of Commerce and Economics, Mumbai

ABSTRACT

We observe a potential expansion in the newly established sector of financial influencers in the financial world where young people look for other sources for their own financial investments. The emergence of personal finance influencers may be partially linked to the rising use of social media to seek financial advice. The purpose of this study was to determine if those who have the potential to influence financial decisions really do so and to comprehend the warnings that financial influencers gloss over when describing various financial topics. Secondary and primary sources were used to gather the data for this study. A tailored questionnaire that was distributed to the respondents was used to gather primary data. Reviews from numerous study papers, publications, and newspapers make up secondary data. Some of the findings of this research paper conclude that financial influencers should deliver material that meets investor expectations and the researcher's opinion is that novice investors should be well-informed when observing or following various financial influencers while making financial judgements.

KEYWORDS

Gen Z, Financial influencers, Financial decisions. Social media

INTRODUCTION

In the world of finance where youngsters chase for various sources for their personal financial investments, we see a potential growth in the newly formed industry of financial influencers. A social media influencer is a person who uses social media to promote themselves and has gained trust in a particular industry or niche. Through the distribution of their content on social media platforms like Facebook, YouTube, Instagram, and TikTok, they develop a loyal following and audience. Moreover, they might have a podcast or blog. A social media influencer who focuses on providing advice on finances and money is known as a personal finance influencer. The increasing usage of social media to seek financial advice might be partly attributed for the rise of personal finance influencers. Personal finance influencers can monetize a YouTube channel, provide sponsored articles, offer digital goods or courses, or engage in affiliate marketing by disseminating their financial expertise. By the end of this year, India is expected to have a market of Rs 900 crore for influencer marketing. Additionally, about two-thirds of Indians follow influencers. Celebrities receive only 27% of the marketing dollars spent on well-known figures. The bulk of 73%, however, goes to influencer marketing! Whether you like it or not, influencers and influencer marketing are a reality.

Since age is not a factor in defining generational cohorts, the age range of Gen Z will change throughout time. According to the majority of sources, Generation Z was born between 1997 and 2010, hence as of 2020, its age range was generally between 10 and 23. A sizeable fraction of Gen Z's oldest workers currently make up the workforce. The need for personal financial security and education is another tendency that academics have noticed among Generation Z. Many people witnessed their parents' struggles during the Great Recession as children. Because of this, people are worried about their financial future and are getting ready by starting savings accounts and paying off debt.

Prior to a more exact definition of Generation Z, they were sometimes included alongside millennials. It's true that there are certain parallels between the two generations. Some of these similar traits include:

- progressive stances on issues
- acclimating to technology
- Social media presence
- Putting personal finance first

OBJECTIVES

1. To study financial influencers power to alter financial decisions of Gen Z.

2. To analyze the understanding of Gen-Zs financial decisions with the help of financial influencers.
3. To understand the caveats ignored by financial influencers when explaining various financial concepts.
4. To validate GEN-Zs dependence on new age financial influencers as compared to esteemed investment houses.

REVIEW OF LITERATURE

1) Chikhi, I. (n.d.). Financial Influencers and Social Media: The Role of Valuable and Trusted Content in Creating a New Form of Authenticity. *CUNY Academic Works*. https://academicworks.cuny.edu/bb_etds/113/
2) Pham, M. T., Dang, T., Hoang, T. T. H., Tran, T. H., & Ngo, T. H. (2021, January 1). *The Effects of Online Social Influencers on Purchasing Behavior of Generation Z: An Empirical Study in Vietnam.* Journal of Asian Finance, Economics and Business. http://koreascience.or.kr:80/article/JAKO202130254066003.pdf
3) Suryani, W., Tobing, F., & Girsang, Y. (2022, March 2). *Factor Analysis of investment intention: Millennials and Gen Z perspective.* Jurnal Inovasi Ekonomi. https://doi.org/10.22219/jiko.v7i01.20150
4) Appalachian State University. (n.d.). *An Investigation Of The Personal Finance Characteristics Of Gen Z In Secondary Education Programs, ASU NC DOCKS (North Carolina Digital Online Collection of Knowledge and Scholarship).* http://libres.uncg.edu/ir/asu/listing.aspx?id=32620
5) Cristi, S., Birau, R., Afjal, M., & Florescu, I. (2021, December 1). *Evaluating the linkage between Behavioural Finance and Investment Decisions Amongst Indian Gen Z investors...* ResearchGate. https://www.researchgate.net/publication/356799836_Evaluating_the_linkage_between_Behavioural_Finance_and_Investment_Decisions_Amongst_Indian_Gen_Z_investors_Using_Structural_Equation_Modeling

STATEMENT OF THE PROBLEM

During the pandemic many youngsters realized the importance of handling your finances and accumulating money for the future. In order to achieve that it was necessary to have the required financial knowledge and time. This is where financial influencers started to play an important role in terms of educating the young minds and helping them become financially independent. Like all things nothing in this world is free and we wanted to find out how financial influencers profited from this pro bono business. This industry is a relatively new industry and we wanted to explore the benefits and drawbacks of following such financial influencers.

SCOPE OF STUDY

The purpose of this research was to determine the impact that financial influencers have on the financial decisions of Gen Z. The researcher chose the age range of 18-25 for this particular research. This is because the age range of Gen Z's start from 10 all the way to 25. The questionnaire sent out were focused more on college students as they fall into the category of Gen Z. Researcher made sure that the questionnaire was focused more on finance aspect but was easy to understand for people from different fields.

LIMITATIONS OF THE STUDY

1. The target audience was a major limitation since finding people who are into finance and are a part of the Gen Z culture were limited.
2. The data collected was only through google forms. Hence there was no one on one interview.
3. Mumbai is a large and highly populated city the research was limited to the college going students there by ignoring people with a well experienced finance profile.
4. Chances of error in information collected could be high since many wouldn't have disclosed the actual information.

RESEARCH METHODOLOGY

The data for this research was collected through primary and secondary sources. Primary data was collected through a customized questionnaire sent out to the respondents. Secondary data comprised of reviews from different research papers, articles and various newspapers.

DATA ANALYSIS AND INTERPRETATION

Q) AGE

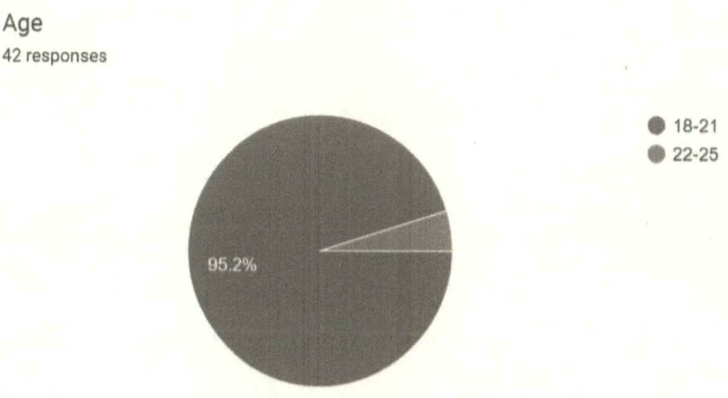

Figure 1

Since our target audience were Gen-Z's, respondents were mainly between the age group of 18 to 25. Out of which 95.2% were between the ages of 18 to 21, and 4.8% were aged between 22 to 25.

Q) PROFESSION

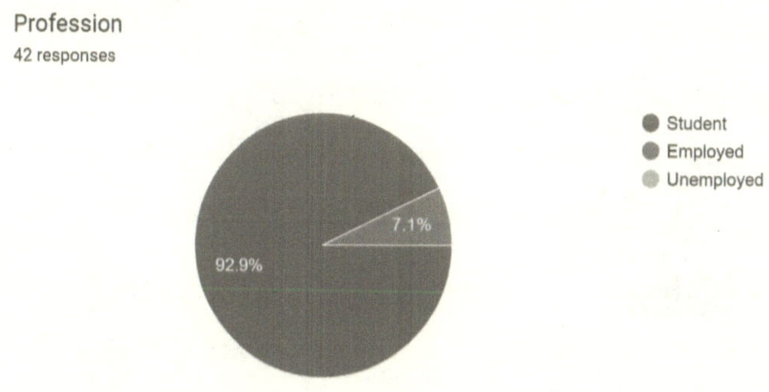

Figure 2

Out of the total respondents, 92.9% were still college goers and the rest had recently got jobs in different companies.

Q) HOW OFTEN DO YOU INVEST?

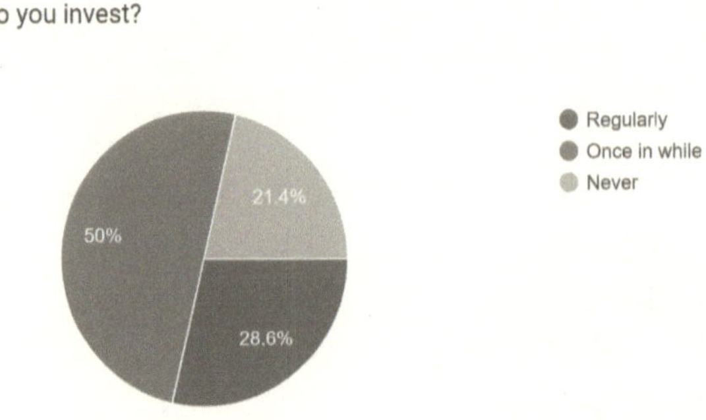

Figure 3

When asked about the frequency of investing in different financial instruments, 50% responded that they used to invest once a while. 28.6% answered that they were regularly investing in different asset classes. 21.4% of people hadn't entered the financial market yet.

Q) DO YOU FOLLOW FINANCIAL INFLUENCERS ON SOCIAL MEDIA?

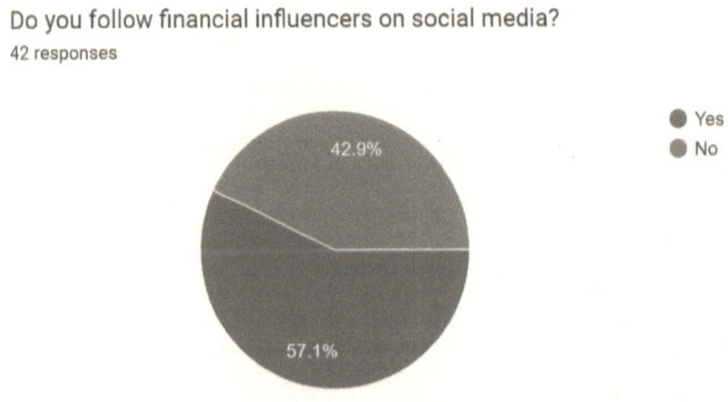

Figure 4

57.1% of the respondents were familiar with different financial influencers and were following them on various social media sites. The rest were not so keen on following the influencers, even though they had heard of them.

Q) WHICH AMONG THE GIVEN SOCIAL MEDIA PLATFORMS DO YOU PREFER THE MOST FOR FINANCIAL ADVICE/KNOWLEDGE?

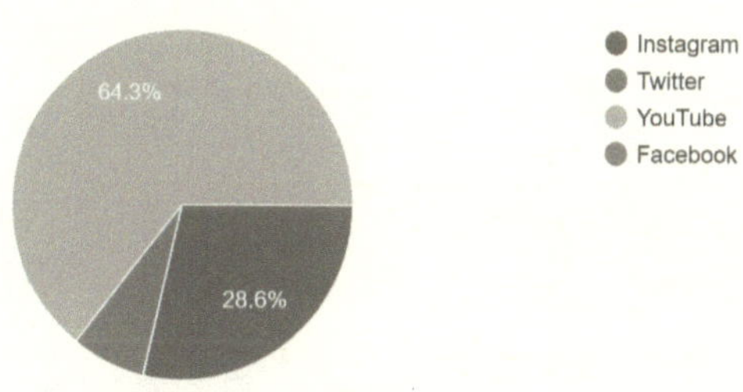

Figure 5

64.3% of people feel that financial influencers should post their content on YouTube. 28.6% are okay with them posting videos on Instagram. Nobody wants influencers to post informational videos on Facebook.

Q) HOW DID YOU GET TO KNOW ABOUT FINANCIAL INFLUENCERS MAKING FINANCIAL LITERACY VIDEOS?

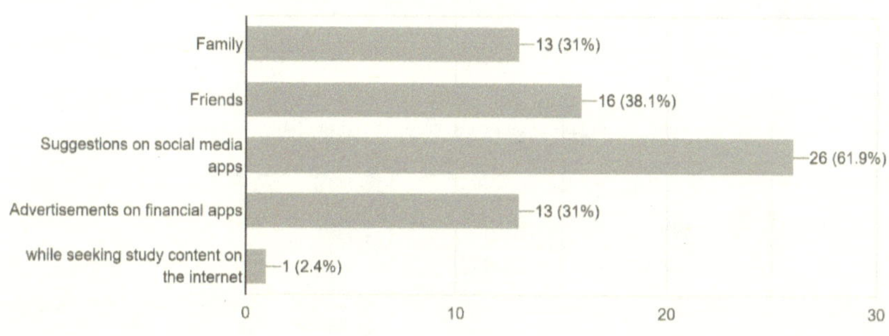

Figure 6

More than half of the respondents got to know about financial influencers through recommendations on social media apps. This shows that influencers leveraged social media to help grow their numbers.

Q) WOULD YOU AGREE THAT FINANCIAL INFLUENCERS DO A GOOD JOB OF SIMPLIFYING COMPLEX FINANCIAL CONCEPTS?

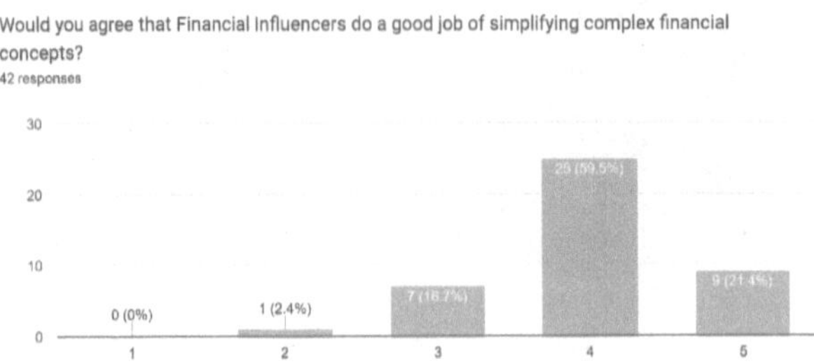

Figure 7

Almost 60% of the respondents feel that the content provided by financial influencers are somewhat to the point and easy to understand. Financial Influencers' main purpose is to simplify different concepts and provide to the masses. And this particular survey shows that they are close to achieving that status.

Q) WOULD YOU AGREE THAT FINANCIAL INFLUENCERS CAN FRAUD GULLIBLE INVESTORS BY NOT MENTIONING THE RISK ASSOCIATED?

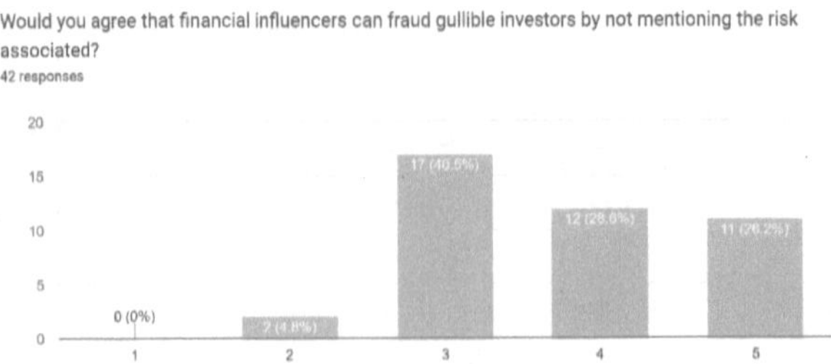

Figure 8

40.5% of the respondents are in two minds about the content put out by the influencers. Surprisingly, 26.2% are fully convinced that financial influencers can easily fraud not-so-smart investors by providing incomplete information about the risk involved in investing.

Q) WOULD YOU AGREE THAT GEN-Z'S HUNGER TO INVEST HAS BOOMED THE FINANCIAL INFLUENCERS' INDUSTRY?

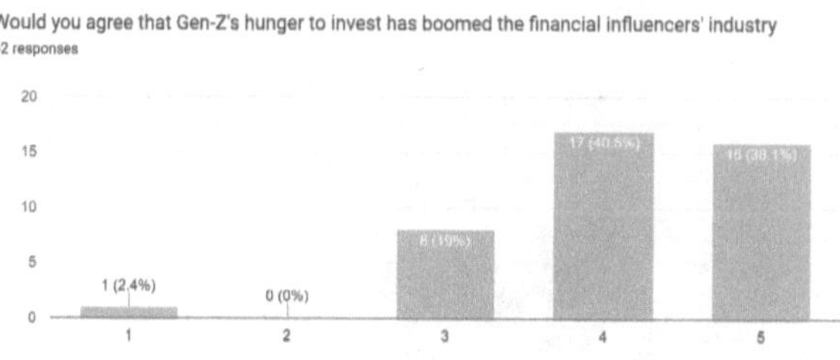

Figure 9

Around 78.6% of the total respondents strongly believe that the industry of financial influencers has seen a meteoric rise due to the demand created by the Gen-Z's. There is also a scope for the industry to rise even further as more and more people are going to start investing and taking help from content put out by the influencers.

Q) HAVE YOU MADE MONEY BY LISTENING TO THESE FINANCIAL INFLUENCERS?

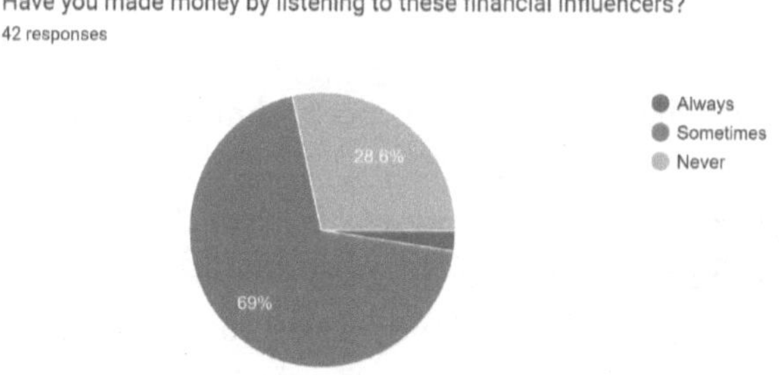

Figure 10

Around 69% of people have made money on some occasions after listening to these financial influencers. This shows that the content put out is accurate most of the times, and can help in financial decisions.

Q) WOULD YOU RECOMMEND OTHERS TO FOLLOW THESE FINANCIAL INFLUENCERS?

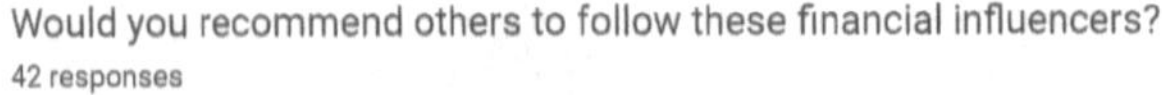

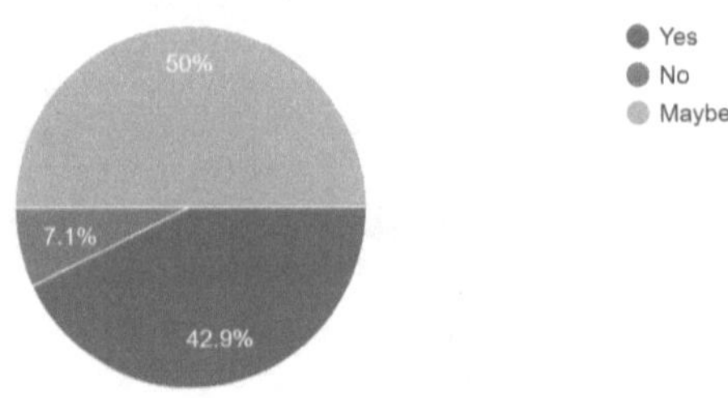

Figure 11

Half of the total respondents are a little bit dicey about suggesting financial influencers to people they know. Close to 43% are fine with recommending influencers for various financial advice. The rest are not so keen on suggesting such influencers to the general public.

RECOMMENDATION

- We recommend Gen Z investors to do their own research, without blindly trusting financial influencers.
- Financial influencers should avoid overhyping trending financial assets to gain reach.
- The content provided by financial influencers should be in line with investor expectations.
- We feel new investors should be well aware while watching or following different financial influencers for their financial decisions.
- Gen Z should take trades on different financial assets only after considering their risk profiles and capital allocation.

CONCLUSION

We can conclude that social media is a very effective platform for financial influencers to put out their content and for new age investors, a better source for gaining financial knowledge. In the rising industry of financial influencers, the number of creators is just going to increase with a view of making it easier and simpler to understand for their viewers and help them gain appropriate financial knowledge. The main aim of investors should be protecting their capital and not expecting super high returns just because influencers were talking about it in their videos.

BIBLIOGRAPHY

1. http://cis01.ucv.ro/revistadestiintepolitice/files/numarul72_2021/5.pdf
2. https://academicworks.cuny.edu/bb_etds/113/
3. https://core.ac.uk/download/pdf/345094277.pdf
4. https://ejournal.umm.ac.id/index.php/JIKO/article/view/20150/11003
5. https://fanbytes.co.uk/finance-influencers/?utm_source=rss&utm_medium=rss&utm_campaign=finance-influencers
6. https://koreascience.kr/article/JAKO202130254066003.pagehttps://koreascience.kr/article/JAKO202130254066003.page
7. https://vested.co.in/blog/influencer-marketing-is-big-should-you-trust-financial-influencers/
8. https://www.bamboohr.com/hr-glossary/generation-z/
9. https://www.businesstoday.in/interactive/immersive/rise-of-the-finfluencers/#:~:text=Simply%20put%2C%20a%20finfluencer%20%E2%80%94%20as,personal%20finance%20and%20mutual%20funds.
10. https://www.newindianexpress.com/magazine/2021/nov/21/the-young-finfluencersnew-age-experts-guide-gen-z-with-financial-planning-2385324.html

Impact of Covid-19 on Business of Britannia Industries Ltd. in India

CHAPTER 29

Author – Amrit Kumar & Parth Lal, Student, IES's Management College and Research Centre, Mumbai

ABSTRACT

Britannia Industries Ltd. (Britannia) is the robust section of FMCG sector in India, products of these brands are frequently consumed by all the segments of the society. During covid-19, business across the globe witnessed slower sales and losses, however Britannia company recorded increased sales and higher returns. Britannia used the digital mode and reached their distributors quickly. The company's Distributor Application, helped them to grow their network and strengthen their business. They also came up with 80:20 rule for the sales of their top products, to ensure easily availability of these products, and helped them to increase their efficiencies and productivity. This paper aims to investigate the COVID-19 outbreak on FMCG sector w.r.t. Britannia. This paper discusses that FMCG sector is unusually affected by many factors such as workers moving back home, logistical problems and changes in buying behaviour. The study is based on data collected from secondary sources. The paper concludes that future of Britannia is very promising and in a strong position to take lead in current FMCG market.

Keyword: FMCG, Covid-19, Pandemic, Sales, Distributor application

INTRODUCTION

The COVID-19 outbreak and spread have dealt a serious damage to the world economy. India is one example of a developing nation that is even more sensitive. Global pandemics have a range of social, economic, and psychological repercussions. The issue in question is COVID 19, which has been blocking most countries throughout the world for about a year, beginning in Asia. India and other developing nations are significantly more sensitive. There have been significant changes in several industries, including the tourism industry's employment rate being affected by travel restrictions and the aviation sector being affected by the reduction in travel demand.**Invalid source specified.**. Like most businesses, FMCG is susceptible to deterioration and unexpected shifts. The FMCG industry in India is a thriving one and is quite popular with consumers. They frequently buy and consume fast due to consumer demand. By days, the industry is expanding in numerous ways. There is a Wadia Group industry, led by Nusli Wadia, includes the Indian company Britannia Industries Ltd, which specialises in the food industry. It is one of the oldest businesses still operating in India and is well recognised for its biscuit offerings. The company sells biscuits, breads, and dairy goods under the Britannia and Tiger brands both domestically and internationally. The company has been embroiled in a number of management-related scandals going back to the circumstances surrounding the Wadia Group's takeover in the early 1990s. But it still commands a sizable portion of the market and is successful. After the first lockdown of march 2020, Industry was adhering to "80:20 rule". The policy was straightforward: 20% of the brands and SKUs, which account for 80% of Britannia's income, were given priority status. Making the shortlist for the largest premium biscuit manufacturer was simple: Good Day and its cream variations, Milk Bikis, Marie Gold, and Nutrichoice. The biscuit manufacturer immediately benefited on four fronts and they to the 80:20 formulae: It increased flexibility in manufacturing capabilities, ensured efficiency in factories and the distance travelled by the products, and brought a laser-sharp attention to execution.**Invalid source specified.**. It also streamlined productivity. Additionally, different industries have been impacted in unique ways. It is important to pay attention to and conduct research on how the FMCG business is changing in relation to everyday life. In this research, we examine the characteristics of change before and after the COVID-19 outbreak based on the performance of the sale and revenue of the major businesses in the Britannia industry combined with the methodologies of data analysis and comparison analysis. This study concentrated on the impact of Covid 19 on the business of Britannia Industries Ltd.

REVIEW OF LITERATURE

Invalid source specified. This paper shows that the worldwide effect of the Coronavirus pandemic is unprecedented, and consequently the impact is much greater in rising economies like India. Fast-moving consumer goods (FMCG) is one of the most significant industries in India, with several companies, including domestic, care, and so on, that are in high demand, regularly used, and services are offered for a minimal cost. This document is a decision to investigate the COVID-19 epidemic in the FMCG sector. It demonstrates that FMCG is unusually influenced by various variables such as labor migration to their original countries, logistical challenges, and changes in the buyer basket such as an explosion in demand for sanitary items and a rise in demand for cosmetics.

Invalid source specified. According to this paper every element of our existence is touched by FMCG products. These things are often used by all segments of society, and a significant amount of their money is spent on them. Aside from that, the sector is a significant contributor to the Indian economy. This industry has had tremendous growth in recent years, even during the recession. Because of its inherent potential and favorable environmental developments, the FMCG sector's future looks bright. This article examines the sector's overview, critical analysis, and future prospects.

Invalid source specified. This paper shows the liquidation position of the companies. Britannia Industries Limited has earned more revenue as comparing to Marico Limited. The solvency position of Britannia Industries Limited is better as comparing to Marico Limited. Marico Limited has to increase their operational level to generate more revenue. Marico Limited must reduce their outside liabilities or they must increase their share capital. The outside liabilities are more as compared to share capital which is not a good capital structure

Invalid source specified. This paper shows that the global economy has been devastated by the Covid19 outbreak, and the Indian economy was not immune. Due to this pandemic and the subsequent lockdown, very few industries, such as the pharmaceutical and FMCG sectors, have shown some positive signs despite the negative trend in India's GDP. No matter how the economy is doing, essential consumer staples will always be there. Particularly during difficult times, whenever an unprecedented circumstance occurs, humans will always attempt to protect themselves, which will undoubtedly result in a high demand for FMCG products. In this paper, we will break down the effect of lockdown in the development of the FMCG area utilizing a portion of the Measurable devices.

RESEARCH METHODOLOGY

The study is descriptive as well as analytical in nature, and it discusses the positive and negative effects of COVID-19 on the Britannia Industry Ltd. Data Sources: The study analyses Britannia Industry Ltd the using secondary data obtained from the NSE. To investigate, sources were gathered from Annual report, magazines, journals, newspapers, and so on.

Data collection period: For analysing the impact of COVID-19 on the Britannia Industry Ltd, data was collected from April 2019 to March 2020 for pre-COVID-19, from April 2020 to March 2021 in COVID-19 and from April 2021 to March 2022. The necessary information required for making this research paper is collected from various magazines, journals, magazine report of This the company and from the website. This quantitative data is collected from secondary data. We have taken the values from the annual report of the company to find the profitability ratios.

DATA ANALYSIS AND INTERPRETATION

PROFIT/LOSS FOR THE PERIOD

During covid, the financial performance of the company was normal, but suddenly during corona, the profitability rose at a different rate. consumer behaviour has changed quite dramatically. During a shutdown, people don't stop spending. In normal conditions, it is street food, we eat in restaurants, we go to malls and eat there, etc. In closed conditions, it was mostly for domestic use and was obviously helpful for the company.

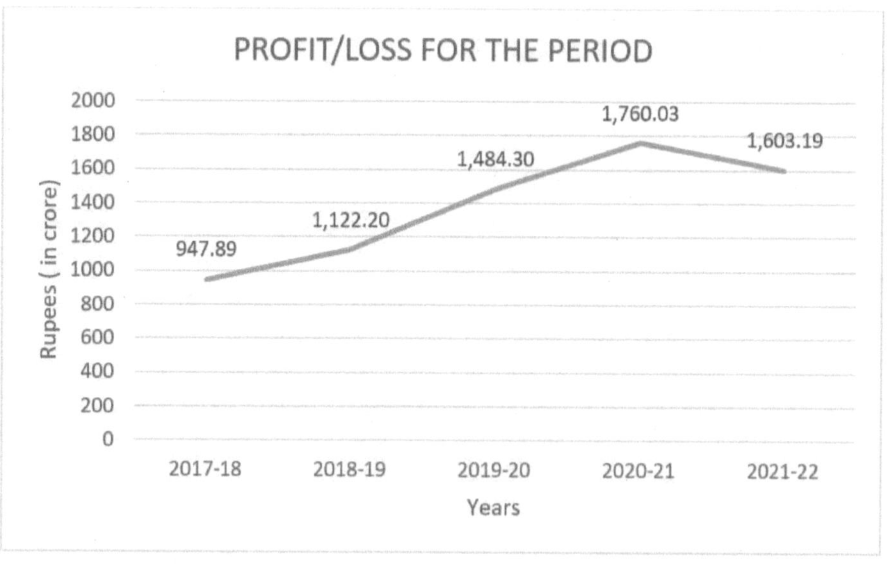

Source: Annual report of Britannia Industry.

BASIC EPS

Earnings per share (EPS) is calculated as a company's earnings divided by shares of common stock outstanding. The resulting numbers serve as an indicator of the company's profitability. It is common for companies to report his earnings per share adjusted for exceptional items and potential share dilution. About 80% of Britannia's revenue comes from biscuits and demand will stabilize he Covid-19 times, as Indians spend more time at home. Base EPS in 2018-19 was Rs.46.71, lower than the previous year, then EPS started to increase due to some innovations and expansion of distribution, continued to grow during Covid, but post-Covid 2021 EPS for -22 fiscal year found to decline again at Rs.66.56

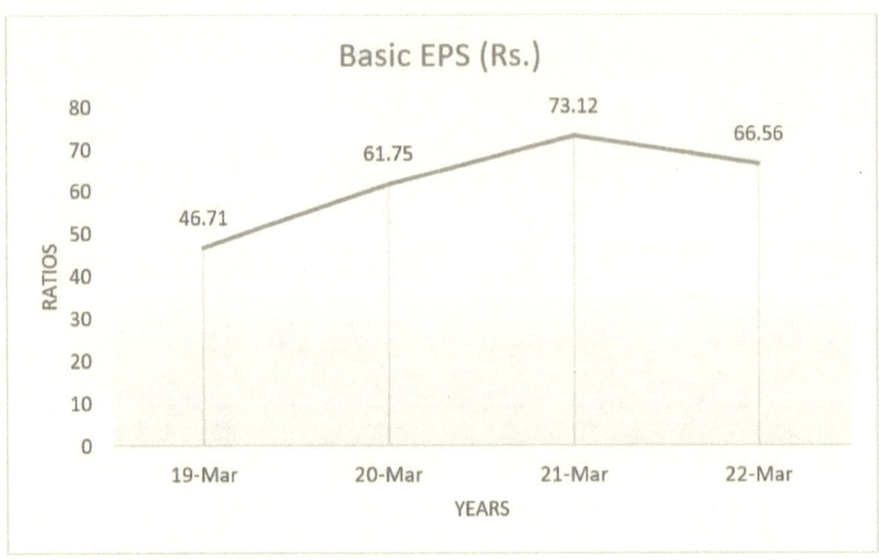

Source: Annual report of Britannia Industry.

PBDIT MARGIN

Britannia Industries Ltd has benefited greatly from increased home consumption when lockdown measures were implemented earlier this year to stem the spread of the coronavirus. His consolidated operating profit for the processed food company in the June quarter was up 26% year-on-year, the best performance among consumer products companies at the time. But that tailwind has eased as lockdowns have eased. September quarter earnings increased 11%, down from 15% and 16.6% earnings growth. The company's operating profit for the full year increased by 15.4% year-on-year. Operating profit margin declined, falling from 15.3% in FY2018 to 15.7% in FY2019. The company's operating profit increased by 5.4% year-on-year in the same year. Operating profit margin declined, falling from 15.7% in FY2019 to 15.7% in FY2020. The company's operating profit fell by 12.3% in the same year. The operating margin declined, from 19.1% in FY21 to 15.6% in FY22.

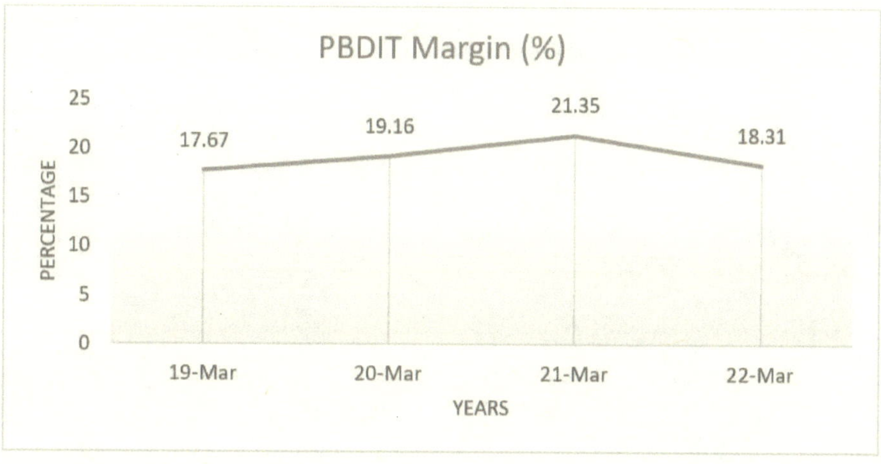

Source: National Stock Exchange

EQUITY SHARE DIVIDEND

The ratio between the total amount of dividends given to shareholders and the company's net income is known as the dividend pay out ratio. It is the portion of earnings that are distributed as dividends to shareholders. The corporation keeps the money that is not distributed to shareholders to pay down debt or to reinvest in its core businesses. Sometimes, it's just referred to as the pay out ratio. Britannia Industry Ltd yield a huge profit in the first quarter of 2020 and in whole 2020-21 financial year, they gave high dividends to their shareholders. Interim Dividend @ 3500% declared on April 23, 2020, i.e., Rs.35 per Equity Share of Rs.1/- each for FY 2019-20. At their meeting on 2 April 2021, the dividend was 6200%, i.e., Rs. 62 per equity share of Rs.1/- each. The total dividend payment for fiscal year 2020-21 is Rs. 3,491.41 crores. Dividend is 5650%, i.e. Rs.56.50 per equity share of face value of Rs.1 each, for the fiscal year 2021-22, for consideration and approval by the Members at the Company's upcoming Annual General Meeting.

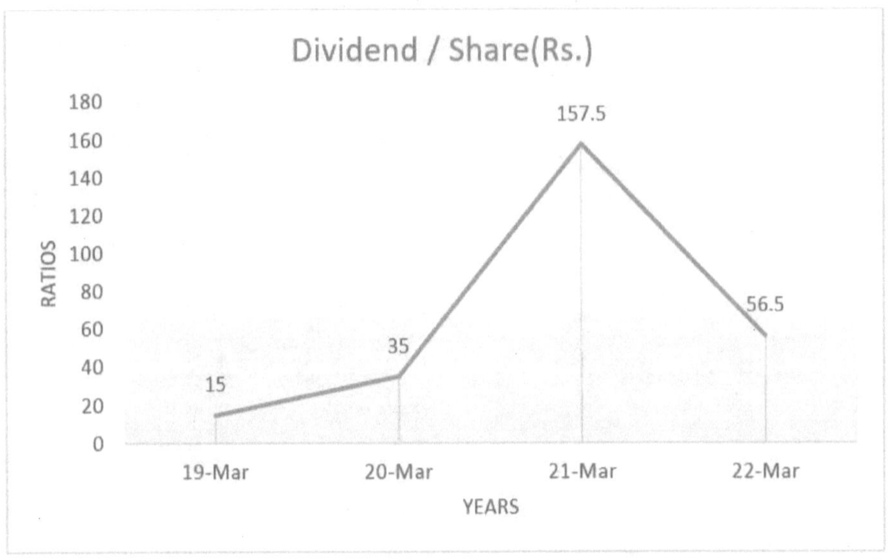

Source: Annual report of Britannia Industry.

RSI

In technical analysis, the relative strength index (RSI) is a momentum indicator. The RSI measures the speed and magnitude of a security's recent price changes to determine whether it is overvalued or undervalued. In 2019 the more than two times the lower limit had broken and share is oversold and also many of the times the RSI is close to 70 and here also two times the stock crossed upper limit so the fluctuation high, in 2020 at the starting of the fiscal year stock price had started to decrease but got stabilised near the 40-50. And after the lockdown stock once again hit the lower limit go to very low, and once again bounce back and in third quarter and hit the upper limit. This fluctuation is continued up to the last quarter of the 2020-21

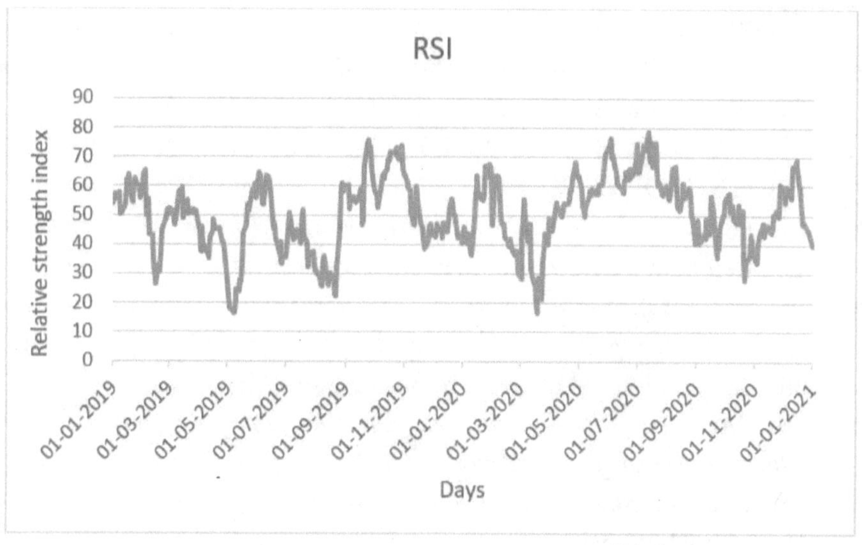

Source: National Stock exchange

CONCLUSION

The findings of the study indicate that the spread and popularity of COVID-19 have encouraged customers to gradually transition their consumption channels from online to offline, creating a new consumption pattern. The strategy of 80:20 followed by the Britannia industry is the one of the biggest reason for the jump in revenue of the company. From the various parameter as profit/loss of the period, EPS, PBDIT, Equity share dividend, and also the Relative Strength Index (RSI) results clearly show that the market has changed significantly since COVID19. The RSI has increased slightly due to the surge in demand for certain products. As a result of all analysis, COVID 19 adversely affected the FMCG sector but Britannia Industry performance is not affected too much. Therefore, the above results show the strategy followed by the Britannia for the availability of the product in the market is so strategical their supply chain was works very smartly but after covid their declining performance is the matter of concern for the company. so there are some needs of flexible plans to deal with the future.

REFERENCES

Masurali A., S. P. (2018). *Perception and Awarness level of Potential Customers towards Electric Cars.* INTERNATIONAL JOURNAL FOR RESEARCH IN APPLIED SCIENCE AND ENGINEERING TECHNOLOGY.

Pritam K. Gujarathi, V. A. (2018). *Electric Vehicles in India: Market Analysis with Consumer Perspective,.* Surat: River Publishers.

Putri, B. &. (2021). *Factors Affecting E-Scooter Sharing Purchase Intention: An Analysis Using Unified Theory of Acceptance and Use of Technology 2.* International Journal of Creative Business and Management.

roche, M. M. (2010). *Public attitude towards demand for hydrogen fuel cell vehicles: a review of the evidence and methodological implications.*

Singh, S. (n.d.). *Investigating the Characteristics and Choice of Electric Scooter Users.* Tiruchirappalli .

Comparison of Central Bank Digital Currency with Other Payment Methods

CHAPTER 30

Author – Jay Patel, Sonal Ghanchi & Amin Ayub Kardekar, Student, IES's Management College and Research Centre, Mumbai

ABSTRACT

In India, few months back a new mode of currency is being introduced named as Central Bank Digital Currency (CBDC) also known as E-Rupee. It is a digital token similar to cryptocurrency, issued by central bank. This will provide ease, along with existing modes of payment i.e. cash and electronic payment service used by individuals and financial institutions. This new mode can be used to reduce the use of physical mode of payment (cash/ plastic money) as E-Rupee is traceable also it does not include the printing cost of the currency. This paper gives detailed information about the objectives, choices, advantages and risks of issuing a CBDC in India. Hence, there is a comparison of a general purpose of CBDC with existing means of payment. In recent years, there has been a growing conversation about whether central banks should offer a digital version of cash or not. CBDC is broadly divided into 2 parts, Wholesale and Retail CBDC. In this paper we will mainly focus on Retail CBDC.

Key Words: CBDC, Commercial Bank, Digital Money, E-Rupee, Fiat currency, India, Pilot Project, RBI, Token Based, UPI.

INTRODUCTION

The Indian version of Central Bank Digital Currency (CBDC) is not a new currency but it is an electronic currency i.e. E-Rupee. It is issued by the Central Bank of India (RBI). In this research paper we have compared CBDC with the other modes of payment that are Unified Payments Interface (UPI), Cash,

Net Banking, Digital Wallets and Card Payment. However, the main objective of the Central Bank to launch the CBDC is to reduce the operational costs involved in physical cash management, fostering financial inclusion, efficiency and innovation in payments systems, adding upgradation in cross-border payments and many more.

CBDC is a form of fiat currency and a concept note issued by the Central bank of India. RBI has launched the pilot of CBDC in both Retail and Wholesale segment. The pilot in wholesale segment is known as the Digital Rupee -Wholesale (e₹-W) and the retail segment pilot is known as Digital Rupee-Retail (e₹-R) which was launched on November 1, 2022 and December 01, 2022 respectively, recently the pilot has generated 7,70,000 transactions which consists of 50,000 customers and 5,000 merchants.

In initial stages 4 cities have been chosen for pilot launching which include Mumbai, New Delhi, Bengaluru and Bhubaneswar where sufficient customers are available and it can be extended to Ahmedabad, Gangtok, Guwahati, Hyderabad, Indore, Kochi, Lucknow, Patna and Shimla and certainly 4 banks will participate in retail CBDC pilot and first phase shall commence with four lenders that are, the State Bank of India, ICICI Bank, YES Bank, and IDFC First Bank, four other banks shall join the pilot later that are Bank of Baroda, Union Bank of India, HDFC Bank and Kotak Mahindra Bank.

The offline feature of CBDC is beneficial in all locations specially for remote areas, so this feature will attract the users as this feature is not available in other digital payments mode. In the other payment modes commercial banks act as an intermediary to undertake a transaction between person to person whereas in CBDC there is no such role of a commercial bank. CBDC can be used as a means of payment on the other hand UPI is an enabler provided by 3rd party and government that facilitates electronic transactions and Net Banking is the enabler provided by Commercial Banks for transactions. Card payment systems are provided by financial institutions for payment and leverage. CBDC is a country's national currency regulated by the RBI whereas other payment systems facilitate digital payment, where commercial banks and financial institutions play an important role. So the key difference is that CBDC is digital currency or E-Rupee and UPI, Net Banking, Digital Wallets are the digital payment platforms. Therefore, there are some advantages of CBDCs over other digital payments systems. CBDCs reduce the risk factors to settle the transaction. The Introduction of Cross-border payments feature in CBDC allows an Indian importer to pay its American exporter on a real time basis in digital dollars, without the need of an intermediary.

Following are certain features of CBDC:

- Sovereign currency issued by Central Banks
- Liability on the central bank's balance sheet
- Accepted as a medium of payment, legal tender
- Freely convertible against commercial bank money and cash
- Holders need not have a bank account
- Lowers the cost of issuance of money and transactions

LITERATURE REVIEW

Paulo Rupino Cunha, Paulo Melo and Helder Sebastião - "From Bitcoin to Central Bank Digital Currencies: Making Sense of the Digital Money Revolution"; MDPI publication.

Analysing the path from cryptocurrency to Central Bank Digital Currency (CBDC), to shed some light on dematerialization of money. Characteristics of different CBDC variants are considered namely, wholesale, retail and for the latter, the account-based and token-based-as well as ongoing pilots and open issues. Following article will also be able to enable decision-makers and society to understand the advantages and some risks of CBDC and how CBDC can vary as per technology and economic choices.

SERGHEI MĂRGULESCU PhD, ELENA MĂRGULESCU PhD Faculty of Economics and Business Administration, Nicole Titulescu University of Bucharest; "Traditional Cryptocurrencies and Fiat-Backed Digital Currencies".

Digital payments saw vigorous growth since 2020 and announcement of account based Central Bank Digital Currency. China has launched its digital yuan or DCEP (Digital Currency Electronic Payments) and it will help China to push itself ahead in the digital era. The European Commission and European Central Bank are working together to investigate the policy, legal and technical questions emerging from a possible introduction of a digital Euro. Creating the digital currency is the easy part but linking it with a wider ecosystem to ensure the circulation of money and cash flow. The Central bank will play a major role in CBDC and digital currency will change the face of the entire financial system.

Neha Narula; "Technology Development of Digital Currency"; Cato Journal, Vol. 41, No. 2 (Spring/Summer 2021).

Nowadays Digital Currency is the topic of discussion, technology will play a major role in launching of CBDC. Technology is incredibly important and influences what we can do with policies and what kinds of functionality we can even enable. Largest companies which are most influential on our ways of life are tech companies. CBDC also needs to keep a few aspects for smooth functioning like user privacy along while preventing illicit activities. Central banks at the moment lack the capabilities to rigorously build and test CBDC designs.

The Future of Money: Gearing up for Central Bank Digital Currency, By Kristalina Georgieva, IMF Managing Director Atlantic Council, Washington, DC

This Article talks about the future aspects of Central Bank Digital Currency along with a few considerations that countries need to focus on for the success of CBDC.

Amitoj Singh, David Parapallicherayil John & Arun Pattamookkil Jacob; "A Review of Central Bank Digital Currencies"; Ushus-Journal of Business Management 2022.

This paper focuses on research, whether consumers are actually ready for the digital currency. In most of the countries people are willing to use the CBDC on a large scale. As in the pandemic period the use of cash and cheques has declined and people moved towards digital payment. So such behaviour of people can strengthen the use of CBDC.

RESEARCH METHODOLOGY

For our research we have followed mixed research methodology, it includes both primary and secondary data collection. A sample of 70 respondents were collected for our analysis, where a descriptive method is used. The study was carried out in relation to finding the perspective of people regarding different payment methods in Mumbai, Maharashtra. The study makes extensive use of original data. Using a standard questionnaire, the primary data was gathered. Based on the study's Objectives, this questionnaire was developed. Journals, research papers, publications, Articles and websites served as the sources for the secondary data. Respondents were screened, and their inclusion was solely determined by the depth of their understanding of Digital Payments.

FINDINGS

The following data is collected from the Mumbai area with the sample size of 70 respondents covering different age groups and genders. Most of the respondents are between the age group of 18 to 30 as this age group is more keen to use digital platforms the most.

Question 1: What drives you to use digital mode of payment?

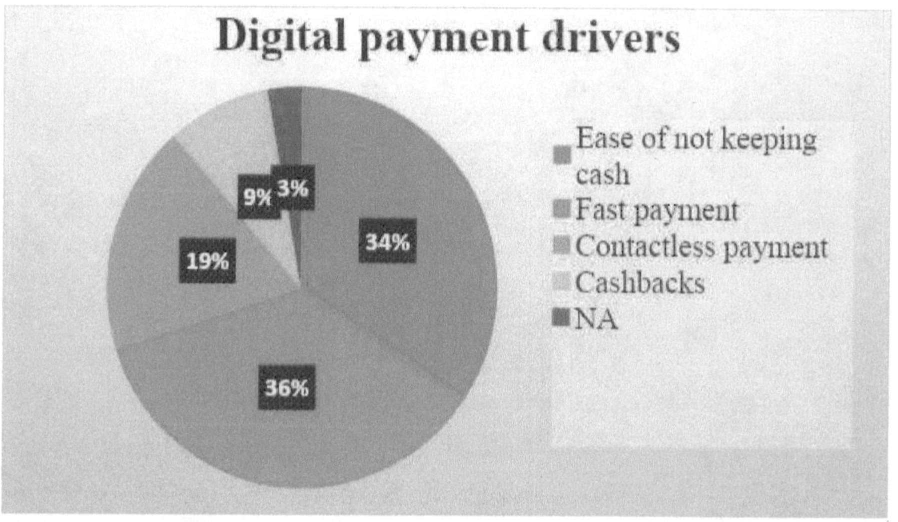

Table No. 1:

Digital payment drivers	Percentage
Ease of not keeping cash	34%
Fast payment	36%
Contactless payment	19%
Cashbacks	8%
NA	3%

Inference:

According to the survey, 36% of respondents use digital payment apps for fast payment, 34% for ease of not keeping cash, 19% for contactless payments, 8% for cashbacks and 3% for NA.

So, from this we can say that to make CBDC successful, ease of not keeping cash, fast payment and contactless payment are the important factors.

QUESTION 2 DO YOU KNOW ABOUT CBDC (E-RUPEE)

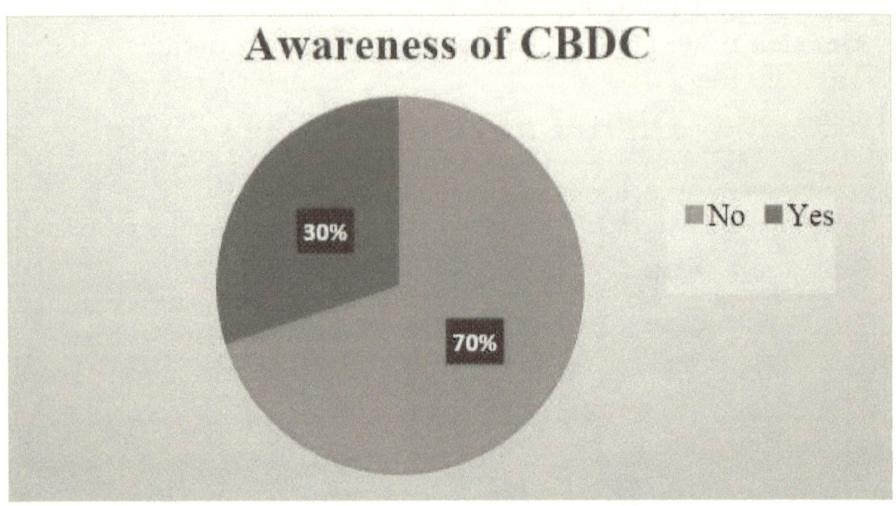

Table No. 2:

Awareness of CBDC	Percentage
Yes	30%
No	70%

INFERENCE

According to the survey, 30% of respondents are aware of the CBDC and 70% are not aware of CBDC.

So from this output we can say that the RBI should create more awareness about CBDC, its concept and features and how normal people can use it and how this will benefit them. As this concept is new and many countries are working on it, the government should increase the number of users using the pilot of CBDC.

As of now there are 50,000 customers and 5000 merchants using the pilot with 7,70,000 transactions taking place till now.

QUESTION 3 WHICH MODE OF PAYMENT DO YOU PREFER MOST?

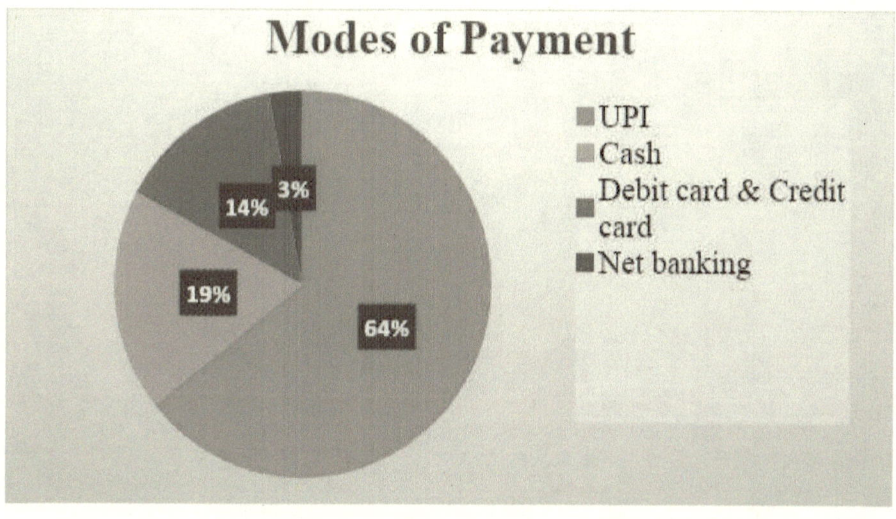

Table No. 3

Mode of Payment	Percentage
UPI	64%
Cash	19%
Debit card & Credit card	14%
Net banking	3%

INFERENCE

According to the survey, most of the respondents use UPI (64%) as a mode of payment, 19% use cash, 14% use Debit card and credit card and only 3% use Net banking.

As most of the respondents use UPI for payment which is used digitally we can say that they will adopt CBDC faster than the rest of the other mode of payment users.

QUESTION 4 MODE OF PAYMENTS USED BY DIFFERENT AGE GROUPS AND GENDERS.

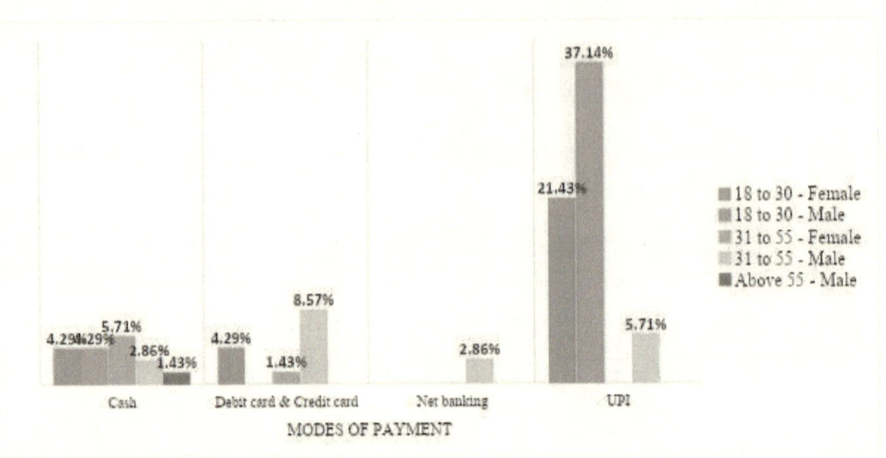

INFERENCE

According to the survey we can say that male from the age group of 18-30 mostly use UPI for payment and from the age group of 31-55 mostly use debit and credit cards and and in Female from the age group of 18-30 mostly use UPI for payments and from 31-55 use cash for payments. So we can say that young and adult males and females are more keen to use digital currency more frequently and can adopt new digital payment systems then other age groups.

DISCUSSION

Benefits of CBDC:

- **Easiness, Efficient and Risk free of payment settlements:**

  In most parts of the world, banks have handled the retail payment systems. However recently, innovative FinTechs have challenged this dominance and changed consumer preference and regulatory intervention. The rising competition in the non-bank financial sectors, with a rising volume payments undertaken by the third parties not directly controlled by the central bank of India, may threaten control and introduce the transaction safety risk. Since the consumer preferences for quicker and cheaper payment systems partly drive this change, so the introduction of electronic currency by the central Banks could provide a suitable way to support the current financial framework.

- **Better visibility and transparency of monetary policy**

The introduction of CBDCs is beneficial for the central bank in that they have better knowledge of financial transactions that are undertaken in real time. Even the central bank can monitor the critical financial data. Furthermore, it provides a great opportunity to enhance the transparency of the central bank's monetary policy framework including its nominal anchor, its tool and operations and its policy strategy. The more effective argument is that CBDCs may have direct connection between the central bank and citizens, which could help and enhance the public's understanding of the role of the central bank and the need for independence.

- **Eradication of black economy, money laundering and tax evasion:**

According to the United Nations the approximate amount of money laundered in one year is 2-5% of global GDP or 800 billion $ to $2 trillion in current US dollars. A lot of illegal activities rely on the dependency of physical cash. According to the BIS report, the introduction of CBDC can trace and detect the transaction of digital money. It could improve the application of rules aimed at anti money laundering and countering the financing of terrorism and possibly help informal economic activities. If token based CBDC is introduced along with the account based variant to increase the degree of privacy to the public, the amount transferable to wallets may be restricted, effectively to stop the use for large scale criminal activities. However, the BIS also mentioned that the impact on fighting illegal activities may not be significant, since a traceable CBDC would not necessarily be the main reason for illegal transaction and informal economic activities.

- **More Involvement of Unbanked and Underbanked**

Financial inclusion is one of the main reasons for introducing the CBDCs mentioned by the central bank. According to the Bank of England "the provision of basic accounts and an electronic payment system by the central bank could make a significant difference to financial inclusion." However, the use of CBDC digital wallets would increase efficiency and justice in the allocation of relief funds.

- **Positive Impact on Macroeconomic**

The wide acceptance of CBDC will reduce the cost of running the payment system. And the activities are like reduction in the frictions and cost associated with the storage, transport and management of cash, reduce tax evasion, corruption, illegal activities, increase financial stability, increase financial inclusion especially in underbanked economy. So overall the advantages of CBDC in the payment systems may reveal to the overall economy with a significant impact on the GDP.

RISKS OF CBDC

- **Affect the business models of commercial banks:**

If central banks begin to compete with the private banking sector for deposits and lending money then the significant deposit balances could shift to the central banks from the commercial bank account, which would impact the balance sheet of the commercial bank. Furthermore, commercial banks could lose the valuable connection with the consumers.

- **Privacy Risks:**

The Current payment system provides a number of levels of privacy from the complete physical cash transaction to full traceable, document verification and monitored bank accounts. The design of the CBDC should also provide high security with unlimited access to information.

- **Faster obsolescence of technology:**

Faster obsolescence of technology could pose a threat to the CBDC ecosystem calling for higher cost of upgrading.

- **Difficult to attain widespread adoption:**

In India many people would not be able to access digital currencies, as adoption of new technology will be difficult for many people and others will not adopt because they don't trust digital currencies. So this would lead to not adopting the digital currency (CBDC).

Conclusion:

From the Research paper we have conclude that CBDC will play a significant role in the upcoming years in the overall payment systems of India. The introduction of CBDC will reduce the role of the commercial banks in the country. The role of CBDC will reduce the illegal activities in the economy, reduce tax evasion, increase in the financial inclusion and the main aim is that it will reduce the operational expense to maintain the physical cash. CBDC once launched on full scale will be majorly accepted by Indian youths as they prefer digital payments over physical cash. RBI has circulated Retail Central Bank Digital Currency pilot which has generated about 770,000 transactions and it includes 50,000 customers and 5,000 merchants. In this research paper we have compared the CBDC with the other modes of payment. The other modes of payment include UPI, Net Banking, E-Wallets and Cards. In India around 69% of people live in rural areas and most of them don't use smartphones so at the initial stage it would be difficult to implement this new digital currency concept. So this will be a big task for the government to implement CBDC in India, also privacy will play a major role in the success of CBDC. But the crucial part of CBDC is that each individual will need to remember a new password/pin to access their account which can be hectic for some of the people in India, mostly the elderly people. Overall the launch of CBDC will be beneficial for the digital growth in India and CBDC will work hand in hand with other modes of payments. Accepting CBDC as regular mode payments will be personal choice of individuals. Introduction of CBDC will boost our Fintech innovation to provide new financial services and to improve the delivery of existing financial services.

REFERENCE

1. Cunha, Melo and Sebastião; [2021]; "From Bitcoin to Central Bank Digital Currencies: Making Sense of the Digital Money Revolution"; MDPIpublication.
2. MĂRGULESCU, MĂRGULESCU [2020] "Traditional Cryptocurrencies and Fiat- Backed Digital Currencies".
3. Narula (2021), "Technology Development of Digital Currency";
4. Singh, John & Jacob [2022]; "A Review of Central Bank Digital Currencies"; Ushus- Journal of Business Management.
5. RBI Concept Note: https://rbi.org.in/Scripts/PublicationReportDetails.aspx?UrlPage=&ID=1218
6. RBI's Digital Rupee: Expected Advantages and Implications https://www.mondaq.com/india/fin-tech/1248676/rbis-digital-rupee-expected- advantages-and-implications
7. Global CBDC Pilot Projects https://www.outlookindia.com/business/here-s-all-you-need-to-know-about-global-cbdc- pilot-projects-news-247588

A Study of Financial Performance Analysis of Hindustan Unilever Limited

CHAPTER 31

Author – Shivani Singh, Neha Shrivastav, Student, IES's Management College and Research Centre, Mumbai

ABSTRACT

Business finance is the cornerstone of every organization. Finance is very important for smooth going of business. Finance controls the policies, activities and decision of every business. Financial performance helps to know the overall performance of the company. This research paper is based on Hindustan Unilever Limited (HUL) which exists in India since past 90 years and is India's largest fast-moving consumer goods company. Hindustan Unilever Limited is subsidiary of Unilever and one of the world's leading suppliers of Food, Home care, personal care and Refreshment product with sales in over 190 countries. Forbes rated Hindustan Unilever Limited as the most innovative company in India and #8 globally. This paper examines the financial performance of Hindustan Unilever Limited by using Liquidity, Profitability Ratios, Leverage Ratios and Turnover ratio of the company. The study to analyse the financial performance of the company was conducted using financial data from the company's annual report for the last three years.

KEYWORDS

"Ratio Analyses, Financial Statement, Annual Report, fundamental Analysis, HUL."

INTRODUCTION

Finance is a term for matters regarding the management, creation, study of money and investment, which is used by individual, company or government. It also deals with the question of how and why and also help how to acquire the money and how to spend or invest the money. Finance majorly has three categories: corporate finance, personnel finance and public finance. Finance is also about overall "system" i.e, the financial market that allow the flow of money, via investments and other financial instruments between and within this area; this "floe" is facilitate by financial services sector.

An Indian manufacturer of consumer goods, Hindustan Unilever Limited (HUL) is headquartered in Mumbai, Maharashtra. It is a subsidiary of the British Dutch business Unilever. It was founded in 1933 as Lever Brothers of the United Kingdom and changed its name to "Hindustan Lever Limited" in 1956 after its constituent organisations merged. In June 2007, the business adopted the name "Hindustan Unilever Limited." Mumbai is where it's headquartered. Foods, beverages, cleaning supplies, personal care items, and water purifiers are just a few of the many products offered by Hindustan Unilever Limited. Through products and services that are beneficial to both them and others, HUL aims to build a better future every day and makes it easier for people to feel good, look good, and enjoy life more. Indian company Hindustan Unilever Limited (HUL)It has 50+ FMCG brands in India and 20 distinct categories such as soaps, detergents, shampoos; skin care, toothpaste, deodorants, cosmetics, tea, coffee, packaged foods, ice cream and water purifiers. HUL is a part of everyday life of millions of consumers across India. It has leading Household brand such as Lux, Lifebuoy, Surf Excel, Rin, Wheel, Fair and Lovely, Pond's, Vaseline, Lakme, Dove, Clinic Plus, Sunsilk, Pepsodent, Close Up, Axe, Kwality Wall's, Bru, Kissan, Knorr. HUL has achieved plastic neutrality in 2021. In the financial year 2021-22 Hul has 50000+ crore turnover and 9/10 households in India use HUL. It is one of the oldest companies operating in the FMCG sector. More than 50% of the consumer consume HUL products. Soap is the important manufacturing industry in the sector of FMCG. On 17th February HUL said its laundry detergent brand, Surf Excel has crossed the 1 billion turnover in the company portfolio HUL is becoming the first brand to cross the milestone. It has the annual revenue of Rs 51,193.00 crore in fiscal. Surf Excel has played the important role now surf excel has accelerated its sustainability jouney with bottles in the liquid now being made for 50% recycled plastic. It is designed by 100% biodegradable actives. We have also analysis it by using SWOT and BCG Matrix.

SWOT ANALYSIS OF HUL

The SWOT analysis of Hindustan Unilever Limited includes internal factors that is Strengths and Weaknesses and external factor that is Opportunities and Threats. We have examine this in terms of internal and external factors. SWOT is a strategic way to analyse that where the companies. It provides key insight both internal and external factor that can effect the performance of organization. It is very useful for the manager of the company to optimize performance, plan for the new opportunities, balance the competition, they try to get the maximum return from the resource which is used.

STRENGTHS

HUGE LINE OF BRAND: HUL has many brand which are mostly used by consumer. It has high brand awareness with broad range of products which includes namely, oral care, personal care, pet food, textile care and household surface care. In the FMCG market, HUL is a market leader. In Indian market it itself is known as a brand. They also applied the supply chain and other things.

MARKET LEADER: It has huge market Share because of high market penetration. HUL manages to have high market share in many product categories. It has strong promoters.

MOST PREFFERED BRAND: From mineral water to soap HUL helps in daily living of 1.3 billion people. It stands in the market with 35+ products which include soap, shampoo, tea, detergent. This helps hul to occupy a large share. Five out of four Indian consumers use HUL products according to the study. It is market leader in the Indian market

WEAKNESS

Declining market share:

There are many competitors than Ghadi and Nirma detergents which is eating up its share of wheel washes.

LIMITED MARKET SHARE:

As there is presence of many others strong FMCG brands HUL market share is limited.

OPPORTUNITIES

AYURVEDIC PRODUCTS: HUL can start manufacturing Ayurveda product under its brand name
PARTNERSHIP: The brand can be strengthening for the long run with the help of Mergers and Acquisitions.

THREATHS

COMPETITORS: As there is an increase in the number of National and Local suppliers, it has become difficult to differentiate their businesses from others.
GOVERNMENT REGULATIONS: Change in any government rules and regulations may effect business practices and policies.

BCG MATRIX OF HUL (HINDUSTAN UNILEVER LTD)

BCG matrix of HUL contains the Dogs, stars, Cash Cows and the Question mark. In this study of BCG matrix of HUL we can analyse the high growth products, company's low growth products, that may attract sales.
DOGS: The Dogs of HUL are: Brooke Bond sehatmand and Taaza
STARS: The stars of HUL are 1. AXE Deodorant 2. Vim 3. Fair and Lovely 4. Lifebuoy 5. Lakme Anti-Ageing 6. Lux 7. Wheel 8. Knorr Soup 9. Kwality walls 10. Kissan jam.
Deodorant AXE contributes 25% of market share (sandhu,2013). all the star products contribute the most to the market share.
CASH COWS:
HUL Cash Cows are daily morning things and fast food, Shampoos, Soaps. Sunsilk has been used by large group of young Indian women.
QUESTIONS:

The HUL question marks are

1. Knorr meal maker
2. Domex
3. Fair and Lovely Men's Active
4. Kissan Ketchup
5. Breeze

LITERATURE REVIEW

SHARMILA.P(2017) in her "A study on financial performance analysis of Hindustan Unilever Limited". The objective of her study was ratio analysis such as Profitability, Liquidity, solvency and Trend analysis of the company. She analyses the financial performance of the company for last five years.

AKASH SURESH (2020) in their study "A study on the financial performance of Hindustan Unilever Limited". The objective of them was to analyses the financial performance of Hindustan Unilever Limited and to find the profitability and liquidity position of the company.

RESEARCH METHODOLOGY

RESEARCH

The research comprises of defining and redefining problems, formulation, hypothesis or suggested solution; collecting, organizing and evaluating data; making deduction and reaching conclusions; and at last carefully testing the conclusion to see if they conform to the forming premise.

OBJECTIVES OF THE STUDY

The study the financial performance of HUL in last three years.

Sub-Objectives:

- To calculate the ratio analysis of the company.
- To figure out the company's profitability.
- To understand the company's financial status.

Tool used: Bar chat and Tables.

SOURCE OF DATA

SECONDARY DATA

The secondary data is a data which is collected by someone else and which have already been passed through the statistical process. Secondary data is gathered from sources including internal documents, books, journal articles, websites, and government publications.

TOOLS USED FOR THE STUDY

- Current ratio

- Return on asset ratio
- Debt to equity ratio
- Debt asset ratio
- Fixed asset ratio
- Inventory turnover ratio

LIMITATION OF THE STUDY

- we have restricted to only last three years' Financial performance of Hindustan Unilever Limited.
- This data may have accuracy problem.
- We have only used Ratio Analyses Technique which have its own limitations and it is based on past data.
- This studies based on historical data and it depends on secondary data which is obtain from www.moneycontrol.com.

FINDINGS

Liquidity Ratio:

1. CURRENT RATIO:

The current ratio is a liquidity ratio that measures a company's ability to pay of its short term debt and obligations, which are typically due within one year. It tells you whether the company has enough current/liquidity asset to repay its short term dues. The following is the current ratio formula.

Current Asset Year (in crores) Existing Liability (in crores) Actual Ratio

Year	Current Asset (in crores)	Current Liability (in crores)	Current Ratio
2019-20	11908	9104	1.31
2020-21	13640	10841	1.26
2021-22	14647	10944	1.34

Source: (Secondary Data)

CURRENT RATIO = CURRENT ASSETS ÷ CURRENT LIABILITIES

INTERPRETATION

From the above table the highest current ratio of 1.34 is found for the year 2021-22 and lowest current ratio of 1.26 is found for the year 2020.21. In the table it is clear that, in all the three-year study period, the ideal ratio is 2:1. But there is a decrease trend from 2019-20 to 2020-21. But again in the year 2021-22 there is a significant increase in current ratio, the current ratio is 1.34:1 indicating that the firm is in an average condition to meet the short term-debt. It is a measure of liquidity which is calculated by CA/CL. The above three years have more than 1 current ratio which indicates that current asset are in excess of current liability.

2. Return on assets (ROA) offers you an understanding of how effectively a business uses its assets to generate revenue. A corporation that has a high return on asset is good at using its assets to produce profits. It is expressed as a percentage and is computed using the formula below:

RETURN ON ASSET (ROA) IN % = (NET INCOME ÷ TOTAL AVERAGE ASSET)

Years	Net Income	Total Asset	Ratio
2019-20	6738	18733.5	0.35
2020-21	7954	25548	0.31
2021-22	8818	28287	0.31

Source: (Secondary Data)

Return on asset (ROA) = Net income / total average asset * 100

Source:(Secondary Data)

INTERPRETATION

From the above table the highest return on asset (ROA) ratio of 0.35:1 is found for the year 2019-20 and the lowest return on asset ratio of 0.31:1 is found for the year 2020-21. Therefore, we can infer that in 2021 and 2022 the return on asset was low as compare to 2020.Basically by the name itself means it is the overall profit of the firm earn through the asset.

3. DEBT TO EQUITY RATIO:

The debt to equity ratio denotes how much debt a corporation has compared to its equity. If debt to equity ratio is greater than 1 than it means that a company as more debt than equity, while a ratio lower than 1 means that the equity is more than debt. The ratio of 1 indicates that a company as equal portion of debt and equity.

Years	Total Liability	Total Equity	Ratio
2020	11571	8031	1.4
2021	20862	47434	0.4
2022	20977	48760	0.4

Source: (Secondary Data)

Debt to equity ratio = total liabilities / total equity

INTERPRETATION

From the above table the highest debt equity ratio 1.4 is found for the year 2019-20 and the lowest debt equity ratio 0.4 is found for the year 2021 and 2022. In the table it is clear that in all the three years' study period, the debt was high in 2020 is state that the company had more debt than equity and in 2021 and 2022 the portion of equity was more than the debt. It measures the ratio of total debt or long term to shareholder's equity. The Debt of the firm is quiet low as compare to 2020. This ratio shows the amount of debt company has with respect to its net worth.

Here the ratio is decreasing and it is close to zero so it is very good sign for the company.

4. DEBT ASSET RATIO:

Debt asset ratio is same as debt to equity ratio, the proportion of debt to debt of asset of company. The lesser the debt to asset ratio, the better.

Years	Total Liability	Total Asset*100	Ratio
2019-20	19602	11571	1.69
2020-21	20682	68116	0.30
2021-22	20977	69737	0.30

Source: (Secondary Data)

Debt asset ratio =Total Liabilities / Total asset *100

INTERPRETATION

It signifies that the higher a company's in debt-to-total asset ratio, the more it is said to be debt. A debt to asset ratio of 1.69 indicates that approx. 1.69 percent of asset was owned by HUL is by finance using debt capital. In 2021 and 2022 the Debt Asset Ratio is quite low as compare to previous one. This ratio shows the amount of debt company has with respect to its net assets is low in the year 2021 and 2022.

As company has very low amount of debt so debt to asset ratio is close to 0 which is good sign for the company.

5. FIXED ASSET TURNOVER RATIO:

It is connected between the operating income of the company and its fixed asset. The ratio used to determine how much a sale a company make using its fixed asset such as machinery, capital work in progress, equipment. The higher the fixed turnover it is better.

Years	Sale	Fixed Asset	Ratio
2019-20	38273	6219	6.15
2020-21	45996	7518	6.12
2021-22	51193	8692	5.89

Source: (Secondary Data)

Fixed asset turnover = revenue from sales / fixed asset

INTERPRETATION

It shows how efficient a company is at generating sales from the existing fixed asset. From the above table we can analyse that in 2020 the sale of a companies was 6.15% of return on investment using its fixed asset. And in 2021 and 2022 the turnover much better than previous year. Company is efficiently utilizing its fixed asset in generating sales.

6. INVENTORY TURNOVER RATIO:

It shows the number of times a company has managed to sell its stock of finished goods. It is done on specific period of time

INVENTORY TURNOVER RATIO= REVENUE FROM SALES / AVERAGE INVENTORY

Years	Revenue From Sale	Average Inventory	Ratios
2020	38273	2529	15.1
2021	45996	4701	9.8
2022	51193	5581	9.2

Source: (Secondary Data)

INTERPRETATION

The above figure shows that in a financial year 2019-20, HUL has managed to sell the entire stock of finished goods approximately 15 times. In 2021 and 2022 they managed to sell the entire stock of finished goods by 9 times. It indicates how fast inventory is sold, if the ratio is high from the viewpoint of liquidity then it is good and vice-versa. This ratio indicates that inventory management in the company.

As this ratio is decreasing in 2021-2022 as compared to previous year 2020-2021 which shows that company has not able to manage its inventory and convert its inventories into sales. Higher the ratio is better. Here we can say that ratio in 2022 is decreasing because average inventory is increased it means that company has accumulated more inventory as compared to previous year and sales are also increasing which Is a good sign for the company.

Scope for further research of HUL:

Sustainability and Environmental Impact: Investigate HUL's initiatives and strategies for sustainable practices, including waste reduction, water conservation, renewable energy adoption, and carbon footprint reduction. Assess the effectiveness and impact of these initiatives on the environment.

Market Expansion and Growth Strategies: Analyse HUL's expansion plans and strategies to enter new markets or expand existing ones, both within India and internationally. Assess the factors influencing their market selection and evaluate the outcomes of these expansion efforts.

Consumer Behaviour and Market Trends: Study consumer preferences, buying patterns, and market trends in the sectors where HUL operates. Explore the impact of changing consumer behavior, shifting demographics, and emerging market trends on HUL's product portfolio, marketing strategies, and brand positioning.

Digital Transformation and E-commerce: Examine HUL's digital transformation initiatives, including its online presence, e-commerce strategies, and use of technology for supply chain management and customer engagement. Evaluate the effectiveness of these initiatives in enhancing customer experience and driving business growth.

Product Innovation and R&D: Explore HUL's research and development activities, focusing on product innovation, formulation, and development of new technologies. Assess the impact of innovation on HUL's market competitiveness, product portfolio diversification, and revenue growth.

Social Impact and Corporate Social Responsibility (CSR): Investigate HUL's CSR initiatives and their impact on society, including projects related to education, healthcare, hygiene, and rural development. Evaluate the effectiveness and long-term sustainability of these initiatives.

SUMMARY AND CONCLUSIONS

From the study we mainly concentrated on the Financial performance of the company of Hindustan Unilever Limited. Total revenue for the financial year 2019-2020 was Rs.40415 Crore. There was increase in the growth rate by 17.38% in the year 2020-2021. We also saw that in 2022 the turnover crosses by Rs 50336 crore up by 11% with the volume growth of 3%. PAT at 8188 crores was up by 11%. They have grown competitively and protected their business by balancing the margin in a healthy range. Their performance is directly reflective of their strategic clarity. But they are concern around significant inflation and their slowing growth of market. They are confident and well-focused on delivering a though competitive, Profitable and Responsible growth.

REFERENCES

Kakani, R. K., Saha, B., & Reddy, V. N. (2001). Determinants of financial performance of Indian corporate sector in the post-liberalization era: an exploratory study. *National Stock Exchange of India Limited, NSE Research Initiative Paper*, (5).

Khan, M. M. (2021). Financial Performance of FMCG companies-Post COVID-19. *International Journal of Economics and Management Systems, 6*.

Knight, R., & Bertoneche, M. (2000). *Financial performance*. Elsevier.

Bhunia, A., Mukhuti, S. S., & Roy, S. G. (2011). Financial performance analysis-A case study. *Current Research Journal of Social Sciences, 3*(3), 269-275.

Beg, K. (2018). Impact of accounting information system on the financial performance of selected FMCG companies. *Asian Journal of Applied Science and Technology, 2*(3), 08-17.

Paswan, R. K. (2016). Financial Performance of FMCG Companies in India: A Comparative Study. *ANVESHAK, 5*(2), 117.

Das, S. (2019). Cash flow ratios and financial performance: A comparative study. *Accounting, 5*(1), 1-20.

A Comparative Study on the Impact of Internship in Enhancing Skills of Undergraduate Students of in the Mumbai

Author – Manasi Parab & Vardhini Ramchandran, Student, SIES College of Commerce and Economics, Mumbai

ABSTRACT

In the modern world, internships are crucial for improving students' overall skills. As a result, India's Union Cabinet launched the National Education Policy on July 29, 2020. The NEP 2020 suggested that students at all higher education institutions will be given opportunities for internships with local industries, businesses, and the arts as part of a holistic education. This study examines if a student actually needs to complete an internship or whether their college curriculum is adequate for them to enhance their skills. An online survey method containing 18 questions was used to get information from the respondents. 94 students filled out the survey that was distributed via MyForm App. This research does not cover all types of skills. This study only considers students who are currently pursuing their undergraduate degrees. The data is collected from 94 respondents only. The research is based on an online survey and questionnaire. Students who completed internships thrive in leadership and communication abilities, whereas those who did not complete internships excel in social skills. However, both groups have similarly strong decision-making abilities.

Keyword: Internship, social skills, life skills, undergraduates, commerce.

INTRODUCTION OF INTERNSHIP

Meaning

Nowadays, an internship is an important component of students' education. Students that do internships increase their knowledge by being exposed to a professional environment. It helps to link theoretical knowledge with the practical world. Shortly, internships have emerged as a crucial means of developing abilities and gaining office experience prior to landing a real job. Since they are already familiar with the workplace, companies frequently choose to hire their top interns instead of spending time and money on training new hires.

Before employing a candidate, an employer will check for a few skills. These skills include Leadership, social, decision-making, communication, etc. As a result, India's Union Cabinet launched the National Education Policy on July 29, 2020. The NEP 2020 suggested that students at all higher education institutions will be given opportunities for internships with local industries, businesses, and the arts as part of a holistic education. Before employing a candidate, an employer will check for a few skills. A student needs leadership, social, decision-making, communication, and employability skills even if they perform well academically.

BENEFITS OF INTERNSHIP TO STUDENTS

1. Job experience
2. Helps in choosing a suitable career path.
3. Best way to put theoretical knowledge into practice.
4. Skill Development
5. Networking with professionals
6. Resume building.
7. Obtain information beyond that found in book.
8. Can earn/obtain credits for the semester.

DEFINITION

- According to Oxford Dictionary, an Internship is – "a period during which a student or new graduate gets practical experience in a job, for example during the summer holiday."
- Leadership skills: "Successful leadership is leading with the heart, not just the head. They possess qualities like empathy, compassion, and courage." –

Bill George, Professor at Harvard Business School. Leadership skills are the abilities to motivate teams, delegate responsibilities, respond to feedback and solve problems. Most people can learn how to be a good leader in any role or level. Almost any positive soft skill might be considered a leadership skill.

- Interpersonal Skills: Our ability to engage and communicate with one another through gestures, body language, and outward appearance is referred to as social skills. In both a personal and professional setting, social skills are crucial. You may succeed in your career, excel in interviews, reach your career goals, and grow your professional network by having great social skills.
- Decision-making skills: "In any moment of decision, the best thing you can do is the right thing, the next best thing is the wrong thing, and the worst thing you can do is nothing." Theodore Roosevelt.

The term problem solving and decision making is often used in the workplace interchangeably but is not the same. As the term suggests, problem-solving begins with problem identification, whereas decision-making skills are necessary for solving problems. The ability of employees to take decisions is influenced not only by knowledge and experience but also by the structural empowerment prevailing in the organization

- Communication Skills: Communication skills are defined as the skills that help us speak, listen, observe and empathize with others by using verbal and non-verbal communication in an effective manner. Verbal communication skills include the way you use written or spoken words while non-verbal communication refers to your body language, facial expressions sorts of nonverbal signals.
- Problem-solving skills: Problem-solving skills help you determine the source of a problem and find an effective solution. Although problem-solving is often identified as its own separate skill, there are other related skills that contribute to this ability.
- Creative-thinking skills: Creative thinking refers to using abilities and soft skills to come up with new solutions to problems. Creative thinking skills are techniques used to look at the issue from different and creative angles, using the right tools to assess it and develop a plan.

REVIEW OF LITERATURE

Sr. No	Authors	Title	Year	Country	Sample	Methodology	Key Findings
1.	Manjunath S, M B Shrava, Dechakka B B	A study on assessment of Skill Gap to enhance workforce performance	April 2019	India	Studied 101 responses of front-line employees of Sanria Engineering and Consulting Pvt Ltd.	Content analysis using simple random sampling technique, ANOV, Regression Analysis, Coefficients, Correlation and Gap Analysis, mean.	There is a relationship between the skills considered such as technical skills, communication skills, inter-personal skills and decision-making skills. All the above-mentioned skills had an impact on the performance of the employees except technical skills.
2.	Goplani Mala, Gupta Akash and Sabhani Jewel	A study on impact of Internship on regular studies of Undergraduate students	March 2020	India	Studied responses of 319 undergraduate students of Self-financing course.	Questionnaire survey	Majority students felt that internships are not helpful to understand the college syllabus. Majority of students were able to cope up with internship even during exams. Students enhance their professional skills through internships, which help them apply practical knowledge.

Sr. No	Authors	Title	Year	Country	Sample	Methodology	Key Findings
3.	Elisa, K Mutiara, A Hamida, M Syukri, H Mazlina & Musdar	The contribution of Internship towards soft skills competencies of Pre-service teachers.	2019	Indonesia	Studied 36 physics students of 2014 academic year of Universitas Syiah Kuala and University of Serambi Mekkah	SPSS, correlation coefficient formula, product moment correlation.	Apprenticeship value has a positive contribution to students' soft-skill competencies. The results of the correlation between students soft-skill competencies and internship scores are very weak.
4.	Ilias Kapareliotis, Katerina Voutsina and Athanasios Patsioti	Internship and employability prospects: assessing student's work readiness	January, 2019	Greece	Studied 74 students' responses from an Institution of Higher education in Greece.	Online survey.	Students who attend internship programs assessed positively all aspects of the work readiness construct. They were able to effectively apply basic academic skills, high-order skills and professional skills required by employers on the job and placed greater importance to the intrinsic rewards than the extrinsic ones
5.	Prajapati& Amit Kantilal	An empirical investigation of the relationship between internship programmes and employment marketability of Management students.	Aug, 2013	India	Studied response of 350 students of management affiliated to Mumbai university.	Statistical Analysis, Scaling technique, Questionnaire survey.	The employer assigns or attributes successful job performance to experiential learning through internship.

RESEARCH GAP

In studies involving undergraduates, there are few that validate internships in terms of life and social skills. We, therefore, filled the gap by assessing how internships affect various skills. Additionally, insufficient study has been done on the effectiveness of college curriculam in developing students' skills in Mumbai suburbs.

OBJECTIVES

1. To evaluate the impact of internships on students' life skills.
2. To evaluate the impact of internships on students' social skills.
3. To assess whether the college curriculum is sufficient for enhancing students' skills.

SCOPE

The study is limited to the age group of 18-21 years. Data is collected from undergraduate students studying in colleges in Mumbai city. An online survey was conducted to determine the number of students carrying out internships and their skills. A total of 18 questions were included which were answered by 94 students.

RESEARCH METHODOLOGY

DATA COLLECTION

1. Primary Data: An online survey method was used to get information from the respondents. 94 students filled out the survey that was distributed via MyForm. Focused group interview helped to know the views of students who did internships (50%)
2. Secondary Data: Secondary data was gathered through publications, the internet, and a variety of other sources.

Sample size: A random sample of 94 students from commerce department of various colleges in Mumbai suburbs were selected for this survey.

Data collection tool: A questionnaire was circulated among 94 respondents, in which questions were asked on a Likert scale of 1-5, 1 being Strongly disagree/Not at all like me to 5 being Strongly agree/Exactly like me.

DATA ANALYSIS AND INTERPRETATION

Considerations:

1. The data consists of two types of students:
   a. Students who did an internship
   b. Students who did not do an internship.

The researchers named "Students who did an internship" as **Category A** whereas "Students who did not do an internship" as **Category B.**

2. The researchers have considered an equal number of Category A (47 respondents) and Category B (47 respondents) to get relevant outcomes.

Assumption:

1. The researchers have assumed that all the respondents are academically good.
2. The researchers have assumed that participation in a variety of activities throughout college helped Category B strengthen their leadership, communication, social, and decision-making skills. Their skills have improved as a result of several projects, presentations, college fests, debate competitions, and other activities.

SOCIAL SKILLS

LEADERSHIP SKILLS

1. **Which of the Following Best Describes You as a Child?**

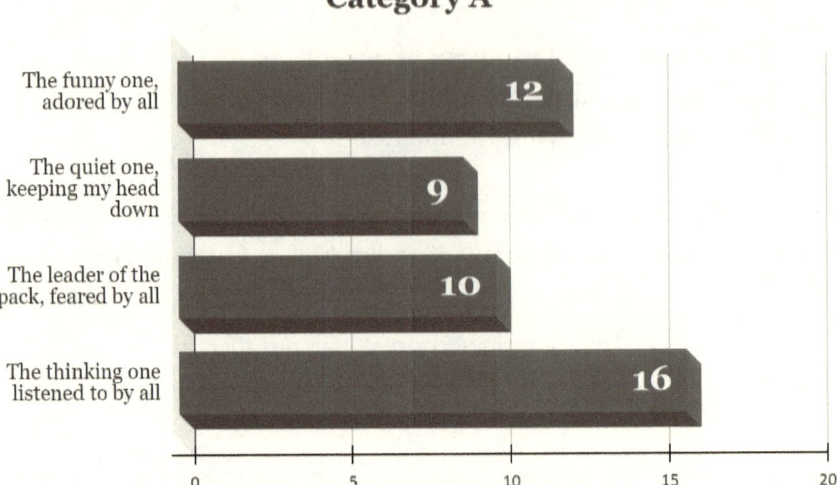

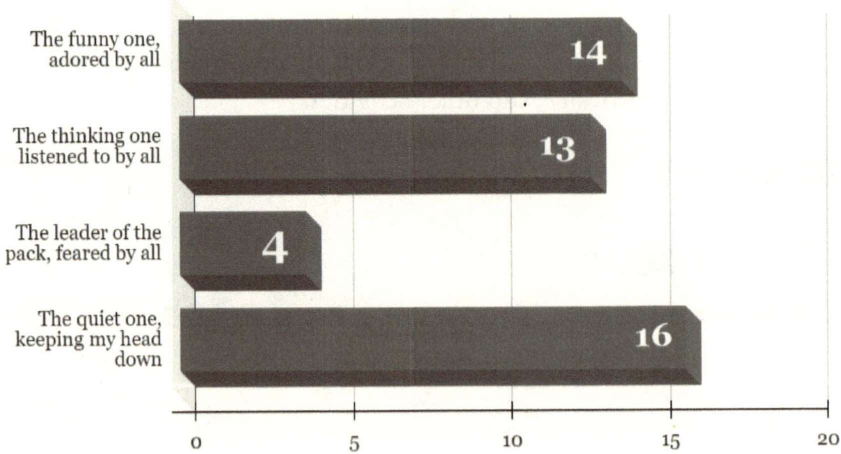

In order to determine if a response is a leader or not, this question aims to grasp their qualities as children. Researchers claim that a leader is someone who thinks and is listened to by others. 16 responders in category A possess the quality of a leader, compared to just 13 in category B. Most respondents in category B are quiet people who keep their heads down, which is the exact opposite of being a leader.

2. I think that personal feelings shouldn't be allowed to get in the way of performance and productivity.

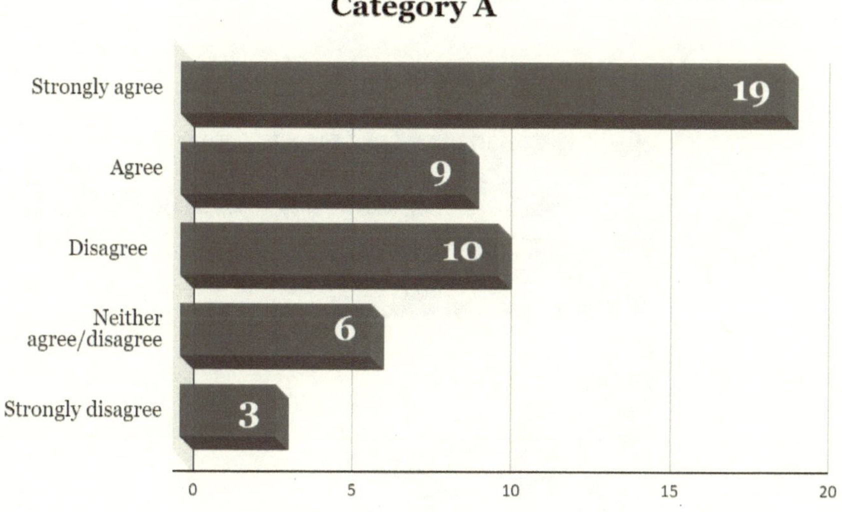

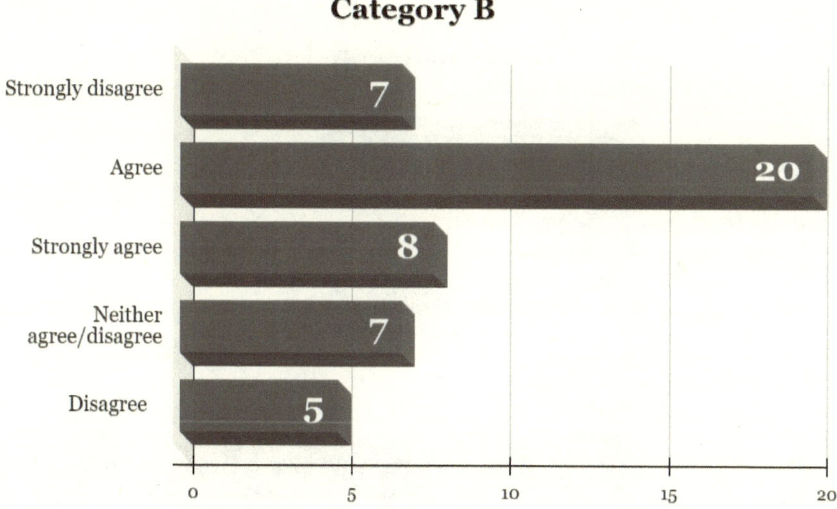

The purpose of this question is to better understand the respondents' viewpoint on allowing personal feelings to interfere with performance and productivity. Typically, a leader won't permit their personal feelings to influence their work because it could have a detrimental impact. Both categories in this question agree that work performance and productivity shouldn't be compromised by personal feelings.

3. **I think time spent worrying about team morale is time that's wasted.**

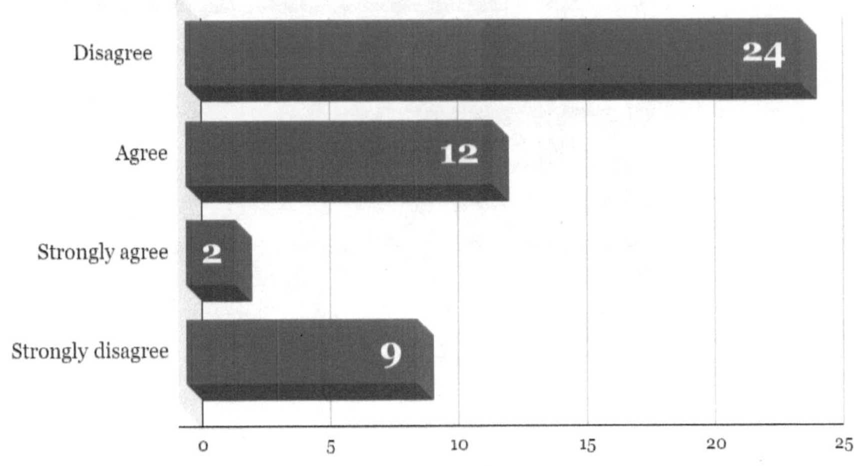

Category B

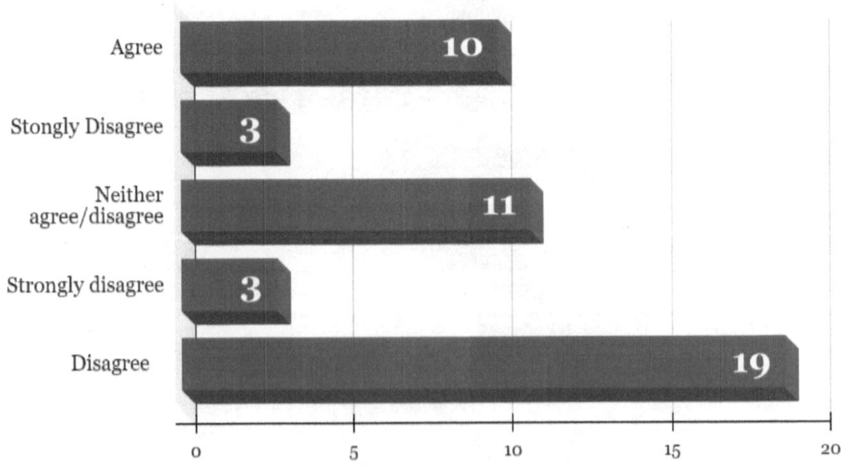

This question seeks to ascertain how both categories feel about team morale. A leader should ideally be considerate of the individuals they are responsible for. They value collaboration and constantly take into account the ideas and opinions of others. The majority of responders in category A believe that investing time in team morale is crucial.

INTERPERSONAL SKILLS

4. **When people are speaking, I spend as much time watching their movements as I do listening to them.**

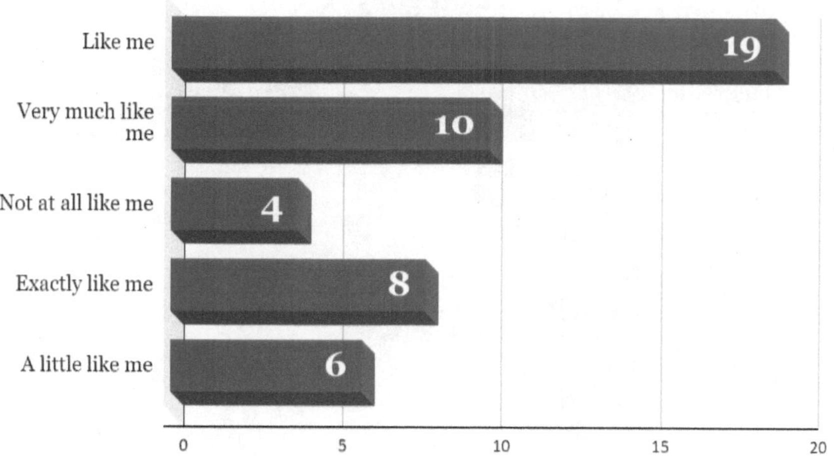

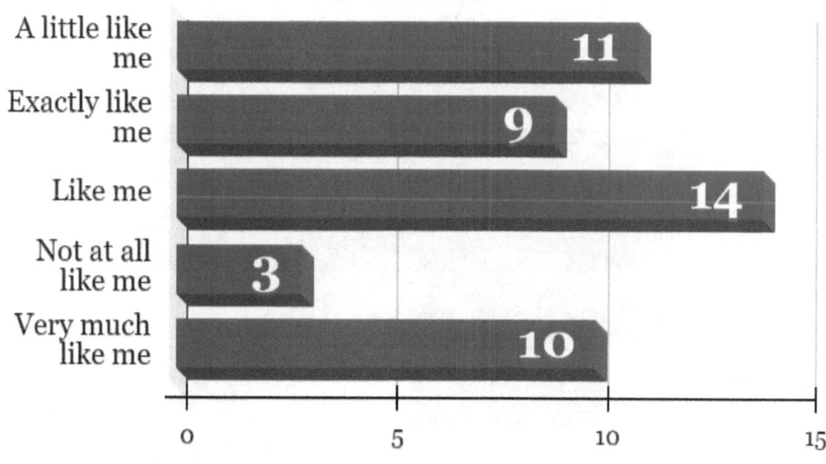

Understanding and interpreting a person's body language helps us interpret their words. Occasionally, a person's body language could contradict what they are saying. The majority of Category A respondents spent time observing the speaker's motions while listening.

5. When I'm with a group of friends, I am often the spokesperson for the group.

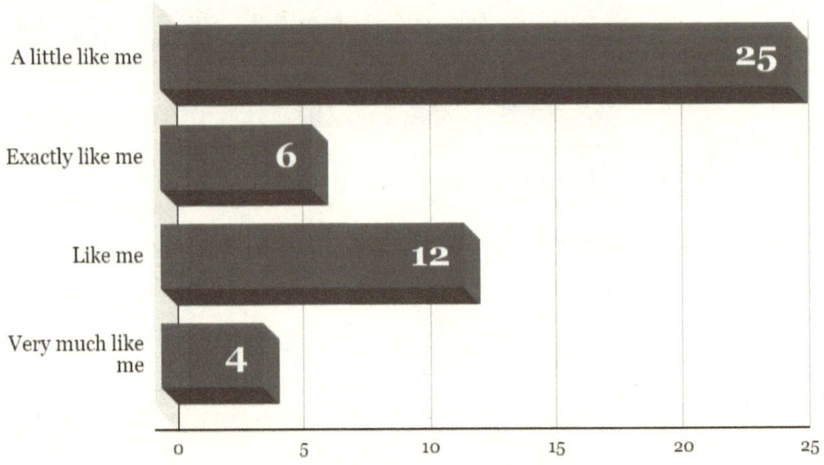

Category B

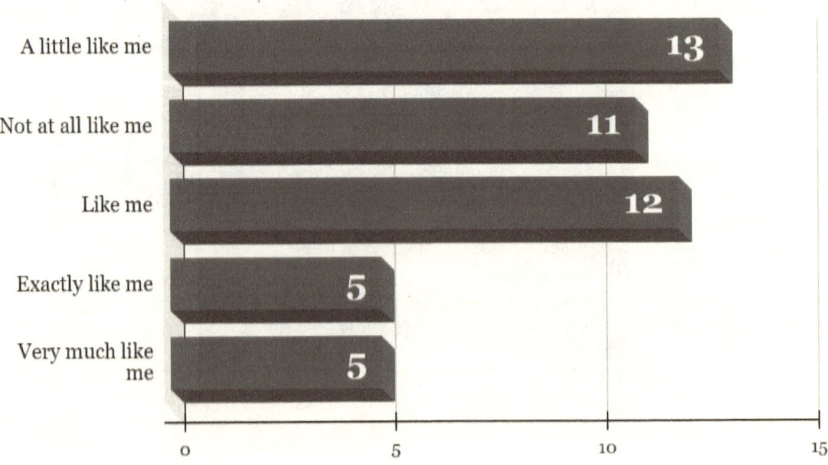

This question aims to ascertain the respondents' place in a larger group of people. A spokesperson, also known as a spokesman or spokeswoman, is someone who speaks on behalf of others. In most conversations, they take the lead. As shown in the charts, the majority of responders in category A state that they are not the group's spokesperson. However, category B asserts that they occasionally serve as the spokesperson.

6. **I would much rather take part in a political discussion than observe and analyze what the participants are saying.**

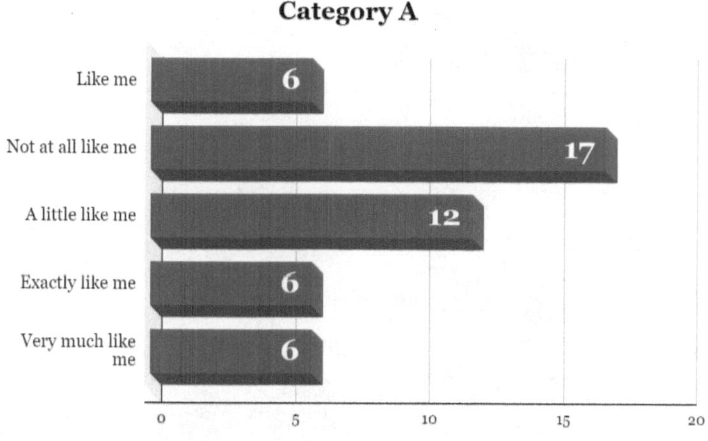

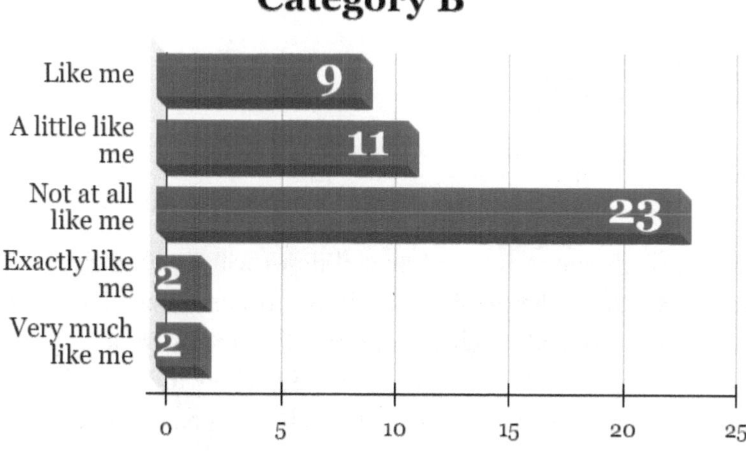

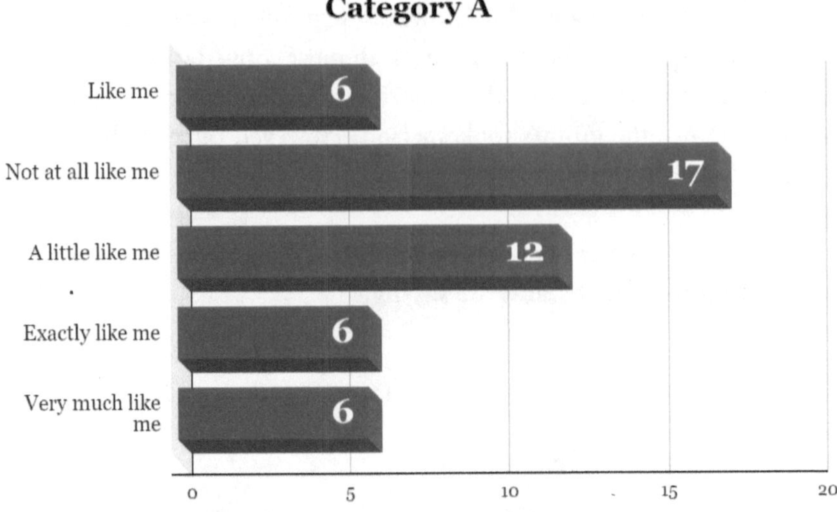

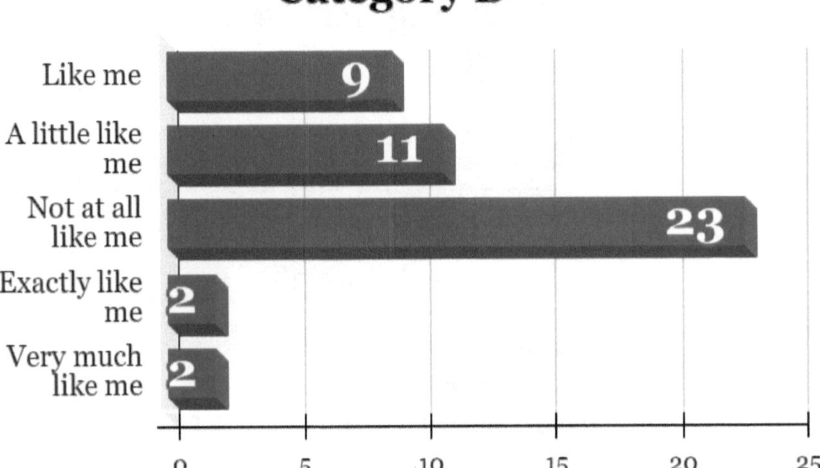

A person with strong interpersonal abilities will never engage in political debates. Even then, they'll make an effort to comprehend the viewpoints of the participants and reach a decision. The majority of respondents in Category B claim that the statement contradicts how they feel about political discussions. They listen and observe what is being spoken by the participants. Only 17 respondents from category A, on the other hand, claim not to engage in political discourse; nevertheless, 12 respondents claim to engage in political discourse to some extent but do not watch the participants.

COMMUNICATION SKILLS

7. **What I say is more important than how I say it.**

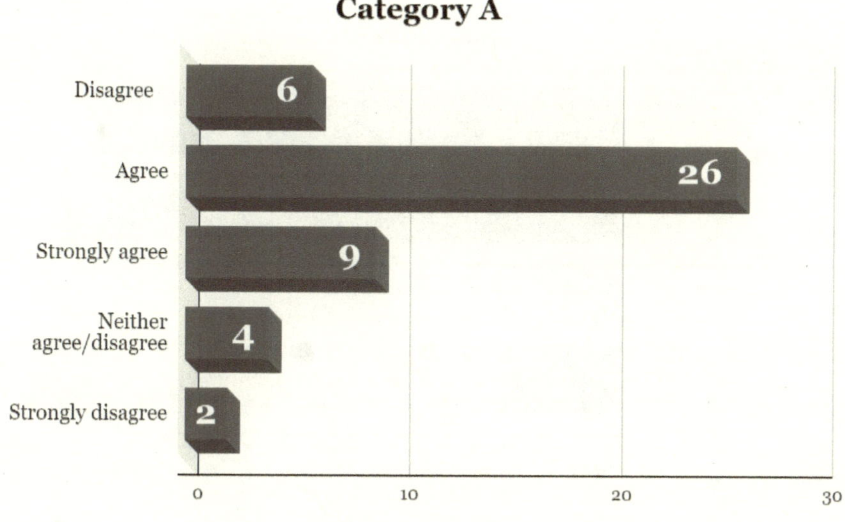

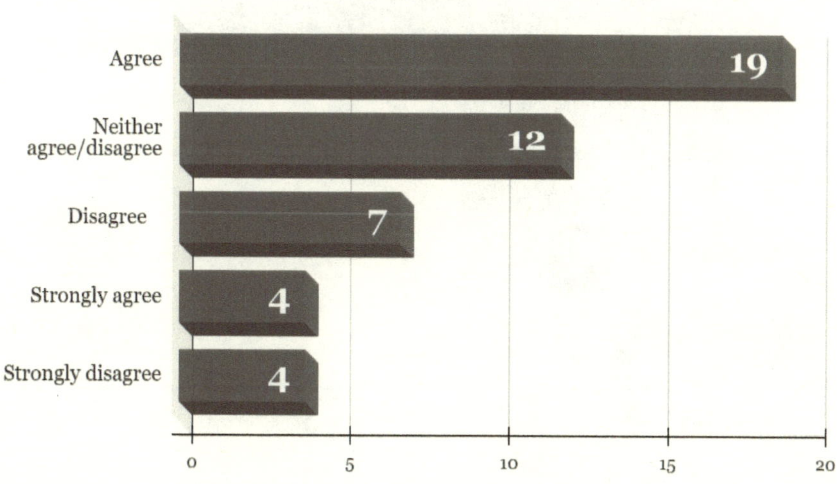

The speaker's voice modulation, body language, clarity of ideas, etc., all play a role in effective communication. This enquiry aims to gauge the respondents' communication abilities. From category A, 26 people concur with the statement. Contrarily, 19 respondents from group B say they concur with the assertion.

8. I am uncomfortable with silence and quick to fill gaps in the conversation.

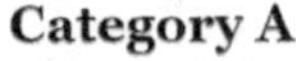

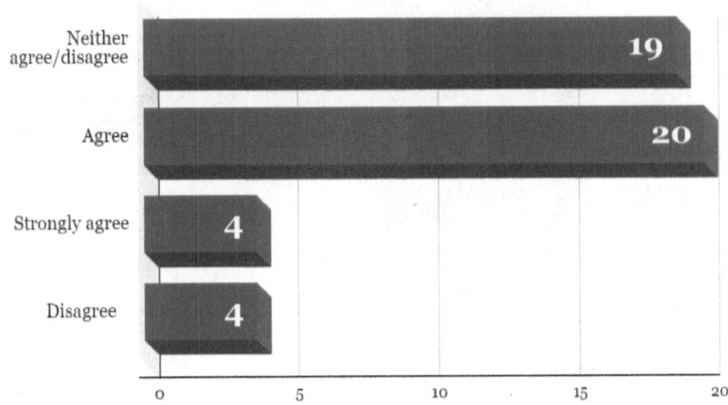

Category B

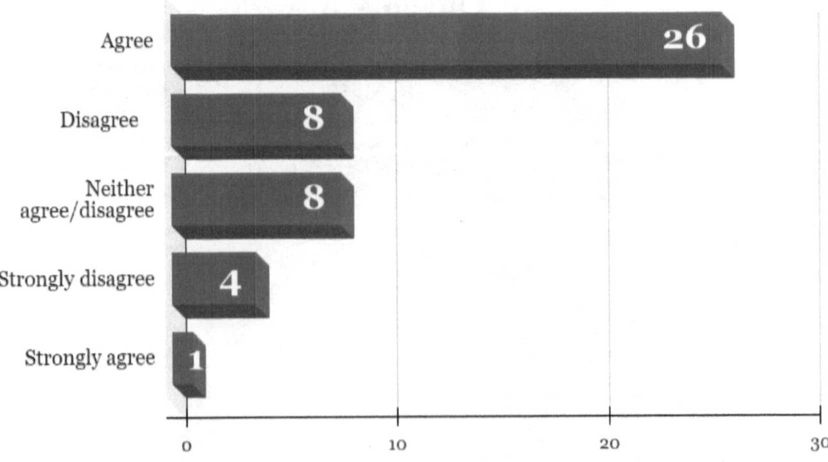

A person with good communication skills will constantly look for methods to keep the conversation interesting. Additionally, they make sure that everyone shares their opinions during the conversation. Numerous category B respondents concur that they fill in the conversation's gaps swiftly. On the other hand, Category B is neutral regarding the assertion.

9. **If I don't understand something, I tend to keep this to myself and figure it out later.**

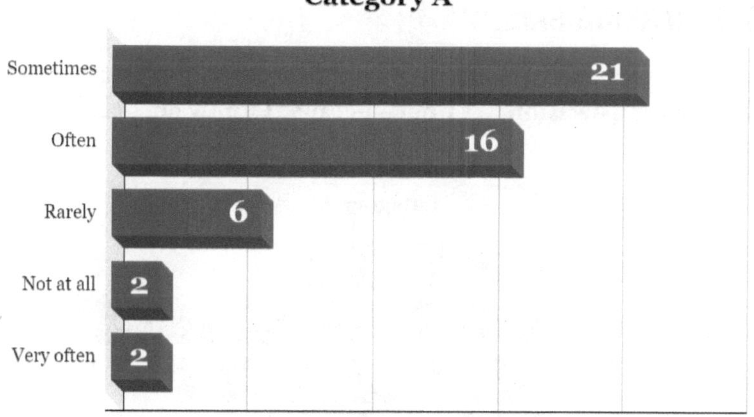

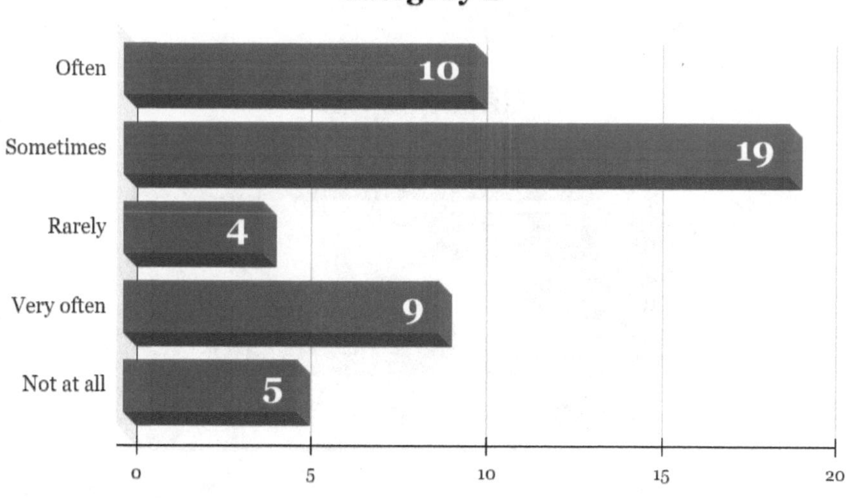

It is common for people to not fully comprehend everything; therefore it is possible that one will encounter such situation and decide to handle things on your own until they can't resolve them. Therefore, it is totally acceptable if it occurs occasionally, but it should not happen that frequently. Here, we can see that Category A respondents entirely agree with the statement made above and only occasionally come up with answers on their own, whereas Category B respondents do so quite frequently.

LIFE SKILLS

DECISION-MAKING SKILLS

10. **After I make a decision, it's final – because I know my process is strong.**

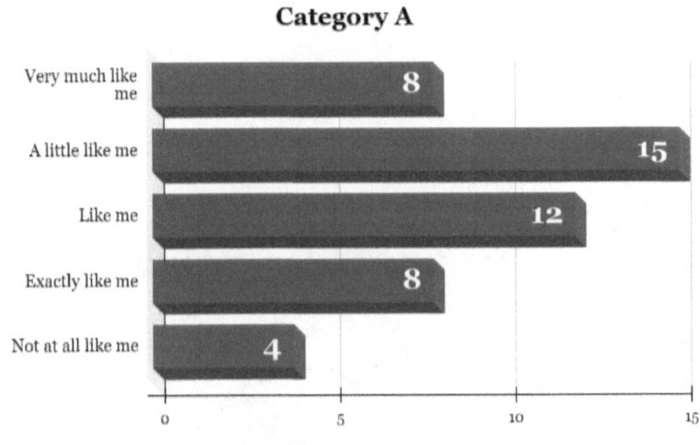

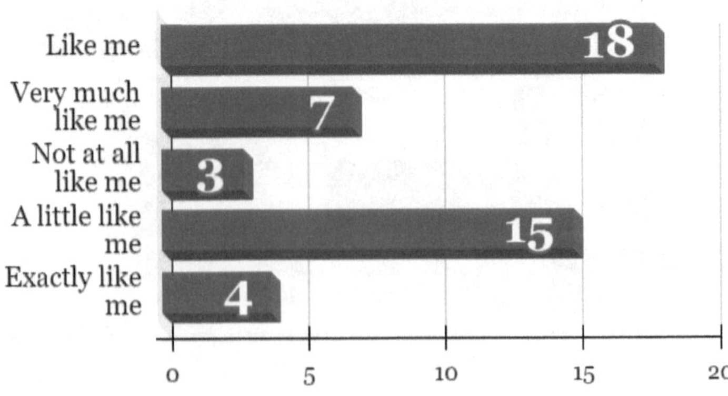

One of the most essential talents assessed while testing skills is decision-making ability. Therefore, one should feel confidence in their choice and that their thought process while selecting it. Thus, it is clear that Category A is not very confident in their decisions, whereas Category B is quite confident in both its decisions and its reasoning.

11. **I rely on my own experience to find potential solutions.**

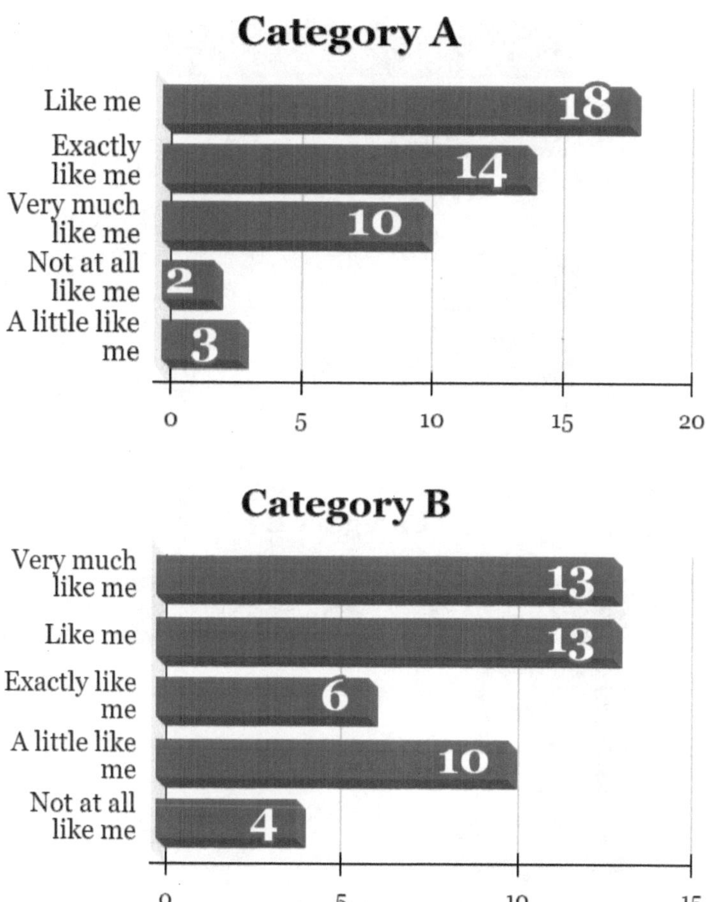

As it was previously stated, one should always have faith in their own judgement. A person should therefore rely on their own experience rather than that of others while looking for potential solutions. Here, we can see that Category A is assured and rely on their own experience, while Category B lacks confidence in their own experience.

12. **I evaluate the risks associated with each alternative before making a decision.**

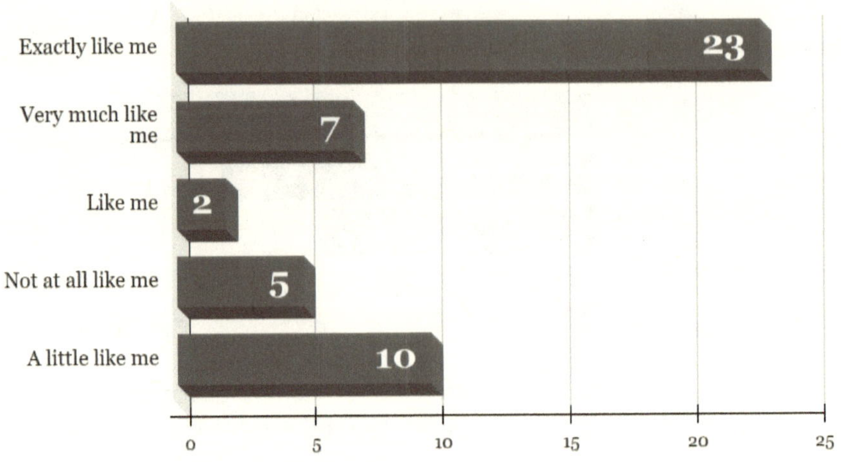

Category B

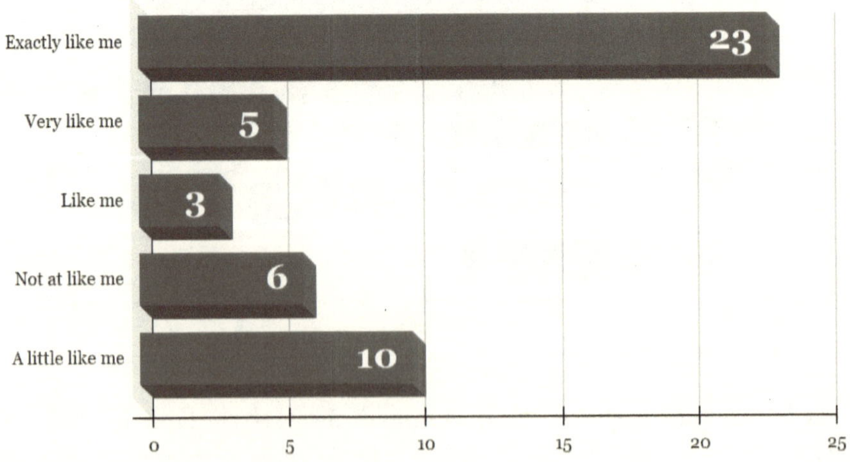

Finding options, analysing the risks connected with each one, and selecting the most advantageous alternative are all necessary steps in making effective decisions. Regarding the following statement, both categories have the same opinion. Before choosing one option over another, they weigh the risks involved.

PROBLEM-SOLVING SKILLS

13. **I think that involving many people to generate solutions can make the process more complicated than it needs to be.**

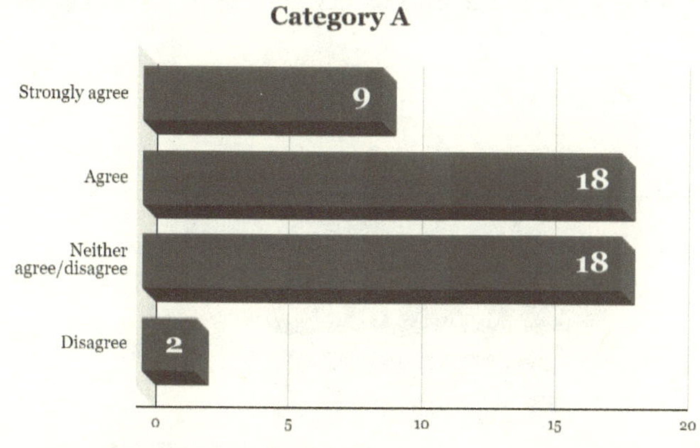

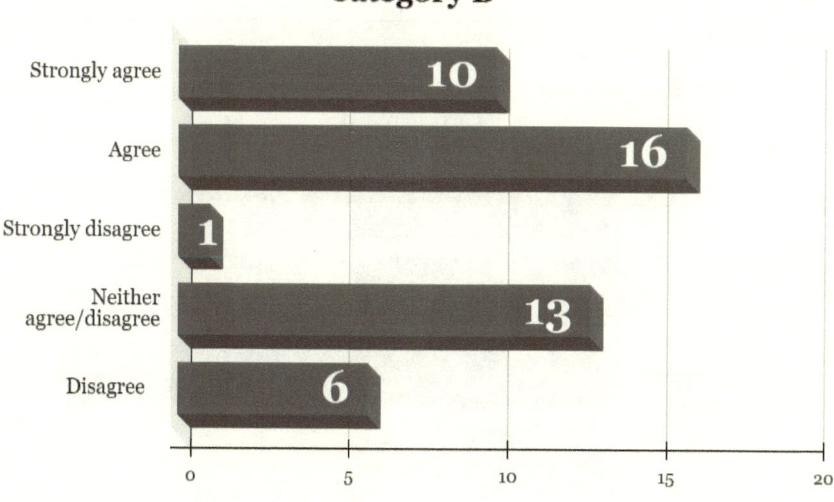

As is frequently stated, unity is strength. However, it doesn't always work. It is true that we need the opinions of many different people in order to find solutions for various problems. When too many people are involved in developing solutions, it can result in a chaotic situation. In the end, new problems may arise without getting solution for the old ones. Hence, here we can see that Category A respondents entirely concur with the statement that enlisting the help of many people in the search for solutions can make the process rather difficult, while Category B respondents appear to disagree only somewhat with the statement.

14. **Making a decision is the end of my problem-solving process.**

Category A

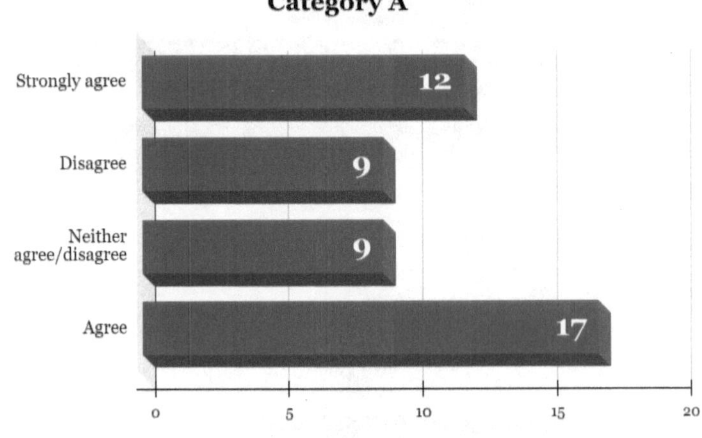

Category B

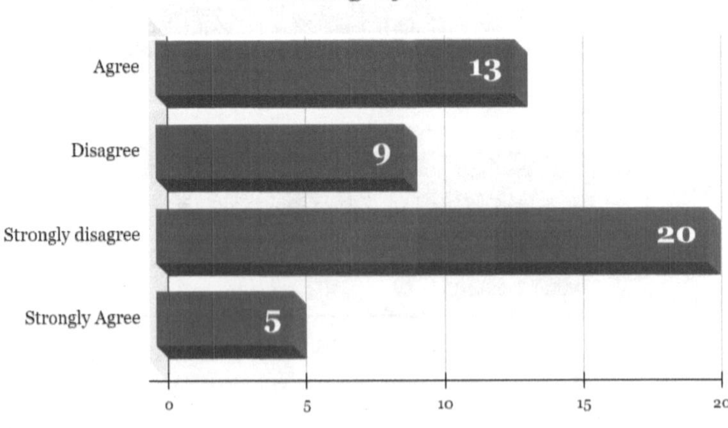

Ideally, one should evaluate the circumstances after making a decision and revise it as necessary. The majority of respondents in category B agree that fixing a problem is a process that doesn't conclude with a decision. But most respondents in group A concur that making a decision marks the conclusion of the problem-solving process.

15. **I evaluate potential solutions carefully and thoroughly against a predefined standard.**

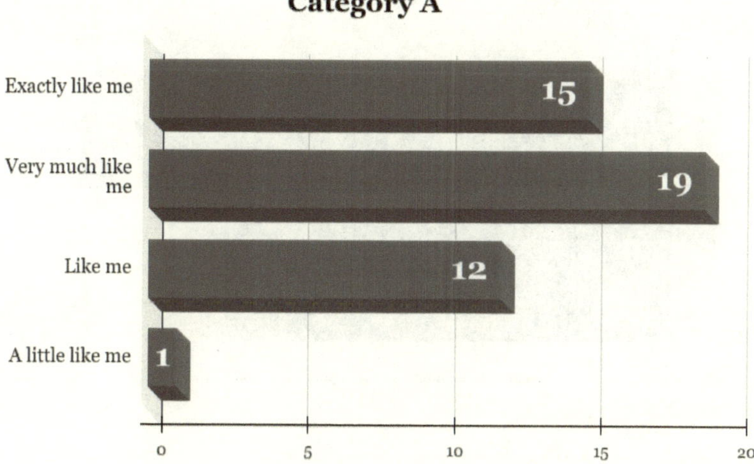

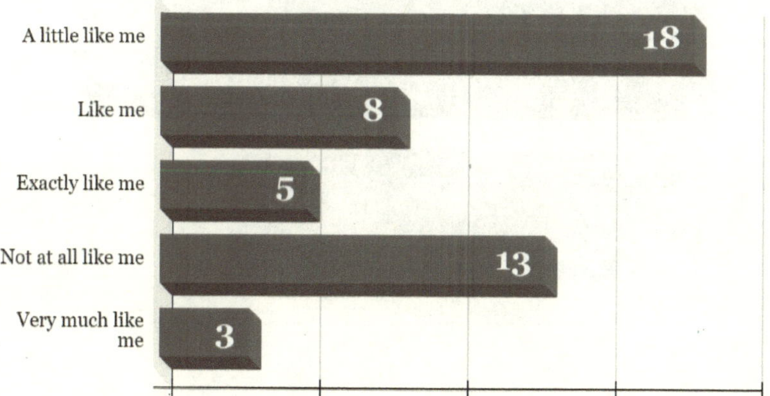

Even though one is confident in offering a potential solution, he or she must carefully evaluate it and make sure it adheres to predetermined criteria. As a result, we can see that Category A respondents agree with the statement made and consistently follow it to guide their search for solutions, whereas Category B respondents only occasionally follow it.

CREATIVE THINKING SKILLS

16. **I try to find ways of doing things even when they sound impossible.**

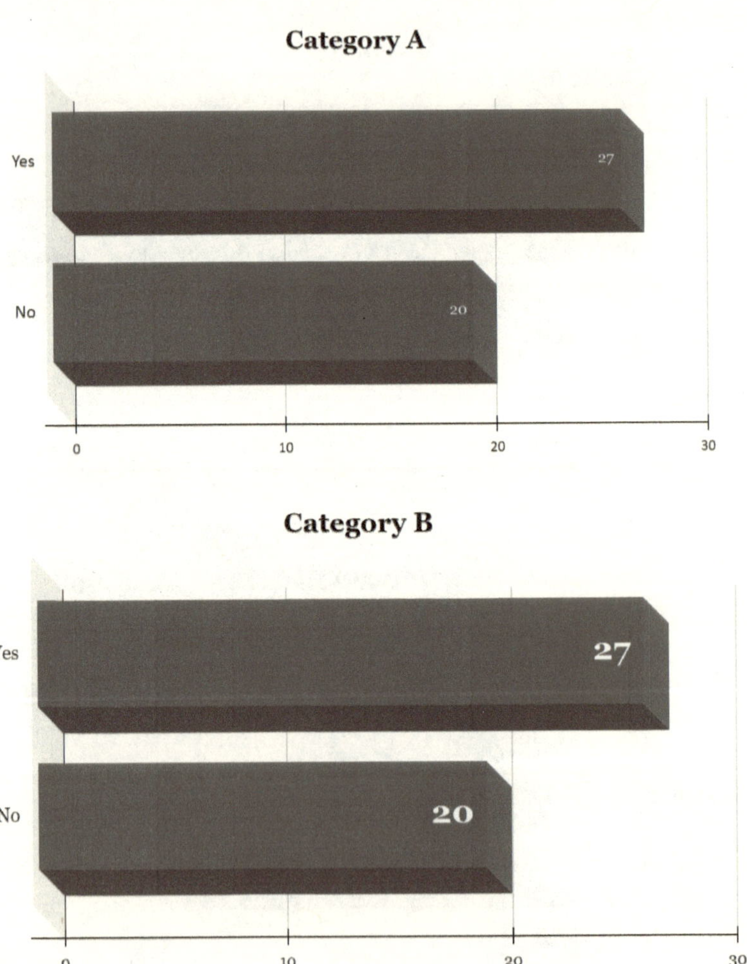

One should always try different approaches or solutions to things that appear to be impossible. This will drastically enhance one's creative thinking skills. As a result, we can see that categories A and B both agree with the statement made above. Thus, it is also possible to draw the conclusion that both categories possess strong creative thinking abilities.

17. **I enjoy discussions with people with different viewpoints.**

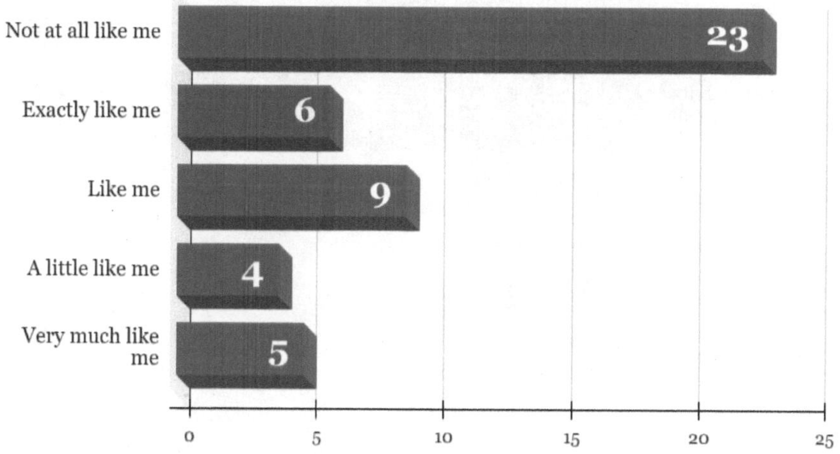

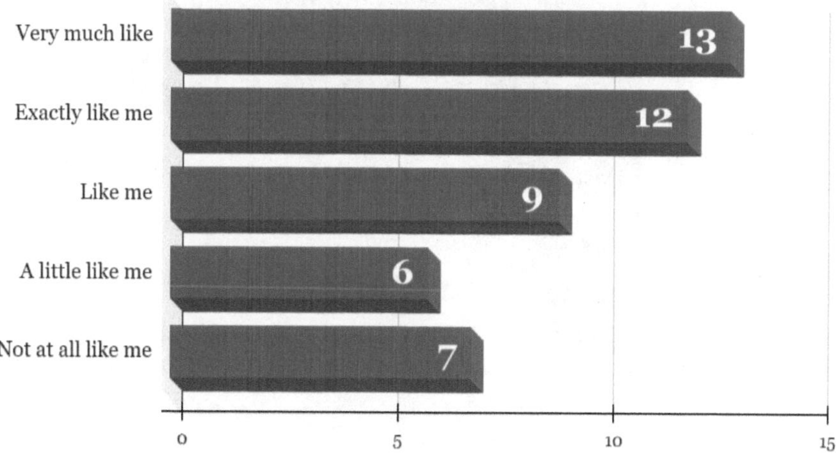

Discussion with those who hold diverse opinions broadens one's thinking, stimulating creativity. It aids in comprehending people's various perspectives and how they think. Most respondents of category B value discussions with others who hold diverse viewpoints.

18. **I try out several ideas before settling on a solution to any problem.**

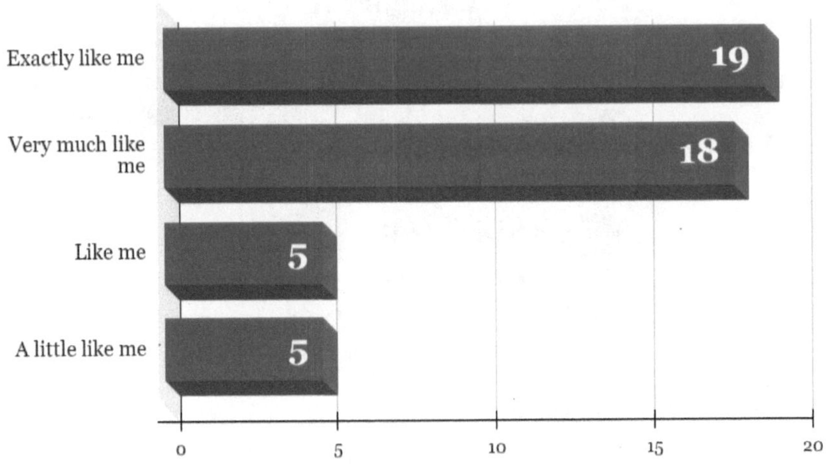

Category B

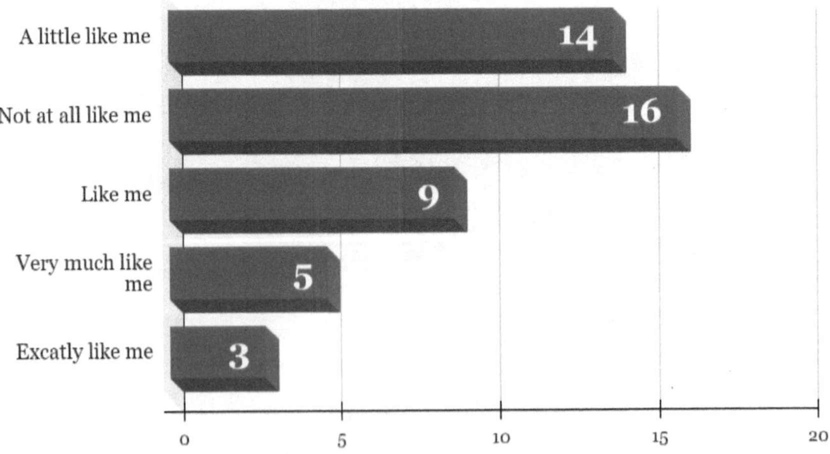

To tackle a problem, one needs to use several alternative strategies. Before choosing a solution to a problem, Category A claims to have tried various different approaches. Category B, however, proceeds with just one solution.

LIMITATIONS

1. The universe of this study is restricted to colleges in Mumbai.
2. This research does not cover all types of skills.
3. This study only considers students who are currently pursuing their undergraduate degrees.
4. The data is collected from 94 respondents only.
5. Time constraints.
6. The research is based on an online survey and questionnaire.

FINDINGS

Through data analysis, the researchers have found that through their responses to the questions, Category A respondents demonstrate their ability to lead, communicate, and solve problems. However, both groups are equally capable in terms of interpersonal, critical thinking, and decision-making skills.

RECOMMENDATIONS

Some of the suggestions in this section are given by the responders.

1. Through books, campaigns, internet ads, and television commercials, the government can raise awareness among students of the advantages of internships.
2. A number of internship programs that the Indian government has developed need to be promoted.
3. The educational system must make internship as a required fieldwork assignment which will increase their communication and social skills.
4. Pass a law requiring a minimum stipend because most interns do so in hopes of earning a little extra money while they are still studying.
5. Colleges should work harder and partner with more companies so that students can obtain internships through on-campus interviews.
6. The government should mandate that at least 10% of a company's personnel be interns.
7. Government should create a dedicated website that serves as a conduit between students and businesses looking for interns, ensuring that no student is taken advantage of.

8. In nations like the UK, a student is only permitted to work a maximum of 20 hours per week during the academic year and full-time during vacation periods. The Indian government could similarly enact such regulations to help students balance their education and internships.

CONCLUSION

This research concludes that students who have completed internships thrive in leadership communication and problem-solving skills. However, both groups have similarly strong decision-making, interpersonal and creative thinking abilities. A student needs to possess all of the mentioned skills in order to be employed. However, category B lacks the leadership, communication and problem-solving skills that are essential for developing employability. In order to be employable, students should complete an internship. Internships for students can be made available through collaboration between the government, universities, and industry.

BIBLIOGRAPHY

- Manjunath S1*, M B Shravan2, Dechakka B B3 (2019), A Study on Assessment of Skill Gap to Enhance Workforce Performance, International Journal of Management, Technology And Engineering, ISSN NO : 2249-7455
- Ilias Kapareliotis, Katerina Voutsina and Athanasios Patsiotis, (2019), Internship and employability prospects: assessing student's work readiness, Higher Education, Skills and Work-Based Learning, Vol. 9 No. 4, pp. 538-549
- Sarika Joshi, Honey Tyagi, (2019), A Study on Student's Perception About Internship Program and Its Impact on Their Personality, With Reference to Hotel Management Students of Pune Region, A Journal of Hospitality 5 (2) 2019, 67-74
- S. Nayana Tara, N.S. Sanath Kumar (2016), Skill development in India: In conversation with S. Ramadorai, Chairman, National Skill Development Agency & National Skill Development Corporation; former CEO, MD and Vice Chairman, Tata Consultancy Services, IIMB Management Review, 1–9, http://dx.doi.org/10.1016/j.iimb.2016.10.003
- Lavina Sharma and Asha Nagendra, (2016), Skill Development in India: Challenges and Opportunities, Indian Journal of Science and Technology,

Vol 9(48), DOI: 10.17485/ijst/2016/v9i48/107324, ISSN (Print) : 0974-6846

- Thiyazan Sultan Ahmed Al-Qubati, (2021), The Role Of Internship Programs In Enhancing Graduates' Employability, DOI:10.13140/RG.2.2.27784.75529
- Frederick F. Patacsil, Christine Lourrine S. Tablatin, (2017), Exploring The Importance Of Soft And Hard Skills As Perceived By It Internship Students And Industry: A Gap Analysis, Journal of Technology and Science Education JOTSE, 2017 – 7(3), https://doi.org/10.3926/jotse.271
- Elisa, K Mutiara, A Hamid, M Syukri, H Mazlina and Musdar, (2019), The contribution of Internship toward soft skill competencies of pre-service teachers, Journal of Physics: Conf. Series 1460 (2020) 012115, doi:10.1088/1742-6596/1460/1/012115
- Washor, Kim Stack, "Bridging The Soft-Skill Gap From Education To Employment Through Internships" (2015), https://digitalcommons.uri.edu/oa_diss/318

The Impact of Brand on Customer Behavior and Their Perceptions

CHAPTER 33

Author – Mansi Kotian, Risha Poojary, Kinjal Kurdia, Student & Prof. Falguni Mathews, Assistant Professor, SIES College of Commerce and Economics, Mumbai

ABSTRACT

The concept "brand image" has drawn significant attention from academics and practitioners since it was put forward, because it played an important role in marketing activities. Although brand image was recognized as the driving force of brand asset and brand performance, few studies have elaborated on the relationship between brand image and consumer perception from the consumer perspective. Based on the brand image theories, this study reviewed extant studies about the impact of brand image on consumers from the perspective of customer equity. Secondary and primary sources were used to gather the data for this study. A tailored questionnaire that was distributed to the respondents was used to gather primary data. It also presented the shortcomings of current research and pointed out the trends for future study.

KEYWORDS: Consumer Behavior, Consumer Perception, Brand Image, and Satisfaction.

INTRODUCTION

Brand image has been studied extensively since the 20th century due to its importance in building brand equity. In the increasingly competitive world marketplace, companies need to have a deeper insight into consumer behavior and educate consumers about the brand in order to develop effective marketing strategies. Brand is something that remains with us when our factory is burned". These are the words of David Ogilvy, who is considered the father of advertising. Brands are important to brand owners at two quite different levels. Firstly, they serve as a focus for consumer loyalty and therefore develop as assets that ensure uterus demand and hence future cash flow. They thus introduce stability into businesses, help guard against competitive encroachment, and allow investment and planning to take place with increased confidence. Brands are business assets that are legally protected and shielded from duplication. They are valuable, rare, non-substitutable and provide sustainable competitive advantages- and, therefore, superior financial performances. A brand is built over time by the impression one has of the company, its products or services, and confirmed experiences. People use brands to categorize their choices. On the basis of existing definitions of the brand, we define it as "a perceptible sign of the organization and its products to the human senses, through which the consumer is able to differentiate an organization and its products from others".

Brand image is the key driver of brand equity, which refers to consumers' general perceptions and feelings about a brand and has an influence on consumer behavior. For marketers, whatever their companies' marketing strategies are, the main purpose of their marketing activities is to influence consumers' perception and attitude toward a brand, establish the brand image in consumers' mind, and stimulate consumers' actual purchasing behavior of the brand, therefore increasing sales, maximizing the market share and developing brand equity.

REVIEW OF LITERATURE

- Abdul-Talib, A. N. and Arshad, S. (2020) gave advertisers assorted methods to interface with their objective market and viral promoting is one of those minimal effort methods. The motivation behind this study is to investigate how popular showcasing impacts purchase expectations. Online media is one of the fundamental pointers that impact customers to purchase intentions. In any case, brand loyalty, one of the significant segments of CBBE, is concentrated as far as customers' purchase expectations. This study also centers around recognizing the job of viral showcasing in creating positive brand equity in customers' outlooks.
- Balderaz, B.G.B. and Campos, K.P. (2020) tried to decide whether there is a huge contrast fair and square of internet shopping fulfillment when broken down as indicated by the profile of respondents. This study used

the non-trial quantitative exploration utilizing expressive connection research plan. Organized study survey was utilized as the examination instrument. Utilizing T-test and Analysis of Variance, the result uncovered that there is a huge distinction on internet shopping fulfillment regarding gross month to month pay.

- Cheun, B. G. and Park, H.S. (2020) inspected the impacts of insurance agency's CSR exercises on customer-based brand resources and customers' aim to follow through on charge costs to distinguish the chance of CSR exercises as an insurance agency's separated showcasing methodologies. All through gathering 510 overviews, this study has demonstrated that monetary and beneficent exercises had an impact on customer-based brand resources, likewise financial and natural exercises had an impact on the goal to address premium costs. Also, the interceding job of the customer-based brand resource among monetary and altruistic exercises and aim to pay charges was demonstrated. In conclusion, it was affirmed that the degree of SNS utilization directs the connection between financial exercises and customer-based brand resources. Based on the results, this study gives insurance agencies a compelling advertising methodology of the CSR program.
- Cheung, M.L. et al. (2020) analyzed the viability of online media brand correspondence and serious conveyance methodology on the consumer-based brand equity measurements, likewise representing the direct impact of product contribution. The hypothetical system is tried utilizing 210 consumers purchased from an electronic-machine store or active wear shop (low inclusion) in a shopping center. Information examination utilized incomplete least squares – underlying condition displaying Be that as it may, conflicting with past investigations, there is just halfway help for the effect of client created web-based media correspondence on measurements. It empowers directors and scholastics to more readily comprehend the consolidated adequacy of web-based advertising and conveyance force, just as the directing impact of product-inclusion level for better asset distribution.
- Inar K. (2020) opined that the building and keeping up brand equity is significant and fundamental in the present industry when the idea is considered to incorporate all material and non-material values of business. In spite of the fact that there has been expanding conversation on brand equity building, the lion's share of the current investigations has neglected

to fabricate CBBE ideas or characterize the particular components of CBBE. Hence, related writing has presented different CBBE models. The motivation behind this examination is to survey distinctive customer based brand equity models from scholastic writing to have a more integrative conceptualization for understanding brands in the lodging industry. It has shown that there are more requests for additional examinations of CBBE models with regards to continually changing customer needs and lodging industry and this viewpoint empowers advertising chiefs to utilize a viable technique in arrangement and impacting customer perspectives and practices.

- Duman, T. et al. (2018) tried to break down the role of emotional factors in brand reverberation with regards to an objective brand. Keller's brand reverberation model (Keller, 2013) was utilized to recognize the role of emotional factors in the brand equity chain. The research was led on the 'Sarajevo' brand, with the desire that emotional factors would be more compelling for brand reverberation than intellectual factors. Sarajevo is recognized as the focal point of the war that resulted in the breakdown of the Republic of Yugoslavia in the 1990s, and feelings towards the enduring of regular people under attack are as yet predominant. The research theory was tested with information from 286 Turkish guests. A Turkish example was picked to test the theory because of the way that the Turkish and Bosnian populaces have solid, authentic ties with one another, and 19 Sarajevo speaks to a sincerely solid objective for the Turkish populace. Findings together are utilized to propose methodologies for Sarajevo advertisers, out of which utilizing the passionate parts of the city in objective marketing is by all accounts the most persuasive.

OBJECTIVES OF STUDY

1. To identify and define different factors of impact of brand which have a great impact on the purchase behavior of customers in the retail industry.
2. To evaluate how these factors of brand image affect the purchase behavior of customers.
3. To understand the Impact of Brand perception on Consumer Purchase Behavior

4. To analyze the actual impact of branding on consumers purchase behavior in the market.
5. To provide some suggestions regarding how brand image can be a more effective business strategy to influence consumers purchase behavior positively.

SCOPE OF STUDY

Many studies have been done regarding the impact of brand image on consumers' purchase behavior or relationships, but there are still some important insights that have remained uncovered by prior studies. This study is significant in the sense that the author will try to provide complete information about the brand's image and its true impact on consumers' purchase behavior. Moreover, this study would be significant for retailers in order to develop a sound brand image within the industry by designing and implementing effective policies for influencing consumers' behavior positively. The researchers would also benefit from this study, as it would open a new opportunity to conduct further extensive studies in this research area.

Brand image has become important for every business as it helps fulfill its motives. Brand image is paramount to brand performance, as a good image brings good profits. Every business firm strives to build a strong brand image due to several benefits, such as- i) ensuring more sales revenue as new customers are attracted to the brand; ii) making it easy to launch new products under the same brand; iii) increasing brand awareness and value; iv) boosting the confidence of existing customers and making them loyal to the brand; and v) developing better business customer relationships. For example- Rolls-Royce is the best premium brand to be exclusive to influential customers because Rolls-Royce ensures its product quality in addition to making product differentiation that increases its gross sales by 27%. Moreover, the brand identity, brand trust and competitive market price make the Rolls-Royce as one of the best premium brands within automobile industry

RESEARCH METHODOLOGY

In this research, data from primary and secondary sources has been gathered as a form of evidence, and all the information has been properly aligned with the topic, aim, and objectives of the research work. With proper analysis, data interpretation has been produced for a better understanding of the collected data. As the aim of the research is to identify the impact of brand image on customer purchase behaviors, the research questions in the primary data are designed in this way. The survey will help the researcher understand the customer's viewpoint.

The main aim of the survey was to find out whether the brand has an impact on the consumer decision-making process in the consumer market or not and if there is a relationship between the age category and the purchase decision. The partial aims of the survey were to examine the role of brand in customer decision making-process in several specific areas (brand awareness, brand recognition, customer preferences, and motivation to purchase the product of a particular brand).

STATEMENT OF PROBLEM

In order to enhance consumer brand perception for green consumers, brand performance will need to be augmented across the various cognitive, behavioral, and affective components. It is vital for companies to keep collecting consumer responses and identify whether they need to improve brand performance to enhance the consumer experience or strengthen consumer belief in the brand. Companies need to focus on improving consumer brand knowledge to ensure that consumers prefer the respected green brand and have positive feelings for it.

Though many companies are able to have better products, they are sometimes unable to compete in the market due to poor branding activities. Thus, strong brands have the potential to generate long term and loyal customers, which would eventually lead to an increase in sales in the future. As a result of the challenges in managing brands and their benefits, the research will bring into focus a critical evaluation of branding and its role or impact in the purchase decision making process of consumers.

DATA ANALYSIS AND INTERPRETATION

Q.1)

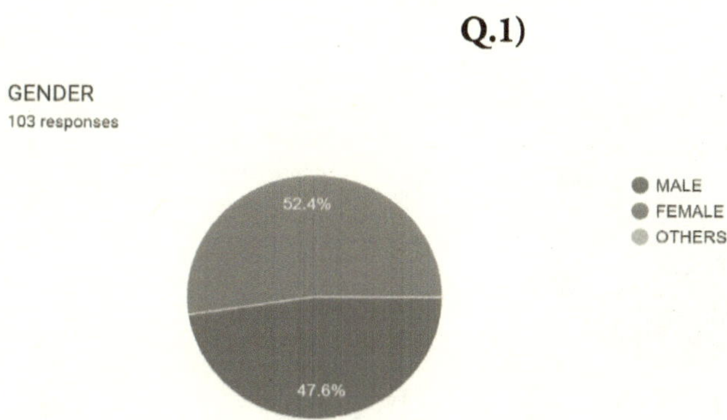

Inference: In this figure, we can see that 52.4% of the responses are female and the remaining 47.6% are male.

Q.2)

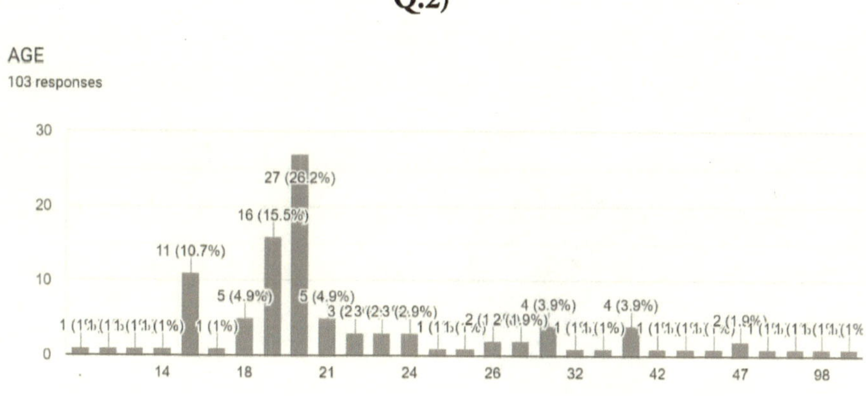

Inference: We can observe that most of the respondents are between the ages of 20-30. This shows that most of the people who answered our survey were youth. As a result,we should keep in mind that most of the responses are coming from younger and generally more open minded generations.

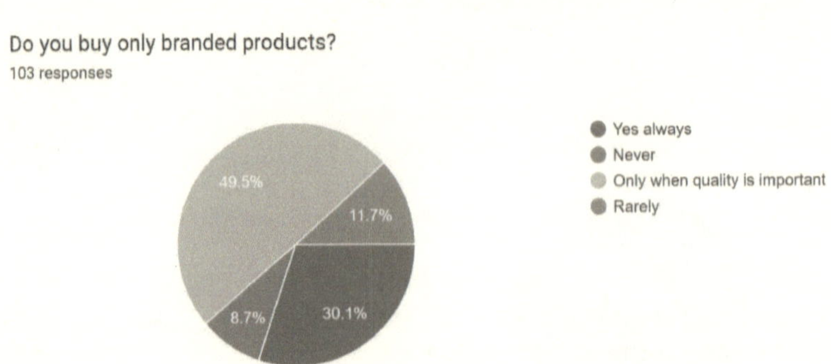

Inference: In this figure, we can see that 49.5% of the responses go for branded products only when quality is important, 30.1% buy branded products, 11.7% of the responses rarely use branded products and the remaining 8.7% don't buy branded products.

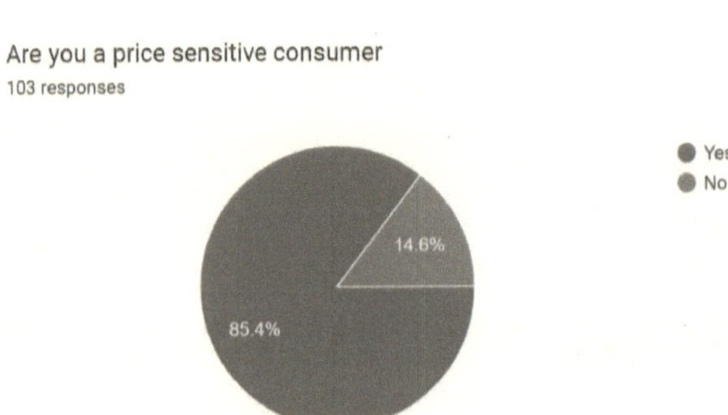

Inference: In this figure, we can observe that out of 103 respondents, 85.4% of the sample population are price sensitive, whereas 14.6% of the respondents don't care about the price.

Q.5)

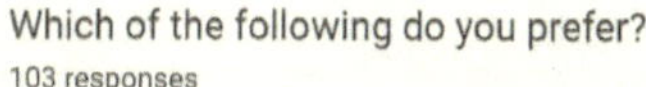

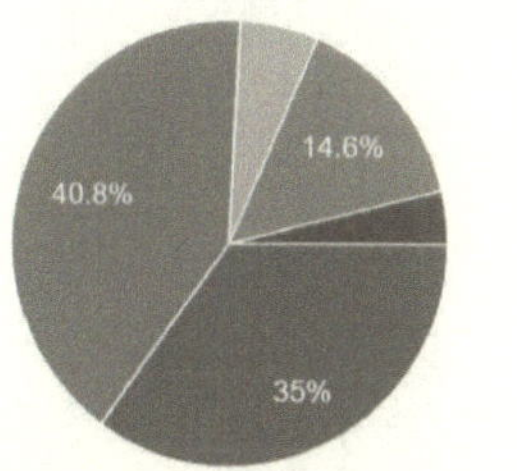

Inference: Looking at this figure, we can see that most of the people are preferring products from companies with good warranty and sale service, which counts to 40.8%, and 35% of the responses are going for products from bigger companies with broader distribution, then 14.6% are going for products belonging to companies with a good brand image, 6% are choosing products from local companies with better prices and slightly lower quality, and the remaining responses are going for others. A large number of people prefer products from companies with good warranties and after sales services; 35% prefer products from bigger companies with broader distribution.

Q.6)

Does the country of origin affect your product purchase decision?
103 responses

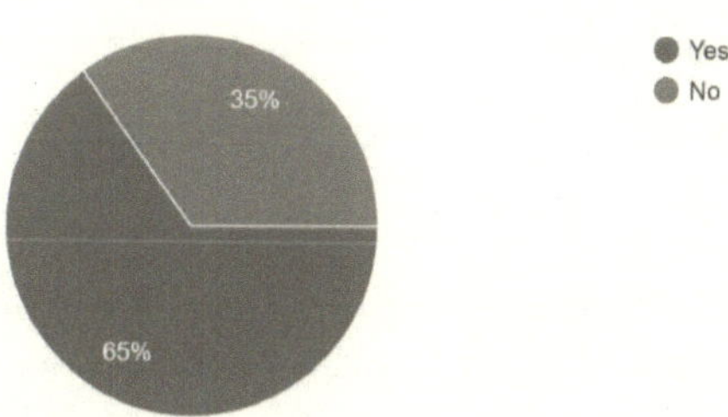

Inference: As we can clearly see in this figure, the percentage of people buying a particular product based on the origin of the country is higher.

It accounts for 65% of people caring about the country of origin, and the remaining 35% not really caring about the country of origin of a product.

Q.7)

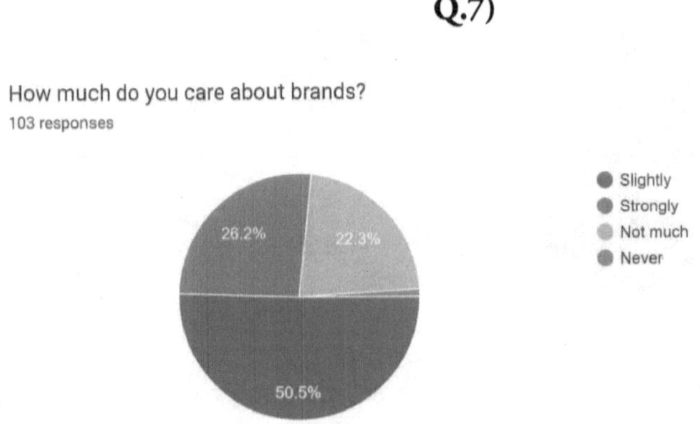

Inference: In this figure, we can see that 26.2% of the respondents strongly care about the brands and 22.3% of the respondents don't.

Q.8)

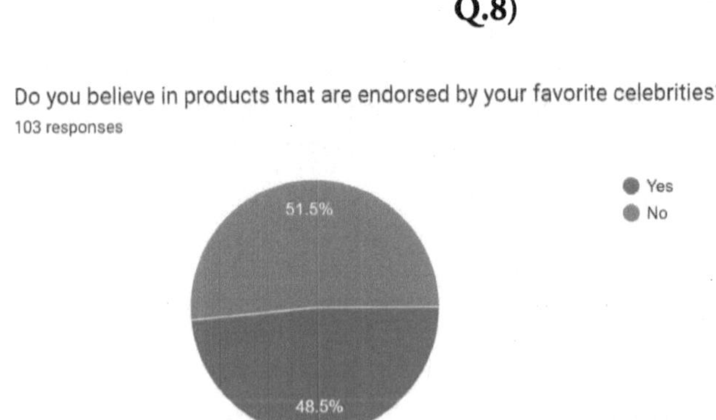

Inference: In this figure, we can see that 51.5% of the respondents believe in products that are endorsed by their favorite celebrities, and the remaining 48.5% of the respondents don't believe in products endorsed by celebrities.

Q.9)

Apart from the direct benefit of the product, what else do you look for in the product ?

103 responses

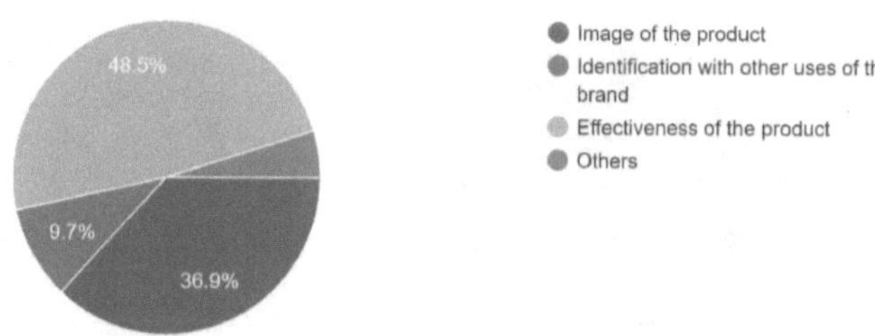

Inference: As we can see in this figure, the major responses, which are 48.5%, look for the effectiveness of the product, whereas 36.9% look for the image of the product, and 9.7% of the responses look for the identification with other uses of the brand.

Q.10)

Will you stick to the same product if their price is increased ?

103 responses

Inference: In this figure, we can see that the major response, 78.6%, will stick to a particular product even though there is an increase in price, and the remaining won't.

Q.11)

What influences customers to buy a particular product ?
103 responses

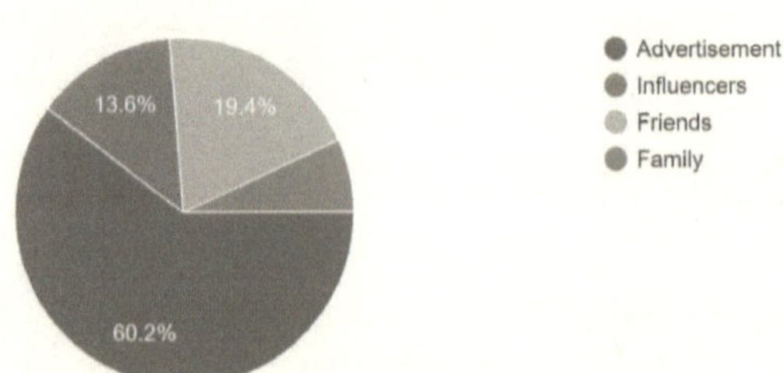

Inference: As we can see in this figure, 60.2% of the responses are influenced by advertisements; the next 19.4% are influenced by friends; 13.6% are influenced by influencers; and the remaining 7% are influenced by family.

Q.12)

What are your preference that attracts you the most to buy a particular brand ?
103 responses

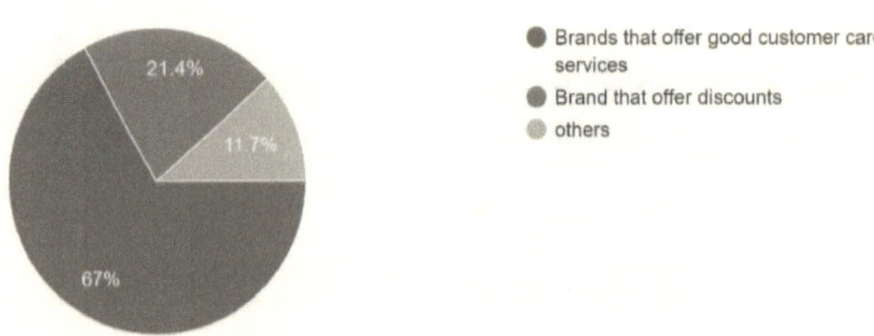

In the above figure, 67% prefer brands that offer good consumer care services, whereas 21.4% prefer brands that offer discounts.

Q.13)

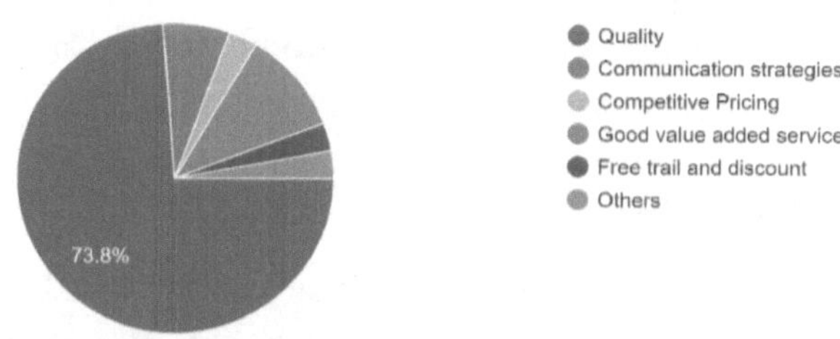

Inference: By seeing this figure, we can conclude that the respondents are inclined towards quality of the goods,73.8% prefer quality,after that good value added services etc.

RECOMMENDATION

1. Enrich the Connotation of Brand Image

Brand emotion is the cultural implication embodied in a brand, and emotional branding is a highly effective way to cause customer reactions, sentiments, and moods, ultimately forming connection and loyalty with the brand. Even the traditional brand management pattern based on customer perception now incorporates emotional branding.

In the unprecedentedly competitive marketplace, brand emotion is the bond between the brand and the customer and the key to expanding the market. Future studies could explore the relationship between brand image and consumer behavior from a brand new perspective—brand emotion.

2. Brand Image, Customer Satisfaction and Customer Loyalty

The relationship between brand image and customer satisfaction has been studied extensively. However, a majority of these researches were conducted in the service industry, such as hotels, supermarkets and banks, etc. Whether the results generated from the service industry can be applied to other contexts (e.g., manufacturing industry, finance industry, real estate industry, etc.) remains to be examined.

Although the positive impact of brand image on customer satisfaction and loyalty has been proven, there are still disagreements between different research studies. Specifically, some studies prove that brand image not only influences customer loyalty directly but also impacts it through other mediating factors. However, some research results demonstrate that brand image exerts no direct influence on customer loyalty, but it can impact customer loyalty via customer satisfaction. Future studies should further discuss the interrelationships among brand image, customer satisfaction, and customer loyalty, and identify a more comprehensive indicator for consumer behavior.

LIMITATION OF STUDY

1. The one limitation of this study that can be stated here, is that the research method is qualitative, which indicates that the outcomes might be a little too generalized. The research has collected data from secondary and primary data collection. However, only surveys have been conducted via online methods. The interview method has not been adopted here, which can be seen as a limitation of the study. The use of open-ended questions through an interview could have further supplemented the findings, since a wider population could have been accessed.
2. One of the limitations of our study is that we have studied the responses of only 103 responses.

CONCLUSION

In conclusion, we have to stress the fact that brand is a factor that has an impact on the consumer purchase decision-making process. Brands provide information about products and create associations that affect the mind of the consumer during the purchase process. A very important category of consumer behavior research is brand awareness. Suitable forms of marketing activities as a whole can create positive brand associations and start a purchase action for positively seen brands. A brand represents a certain value in the mind of the consumer. Without the psychological linkage, a product or a service would be indistinguishable from each other. Our survey was aimed at assessing the impact of a brand on consumer behavior. More than half of respondents choose their products or services by brand. Participating survey respondents stated that quality is the key factor in their decision-making process when purchasing a brand. A higher quality of products, national pride, support of the Slovak economy, and support of domestic producers were the most frequently mentioned reasons for purchasing.

Based on the above discussion of the impact of brand image on consumer purchase behavior, it can be concluded that brand image plays an important role in the consumer's behavior. It is an important aspect of the organization's image and reputation. In this report, it has been found that to make customers satisfied, the organization needs to improve its brand image. The result or outcome of this research can help companies enhance their brand image and achieve high customer satisfaction. The implication of the studies for other organizations is that there is an influx of products available on the current market, so customers are making their buying decisions based on the brand image instead of the products. This study is helpful because other companies will recognize the importance of enhancing brand image and influencing consumer purchasing behavior. It has been found that keeping products available in attractive packaging will enhance the brand's image among consumer behavior. More than half of respondents choose their products or services by brand. Participating survey respondents stated that quality is the key factor in their decision-making process when purchasing a brand. A higher quality of products, national pride, support of the economy, and support of domestic producers were the most frequently mentioned reasons for purchasing.

BIBLIOGRAPHY

- **Papers discussed in the literature review section:**
  1. **Abdul-Talib, A. N. and Arshad, S. (2020)**
  2. **Balderaz, B.G.B. and Campos, K.P. (2020)**
  3. **Cheun, B. G. and Park, H.S. (2020)**
  4. **Cheung, M.L. et al. (2020)**
  5. **Inar K. (2020)**
  6. **Duman, T. et al. (2018)**
- https://www.researchgate.net/publication/354753850_The_Service_Quality_Effect_on_Corporate_Reputation_Customers_Satisfaction_and_Loyalty
- https://www.researchgate.net/publication/342383269_The_Impact_of_Brand_Relationships_on_Corporate_Brand_Identity_and_Reputation-An_Integrative_Model
- https://www.researchgate.net/publication/314546961_Impact_of_Brand_on_Consumer_Behavior
- https://www.scirp.org/html/6-1530143_53297.htm

www.ingramcontent.com/pod-product-compliance
Lightning Source LLC
LaVergne TN
LVHW091247150826
845673LV00006B/1347

* 9 7 9 8 8 9 1 3 3 4 3 2 8 *